The Principal
Navigations Voyages Traffiques and
Discoveries of the English Nation

In Twelve Volumes

Volume VII

Photogravure by Annan & Sons, Glasgow.

THE EARL OF CUMBERLAND.

The Principal
Navigations Voyages
Traffiques & Discoveries
of the English Nation

Made by Sea or Over-land to the
Remote and Farthest Distant Quarters
of the Earth at any time within the
compasse of these 1600 Yeeres

By

RICHARD HAKLUYT
Preacher, and sometime Student of
Christ-Church in Oxford

VOLUME VII

REPRINTS OF ECONOMIC CLASSICS

Augustus M. Kelley · Publishers
NEW YORK 1969

FIRST EDITION 1589
SECOND EDITION 1598-1600

THIRD EDITION 1903-1905
(GLASGOW: James MacLehose & Sons, 1904)

Reprinted 1969 by
AUGUSTUS M. KELLEY · PUBLISHERS
NEW YORK NEW YORK 10010

LIBRARY OF CONGRESS CATALOGUE CARD NUMBER

70-75411

Printed in the United States of America

THE TABLE

THE TABLE

THE TABLE

THE TABLE

THE TABLE

A Catalogue of the Voyages—*Continued.*

THE TABLE

ILLUSTRATIONS

ILLUSTRATIONS

Sir Richard Grenville or Greynville belonged to a
Cornish family and was born about 1541. He was
a cousin of Sir Walter Raleigh. In 1571 he sat in
Parliament as member for Cornwall. He made his
first sea voyage in May 1585 when he commanded
a fleet of seven ships intended for the settlement of
Virginia. On his way home 'he tooke a Spanish
ship of 300 tunne richly loaden, boording her with
a boate made with boards of chests, which fell
asunder, and sunke at the ships side, assoone as
ever he and his men were out of it.' In
1586 he made another voyage to Virginia. In 1588
he was engaged in planning measures of defence for
the western counties in anticipation of the Spanish
Armada. In 1591 the action off the Azores took
place which resulted in the loss of the 'Revenge'
and his death. The portrait here reproduced is
taken from the British museum copy of Holland's
Heroologia published in London in 1620.

Linschoten was born at Haarlem about 1563, but it was
from Enkhuizen, whither his parents had removed,
that in 1576 Linschoten set out on the travels which
have made his name famous. He first went to Spain
where he stayed six years ; next he joined the
Spanish fleet for the East Indies and was at Goa in
1583 when John Newbery and Ralph Fitch arrived
as prisoners from Ormuz. His account of their
escape is given in Volume V page 505 of this edition.
In 1591 he was at Terceira in the Azores when the
Spanish fleet put in for repairs after the action with
the 'Revenge,' and his 'large testimony' of the
fight as related to him by the Spaniards, with the
description of the great storm which followed it, will
be found at page 80. In 1594-5 he accompanied
Barents in his voyages to the Arctic regions. He
died in 1611. The portrait is taken from a copy in

ILLUSTRATIONS

the British Museum of Boissardi's *Bibliotheca sive Thesaurus Virtutis* published at Frankfort in 1628.

This, the only known map by Sir Humphrey Gilbert now in existence, is taken from the copy in the British Museum of his *Discourse of a Discoverie of a new passage to Cathaia* published in London in 1576. It was 'made onelye for the particular declaration of this discovery.'

Frobisher was born about 1535. He made his first voyage, to Guinea, in 1554. In 1571 he was employed in sea service off the coast of Ireland, where he attracted the notice of Sir Humphrey Gilbert. On the grant of a charter to the Company of Cathay in 1577 he was appointed Captain-general and admiral of the Company's fleet. In 1576-78 he was occupied in his voyages in search of the North-west passage. In 1580 he was made clerk of Her Majesty's ships. In September 1585 he sailed for the West Indies in Drake's expedition as vice-admiral on the 'Primrose'. He was in command of the 'Triumph' against the Armada in 1588 and was knighted by Lord Howard of Effingham for 'that hee had valiantly and discreetly behaved himself' in the fight on the 25th July. In 1594 in the 'Dreadnought' he was employed at the relief of Brest and Crozon, was wounded in the hip while landing his men at Crozon, and taken back to Plymouth where he died shortly after his arrival. The portrait is taken from the copy in the British Museum of Holland's *Heroologia*, 1620.

This map, made to illustrate George Best's Discourse 'to proove all partes of the worlde habitable,' is taken from the British Museum copy of *A True*

According to the fragment of Autobiography preserved in the British Museum, Michael Lock or Lok was born in 1532. He says: 'My late father, Sr William Lok, knight, alderman of London, kept me at scholes of grammer in England till I was xiii yeres old, which was A^o. Dni, 1545, and he being sworn servant to King Henry the VIIIth his mercer and also his agent beyond the seas dyvers affayres, he then sent me over seas to Flanders and France to learn those languages and to know the world. Synce which tyme I have contynued these xxxii yeres in travaile of body and study of mynde, following my vocation in the trade of merchandise, whereof I have spent the first xv yeres in contynuall travaile of body, passing through allmost all the cuntrees of Christianity. Namely out of England, into Scotland, Ireland, Flanders, Germany, France, Spayne, Italy and Greece, both by land and by sea, not without great labo^{rs}, cares, dangers and expenses of mony incident; having had the charge (as capitayn) of a great ship of burden 1000 tuns, by the space of more then iii yeres in dyvers voyages in the Levant seas, wherewithall I returned into England. In which travailes, besides the knowledge of all those famous common languages of those cuntries, I sought allso for the knowledge of the state of all their common wealths, chiefly in all matters apperteining to

xiv

ILLUSTRATIONS

the traffique of merchants. And the rest of my tyme I have spent in England under the happy raigne of the Queenes Matie now being.' Lock was one of the promoters of Frobisher's voyages and was greatly impoverished through their failure financially. He was imprisoned in the Fleet at the instance of William Borough in 1581. He died about 1615. The map, which is dedicated to Sir Philip Sidney, is taken from the copy in the Hunterian Library, University of Glasgow, of the *Divers Voyages touching the discoverie of America*, published by Hakluyt in 1582.

John Davis, or Davys, 'the Navigator,' was born at Sandridge about 1550. He was a neighbour and companion of Humphrey and Adrian Gilbert. In 1585-6 he made his voyages in search of the North-west passage, and on his return home from his first voyage in 1585 he wrote this letter to Sir Francis Walsingham. In 1589 he joined the Earl of Cumberland's expedition off the Azores, and in 1591 he went with Thomas Cavendish as Rear-admiral on the 'Desire.' In 1598 he was pilot of a Dutch ship, the 'Lion,' and in 1600 was appointed Pilot-major of the first East Indian fleet under Captain James Lancaster. In 1605, when pilot of the 'Tiger' under Sir Edward Michelborne, his ship was treacherously attacked by Japanese pirates near Bintung, in the Straits of Malacca, and he was killed. He wrote a treatise on navigation, the *Seaman's Secrets*, first published in 1594, and the *Worldes Hydrographical Description*, published in 1595, and he invented the 'backstaff,' for taking the altitude of the sun.

The following is the translation of the letter, which is reproduced from the original in the British Museum :

ILLUSTRATIONS

'Right honorable most dutyfully craving pardon for this my rashe boldnes, I am herby, according to my duty, to signyfy unto yor honor that the north-west passage is a matter nothing doubtfull, but at any tyme almost to be passed, the sea navigable, voyd of yse, the ayre tollerable, and the waters very depe. I have also found an yle of very grate quantytie, not in any globe or map dyscrybed, yelding a sufficient trade of furre and lether, and although this passage hath bine supposed very impassible, yeat through Gods mercy, I am in experience ann ey wyttnes to the contrary, yea in this most desperate clymate; which, by Gods help, I wyll very shortly most at large revele unto yor honor as sone as I can possible take order for my maryners and shipping. Thus depending up^n yor honors good favor, I most humbly comytt you to God this third of October.

Yo^r honors for ever most dutyfull

JOHN DAVYS.'

Map of the Earl of Cumberland's Voyage to the Azores, by Edward Wright, 1589, . .

'The excellent Mathematician and Enginier Master Edward Wright' was born at Garveston, Norfolk, about 1558. He went up to Caius College Cambridge in 1576, graduated B.A. in 1580-1, M.A. in 1584 and was a fellow from 1587-96. He accompanied the Earl of Cumberland to the Azores in 1589 and wrote the account of the voyage. It is now generally held that he was the discoverer of the so-called 'Mercator's' projection. He was appointed lecturer on navigation to the East India Company. He died in 1615. The map here reproduced was made by Wright to illustrate the Earl of Cumberland's Voyage to the Azores in 1589 and is taken from a copy of his *Certain Errors in Navigation* published in London in 1599, now in the Grenville Library in the British Museum.

THE SEVENTH VOLUME

OF THE

Principall Navigations, Voyages, Traffiques and Discoveries of the English Nation

Made to the South and South-east quarters of the
World, and the Voyages undertaken for the
finding of a Northwest Passage, with
the directions, letters, privileges
discourses, and observations
incident to the same

The voiage of the right honorable George Erle of Cumberland to the Azores, &c. Written by the excellent Mathematician and Enginier master Edward Wright.

He right honorable the Erle of Cumberland having at his owne charges prepared his small Fleet of foure Sailes onely, viz. The Victorie one of the Queenes ships royall; the Meg and Margaret small ships, (one of which also he was forced soone after to send home againe, finding her not able to endure the Sea) and a small Caravell, and having assembled together about 400 men (or fewer) of gentlemen, souldiers, and saylers, embarked himself and them, and set saile from the Sound of Plimmouth in Devonshire, the 18 day of June 1589. being accompanied with these captaines and gentlemen which hereafter folow.

Captaine Christopher Lister a man of great resolution, captaine Edward Carelesse, *aliâs* Wright, who in sir Francis Drakes West-Indian voyage to S. Domingo and Carthagena, was captaine of the Hope. Captaine Boswell, M. Mervin, M. Henry Long, M. Partridge, M. Norton, M. William Mounson captaine of the Meg, and his viceadmirall, now sir William Mounson, M. Pigeon captaine of the Caravell.

About 3 dayes after our departure from Plimmouth we met with 3 French ships, whereof one was of Newhaven, another of S. Malos, and so finding them to

be Leaguers & lawful Prises, we tooke them and sent
two of them for England with all their loding, which was
fish for the most part from New-found-land, saving
that there was part thereof distributed amongst our small
Fleet, as we could find Stowage for the same : and in
the third, all their men were sent home into France.
The same day & the day folowing we met with some
other ships, whom (when after some conference had with
them, we perceived plainly to bee of Roterodam and
Emden, bound for Rochell) we dismissed.

The 28 and 29 dayes we met divers of our English
ships, returning from the Portugall voiage which my
lord relieved with victuals. The 13 day of July being
Sonday in the morning, we espied 11 ships without
sight of ye coast of Spaine, in the height of 39 degrees,
whom wee presently prepared for, & provided to meet
them, having first set forth captaine Mounson in the
Meg, before us, to descry whence they were. The Meg
approching neere, there passed some shot betwixt them,
[II. ii. 156.] whereby, as also by their Admiral and Viceadmirall
putting foorth their flags, we perceived that some fight
was likely to follow. Having therefore fitted our selves
for them, we made what hast we could towards them
with regard always to get the wind of them, and about
10 or 11 of the clocke, we came up to them with the
Victory. But after some few shot & some litle fight
passed betwixt us, they yeelded themselves, & the masters
of them all came aboord us, shewing their several Pas-
ports from the cities of Hamburg and Lubeck, from
Breme, Pomerania and Calice.

They had in them certaine bags of Pepper & Syna-
mom, which they confessed to be the goods of a Jew
in Lisbon, which should have bene caried by them into
their country to his Factor there, and so finding it by
their owne confession to be lawful Prise, the same was
soone after taken and devided amongst our whole company, the value wherof was esteemed to be about 4500
pounds, at two shillings the pound.

2

The 17 day the foresaid ships were dismissed, but 7 of their men that were willing to go along with us for sailers, we tooke to helpe us, and so held on our course for the Azores.

The 1 of August being Friday in the morning, we had sight of the Iland of S. Michael, being one of the Eastermost of the Azores toward which we sailed all that day, and at night having put foorth a Spanish flag in our main-top, that so they might the lesse suspect us, we approched neere to the chiefe towne and road of that Iland, where we espied 3 ships riding at anker and some other vessels: all which we determined to take in the darke of the night, and accordingly attempted about 10 or 11 of the clocke, sending our boats well manned to cut their cables and hausers, and let them drive into the sea. Our men comming to them, found yᵗ one of those greatest ships was the Falcon of London being there under a Scottish Pilot who bare the name of her as his own. But 3 other smal ships that lay neere under the castle there, our men let loose and towed them away unto us, most of the Spaniards that were in them leaping over-boord and swimming to shore with lowd and lamentable outcries, which they of the towne hearing were in an uprore, and answered with the like crying. The castle discharged some great shot at our boats, but shooting without marke by reason of the darknesse they did us no hurt. The Scots likewise discharged 3 great pieces into the aire to make the Spaniards thinke they were their friends and our enemies, and shortly after the Scottish master, & some other with him, came aboord to my lord doing their dutie, and offring their service, &c. These 3 ships were fraught with wine and Salletoile from Sivil.

3 ships forcibly towed out of harbour

The same day our Caravel chased a Spanish Caravel to shore at S. Michael, which caried letters thither, by which we learned that the Caraks were departed from Tercera 8 dayes before.

The 7 of August we had sight of a litle ship which

wee chased towards Tercera with our pinnasse (the weather being calme) and towards evening we overtooke her, there were in her 30 tunnes of good Madera wine, certaine woollen cloth, silke, taffata, &c. The 14 of August we came to the Iland of Flores, where we determined to take in some fresh water and fresh victuals, such as the Iland did affoord. So we manned our boats with some 120 men and rowed towards the shore; whereto when we approched the inhabitants that were assembled at the landing place, put foorth a flag of truce, whereupon we also did the like.

When we came to them, my Lord gave them to understand by his Portugall interpreter, that he was a friend to their king Don Antonio, and came not any way to injury them, but that he ment onely to have some fresh water and fresh victuals of them, by way of exchange for some provision that he had, as oile, wine, or pepper, to which they presently agreed willingly, & sent some of their company for beeves and sheepe, and we in the meane season marched Southward about a mile to Villa de Santa Cruz, from whence all the inhabitants yong and old were departed, and not any thing of value left. We demanding of them what was the cause hereof, they answered, Feare; as their usuall maner was when any ships came neere their coast.

We found that part of the Iland to be full of great rockie barren hils and mountains, litle inhabited by reason that it is molested with ships of war which might partly appeare by this towne of Santa Cruz (being one of their chiefe townes) which was all ruinous, and (as it were) but the reliques of the ancient towne which had bene burnt about two yeeres before by certaine English ships of war, as the inhabitants there reported.

At evening as we were in rowing towards the Victory, an huge fish pursued us for the space well nigh of two miles together, distant for the most part from the boats sterne not a speares length, and sometimes so neere that the boat stroke upon him, the tips of whose finnes

4

about the ghils (appearing oft times above the water) were by estimation 4 or 5 yards asunder, and his jawes gaping a yard and an halfe wide, which put us in feare of overturning the pinnasse, but God bee thanked (rowing as hard as we could) we escaped.

When we were about Flores a litle ship called the Drake, brought us word that the Caraks were at Tercera, of which newes we were very glad, & sped us thitherward with all the speed we could: and by the way we came to Fayal road the seven and twentieth day of August, [II. ii. 157.] after sunne set, where we espied certaine shippes ryding at anker, to whom we sent in our Skiffe with Captaine Lister and Captaine Monson in her to discover the roaders: and least any daunger should happen to our boate, we sent in likewise the Sawsie Jacke and the small Caravell; but the wind being off the shoare, the shippes were not able to fet it so nigh as the Spaniards ride, which neverthelesse the boate did, and clapped a shippe aboord of two hundred and fiftie tunnes, which caried in her fourteene cast peeces, and continued fight alone with her for the space of one houre untill the comming up of other boates to the reskue of her, which were sent from the shippes, and then a fresh boording her againe one boate in the quarter, another in the hause, wee entred her on the one side, and all the Spaniards lept overboord on the other, save Juan de Palma the Captaine of her and two or three more, and thus we became possessors of her. This shippe was mored to the Castle which shot at us all this while: the onely hurt which we received of all this shot was this, that the master of our Caravell had the calfe of his legge shot away. This shippe was laden with Sugar, Ginger, and hides lately come from S. Juan de Puerto Rico; after we had towed her cleare off the castle, we rowed in againe with our boats, and fetched out five small ships more, one laden with hides, another with Elephants teeth, graines, coco-nuts, and goates skins come from Guinie, another with woad, and two with dogge-fish, which two last we let drive in the sea making none account of them. The other foure we sent for England the 30 of August.

At the taking of these Prizes were consorted with us some other small men of warre, as Maister John Davis, with his shippe, Pinnesse, and Boate, Captaine Markesburie with his ship, whose owner was Sir Walter Ralegh, the Barke of Lime, which was also consorted with us before.

The last of August in the morning we came in sight of Tercera, being about some nine or ten leagues from shoare, where we espied comming towards us, a small boat under saile, which seemed somewhat strange unto us, being so farre from land, and no shippe in sight, to which they might belong: but comming neere, they put us *An escape of 8. Englishmen from Tercera.* out of doubt, shewing they were English men (eight in number) that had lately beene prisoners in Tercera, and finding opportunitie to escape at that time, with that small boat committed themselves to the sea, under Gods providence, having no other yard for their maine saile, but two pipe staves tyed together by the endes, and no more provision of victuals, then they could bring in their pockets and bosomes. Having taken them all into the Victorie, they gave us certaine intelligence, that the Carackes were departed from thence about a weeke before.

Thus beeing without any further hope of those Caraks, we resolved to returne for Fayall, with intent to surprize the towne, but untill the ninth of September, we had either the winde so contrary, or the weather so calme, that in all that time, we made scarce nine or ten leagues way, lingring up and downe not farre from Pico.

The tenth of September, being Wednesday in the afternoone, wee came againe to Fayal roade. Whereupon immediatly my Lord sent Captaine Lister, with one of Graciosa (whom Captaine Munson had before taken) and some others, towards Fayal, whom certaine of the Inhabitants met in a boat, and came with Captaine Lister to my Lord, to whom hee gave this choice: either to

6

suffer him quietly to enter into the platforme there without resistance, where he and his companie would remaine a space without offering any injurie to them, that they (the Inhabitants) might come unto him and compound for the ransome of the Towne; or else to stand to the hazard of warre.

With these words they returned to the towne: but the keepers of the platforme answered, that it was against their oath and allegeance to king Philip to give over without fight. Whereupon my Lord commanded the boates of every ship, to be presently manned, and soone after landed his men on the sandie shoare, under the side of an hill, about halfe a league to the Northwards from the platforme: upon the toppe of which hill certaine horsemen and footmen shewed themselves, and other two companies also appeared, with ensignes displayed, the one before the towne upon the shore by the sea side, which marched towards our landing place, as though they would encounter us; the other in a valley to the Southwards of the platforme, as if they would have come to helpe the Townesmen: during which time, they in the platforme also played upon us with great Ordinance. Notwithstanding my L. (having set his men in order) marched along the sea shore, upon the sands, betwixt the sea & the towne towards the platforme for the space of a mile or more, & then the shore growing rockie, & permitting no further progresse without much difficultie, he entred into the towne & passed through the street without resistance, unto the platforme; for those companies before mentioned at my Lo. approching, were soone dispersed, and suddenly vanished.

The taking of the towne and platforme of Fayal.

Likewise they of the platforme, being all fled at my Lordes comming thither, left him and his company to scale the walles, to enter and take possession without resistance.

[II. ii. 158.]

In the meane time our shippes ceased not to batter the foresaid Towne and Platforme with great shotte, till such time as we saw the Red-Crosse of England flourishing upon the Forefront thereof.

This Fayal is the principall towne in all that island,
& is situate directly over against the high and mighty
mountaine Pico, lying towards the West Northwest from
that mountaine, being devided therefrom by a narrow
Sea, which at that place is by estimation about some
two or three leagues in bredth betweene the Isles of
Fayal and Pico.

The towne conteyned some three hundred housholds,
their houses were faire and strongly builded of lime
and stone, and double covered with hollow tyles much
like our roofe-tyles, but that they are lesse at the one
end then at the other.

Every house almost had a cisterne or well in a garden
on the backe side: in which gardens grew vines (with
ripe clusters of grapes) making pleasant shadowes, and
Tabacco nowe commonly knowen and used in England,
wherewith their women there dye their faces reddish, to
make them seeme fresh and young: Pepper Indian and
common; figge-trees bearing both white and red figges:
Peach trees not growing very tall: Orenges, Limons,
Quinces, Potato-roots, &c. Sweete wood (Cedar I
thinke) is there very common, even for building and
firing.

My Lord having possessed himselfe of the towne
and platforme, and being carefull of the preservation
of the towne, gave commandement, that no mariner or
souldier should enter into any house, to make any spoyle
thereof. But especially he was carefull that the Churches
and houses of religion there should be kept inviolate,
which was accordingly performed, through his appointment of guarders and keepers for those places: but
the rest of the towne eyther for want of the former
inhibition, or for desire of spoyle & prey, was rifled,
& ransacked by the souldiers & mariners, who scarcely
left any house unsearched, out of which they tooke
such things as liked them, as chestes of sweete wood,
chaires, cloth, coverlets, hangings, bedding, apparell: and
further ranged into the countrey, where some of them

8

also were hurt by the inhabitants. The Friery there conteyning and maintayning thirtie Franciscan Friers (among whom we could not finde any one able to speake true Latine) was builded by a Fryer of Angra in Tercera of the same order, about the yeare of our Lord one thousand five hundred and sixe. The tables in the hall had seates for the one side onely, and were alwayes covered, as readie at all times for dinner or supper.

From Wednesday in the afternoone, at which time we entred the towne, til Saturday night, we continued there, untill the Inhabitants had agreed and payed for the ransome of the towne, two thousand duckats, most part whereof was Church-plate.

We found in the platforme eight and fiftie yron peeces of Ordinance, whereof three and twentie (as I remember) or more were readie mounted upon their carriages, betweene Barricadoes, upon a platforme towardes the sea-side, all which Ordinance wee tooke, and set the platforme on fire, and so departed: My Lord having invited to dinner in the Victorie, on the Sunday following, so many of the Inhabitants as would willingly come (save onely Diego Gomes the Governour, who came but once onely to parle about the ransome) onely foure came and were well entertained, and solemnely dismissed with sound of drumme and trumpets, and a peale of Ordinance: to whom my Lord delivered his letter subscribed with his owne hand, importing a request to all other Englishmen to abstaine from any further molesting them, save onely for fresh water, and victuals necessary for their intended voyage. During our abode here (viz. the 11 of September) two men came out of Pico which had beene prisoners there: Also at Fayal we set at libertie a prisoner translated from S. Jago who was cousin to a servant of Don Anthonio king of Portugall in England: These prisoners we deteyned with us.

On Munday we sent our boates a shore for fresh water, which (by reason of the raine that fell the former night) came plentifully running downe the hilles, and would

otherwise have beene hard to be gotten there. On
Tuesday likewise having not yet sufficiently served our
turnes, we sent againe for fresh water, which was then
not so easie to be gotten as the day before, by reason
of a great winde: which in the afternoone increased also
in such sort, that we thought it not safe to ride so neere
the land; whereupon we weyed anker and so departed
Northwest and by west, alongst the coast of Fayal Island.
Some of the Inhabitants comming aboord to us this day,
tolde us that alwayes about that time of the yeere such
windes West Southwest blew on that coast.

This day, as we sayled neere Saint Georges Island, a
huge fish lying still a litle under water, or rather even
therewith, appeared hard by a head of us, the sea breaking upon his backe, which was blacke coloured, in such
sort as deeming at the first it had beene a rocke, and the
[II. ii. 159.] ship stemming directly with him, we were put in a
sudden feare for the time: till soone after we saw him
move out of the way.

The 16 of September in the night it lightened much,
whereupon there followed great winds and raine, which
continued the 17 18 19 20 and 21 of the same. The 23
of September we came againe into Faial road to weigh an
anker which (for haste and feare of foule weather) wee
had left there before, where we went on shore to see the
towne, the people (as we thought) having now setled
themselves there againe, but notwithstanding many of
them through too much distrustfulnesse, departed and
prepared to depart with their packets at the first sight
of us: untill such time as they were assured by my
Lord, that our comming was not any way to injury
them, but especially to have fresh water, and some other
things needefull for us, contenting them for the same.

So then we viewed the Towne quietly, and bought
such things as we desired for our money as if we had
bene in England. And they helped to fill us in fresh
water, receiving for their paines such satisfaction as contented them.

The 25 day we were forced againe to depart from thence, before we had sufficiently watered, by reason of a great tempest that suddenly arose in the night, in so much, that my Lord himselfe soone after midnight raysed our men out of their Cabines to wey anker, himselfe also together with them haling at the Capsten, and after chearing them up with wine.

The next day we sent our Caravell and the Sawsie-Jacke to the road of Saint Michael, to see what they could espie: we following after them upon the 27 day, plying to and fro, came within sight of S. Michael, but by contrary windes the 28 29 and 30 dayes wee were driven to leewarde, and could not get neere the Island.

The first of October wee sayled alongst Tercera, and even against Brasill (a promontorie neere to Angra the strongest Towne in that Island) wee espied some boates comming to the Towne, and made out towardes them: but being neere to the lande they ranne to shoare and escaped us.

In the afternoone we came neere to Graciosa, where-upon my Lord foorthwith sent Captain Lister to the Ilanders, to let them understand that his desire was onely to have water and wine of them, and some fresh victuals, and not any further to trouble them. They answered they could give no resolute answere to this demaund, untill the Governors of the Iland had con-sulted therupon, and therefore desired him to send againe to them the next day.

Upon the second day of October early in the morning, we sent forth our long boat and Pinnesse, with emptie Caske, and about some fiftie or sixty men together with the Margaret, and Captaine Davis his shippe: for we now wanted all the rest of our consortes. But when our men would have landed, the Ilanders shot at them, and would not suffer them. And troupes of men appeared upon land, with ensignes displayed to resist us: So our boates rowed alongst the shoare, to finde some place where they might land, not with too much

11

disadvantage: our shippes and they still shooting at the Ilanders: but no place could be founde where they might land without great perill of loosing many of their lives, and so were constrayned to retire without receiving any answere, as was promised the day before. We had three men hurt in this conflict, whilest our boates were together in consulting what was best to be done: two of them were stroken with a great shot (which the Ilanders drew from place to place with Oxen) wherewith the one lost his hand, and the other his life within two or three dayes after: the third was shot into his necke with a small shot, without any great hurt.

With these newes our company returned backe againe at night, whereupon preparation was made to goe to them againe the next day: but the day was farre spent before we could come neere them with our ship: neither could we finde any good ground to anker in, where we might lye to batter the Towne, and further we could finde no landing place, without great danger to loose many men: which might turne not only to the overthrow of our voiage, but also put the Queenes ship in great perill for want of men to bring her home. Therefore my Lord thought it best to write to them to this effect: That he could not a litle marvell at their inhumanitie and crueltie which they had shewed towards his men, seeing they were sent by him unto them in peaceable manner to receive their answere which they had promised to give the day before: and that were it not for Don Antonio their lawfull king his sake, he could not put up so great injury at their hands, without just revengement upon them: notwithstanding for Don Antonio his sake, whose friend he was, he was yet content to send to them once againe for their answere: At night Captaine Lister returned with this answere from them. That their Gunner shot off one of their peeces, which was charged with pouder onely, and was stopped; which our men thinking it had bin shot at them, shot againe, and so beganne the fight: [II. ii. 160.] and that the next morning they would send my Lord a

12

resolute answere to his demaunde, for as yet they could not knowe their Governours minde herein. The next morning there came unto us a boate from the shoare with a flagge of truce, wherein were three of the chiefe men of the Island, who agreed with my Lorde that hee should have of them sixtie buttes of wine, and fresh victuals to refresh himselfe and his companie withall: but as for fresh water, they could not satisfie our neede therein, having themselves little or none, saving such as they saved in vessels or cisternes when it rayned, and that they had rather give us two tunnes of wine then one of water: but they requested that our souldiers might not come on shoare, for they themselves would bring all they had promised to the water-side, which request was graunted, we keeping one of them aboord with us untill their promise was performed, and the other we sent to shoare with our emptie Caske, and some of our men to helpe to fill, and bring them away with such other provision as was promised: so the Margaret, Captaine Davis his shippe, and another of Weymouth stayed ryding at anker before the Towne, to take in our provision. This shippe of Weymouth came to us the day before, and had taken a rich Prize (as it was reported) worth sixteene thousand pound, which brought us newes that the West-Indian Fleete was not yet come, but would come very shortly. But we with the Victorie put off to sea, and upon Saturday the fourth of October, we tooke a French shippe of Saint Malo (a citie of the unholy league) loden with fish from Newfoundland: which had beene in so great a tempest, that she was constrayned to cut her mayne mast overboord for her safetie, and was now comming to Graciosa, to repaire her selfe. But so hardly it befell her, that she did not onely not repaire her former losses, but lost all that remayned unto us. The chiefe of her men we tooke into our ship, and sent some of our men, mariners, and souldiers into her to bring her into England.

Upon the Sunday following at night, all our pro-

mised provision was brought unto us from Gratiosa:
and we friendly dismissed the Ilanders with a peale of
Ordinance.

Upon Munday, Tuesday, and Wednesday, we plyed
to and fro about those Islandes, being very rough weather.
And upon Thursday at night, being driven some three
or foure leagues from Tercera, we saw fifteene saile of
the West-Indian Fleete comming into the Haven at
Angra in Tercera. But the winde was such, that for the
space of foure dayes after, though wee lay as close by the
winde as was possible, yet we could not come neere them.
In this time we lost our late French Prize, not being able
to lie so neere the winde as we, and heard no more
of her till we came to England where shee safely arrived.
Upon Munday we came very neere the Havens mouth,
being minded to have runne in amongst them, and to
have fetched out some of them if it had beene possible:
But in the end this enterprise was deemed too daungerous, considering the strength of the place where they
rode, being haled and towed in neerer the towne, at the
first sight of our approching, and lying under the protection of the Castle of Brasill, on the one side (having
in it five and twentie peeces of Ordinance) and a fort
on the other side wherein were 13 or 14 great brasse
pieces. Besides, when we came neere land the winde
prooved too scant for us to attempt any such enterprise.

Upon Tuesday the fourteenth of October we sent our
boate to the roade to sound the depth, to see if there
were any ankoring place for us, where we might lie
without shot of the Castle and Fort, and within shot of
some of those shippes, that we might either make them
come out to us, or sinke them where they lay. Our
boate returned having found out such a place as we
desired, but the winde would not suffer us to come
neere it, and againe if we could have ankored there, it
was thought likely that they would rather runne themselves a ground to save their lives and liberties, and some
of their goods, then come foorth to loose their liberties

and goods to us their enemies. So we shot at them
to see if we could reach them, but it fell farre short.
And thus we departed, thinking it not probable that they
would come foorth so long as we watched for them before
the havens mouth, or within sight of them. For the
space of five dayes after we put off to sea, and lay without
sight of them, and sent a pinnesse to lie out of sight
close by the shore, to bring us word if they should come
foorth. After a while the Pinnesse returned and tolde
us that those ships in the Haven had taken downe their
sayles, and let downe their toppe mastes: so that wee
supposed they would never come foorth, till they perceived us to bee quite gone.

Wherefore upon the 20 of October, hearing that there
were certaine Scottish ships at Saint Michael, we sayled
thither, and found there one Scottish roader, and two
or three more at Villa Franca, the next road a league
or two from the towne of S. Michael, to the Eastwards:
of whom we had for our reliefe some small quantitie
of wine (viz. some five or sixe buttes of them all) and
some fresh water, but nothing sufficient to serve our
turne.

Upon Tuesday the one and twentieth of October, we
sent our long boate to shore for fresh water at a brooke
a little to the Westwards from Villa Franca.

But the Inhabitants espying us came downe with two [II. ii. 161.]
Ensignes displayed, and about some hundred and fiftie
men armed, to withstand our landing. So our men
having spent all their pouder upon them in attempting
to land, and not being able to prevaile at so great oddes,
returned frustrate.

From hence we departed towardes Saint Maries Island,
minding to water there, and then to goe for the coast
of Spaine. For we had intelligence that it was a place
of no great force, and that we might water there very
well: therefore upon Friday following, my Lord sent
Captaine Lister, and Captaine Amias Preston now Sir
Amias Preston (who not long before came to us out

of his owne shippe, and she loosing us in the night, hee
was forced to tarry still with us) with our long boate
and Pinnesse, and some sixtie or seventie shotte in them,
with a friendly letter to the Ilanders, that they would
grant us leave to water, and we would no further trouble
them.

So we departed from the Victorie for the Iland, about
nine of the clocke in the forenoone, and rowed freshly
untill about 3 a clocke afternoone. At which time our
men being something weary with rowing, and being
within a league or two of the shore, and 4 or 5 leagues
from the Victorie, they espied (to their refreshing) two
ships ryding at anker hard under the towne, whereupon
having shifted some 6 or 7 of our men into Captaine
Davis his boate, being too much pestered in our owne,
and retayning with us some 20 shot in the pinnesse,
we made way towardes them with all the speede we
could.

By the way as we rowed we saw boates passing betwixt
the roaders and the shore, and men in their shirtes
swimming and wading to shoare, who as we perceived
afterwardes, were labouring to set those shippes fast on
ground, and the Inhabitants as busily preparing themselves for the defence of those roaders, their Iland, and
themselves. When we came neere them, Captaine Lister
commaunded the Trumpets to be sounded, but pro-
hibited any shot to be discharged at them, untill they
had direction from him : But some of the companie,
either not well perceiving or regarding what he sayd,
immediatly upon the sound of the Trumpets discharged
their pieces at the Islanders, which for the most part lay
in trenches and fortefied places unseene, to their owne
best advantage : who immediatly shot likewise at us,
both with small and great shot, without danger to
themselves : Notwithstanding Captaine Lister earnestly
hastened forward the Saylers that rowed, who beganne to
shrinke at that shot, flying so fast about their eares, and
himselfe first entring one of the shippes that lay a litle

further from shoare then the other, we spedily followed
after him into her, still plying them with our shot. And
having cut in sunder her Cables and Hausers, towed her
away with our Pinnesse. In the meane time Captaine
Davis his boate overtooke us and entred into the other
shippe, which also (as the former) was forsaken by all her
men : but they were constrayned to leave her & to come
againe into their boate (whilest shot and stones from
shoare flew fast amongst them) finding her to sticke so
fast a grounde, that they could not stire her : which
the Townesmen also perceiving, and seeing that they
were but fewe in number, and us (busied about the
other ship) not comming to ayde them, were preparing
to have come and taken them. But they returned unto
us, and so together we came away towards the Victory,
towing after us the Prize that we had now taken, which
was lately come from Brasill, loden with Sugar.

In this fight we had two men slaine and 16 wounded :
and as for them, it is like they had litle hurt, lying for
the most part behind stone walles, which were builded
one above another hard by the sea side, upon the end
of the hill whereupon the Towne stoode betwixt two
valleyes. Upon the toppe of the hill lay their great
Ordinance (such as they had) wherewith they shot leaden
bullets, whereof one pierced through our Prizes side,
and lay still in the shippe without doing any more harme.

The next day we went againe for water to the same
Iland, but not knowing before the inconvenience and
disadvantage of the place where we attempted to land,
we returned frustrate.

The same night the 25 of October we departed for
S. Georges Iland for fresh water, whither we came on
Munday following October 27, and having espied where
a spout of water came running downe : the pinnesse and
long boate were presently manned and sent under the
conduct of Captaine Preston, and Captaine Munson, by
whom my Lord sent a letter to the Ilanders as before,
to grant us leave to water onely, and we would no

further trouble them: notwithstanding our men comming on shoare found some of the poore Ilanders, which for feare of us hid themselves amongst the rockes.

And on Wednesday following our boats returned with fresh water, whereof they brought only sixe tunnes for the Victorie, alleaging they could get no more, thinking [II. ii. 162.] (as it was supposed) that my Lord having no more provision of water and wine, but onely 12 tunnes, would not goe for the coast of Spaine, but straight for the coast of England, as many of our men greatly desired: notwithstanding my Lord was unwilling so to doe, and was minded the next day to have taken in more water: but through roughnesse of the seas and winde, and unwillingnesse of his men it was not done. Yet his Hon. purposed not to returne with so much provision unspent, and his voyage (as he thought) not yet performed in such sort as mought give some reasonable contentment or satisfaction to himselfe and others.

Therefore because no more water could now conveniently be gotten, and being uncertaine when it could be gotten, and the time of our staying aboord also uncertaine, the matter being referred to the choyse of the whole companie, whither they would tarrie longer, till wee might be more sufficiently provided of fresh water, or goe by the coast of Spaine for England, with halfe so much allowance of drinke as before, they willingly agreed that every mease should bee allowed at one meale but halfe so much drinke as they were accustomed (except them that were sicke or wounded) and so to goe for England, taking the coast of Spaine in our way, to see if we could that way make up our voyage.

Upon Saturday Octob. 31 we sent the Margaret (because she leaked much) directly for England, together with the Prize of Brasile which we tooke at S. Marie, and in them some of our hurt and wounded men or otherwise sicke were sent home as they desired, for England: but Captaine Monson was taken out of the Megge into the Victorie.

18

So we held on our course for the coast of Spaine
with a faire winde and a large which before we seldome
had. And upon Twesday following being the 4 of
Novemb. we espied a saile right before us, which we
chased till about three a clocke in the afternoone, at
which time we overtaking her, she stroke sayle, and
being demaunded who was her owner and from whence
she was, they answered, a Portugall, and from Pernan-
bucke in Brasile. She was a ship of som 110 tuns
burden, fraighted with 410 chestes of Sugar, and 50
Kintals of Brasill-wood, every Kintall contayning one
hundred pound weight: we tooke her in latitude nine
and twentie degrees, about two hundred leagues from
Lisbone westwards: Captaine Preston was presently sent
unto her, who brought the principall of her men aboord
the Victorie, and certaine of our men, mariners and
souldiers were sent aboord her. The Portugals of this
Prize told us that they saw another ship before them
that day about noone. Having therefore dispatched all
things about the Prize aforesaid and left our long boat
with Captaine Davis, taking his lesser boat with us,
we made way after this other ship with all the sayles
we could beare, holding on our course due East, and
giving order to Captaine Davis his ship and the Prize
that they should follow us due East, and that if they
had sight of us the morning following they should
follow us still: if not, they should goe for England.

The next morning we espied not the sayle which we
chased, and Captaine Davis his ship and the Prize were
behinde us out of sight: but the next Thursday the
sixt of November (being in latitude 38 degrees 30
minutes, and about sixtie leagues from Lisbone westwards) early in the morning Captaine Preston descried
a sayle some two or three leagues a head of us, after
which we presently hastened our chase, and overtooke
her about eight or nine of the clocke before noone.
She came lately from Saint Michaels roade, having beene
before at Brasill loden with Sugar and Brasile. Having

sent our boat to them to bring some of the chiefe of
their men aboord the Victorie, in the meane time whilest
they were in comming to us one out of the maine toppe
espied another saile a head some three or foure leagues
from us. So immediately upon the returne of our boate,
having sent her backe againe with some of our men
aboord the prize, we pursued speedily this new chase,
with all the sayles we could packe on, and about
two a clocke in the afternoone overtooke her: she had
made provision to fight with us, having hanged the
sides of the ship so thicke with hides (wherewith
especially she was loden) that musket shot could not have
pearced them: but yer we had discharged two great
pieces of our Ordinance at her, she stroke sayle, and
approching neerer, we asking of whence they were, they
answered from the West-Indies, from Mexico, and Saint
John de Lowe (truely called Ulhua.) This ship was
of some three or foure hundred tunnes, and had in her
seven hundred hides worth tenne shillings a peece: sixe
chests of Cochinell, every chest houlding one hundred
pound weight, and every pound worth sixe and twentie
shillings and eight pence, and certaine chests of Sugar
and China dishes, with some plate and silver.

The Captaine of her was an Italian, and by his behaviour seemed to be a grave, wise, and civill man:
he had put an adventure in this shippe five and twentie
thousand Duckats. Wee tooke him with certaine other
of her chiefest men (which were Spaniards) into the
Victorie: and Captaine Lister with so manie other of
[II. ii. 163.] the chiefest of our Mariners, souldiers, and saylers as
were thought sufficient, to the number of 20. or there
abouts, were sent into her. In the meane time (we
staying) our other prizes which followed after, came up
to us. And nowe wee had our hands full and with
joy shaped our course for England, for so it was thought
meetest, having now so many Portugals, Spaniards and
Frenchmen amongst us, that if we should have taken
any more prizes afterwards, wee had not bene well able

to have manned them without endangering our selves. So about 6. of the clocke in the afternoone (when our other prize had overtaken us) wee set saile for England. But our prizes not being able to beare us company without sparing them many of our sailes, which caused our ship to rowle and wallow, in such sort that it was not onely very troublesome to us, but, as it was thought, would also have put the maine Maste in danger of falling overboord: having acquainted them with these inconveniences, we gave them direction to keepe their courses together, folowing us, and so to come to Portsmouth. We tooke this last prize in the latitude of 39. degrees, and about 46. leagues to the Westwards from The Rocke.

She was one of those 16. ships which we saw going into the haven at Angra in Terçera, October 8. Some of the men that we tooke out of her tolde us, that whilest wee were plying up and downe before that haven, as before was shewed, expecting the comming foorth of those shippes, three of the greatest and best of them, at the appointment of the Governour of Terçera, were unloden of their treasure and marchandize. And in every of them were put three hundred Souldiers, which were appointed to have come to lay the Victory aboord in the night, and take her: but when this should have bene done the Victory was gone out of their sight.

Now we went meerily before the winde with all the sailes we could beare, insomuch that in the space of 24. houres, we sailed neere 47. leagues, that is sevenscore English miles, betwixt Friday at noone and Saturday at noone (notwithstanding the shippe was very foule, and much growne with long being at Sea) which caused some of our company to make accompt they would see what running at Tilt there should bee at Whitehall upon the Queenes day. Others were imagining what a Christmas they would keepe in England with their shares of the prizes we had taken. But so it befell, that we kept a colde Christmas with the Bishop and his clearks (rockes that lye to the Westwards from Sylly, and the Westerne parts of England:) For soone after the wind scanting came about to the Eastwards (the worst part of the heavens for us, from which the winde could blow) in such sort, that we could not fetch any part of England. And hereupon also our allowance of drinke, which was scant ynough before, was yet more more scanted, because of the scarcitie thereof in the shippe. So that now a man was allowed but halfe a pinte at a meale, and that many times colde water, and scarce sweete. Notwithstanding this was an happie estate in comparison of that which followed: For from halfe a pinte we came to a quarter, and that lasted not long neither, so that by reason of this great scarcitie of drinke, and contrarietie of winde, we thought to put into Ireland, there to relieve our wants. But when wee came neere thither, lying at hull all night (tarrying for the daylight of the next morning, whereby we might the safelyer bring our ship into some convenient harbour there) we were driven so farre to lee-ward, that we could fetch no part of Ireland, so as with heavie hearts and sad cheare, wee were constreined to returne backe againe, and expect till it should please God to send us a faire winde either for England or Ireland. In the meane time we were allowed every man three or foure spoones full of vineger to drinke at a meale: for other drinke we had none, saving onely at two or three meales, when we had in stead hereof as much wine, which was wringed out of Wine-lees that remained. With this hard fare (for by reason of our great want of drinke, wee durst eate but very litle) wee continued for the space of a fourtnight or thereabouts: Saving that now and then wee feasted for it in the meane time: And that was when there fell any haile or raine: the haile-stones wee gathered up and did eate them more pleasantly then if they had bene the sweetest Comfits in the world; The raine-drops were so carefully saved, that so neere as wee coulde, not one was lost in all our shippe. Some hanged up sheetes tied

with cordes by the foure corners, and a weight in the
midst that the water might runne downe thither, and so
be received into some vessell set or hanged underneth :
Some that wanted sheetes, hanged up nakins, and cloutes,
and watched them till they were thorow wet, then wring-
ing and sucking out the water. And that water which
fell downe and washed away the filth and soyling of the
shippe, trod under foote, as bad as running downe the
kennell many times when it raineth, was not lost I warrant
you, but watched and attended carefully (yea sometimes
with strife and contention) at every scupper-hole, and
other place where it ranne downe, with dishes, pots, cannes,
and Jarres, whereof some drunke hearty draughts even
as it was, mud and all, without tarrying to clense or
settle it : Others clensed it first, but not often, for it
was so thicke and went so slowly thorow, that they
might ill endure to tary so long, and were loth to loose
too much of such precious stuffe : some licked with
their tongues (like dogges) the boards under feete, the
sides, railes, and Masts of the shippe : others that were
more ingenious, fastened girdles or ropes about the [II. ii. 164.]
Mastes, dawbing tallow betwixt them and the Maste
(that the raine might not runne downe betweene) in
such sort, that those ropes or girdles hanging lower on
the one side then on the other, a spout of leather was
fastened to the lowest part of them, that all the raine
drops that came running downe the Maste, might meete
together at that place, and there be received.

Hee that got a canne of water by these meanes was
spoken of, sued to, and envied as a rich man. Quàm
pulchrum digito monstrari & dicier hic est? Some of the
poore Spaniards that we had taken (who notwithstanding
had the same allowance that our owne men had) would
come and crave of us, for the love of God, but so much
water as they could holde in the hollow of their hand :
and they had it, notwithstanding our great extremitie,
to teache them some humanitie in stead of their accustomed barbaritie, both to us and other nations heretofore.

They put also bullets of lead into their mouthes to slake their thirst.

Now in every corner of the shippe were heard the lamentable cries of sicke and wounded men sounding wofully in our eares, crying out and pitifully complaining for want of drinke, being ready to die, yea many dying for lacke thereof, so as by reason of this great extremitie we lost many more men, then wee had done all the voyage before: having before this time bene so well and sufficiently provided for, that we lived in maner as well and healthfully, and died as few as if wee had bene in England, whereas now lightly every day some were cast overboord.

But the second day of December 1589. was a festivall day with us, for then it rained a good pace, and wee saved some pretie store of raine water (though wee were well wet for it, and that at midnight) and filled our skins full besides: notwithstanding it were muddie and bitter with washing the shippe, but (with some sugar which we had to sweeten it withall) it went merrily downe, yet remembred we and wished for with all our hearts, many a Conduit, pumpe, spring, & streame of cleare sweete running water in England: And how miserable wee had accompted some poore soules whom we had seene driven for thirst to drinke thereof, and how happy we would now have thought our selves if we might have had our fills of the same: yet should wee have fared the better with this our poore feasting, if we might have had our meate and drinke (such and so much as it was) stand quietly before us: but beside all the former extremities, wee were so tossed and turmoiled with such horrible stormie and tempestuous weather, that every man had best holde fast his Canne, cup, and dish in his hands, yea and himselfe too, many times, by the ropes, railes, or sides of the ship or else he should soone finde all under feete.

Herewith our maine saile was torne from the yarde and blowne overboord quite away into the sea without recovery, and our other sailes so rent and torne (from side to side some of them) that hardly any of them escaped hole. The raging waves and foming surges of the sea came rowling like mountaines one after another, and overraked the waste of the shippe like a mightie river running over it, whereas in faire weather it was neere 20. foote above the water, that nowe wee might cry out with the princely Prophet Psalme 107. vers. 26. They mount up to heaven, and descend to the deepe, so that their soule melteth away for trouble: they reele too and fro, and stagger like a drunken man, and all their cunning is gone. With this extremitie of foule weather the ship was so tossed and shaken, that by the craking noise it made, and by the leaking which was now much more then ordinary, wee were in great feare it would have shaken in sunder, so that now also we had just cause to pray a litle otherwise then the Poet, though marring the verse, yet mending the meaning.

Deus maris & Cœli, quid enim nisi vota supersunt,
    Solvere quassatæ parcito membra ratis.

Notwithstanding it pleased God of his great goodnesse to deliver us out of this danger. Then forthwith a new maine saile was made and fastened to the yard, and the rest repaired as time and place would suffer: which we had no sooner done, but yet againe wee were troubled with as great extremitie as before, so that againe we were like to have lost our new maine saile, had not Master William Antony the Master of the ship him-selfe (when none else would or durst) ventured with danger of drowning by creeping along upon the maine yarde (which was let downe close to the railes) to gather it up out of the sea, and to fasten it thereto, being in the meane while oft-times ducked over head and eares into the sea.

These stormes were so terrible, that there were some in our company, which confessed they had gone to seas for the space of 20. yeeres, and had never seene the like, and vowed that if ever they returned safe home, they would never come to Sea againe.

The last of November at night we met with an English ship, out of which (because it was too late that night) it was agreed that we should have had the next morning two or three Tunnes of wine, which, as they said, was al the provision of drink they had, save only [II. ii. 165.] a But or two, which they must needs reserve for their owne use: but after that, we heard of them no more, till they were set on ground upon the coast of Ireland, where it appeared that they might have spared us much more then they pretended they could, so as they might wel have relieved our great necessities, and have had sufficient for themselves besides, to bring them into England.

The first of December at night we spake with another English ship, and had some beere out of her, but not sufficient to carry us into England, so that wee were constrained to put into Ireland, the winde so serving.

The next day we came to an anker, not far from the S. Kelmes under the land & winde, where we were somewhat more quiet, but (that being no safe harbour to ride in) the next morning wee went about to weigh anker, but having some of our men hurt at the Capsten, wee were faine to give over and leave it behinde, holding on our course to Ventrie haven, where wee safely arrived the same day, that place being a very safe and convenient harbor for us, that now wee might sing as we had just cause, They that goe downe to the Sea, &c.

So soone as we had ankered here my Lord went foorthwith to shoare, and brought presently fresh water and fresh victuals, as Muttons, pigges, hennes, &c. to refresh his company withall. Notwithstanding himselfe had lately bene very weake, and tasted of the same extremitie that his Company did: For in the time of our former want, having a little fresh water left him remaining in a pot, in the night it was broken, and the water drunke and dried up. Soone after the sicke and wounded men were carried to the next principall Towne, called Dingenacush, being about three miles distant from the foresaide haven, where our shippe roade, to the Eastwards, that there they might be the better refreshed, and had the Chirurgians dayly to attend upon them. Here we wel refreshed our selves whilest the Irish harpe sounded sweetely in our eares, and here we, who for the former extremities were in maner halfe dead, had our lives (as it were) restored unto us againe.

This Dingenacush is the chiefe Towne in al that part of Ireland, it consisteth but of one maine streete, from whence some smaller doe proceede on either side. It hath had gates (as it seemeth) in times past at either ende to open and shut as a Towne of warre, and a Castle also. The houses are very strongly built with thicke stone walles, and narrow windowes like unto Castles: for as they confessed, in time of trouble, by reason of the wilde Irish or otherwise, they used their houses for their defence as Castles. The castle and all the houses in the Towne, save foure, were won, burnt, and ruinated by the Erle of Desmond. These foure houses fortified themselves against him, and withstood him and all his power perforce, so as he could not winne them.

There remaineth yet a thicke stone wall that passeth overthwart the midst of the streete which was a part of their fortification. Notwithstanding whilest they thus defended themselves, as some of them yet alive confessed, they were driven to as great extremities as the Jewes, besieged by Titus the Romane Emperour, insomuch that they were constrained to eat dead mens carcases for hunger. The Towne is nowe againe somewhat repaired, but in effect there remaine but the ruines of the former Towne. Commonly they have no chimneis in their houses, excepting them of the better sort, so that the smoake was very troublesom to us, while we continued there. Their fewell is turfes, which they have very good, and whinnes or furres. There groweth little wood thereabouts, which maketh building chargeable there: as also want of lime (as they reported) which they are faine to fetch from farre, when they have neede thereof. But of stones there is store ynough, so that with them they commonly make their hedges to part ech mans ground from other; and the ground seemeth to be nothing else within but rockes and stones: Yet it is very fruitfull and plentifull of grasse, and graine, as may appeare by the abundance of kine and cattel there: insomuch that we had good muttons (though somewhat lesse then ours in England) for two shillings or five groates a piece, good pigges and hennes for 3. pence a piece.

The greatest want is industrious, painefull, and husbandly inhabitants to till and trimme the ground: for the common sort, if they can provide sufficient to serve from hand to mouth, take no further care.

Of money (as it seemeth) there is very small store amongst them, which perhaps was the cause that made them double and triple the prizes of many things we bought of them, more then they were before our comming thither.

Mines in Ireland.
Good land was here to be had for foure pence the Acre yeerely rent. There are Mines of Alome, Tinne, brasse, and yron. Stones wee sawe there as cleare as Christall, naturally squared like Diamonds.

That part of the Countrey is all ful of great mountaines and hills, from whence came running downe the pleasant streames of sweete fresh running water. The naturall hardnesse of that Nation appeareth in this, that their small children runne usually in the middest of Winter up and downe the streetes bare-foote and bare-
[II. ii. 166.] legged, with no other apparell (many times) save onely a mantell to cover their nakednesse.

The chiefe Officer of their Towne they call their Soveraigne, who hath the same office and authoritie

among them that our Maiors have with us in England,
and hath his Sergeants to attend upon him, and beare
the Mace before him as our Maiors.

We were first intertained at the Soveraignes house,
which was one of those 4. that withstood the Erle of
Desmond in his rebellion. They have the same forme
of Common prayer word for word in Latin, that we have
here in England. Upon the Sunday the Soveraigne
commeth into the Church with the Sergeant before him,
and the Sheriffe and others of the Towne accompany
him, and there they kneele downe every man by himselfe
privately to make his prayers. After this they rise and
go out of the Church againe to drinke, which being
done, they returne againe into the Church, and then the
Minister beginneth prayers.

Their maner of baptizing differeth something from
ours: part of the service belonging thereto is repeated in
Latin, and part in Irish. The Minister taketh the child
in his hands, and first dippeth it backwards, and then
forwards, over head and eares into the cold water in the
midst of Winter, whereby also may appeare their naturall
hardnesse, (as before was specified.) They had neither
Bell, drum, nor trumpet, to call the Parishioners together,
but they expect till their Soveraigne come, and then they
that have any devotion follow him.

They make their bread all in cakes, and, for the tenth
part, the bakers bake for all the towne.

We had of them some 10. or 11. Tunnes of beere for
the Victory, but it proved like a present purgation to
them that tooke it, so that we chose rather to drinke
water then it.

The 20. of December we loosed from hence, having
well provided our selves of fresh water, and other things
necessary, being accompanied with sir Edw. Dennie, his
Lady, and two yong sonnes.

This day in the morning my Lord going ashoare to
dispatch away speedily some fresh water that remained
for the Victory, the winde being very faire for us,

brought us newes that there were 60. Spanish prizes taken and brought to England. For two or three dayes wee had a faire winde, but afterwards it scanted so, that (as I said before) we were faine to keepe a cold Christmas with The Bishop and his clearkes.

After this we met with an English ship, that brought us joyful news of 91. Spanish prizes that were come to England: and sorrowfull newes withall, that the last and best prize we tooke, had suffered shipwracke at a place upon the coast of Cornwal which the Cornish men cal *Captaine Lister drowned.* Als Efferne, that is, Hel-cliffe, and that Captaine Lister and all the men in the ship were drowned, save 5. or 6. the one halfe English, the other Spanish that saved themselves with swimming: but notwithstanding much of the goods were saved, and reserved for us, by sir Francis Godolphin, and the worshipful gentlemen of the Countrey there. My Lord was very sorry for Captaine Listers death, wishing that he had lost his voyage to have saved his life.

The 29. of December we met with another shippe, that tolde us the same newes, and that sir Martin Frobisher, & Captaine Reymond had taken the Admirall and vice-Admirall of the Fleet that we espied going to Terçera haven. But the Admiral was sunke with much leaking, neere to the Idy Stone, a rocke that lieth over against Plimouth sound, and the men were saved.

This ship also certified us that Captaine Prestons ship had taken a prize loden with silver. My Lord entred presently into this ship, & went to Falmouth, and we held on our course for Plimouth. At night we came neere to the Ram-head (the next Cape Westwards from Plimouth sound) but we were afraid to double it in the night, misdoubting the scantnesse of the winde. So we stood off to Sea halfe the night, and towards morning had the winde more large, and made too little spare thereof, that partly for this cause, and partly through mistaking of the land, wee were driven so much to leewards, that we could not double that Cape: Therefore

we returned backe againe, and came into Falmouth haven,
where wee strucke on ground in 17. foote water : but it
was a low ebbe, and ready againe to flowe, and the
ground soft, so as no hurt was done. Here with gladnesse wee set foote againe upon the English ground (long
desired) and refreshed our selves with keeping part of
Christmas upon our native soile.

The valiant fight performed by 10. Merchants ships of London, against 12. Spanish gallies in the Straights of Gibraltar, the 24. of April 1590.

IT is not long since sundry valiant ships
apperTaining to the Marchants of London,
were fraighted & rigged forth, some for
Venice, some for Constantinople, & some
to sundry other places of trafique, among
whom these ensuing met within the
Straights of Gibraltar, as they were
taking their course homewards, having before escaped all
other danger. The first whereof was the Salomon
apperteining to M. Alderman Barnam of London, and
M. Bond, and M. Twyd of Harwich ; which went foorth
the first day of February last. The second was the
Margaret and John belonging to M. Wats of London :
The thirde was the Minion : The fourth was the
Ascension. The fifth was the Centurion of Master
Cordal : The sixt the Violet : the seventh the Samuel :
the eight the Crescent : the ninth the Elizabeth : and the
10. was the Richard belonging to M. Duffield. All
these ships being of notable and approved service, comming neere to the mouth of the Straights hard by the
coast of Barbary, descried twelve tall Gallies bravely
furnished and strongly provided with men and munition,
ready to seaze upon these English ships : which being
perceived by the Captaines and Masters thereof, wee
made speedy preparation for the defence of our selves,

[II. ii. 167.]

February
1590.

31

still waiting all the night long for the approching of the enemie. In the morning early being the Tuesday in Easter weeke, and the 24 of April 1590. according to our usual. customes, we said Service and made our prayers unto Almightie God, beseeching him to save us from the hands of such tyrants as the Spaniards, whom we justly imagined to be, and whom we knew and had found to be our most mortall enemies upon the Sea. And having finished our prayers, and set our selves in a readinesse, we perceived them to come towards us, and that they were indeede the Spanish Gallies that lay under the conduct of Andre Doria, who is Vice-roy for the King of Spaine in the Straights of Gibraltar, and a notable knowne enemie to all Englishmen. So when they came somewhat neerer unto us, they waved us a maine for the King of Spaine, and wee waved them a maine for the Queene of England, at which time it pleased Almightie God greatly to incourage us all in such sort, as that the neerer they came the lesse we feared their great multitudes and huge number of men, which were planted in those Gallies to the number of two or three hundred men in ech Gallie. And it was thus concluded among us, that the foure first and tallest ships should be placed hindmost, and the weaker & smallest ships formost, and so it was performed, every man being ready to take part of such successe as it should please God to send.

At the first encounter the Gallies came upon us very fiercely, yet God so strengthened us, that if they had bene ten times more, we had not feared them at all. Whereupon the Salomon being a hot shippe, and having sundry cast pieces in her, gave the first shotte in such a sowre sort, as that it shared away so many men as sate on the one side of a Gallie, and pierced her through in such maner, as that she was ready to sinke, which made them to assault us the more fiercely. Whereupon the rest of our shippes, especially the foure chiefest, namely, the Margaret and John, the Minion, and the Ascension

followed, and gave a hot charge upon them, and they
at us, where began a hot and fierce battaile with great
valiancie the one against the other, and so continued for
the space of sixe houres. About the beginning of this
our fight there came two Flemings to our Fleet, who
seeing the force of the Gallies to be so great, the one of
them presently yeelded, strooke his sailes, and was taken
by the Gallies, whereas if they would have offered themselves to have fought in our behalfe and their owne
defence, they needed not to have bene taken so cowardly
as they were to their cost. The other Fleming being
also ready to performe the like piece of service began to
vaile his sailes, and intended to have yeelded immediatly.
But the Trumpetter in that shippe plucked foorth his
faulchion and stepped to the Pilote at the helme, and
vowed that if he did not speedily put off to the English
Fleete, and so take part with them, he would presently
kill him: which the Pilote for feare of death did, and so
by that meanes they were defended from present death,
and from the tyrannie of those Spaniards, which doubtlesse they should have found at their handes.

Thus we continued in fight sixe houres and somewhat
more, wherein God gave us the upper hand, and we
escaped the hands of so many enemies, who were constrained to flie into harbour and shroude themselves from
us, and with speed to seeke for their owne safetie. This
was the handie worke of God, who defended us all from
danger in such sort, as that there was not one man of us
slaine. And in all this fierce assault made upon us by
the Spanish power, wee sustained no hurt or damage at
all more then this, that the shrouds and backestay of the
Salomon, who gave the first and last shot, and galled
the enemie shrewdly all the time of the battell, were
cleane striken off.

The battel being ceased, we were constrained for want
of wind to stay and waft up and downe, and then went
backe againe to Tition in Barbary, which is six leagues
off from Gibraltar, and when we came thither we found

the people wonderous favourable to us, who being but Moores and heathen people shewed us where to have fresh water and al other necessaries for us. And there we had such good intertainment, as if we had bene in any place of England.

The governour was one that favoured us greatly, whom wee in respect of his great friendship presented with giftes and such commodities as we had in our custodie, which he wonderfully wel accepted of: and here we stayed foure dayes.

After the battell was ceased, which was on Easter Tuesday, we stayed for want of winde before Gibraltar, untill the next morning, where wee were becalmed, and [II. ii. 168.] therefore looked every houre when they would have sent foorth some fresh supply against us, but they were farre unable to doe it, for all their Gallies were so sore battered, that they durst not come foorth of the harbour, by reason of our hot resistance which they so lately before had received. Yet were they greatly urged thereunto by the Governour of the said Towne of Gibraltar.

At our being at Tition in Barbary, there we heard report of the hurt that wee had done to the Gallies, for at our comming from them wee could not well discerne any thing at all by reason of the smoake which the powder had made: there we heard that we had almost spoiled those twelve Gallies by shooting them cleane through, that two of them were ready to sinke, and that wee had slaine of their men such great abundance, as that they were not able to furnish forth any more Gallies at all for that yeere.

Thus after we came from Tition, we assayed to depart the Straight three severall times, but could not passe, yet, God be thanked, the fourth time wee came safely away, and so sailed with a pleasant winde untill wee came upon the coast of England, which was in the beginning of the moneth of July 1590.

The valiant fight performed in the Straight of
Gibraltar, by the Centurion of London, against
five Spanish Gallies, in the moneth of April
1591.

N the moneth of November 1590, there
were sundry shippes appertaining to
severall Marchants of London, which
were rigged and fraught foorth with
marchandize, for sundry places within
the Straight of Gibraltar: who, together
having winde and weather, which oft-
time fell out very uncertaine, arrived safely in short
space, at such places as they desired. Among whom was
the Centurion of London, a very tall shippe of burden,
yet but weakely manned, as appeareth by this discourse
following.

This aforesaid shippe called The Centurion safely
arrived at Marseils, where after they had delivered their
goods, they stayed about the space of five weekes, and
better, and then tooke in lading, intending to returne to
England.

Now when the Centurion was ready to come away
from Marseils, there were sundry other shippes of smaller
burden which entreated the Master thereof, (whose name
is Robert Bradshaw, dwelling at Lime-house) to stay a
day or two for them, untill they were in a readinesse to
depart with them, thereby perswading them, that it would
be farre better for them to stay and goe together in
respect of their assistance, then to depart of themselves
without company, and so happily for want of aide fall
into the hands of their enemies in the Spanish Gallies.
Upon which reasonable perswasion, notwithstanding that
this shippe was of such sufficiencie as they might hazard
her in the danger of the Sea, yet they stayed for those
litle shippes, according to their request, who together did
put to Sea from Marseils, and vowed in generall not to

35

flie one from another, if they should happen to meete with any Spanish Gallies.

These small shippes, accompanied with the Centurion, sayling along the coast of Spaine, were upon Easter day in the Straight of Gibraltar suddenly becalmed, where immediatly they saw sundry Gallies make towards them, in very valiant and couragious sort: the chiefe Leaders and souldiers in those Gallies bravely apparelled in silke coates, with their silver whistles about their neckes, and great plumes of feathers in their hattes, who with their Calivers shot at the Centurion so fast as they might: so that by 10. of the clocke and somewhat before, they had boorded the Centurion, who before their comming had prepared for them, and intended to give them so soure a welcome as they might. And thereupon having prepared their close fights, and all things in a readinesse, they called upon God, on whom onely they trusted: and having made their prayers, and cheered up one another to fight so long as life endured, they beganne to discharge their great Ordinance upon the Gallies, but the little shippes durst not come forward, but lay aloofe, while five Gallies had boorded them, yea and with their grapling irons made their Gallies fast to the said shippe called the Centurion.

The Gallies were grapled to the Centurion in this maner, two lay on one side, and two on another, and the Admirall lay full in the sterne, which galled and battered the Centurion so sore, that her maine Maste was greatly weakened, her sailes filled with many holes, and the Mizzen and sterne made almost unserviceable.

During which time there was a sore and deadly fight on both sides, in which the Trumpet of the Centurion sounded foorth the deadly points of warre, and encouraged them to fight manfully against their adversaries: on the contrary part, there was no warlike Musicke in the

[II. ii. 169.] Spanish Gallies, but onely their whistles of silver, which they sounded foorth to their owne contentment: in which fight many a Spaniard was turned into the Sea, and they

in multitudes came crauling and hung upon the side of
the shippe, intending to have entred into the same, but
such was the courage of the Englishmen, that so fast
as the Spaniards did come to enter, they gave them such
entertainment, that some of them were glad to tumble
alive into the Sea, being remedilesse for ever to get
up alive. In the Centurion there were in all, of men
and boyes, fourtie and eight, who together fought most
valiantly, and so galled the enemie, that many a brave
and lustie Spaniard lost his life in that place.

The Centurion was fired five severall times, with wilde
fire and other provision, which the Spaniards threw in
for that purpose: yet, God be thanked, by the great
and diligent foresight of the Master it did no harme
at all.

In every of the Gallies there were about 200.
souldiers: who together with the shot, spoiled, rent,
and battered the Centurion very sore, shot through her
maine Maste, and slew 4. of the men in the said shippe,
the one of them being the Masters mate.

Ten other persons were hurt, by meanes of splinters
which the Spaniards shotte: yea, in the ende when their
provision was almost spent, they were constrained to
shoote at them hammers, and the chaines from their
slaves, and yet God bee thanked, they received no more
domage: but by spoyling and overwearying of the
Spaniards, the Englishmen constrained them to ungrapple
themselves, and get them going: and sure if there had
bene any other fresh shippe or succour to have relieved
and assisted the Centurion, they had slaine, suncke, or
taken all those Gallies and their Souldiers.

The Dolphin lay a loofe off and durst not come
neere, while the other two small shippes fledde away,
so that one of the Gallies went from the Centurion
and set upon the Dolphin, which shippe immediatly
was set on fire with their owne powder, whereby both
men and shippe perished: but whether it was with their
good wills or no, that was not knowen unto the Cen-

turion, but sure, if it had come forward, and bene an
aide unto the Centurion, it is to bee supposed that it
had not perished.

Five houres and a halfe this fight continued, in which
time both were glad to depart onely to breath themselves,
but when the Spaniards were gone, they never durst
returne to fight: yet the next day sixe other Gallies
came and looked at them, but durst not at any hand
meddle with them.

Thus God delivered them from the handes of their
enemies, and gave them the victory: for which they
heartily praised him, and not long after safely arrived
in London.

☞ There were present at this fight Master John
Hawes Marchant, and sundry other of good
accompt.

A report of the trueth of the fight about the
Isles of Açores, the last of August 1591.
betwixt the Revenge, one of her Majesties
shippes, and an Armada of the king of Spaine;
Penned by the honourable Sir Walter Ralegh
knight.

Ecause the rumours are diversly spred,
as well in England as in the Lowe
countreis and elsewhere, of this late
encounter betweene her Majesties ships
and the Armada of Spaine; and that the
Spaniards according to their usuall maner,
fill the world with their vaine-glorious
vaunts, making great apparance of victories, when on the
contrary, themselves are most commonly and shamefully
beaten and dishonoured; thereby hoping to possesse the
ignorant multitude by anticipating & forerunning false
reports: It is agreeable with all good reason, for mani-
festation of the truth, to overcome falshood and un-
trueth; that the beginning, continuance and successe of

this late honourable encounter of Sir Richard Greenvil, and other her Majesties Captaines, with the Armada of Spaine; should be truely set downe and published without partialitie or false imaginations. And it is no marveile that the Spaniard should seeke by false and slanderous pamphlets, advisoes and Letters, to cover their owne losse, and to derogate from others their due honors, especially in this fight being performed far off: seeing they were not ashamed in the yeere 1588. when they purposed the invasion of this land, to publish in sundry languages in print, great victories in wordes, which they pleaded to have obteined against this Realme; and spred the same in a most false sort over all parts of France, Italy, and elsewhere. When shortly after it was happily manifested in very deed to al Nations, how their Navy which they termed invincible, consisting of 140. saile of shippes, not onely of their owne kingdome, but strengthened with the greatest Argosies, Portugal Caracks, Florentines, and huge hulks of other Countreis, were by 30. of her Majesties owne ships of war, and a few of our owne Marchants, by the wise, valiant, [II. ii. 170.] and advantagious conduct of the L. Charles Howard high Admirall of England, beaten and shuffled together; even from the Lizard in Cornwall first to Portland, where they shamefully left Don Pedro de Valdes, with his mighty ship; from Portland to Cales, where they lost Hugo de Moncado, with the Gallias of which he was Captaine, and from Cales, driven with squibs from their anchors, were chased out of the sight of England, round about Scotland and Ireland. Where for the sympathie of their barbarous religion, hoping to finde succour and assistance, a great part of them were crusht against the rocks, and those other that landed, being very many in number, were notwithstanding broken, slaine, and taken, and so sent from village to village coupled in halters, to be shipped into England. Where her Majestie of her Princely and invincible disposition, disdaining to put them to death, and scorning either to retaine or entertaine them: they were all sent backe againe to their countreys, to witnes and recount the worthy achievements of their invincible and dreadfull Navy: Of which the number of Souldiers, the fearefull burthen of their shippes, the commanders names of every squadron, with all other their magasines of provisions, were put in print, as an Army and Navy unresistable, and disdaining prevention. With all which so great and terrible an ostentation, they did not in all their sailing round about England, so much as sinke or take one shippe, Barke, Pinnesse, or Cockbote of ours: or ever burnt so much as one sheepecote of this land. Whenas on the contrarie, Sir Francis Drake, with onely 800. souldiers not long before, landed in their Indies, and forced Sant-Iago, Santo Domingo, Cartagena, and the forts of Florida.

And after that, Sir John Norris marched from Peniche in Portugall, with a handfull of souldiers, to the gates of Lisbone, being above 40 English miles. Where the Earle of Essex himselfe and other valiant Gentlemen braved the Citie of Lisbone, encamped at the very gates; from whence, after many dayes abode, finding neither promised partie, nor provision to batter; they made retrait by land, in despight of all their Garrisons, both of horse & foote. In this sort I have a little digressed from my first purpose, onely by the necessarie comparison of theirs and our actions: the one covetous of honour without vaunt of ostentation; the other so greedy to purchase the opinion of their owne affaires, and by false rumors to resist the blasts of their owne dishonours, as they will not onely not blush to spread all manner of untruthes: but even for the least advantage, be it but for the taking of one poore adventurer of the English, will celebrate the victory with bonefires in every towne, alwayes spending more in faggots, then the purchase was worth they obtained. When as we never thought it worth the consumption of two billets, when we have taken eight or ten of their Indian shippes at one time, and twentie of the Brasill fleete. Such is the difference betweene true valure, and ostentation: and betweene honorable actions, and frivolous vaineglorious vaunts. But now to returne to my purpose.

The L. Thomas Howard with sixe of her Majesties shippes, sixe victualers of London, the Barke Ralegh, & two or three other Pinnases riding at anker neere unto Flores, one of the Westerly Ilands of the Azores, the last of August in the afternoone, had intelligence by one Captaine Middleton of the approch of the Spanish Armada. Which Middleton being in a very good sailer had kept them company three dayes before, of good purpose, both to discover their forces the more, as also to give advise to my L. Thomas of their approch. Hee had no sooner delivered the newes but the fleete was in sight: many of our shippes companies were on shore in the Ilande; some providing balast for their ships; others filling of water and refreshing themselves from the land with such things as they could either for money, or by force recover. By reason whereof our ships being all pestered and romaging every thing out of order, very light for want of balast, and that which was most to our disadvantage, the one halfe part of the men of every shippe sicke, and utterly unserviceable: for in the Revenge there were ninety diseased: in the Bonaventure, not so many in health as could handle her maine saile. For had not twenty men beene taken out of a Barke of sir George Careys, his being commaunded to be sunke, and those appointed to her, she had hardly ever recovered England. The rest, for the most parte, were in little better state. The names of her Majesties shippes were these as followeth, the Defiance, which was Admiral, the Revenge Viceadmirall, the Bonaventure commaunded by Captaine Crosse, the Lion by George Fenner, the Foresight by M. Thomas Vavasour, and the Crane by Duffild. The Foresight & the Crane being but smal ships; only the other were of the middle size; the rest, besides the Barke Ralegh, commanded by Captaine Thin, were victuallers, and of small force or none. The Spanish

fleet having shrouded their approch by reason of the
Island; were now so soone at hand, as our shippes had
scarce time to way their anchors, but some of them were
driven to let slippe their Cables and set saile. Sir Richard
Grinvile was the last that wayed, to recover the men that
were upon the Island, which otherwise had bene lost.
The L. Thomas with the rest very hardly recovered the
winde, which Sir Richard Grinvile not being able to doe,
[II. ii. 171.] was perswaded by the Master and others to cut his maine
sayle, and cast about, and to trust to the sayling of the
ship; for the squadron of Sivil were on his weather bow.
But Sir Richard utterly refused to turne from the enemie,
alleaging that hee would rather choose to die, then to
dishonour himselfe, his countrey, and her Majesties
shippe, perswading his companie that hee would passe
through the two squadrons, in despight of them, and
enforce those of Sivil to give him way. Which hee
performed upon divers of the formost, who, as the
Mariners terme it, sprang their luffe, and fell under the
lee of the Revenge. But the other course had beene
the better, and might right well have bene answered in
so great an impossibility of prevaling. Notwithstanding
out of the greatnesse of his minde, he could not be
perswaded. In the meane while as hee attended those
which were nearest him, the great San Philip being in
the winde of him, and comming towards him, becalmed
his sailes in such sort, as the shippe could neither make
way, nor feele the helme: so huge and high carged was
the Spanish ship, being of a thousand and five hundreth
tuns. Who after layd the Revenge aboord. When he
was thus bereft of his sailes, the ships that were under
his lee luffing up, also layd him aboord: of which the
next was the Admiral of the Biscaines, a very mighty and
puissant shippe commanded by Brittandona. The sayd
Philip carried three tire of ordinance on a side, and eleven
pieces in every tire. She shot eight forth right out of
her chase, besides those of her sterne ports.

After the Revenge was entangled with this Philip,

42

foure other boorded her; two on her larboord, and two on her starboord. The fight thus beginning at three of the clock in the afternoone, continued very terrible all that evening. But the great San Philip having received the lower tire of the Revenge, discharged with crossebar-shot, shifted her selfe with all diligence from her sides, utterly misliking her first entertainement. Some say that the shippe foundred, but we cannot report it for truth, unlesse we were assured. The Spanish ships were filled with companies of souldiers, in some two hundred besides the mariners; in some five, in others eight hundreth. In ours there were none at all beside the mariners, but the servants of the commanders and some few voluntary gentlemen onely. After many enterchanged volies of great ordinance and small shot, the Spaniards deliberated to enter the Revenge, and made divers attempts, hoping to force her by the multitudes of their armed soulders and Musketters, but were still repulsed againe and againe, and at all times beaten backe into their owne ships, or into the seas. In the beginning of the fight, the George Noble of London having received some shot thorow her by the Armadas, fell under the lee of the Revenge, and asked Sir Richard what he would command him, being but one of the victuallers and of small force: Sir Richard bid him save himselfe, and leave him to his fortune. After the fight had thus, without intermission, continued while the day lasted and some houres of the night, many of our men were slaine and hurte, and one of the great Gallions of the Armada, and the Admirall of the Hulkes both sunke, and in many other of the Spanish shippes great slaughter was made. Some write that sir Richard was very dangerously hurt almost in the beginning of the fight, and lay speechlesse for a time ere hee recovered. But two of the Revenges owne company, brought home in a ship of Lime from the Ilandes, examined by some of the Lordes, and others, affirmed that hee was never so wounded as that hee forsooke the upper decke, till

an houre before midnight; and then being shot into the
bodie with a Musket as hee was a dressing, was againe
shot into the head, and withall his Chirurgion wounded
to death. This agreeth also with an examination taken
by sir Francis Godolphin, of foure other mariners of
the same shippe being returned, which examination, the
said sir Francis sent unto master William Killegrue, of
her Majesties privy Chamber.

But to returne to the fight, the Spanish ships which
attempted to bord the Revenge, as they were wounded
and beaten off, so alwayes others came in their places,
she having never lesse then two mighty Gallions by her
sides, and aboard her: So that ere the morning, from
three of the clocke the day before, there had fifteene
severall Armadas assayled her; and all so ill approved
their entertainement, as they were by the breake of day,
far more willing to harken to a composition, then hastily
to make any more assaults or entries. But as the day
encreased, so our men decreased: and as the light grew
more and more, by so much more grewe our discomforts.
For none appeared in sight but enemies, saving one
small ship called the Pilgrim, commaunded by Jacob
Whiddon, who hovered all night to see the successe:
but in the morning bearing with the Revenge, was
hunted like a hare amongst many ravenous houndes,
but escaped.

All the powder of the Revenge to the last barrell was
now spent, all her pikes broken, fortie of her best men
slaine, and the most part of the rest hurt. In the beginning of the fight shee had but one hundreth free
from sicknes, and fourescore & ten sicke, laid in hold
upon the Ballast. A small troup to man such a ship,
& a weake garrison to resist so mighty an army. By
those hundred al was susteined, the voleis, boordings,
and entrings of fifteen ships of warre, besides those which
[II. ii. 172.] beat her at large. On the contrary, the Spanish were
always supplied with souldiers brought from every
squadron: all maner of Armes and powder at will.

44

Unto ours there remained no comfort at all, no hope,
no supply either of ships, men, or weapons; the Mastes
all beaten over boord, all her tackle cut asunder, her
upper worke altogether rased, and in effect evened shee
was with the water, but the very foundation or bottome
of a ship, nothing being left over head either for flight
or defence. Sir Richard finding himselfe in this distresse, and unable any longer to make resistance, having
endured in this fifteene houres fight, the assault of
fifteene severall Armadas, all by turnes aboord him, and
by estimation eight hundred shotte of great Artillerie,
besides many assaults and entries; and that himselfe
and the shippe must needes be possessed by the enemy,
who were now all cast in a ring round about him.
(The Revenge not able to moove one way or other,
but as she was moved with the waves and billow of
the sea) commaunded the Master gunner, whom hee
knew to be a most resolute man, to split and sinke
the shippe; that thereby nothing might remaine of glory
or victory to the Spaniards: seeing in so many houres
fight, and with so great a Navie they were not able
to take her, having had fifteene houres time, above
ten thousand men, & fiftie and three saile of men of *The Spanish*
warre to performe it withall: and perswaded the com- *53 saile.*
pany, or as many as hee could induce, to yeelde themselves unto God, and to the mercie of none else; but
as they had, like valiant resolute men, repulsed so many
enemies, they should not nowe shorten the honour of
their Nation, by prolonging their owne lives for a few
houres, or a fewe dayes. The Master gunner readily
condescended and divers others; but the Captaine and
the Master were of another opinion, and besought Sir
Richard to have care of them: alleaging that the
Spaniard would be as ready to entertaine a composition,
as they were willing to offer the same: and that there
being divers sufficient and valiant men yet living, and
whose wounds were not mortal, they might do their
Countrey and prince acceptable service hereafter. And

whereas Sir Richard had alleaged that the Spaniards
should never glory to have taken one shippe of her
Majestie, seeing they had so long and so notably
defended themselves; they answered, that the shippe
had sixe foote water in holde, three shot under water,
which were so weakely stopped, as with the first working
of the sea, she must needs sinke, and was besides so
crusht and brused, as shee could never be removed out
of the place.

And as the matter was thus in dispute, and Sir Richard
refusing to hearken to any of those reasons: the Master
of the Revenge (while the Captaine wanne unto him the
greater party) was convoyd aboord the Generall Don
Alfonso Baçan. Who (finding none over hastie to enter
the Revenge againe, doubting least Sir Richard would
have blowne them up and himselfe, and perceiving by
the report of th Master of the Revenge his dangerous
disposition) yeelded that all their lives should be saved,
the company sent for England, & the better sort to
pay such reasonable ransome as their estate would
beare, and in the meane season to be free from Gally
or imprisonment. To this he so much the rather condescended as wel, as I have said, for feare of further
losse and mischiefe to themselves, as also for the desire
he had to recover Sir Richard Greenvil; whom for his
notable valure he seemed greatly to honour and
admire.

When this answere was returned, and that safetie of
life was promised, the common sort being now at the
ende of their perill, the most drew backe from Sir
Richard and the Master gunner, being no hard matter
to disswade men from death to life. The Master gunner
finding himselfe and Sir Richard thus prevented and
mastered by the greater number, would have slaine himselfe with a sword, had he not bene by force with-held
and locked into his Cabben. Then the Generall sent
many boates aboord the Revenge, and divers of our men
fearing Sir Richards disposition, stole away aboord the

Generall and other shippes. Sir Richard thus over-matched, was sent unto by Alfonso Baçan to remoove out of the Revenge, the shippe being marveilous un-savorie, filled with blood and bodies of dead, and wounded men like a slaughter house. Sir Richard answered that hee might doe with his body what he list, for hee esteemed it not, and as he was carried out of the shippe hee swounded, and reviving againe desired the company to pray for him. The Generall used Sir Richard with all humanitie, and left nothing unattempted that tended to his recoverie, highly commending his valour and worthinesse, and greatly bewailing the danger wherein he was, being unto them a rare spectacle, and a resolution sildome approoved, to see one shippe turne toward so many enemies, to endure the charge and boording of so many huge Armadas, and to resist and repell the assaults and entries of so many souldiers. All which and more is confirmed by a Spanish Captaine of the same Armada, and a present actor in the fight, who being severed from the rest in a storme, was by the Lion of London a small ship taken, and is now prisoner in London.

The generall commander of the Armada, was Don Alphonso Baçan, brother to the Marques of Santa Cruz. The admiral of the Biscaine squadron, was Britandona. Of the squadron of Sivil, the Marques of Arumburch. [II. ii. 173.] The Hulkes and Flybotes were commanded by Luis Coutinho. There were slaine and drowned in this fight, well neere one thousand of the enemies, and two speciall commanders Don Luis de sant John, and Don George de Prunaria de Mallaga, as the Spanish captaine con-fesseth, besides divers others of speciall account, whereof as yet report is not made.

The Admirall of the Hulkes and the Ascension of Sivil were both sunke by the side of the Revenge; one other recovered the rode of Saint Michael, and sunke also there; a fourth ranne her selfe with the shore to save her men. Sir Richard died as it is sayd, the second or third day aboord the Generall, and was by them greatly bewailed. What became of his body, whether it were buried in the sea or on the land we know not: the comfort that remayneth to his friends is, that hee hath ended his life honourably in respect of the reputation wonne to his nation and countrey, and of the same to his posteritie, and that being dead, he hath not outlived his owne honour.

For the rest of her Majesties ships that entred not so farre into the fight as the Revenge, the reasons and causes were these. There were of them but sixe in all, whereof two but small ships; the Revenge ingaged past recovery: The Iland of Flores was on the one side, 53 saile of the Spanish, divided into squadrons on the other, all as full filled with souldiers as they could containe: Almost the one halfe of our men sicke and not able to serve: the ships growne foule, unroomaged, and scarcely able to beare any saile for want of balast, having bene sixe moneths at the sea before. If all the rest had entred, all had bene lost: for the very hugenes of the Spanish fleete, if no other violence had beene offered, would have crusht them betweene them into shivers. Of which the dishonour and losse to the Queene had bene farre greater then the spoyle or harme that the enemie could any way have received. Notwithstanding it is very true, that the Lord Thomas would have entred betweene the squadrons, but the rest would not condescend; and the master of his owne ship offred to leape into the sea, rather then to conduct that her Majesties ship and the rest to bee a pray to the enemie, where there was no hope nor possibilitie either of defence or victory. Which also in my opinion had ill sorted or answered the discretion and trust of a Generall, to commit himselfe and his charge to an assured destruction, without hope or any likelyhood of prevailing: thereby to diminish the strength of her Majesties Navy, and to enrich the pride and glory of the enemie. The Foresight of the Queenes commaunded by M. Thomas Vavisor

Mil. aur.

RIHARDVS GRENVILVS

Neptuni proles, qui magni Martis alumnus
Grenuilius patrias sanguine tinxit aquas

SIR RICHARD GRENVILLE

performed a very great fight, and stayed two houres as
neere the Revenge as the weather would permit him,
not forsaking the fight, till he was like to be encompassed
by the squadrons, & with great difficultie cleared himselfe. The rest gave divers voleis of shot, and entred
as farre as the place permitted, and their owne necessities, to keepe the weather gage of the enemie, untill
they were parted by night. A fewe dayes after the fight
was ended, and the English prisoners dispersed into
the Spanish and Indie ships, there arose so great a
storme from the West and Northwest, that all the fleete
was dispersed, as well the Indian fleete which were then
come unto them, as the rest of the Armada that attended
their arrivall, of which 14. saile together with the Revenge, and in her 200 Spaniards, were cast away upon
the Isle of S. Michael. So it pleased them to honor
the buriall of that renowmed ship the Revenge, not
suffering her to perish alone, for the great honour she
atchieved in her life time. On the rest of the Ilandes
there were cast away in this storme, 15 or 16 more of
the ships of warre : and of an hundred and odde saile
of the Indie fleete, expected this yeere in Spaine, what
in this tempest, and what before in the bay of Mexico,
and about the Bermudas, there were 70 and odde consumed and lost, with those taken by our shippes of
London, besides one very rich Indian ship, which set
her selfe on fire, beeing boorded by the Pilgrim, and
five other taken by master Wats his ships of London,
between the Havana and Cape S. Antonio. The fourth
of this moneth of November we received letters from
the Tercera, affirming that there are 3000 bodies of
men remaining in that Iland, saved out of the perished
ships : & that by the Spaniards owne confession, there
are 10000 cast away in this storme, besides those that
are perished betweene the Ilands and the maine. Thus
it hath pleased God to fight for us, and to defend the
justice of our cause, against the ambicious and bloody
pretenses of the Spaniard, who seeking to devoure

all nations, are themselves devoured. A manifest testimony how injust and displeasing, their attempts are in the sight of God, who hath pleased to witnes by the successe of their affaires, his mislike of their bloody and injurious designes, purposed and practised against all Christian princes, over whom they seeke unlawfull and ungodly rule and Empery.

One day or two before this wracke happened to the Spanish fleete, when as some of our prisoners desired to be set on shore upon the Ilandes, hoping to be from thence transported into England, which libertie was formerly by the Generall promised: One Morice Fitz John, sonne of olde John of Desmond, a notable traytour, cousin german to the late Earle of Desmond, was sent to the English from shippe to shippe, to perswade them to serve the King of Spaine. The arguments hee used to induce them were these. The increase of pay which he promised to be trebled: advancement to the better sort: and the exercise of the true Catholique Religion, and safetie of their soules to all. For the first, even the beggerly and unnaturall behaviour of those English and Irish rebels, that served the King in that present action, was sufficient to answere that first argument of rich pay. For so poore and beggerly they were, as for want of apparell they stripped their poore Countrey men prisoners out of their ragged garments, worne to nothing by sixe months service, and spared not to despoyle them even of their bloody shirtes, from their wounded bodies, and the very shooes from their feete; A notable testimonie of their rich entertainment and great wages. The second reason was hope of advancement if they served well, and would continue faithfull to the King. But what man can bee so blockishly ignorant ever to expect place or honour from a forraine King, having no other argument or perswasion then his owne disloyaltie; to be unnaturall to his owne Countrey that bred him; to his parents that begat him, and rebellious to his true Prince, to whose obedience he is bound by oath, by

nature, and by Religion? No, they are onely assured
to be imployed in all desperate enterprises, to bee helde
in scorne and disdaine ever among those whom they
serve. And that ever traitour was either trusted or
advanced I could never yet reade, neither can I at this
time remember any example. And no man coulde have
lesse becommed the place of an Orator for such a purpose,
then this Morice of Desmond. For the Erle his cosen
being one of the greatest subjects in that kingdom of
Ireland, having almost whole Countreis in his possession ;
so many goodly Mannors, castles, and lordships ; the
Count Palatine of Kerry, five hundred gentlemen of his
owne name and family to follow him, besides others (all
which he possessed in peace for three or foure hundred
yeeres) was in lesse then three yeeres after his adhering
to the Spaniards and rebellion, beaten from all his holdes,
not so many as ten gentlemen of his name left living,
himselfe taken and beheaded by a souldier of his owne
nation, and his land given by a Parliament to her
Majestie, and possessed by the English : His other cosen
Sir John of Desmond taken by Master John Zouch, and
his body hanged over the gates of his native Citie to be
devoured by ravens : the thirde brother Sir James hanged,
drawne, and quartered in the same place. If hee had
withall vaunted of his successe of his owne house, no
doubt the argument would have mooved much, and
wrought great effect : which because, hee for that present
forgot, I thought it good to remember in his behalfe.
For matter of Religion it would require a particuler
volume, if I should set downe how irreligiously they
cover their greedy and ambicious pretenses, with that
veile of pietie. But sure I am, that there is no kingdome
or common-wealth in all Europe, but if they be reformed,
they then invade it for religion sake : if it bee, as they
terme Catholique, they pretend title ; as if the Kings of
Castile were the naturall heires of all the world : and so
betweene both, no kingdome is unsought. Where they
dare not with their owne forces to invade, they basely

entertaine the traitours and vacabonds of all Nations:
seeking by those and by their runnagate Jesuits to winne
parts, and have by that meane ruined many Noble houses
and others in this lande, and have extinguished both
their lives and families. What good, honour, or fortune
ever man yet by them atchieved, is yet unheard of, or
unwritten. And if our English Papists doe but looke
into Portugall, against which they have no pretence of
Religion, how the Nobilitie are put to death, imprisoned,
their rich men made a praye, and all sorts of people
captived; they shall finde that the obedience even of the
Turke is easie and a libertie, in respect of the slaverie
and tyrannie of Spaine. What have they done in Sicill,
in Naples, Millaine, and in the Low countreis; who hath
there bene spared for Religion at all? And it commeth
to my remembrance of a certaine Burger of Antwerpe,
whose house being entred by a company of Spanish
souldiers, when they first sacked the Citie, hee besought
them to spare him and his goods, being a good Catholique, and one of their owne partie and faction. The
Spaniards answered, that they knew him to be of a good
conscience for himselfe, but his money, plate, jewels, and
goods, were all hereticall, and therefore good prize. So
they abused and tormented the foolish Fleming, who
hoped that an Agnus Dei had bene a sufficient target
against all force of that holy and charitable nation.
Neither have they at any time as they protest invaded
the kingdomes of the Indies and Peru, and elsewhere,
but onely led thereunto, rather to reduce the people to
Christianitie, then for either gold or Emperie. When as
in one onely Island called Hispaniola, they have wasted
thirtie hundred thousand of the naturall people, besides
many millions else in other places of the Indies: a poore
and harmelesse people created of God, and might have
bene wonne to his knowledge, as many of them were, and
almost as many as ever were perswaded thereunto. The
storie whereof is at large written by a Bishop of their
owne nation called Bartholomew de las Casas, and trans-

lated into English and many other languages, intituled
The Spanish cruelties. Who would therefore repose
trust in such a nation of ravenous strangers, and especially
in those Spaniards which more greedily thirst after
English blood, then after the lives of any other people of [II. ii. 175.]
Europe, for the many overthrowes and dishonours they
have received at our hands, whose weakenesse wee have
discovered to the world, and whose forces at home,
abroad, in Europe, in India, by sea and land, wee have
even with handfulles of men and shippes, overthrowen
and dishonoured. Let not therefore any English man, of
what religion soever, have other opinion of the Spaniards,
but that those whom hee seeketh to winne of our Nation,
he esteemeth base and trayterous, unworthy persons, or
unconstant fooles: and that he useth his pretence of
religion, for no other purpose but to bewitch us from
the obedience of our naturall Prince, thereby hoping in
time to bring us to slavery and subjection, and then none
shall be unto them so odious, and disdayned as the
traitours themselves, who have solde their Countrey to
a stranger, and forsaken their faith and obedience contrarie to nature & religion; and contrarie to that humane
and generall honour, not onely of Christians, but of
heathen and irreligious nations, who have always sus-
tayned what labour soever, and embraced even death
it selfe, for their countrey, Prince, or common-wealth.
To conclude, it hath ever to this day pleased God to
prosper and defend her Majestie, to breake the purposes
of malicious enemies, of forsworne traytors, and of injust
practises and invasions. She hath ever beene honoured
of the worthiest kings, served by faithfull subjects, and
shall by the favour of God, resist, repell, and confound
all whatsoever attempts against her sacred person or
kingdome. In the meane time let the Spaniard and
traytour vaunt of their successe, and wee her true and
obedient vassals, guided by the shining light of her
vertues, shall alwayes love her, serve her, and obey her
to the end of our lives.

53

A particular note of the Indian fleet, expected to have come into Spaine this present yeere of 1591. with the number of shippes that are perished of the same: according to the examination of certaine Spaniards lately taken and brought into England by the ships of London.

He fleete of Nova Hispania, at their first gathering together and setting foorth, were two and fiftie sailes. The Admirall was of sixe hundred tunnes, and the Vice Admirall of the same burthen. Foure or five of the shippes were of nine hundred and 1000 tunnes a peece, some five hundred, and some foure hundred and the least of two hundred tuns. Of this fleet 19 were cast away, and in them 2600 men by estimation, which was done along the coast of Nova Hispania, so that of the same fleet there came to the Havana but 33 sailes.

The fleete of Terra Firma were, at their first departure from Spaine, fiftie sailes, which were bound for Nombre de Dios, where they did discharge their lading, and thence returned to Cartagena, for their healths sake, untill the time the treasure was readie they should take in, at the said Nombre de Dios. But before this fleete departed, some were gone by one or two at a time, so that onely 23 sayles of this fleete arrived in the Havana.

At the Havana there met
{
33 sailes of Nova Hispania.
23 sailes of Terra Firma.
12 sailes of San' Domingo.
9 sailes of the Hunduras.
}

The whole 77 shippes, joyned and set sailes all together at the Havana, the 17 of July, according to our account, and kept together untill they came into the height of thirtie five degrees, which was about the tenth of August, where they found the winde at Southwest chaunged suddenly to the North, so that the sea comming out of the Southwest, and the wind very violent at North, they were put all into great extremitie, and then first lost the Generall of their fleete, with 500 men in her; and within three or foure dayes after, an other storme rising, there were five or sixe other of the biggest shippes cast away with all their men, together with their Vice-Admirall.

And in the height of 38. degrees, about the end of August, grew another great storme, in which all the fleet saving 48. sailes were cast away: which 48. sailes kept together, untill they came in sight of the Islands of Corvo and Flores, about the fift or sixt of September, at which time a great storme separated them: of which number fifteene or sixteene were after seene by these Spanyards to ride at anchor under the Tercera; and twelve or foureteene more to beare with the Island of S. Michael; what became of them after that these Spaniards were taken cannot yet be certified; their opinion is, that very few of the fleet are escaped, but are either drowned or taken. And it is otherwaies of late certified, that of this whole fleete that should have come into Spaine this yeere, being one hundred twentie [II. ii. 176.] and three sayle, there are arrived as yet but five and twentie. This note was taken out of the examination of certaine Spaniardes, that were brought into England by sixe of the ships of London, which tooke seven of the above named Indian Fleete, neere the Islands of Açores.

[A report

A report of Master Robert Flicke directed to
Master Thomas Bromley, Master Richard
Staper, and Master Cordall concerning the
successe of a part of the London supplies sent
to my Lord Thomas Howard to the Isles of
the Azores, 1591.

Orshipfull, my heartie commendations unto
you premised : By my last of the twelfth
of August from this place I advertised
you particularly of the accidents of our
Fleete untill then. It remayneth now to
relate our endevours in accomplishing the
order received for the joyning with my
Lorde Thomas Howard, together with the successe wee
have had. Our departure from hence was the seventeenth
of August, the winde not serving before. The next day
following I caused a Flagge of Counsell to be put foorth,
whereupon the Captaines and Masters of every shippe
came aboord, and I acquainted them with my Commission, firmed by the Right honourable the Lordes of
her Majesties Counsell, and with all the advertisements
of Sir Edward Denny, of my Lordes determination to
remaine threescore leagues to the West of Fayal, spread-
ing North and South betwixt thirtie seven and a halfe or
thirty eight and a halfe degrees. And not finding him
in this heighth to repaire to the Isles of Flores and
Corvo, where a Pinnesse of purpose should stay our
comming untill the last of August, with intent after that
day to repaire to ye coast of Spaine, about the heigth of
The Rocke, some twentie or thirtie leagues off the shoare.
The which being advisedly considered of, having regard
unto the shortnesse of time, by reason of our long abode
in this place, and the uncertainety of the weather to favour
us, it was generally holden for the best and securest way
to meete with my Lorde, to beare with the heigth of The
Rocke, without making any stay upon the coast, and so

directly for the Islands which was accordingly fully agreed and performed. The 28 day wee had sight of the Burlings, and the 29 being thwart of Peniche, the winde serving us, without any stay we directed our course West for the Islands. The 30 day we met with Captaine Royden in the Red-Rose, sometime called the Golden Dragon, separated from my Lorde of Cumberland in a storme: who certified us of 50 sayles of the Spanish kings Armadas to be gone for the Ilands, but could not informe us any newes of my Lord Thomas Howard, otherwise then upon presumption to remaine about the Islandes, and so wee continued our course the winde standing with us.

The 4 of September we recovered Tercera, and ranged along all the Islands, both on the South and North sides the space of foure dayes: during which time it was not our hap to meete with any shipping, whereby either to understand of my Lord, or of the Indian Fleete: hereupon we directed our course to the West from Fayal, according to the instructions of Sir Edward Denny. The 11 day in the plying to the Westwards we descried a sayle out of our maine toppe, and in the afternoone betweene two and three of the clocke having raysed her hull, the weather became calme, so that the ship could not fetch her. I sent off my Skiffe throughly manned, furnished with shot and swords, The Cherubin, and the Margaret and John doing the like. Upon this the sayle stood off againe, and the night approching, our boates lost her and so returned. In this our pursute after the sayle the Centurion being left a sterne, the next morning wee missed her, and spent that day in plying up and downe seeking her. And for as much as every of the ships had received order, that, if by extremity of weather or any other mischance they should be severed from our Fleete, they should meete and joyne at Flores, we, according to the instructions of Sir Edward Denny, proceeded to the finding of my Lord Thomas Howard, being in the heigth appointed and not able to holde the same by reason of

extreme tempestes which forced us to the Isles of Flores
and Corvo, which we made the 14 day in the morning,
and there also joyned againe with the Centurion, whose
company before we had lost: who declared unto us that
the 12 day, being the same day they lost us, they met
with five and forty sailes of the Indian Fleete. The
same night upon these newes we came to an anker betweene Flores and Corvo, and the morow following at
the breake of day, a flagge of Counsell being put out,
the Captaines & Masters came abord me: where, for the
desire to understand some tidings of my Lord, as also the
supplying of our want of water, it was thought good to
send our boats furnished on shore, under the conduct of
Captaine Brothus, and then it was also ordered after our
[II. ii. 177.] departure thence to range along the Southsides of the
Islands to the end we might either understand of my
Lord, or else light on the Indian fleete; and in the missing of our purpose to direct our course for Cape Sant
Vincente.

The boates, according to the foresayd determination,
being sent on shoare, it chaunced that The Costely ryding
uttermost in the roade, did weigh to bring her selfe more
neere among us for the succour of the boates sent off,
and in opening the land discovered two sayles, which we
in the roade could not perceive: whereupon shee gave
us a warning piece, which caused us to wave off our
boates backe, and before they could recover our shippes,
the discryed ships appeared unto us, towardes the which
we made with all haste, and in a very happie houre, as it
pleased God. In that wee had not so soone cleared the
lande, and spoken with one of them, which was a Barke
of Bristoll, who had also sought my Lorde in the heigths
A violent appointed and could not finde him, but a violent storme
storme. arose, in such manner, as if we had remained in the
roade, we had beene in daunger of perishing: and the
same extremely continued during the space of threescore
houres. In which storme I was separated from our
Fleete, except the Cherubin and the Costely, which kept

company with mee. And so sayling among the Ilands, I viewed the roade of Fayal, and finding no Roaders there, went directly for the Isle Tercera.

The nineteenth day in the morning comming unto ye same with intent to edge into the Road, a tempest arose and scanted the winde, that we could not seaze it : from the which being driven we fell among certaine of the Indian Fleete, which the sayde storme dispersed, and put them from the road : whereupon my selfe with the other two ships in companie gave severall chases, and thereby lost the company each of other.

In following our chase above noone we made her to strike and yeelde, being a Portugall, laden with hides, salsa-perilla and Anile. At this very instant we espied another, and taking our Prize with us followed her, and somewhat before night obtayned her, named the Conception, Francisco Spinola being Captaine, which was laden with hides, Cochonillio, and certaine raw silke. And for that the seas were so growen, as neither with boate nor shippe they were to bee boorded, we kept them till fit opportunitie. The same night a litle before day there happened another into our company, supposing us by our two prizes to be of their Fleete, which we untill the morning dissembled.

A Portugall Prize taken.

A rich West-India Prize taken.

The 20 day in the morning, the sayle being shot somewhat a head of us, having a speciall care for the safe keeping of the two former, we purposed to cause our Prizes to put out more sayle thereby to keepe them neere in giving chase to the other : unto the which the Master would not hearken nor be perswaded, but that they would follow us : by the which his wilfulnesse by such time as we had caused the other to yeelde, and sent men aboord, the Conception, Francisco Spinola Captaine being brought a sterne, and having gotten the winde of us, stood off with all her sayles bearing, so as we were forced to make a new chase of her : and had not the winde enlarged upon us we had lost her. In the pursute before we recovered her and brought our selves againe in company of our other Prizes, the whole day was spent, and by this meanes we lost the oportunitie of that day, the weather fitly serving to boord the Portugall Prize, which was in great distresse, and made request to take them being readie to sinke, and, as we well perceived, they ceased not to pumpe day and night: the which ship to all our judgements the same night perished in the sea.

The one and twentie day the Conception, whereof Francisco Spinola was Captaine, being also in a leake, and the same still increasing notwithstanding the continuall pumping, in such sort as not to be kept along above water, I tooke and discharged out of her two and forty chestes of Cochonillio and silkes, and so left her with 11 foote water in holde, and her furniture and 4700 hides, unto the seas.

The other Prize which we have brought into the harborough is named Nostra Sennora de los remedios, whereof Francisco Alvares is Captaine, laden with 16 chests of Cochonillio, certaine fardels of raw silke, and about 4000 hides. Upon the discharge of the goods your worships shall be particularly advertised thereof.

In the boording of the Prizes the disorder of the company was such, as that they letted not presently besides the rifling of the Spaniards to breake open the chests and to purloyne such money as was in them: notwithstanding that it was ordered at convenient leasure to have gone aboord my selfe, and there in the presence of three or foure witnesses to have taken a just account thereof, and the same to have put in safe keeping, according to the effects of articles received in this behalfe.

And whereas there were also certaine summes of money [II. ii. 178.] taken from the company which they had thus purloyned and embeseled, and the same with some other parcels brought aboord my ship, amounting unto 2129 pezoes & a halfe, the company as pillage due unto them demanded to have the same shared, which I refused, & openly at the maine maste read the articles firmed by my Lord Treasurer and my lord Admirall, whereby we

ought to be directed, and that it was not in mee any way
to dispose thereof untill the same were finally determined
at home. Hereupon they mutined and at last grew into
such furie, as that they would have it or els breake downe
the cabbine, which they were also readie to put in practise,
whereby I was forced to yeeld, least the Spaniards which
we had abord being many perceiving the same, might
have had fit opportunitie to rise against us, which, after
their brawles were appeased, they sought to have put in
execution.

By the last advise from Castile the Generall of the
kings Armada which is lately come to sea hath received
commaundement to joyne his Fleete with those of the
Indies, and for to stay altogether at Tercera untill the
15 of October: for that 6 patches with 7 or 8 millions
of the kings treasure will come by that time, or els they
stay their comming from Havana until January next, or
the kings further pleasure therein to be knowen. These
Patches are said to be of 300 tuns the piece, and to cary
30 pieces of brasse, and also of saile reported to have
the advantage of any shipping.

There perished of the Indies Fleete sunke in the sea
before their comming to Flores 11 sailes, whereof the
General was one, and not one man saved. And it is
by the Spaniards themselves presupposed that the stormes
which we had at Flores & at Tercera have devoured
many more of them, whereof in part we were eye
witnesses. And so what by the seas and our men of
warre I presume that of 75 sailes that came from Havana,
halfe of them will never arrive in Spaine.

The 11 day of October at night we came to anker in
the sound of Plimouth, and the next morning with our
Prize came into Cattewater: for which God be thanked:
for that a vehement storme arose, and with such fury
increased, as that the Prize was forced to cut over her
maine maste: otherwise with the violence of the storme,
her ground tackle being bad, she had driven on shore:
which was the most cause that moved me to put in here;

intending now here to discharge the goods without further adventure, and have certified thus much unto my Lord Admirall, and therewith also desired to understande the direction of the Lords of the Counsell together with yours, insomuch as my Lord Thomas Howard is not returned. How the rest of our consorts which were separated from us by weather have sped, or what Prizes they have taken, whereof there is much hope by reason of the scattering of the West Indian Fleete, as yet we are able to say nothing. And thus expecting your answere, and for all other matters referring me unto the bearer Captaine Furtho, I end. Plymouth the 24 of October. 1591.

Your worships loving friend

Robert Flicke.

A large testimony of John Huighen van Linschoten Hollander, concerning the worthy exploits atchieved by the right honourable the Earle of Cumberland, By Sir Martine Frobisher, Sir Richard Greenvile, and divers other English Captaines, about the Isles of the Açores, and upon the coasts of Spaine and Portugall, in the yeeres 1589, 1590, 1591, &c. recorded in his excellent discourse of voiages to the East and West Indies. cap. 96. 97. and 99.

He 22 of July 1589 about Evening, being by the Islands of Flores & Corvo, we perceived 3 ships that made towards us, which came from under the land, which put us in great feare: for they came close by our Admirall, and shot divers times at him, and at another ship of our companie, whereby we perceived them to be Englishmen, for they bare an English flagge upon their maine tops, but none of them shewed to be above 60 tunnes in greatnes. About Evening they followed after us, and all night bore lanternes with candles burning in them at their sternes, although the Moone shined. The same night passing hard by the Island of Fayal, the next day being betweene the Island of S. George that lay on our right hand, and the small Island called Graciosa on our left hand, we espied the 3 English ships still following us y^t tooke counsell together, whereof one sailed backwards, thinking that some other ship had come after us without company, & for a time was out of sight, but it was not long before it came again to ye other two, wherwith they tooke counsel & came all 3 together against our ship, because we lay in the lee of al our ships, & had ye Island of S. George on the one side in stead of a sconce, thinking to deale so with us, that in ye end we should be constrained to run upon the shore, whereof we wanted not much, and in that manner with their [II. ii. 179.] flagges openly displayed, came lustily towardes us, sounding their Trumpets, and sayled at the least three times about us, beating us with Musket and Caliver, and some great pieces, and did us no hurt in the body of our shippe, but spoyled all our sayles and ropes, and to conclude, wee were so plagued by them, that no man durst put foorth his head, and when wee shot off a peece, wee had at the least an houres worke to lade it againe, whereby wee had so great a noise and crie in the shippe, as if we had all bene cast away, whereat the English men themselves beganne to mocke us, and with a thousand jesting words called unto us. In the meane time the other shippes hoised all their sayles, and did the best they could to saile to the Island of Tercera, not looking once behinde them to helpe us, doubting they should come too late thither, not caring for us, but thinking themselves to have done sufficiently so they saved their owne stakes, whereby it may easily be seene what company they keepe one with the other, and what order is among them. In the ende the English men perceiving small

63

advantage against us, (little knowing in what case and feare we were, as also because wee were not farre from Tercera) left us, which made us not a litle to rejoyce, as thinking our selves to bee risen from death to life, although wee were not well assured, neyther yet voyde of feare till we lay in the road before Tercera, and under the safetie of the Portingales fort, and that we might get thither in good time wee made all the sailes we could: on the other side we were in great doubt, because we knew not what they did in the Island, nor whether they were our friends or enemies, and we doubted so much the more, because we found no men of warre nor any Carvels of advise from Portingal, as wee made our accounts to doe, that might convoy us from thence, or give us advise, as in that countrey ordinarily they use to do: and because the English men had bene so victorious in those parts, it made us suspect that it went not well with Spaine: they of the Island of Tercera were in no lesse feare then we, for seeing our fleete, they thought us to bee Englishmen, and that wee came to overrun the Island, because the 3. Englishmen had bound up their flags, and came in company with us: for the which cause the Island sent out two Carvels that lay there with advise from the king, for the Indians ships that should come thither. Those Carvels came to view us, and perceiving what we were, made after us, where-upon the English ships left us, and made towardes them, because the Carvels thought them to be friends, and shunned them not, as supposing them to bee of our company, but we shot foure or five times and made signes unto them that they should make towards the Island, which they presently did. The Englishmen perceiving that, did put forwards into the sea, & so the Carvels borded us telling us that the men of the Island were all in armes, as having received advise from Portugall, that Sir Francis Drake was in readinesse, and woulde come unto those Islands. They likewise brought us newes of the overthrow of the Spanish fleet before England, and that

SOVFRIR POVR PARVENIR · IOANNES HVGONIS A LINSCHOTEN HAERLEMENSIS AETATIS 35 A° 1598

Eoum nobis heîc dat Lynſcotius Orbem,
Lynſcotum, artifici ſculpta tabella manu.

JOHN HUIGHEN VAN LINSCHOTEN

the English men had bene before the gates of Lisbon:
whereupon the king gave us commandement that we
should put into the Island of Tercera, and there lie under
the safety of the Castle until we received further advise
what we should do, or whether we should saile: for that
they thought it too dangerous for us to go to Lisbon.
Those newes put our fleet in great feare, and made us
looke upon eche other not knowing what to say, as being
dangerous for them to put into the road, because it lieth
open to the sea: so that the Indian ships, although they
had expresse commandement from the king, yet they
durst not anker there, but onely used to come thither,
and to lie to and fro, sending their boates on land to
fetch such necessaries as they wanted, without ankering:
but being by necessitie compelled thereunto, as also by
the kings commandement, and for that we understood
the Erle of Cumberland not to bee farre from those
Islands with certaine ships of warre, we made necessitie
a vertue, and entring the road, ankered close under the
Castle, staying for advise and order from the king, to
performe our voyage, it being then the 24. of July,
and S. James day.

The day before the Erle of Cumberland with 6. or
7. ships of war, sailed by the Island of Tercera, and to
their great good fortune passed out of sight, so that
they dispatched themselves in all haste, and for the more
securitie, tooke with them 4. hundred Spaniards, of those
that lay in Garrison in the Island, and with them they
sayled towards Lisbon, having a good wind: so that
within 11 daies after they arrived in the river of Lisbon
with great gladnes & triumph: for if they had stayed but
one day longer before they had entred the river, they
had all beene taken by Captaine Drake, who with 40
ships came before Cascais at the same time that the
Indian ships cast anker in the river of Lisbon, being
garded thither by divers Gallies.

While I remained in Tercera, the Erle of Cumb. came
to S. Marie, to take in fresh water, and some other

victuals: but the inhabitants would not suffer him to have it, but wounded both himselfe & divers of his men, whereby they were forced to depart without having any thing there.

The Erle of Cumberland while I lay in Tercera, came unto the Isle of Graciosa, where himselfe in person, with seven or eight in his company went on land, asking

[II. ii. 180.] certaine beastes, hens, and other victuals, with wine and fresh water, which they willingly gave him, and therewith he departed from thence, without doing them any hurt: for the which the inhabitants thanked him, and commended him for his courtesie, and keeping of his promise.

The same time that the Erle of Cumberland was in the Island of Graciosa, he came likewise to Fayall, where at the first time that he came, they beganne to resist him, but by reason of some controversie among them, they let him land, where he razed the Castle to the ground, and sunke all their Ordinance in the sea, taking with him certaine Caravels and ships that lay in the road, with provision of all things that he wanted: and therewith departed againe to sea. Whereupon the king caused the principall actors therein to be punished, and sent a company of souldiers thither againe, which went out of Tercera, with all kinde of warlike munition, and great shot, making the foretresse up againe, the better to defend the Island, trusting no more in the Portugales.

The 99 Chapter.

THe ninth of October 1589. there arrived in Tercera fourteene ships that came from the Spanish Indies, laden with Cochenile, Hides, Golde, Silver, Pearles, and other rich wares. They were fiftie in companie, when they departed out of the Haven of Havana, whereof, in their comming out of the Channell, eleven sunke in the same Channell by foule weather, the rest by a storme were scattered and separated one from the other. The next day there came another ship of the same companie,

hat sailed close under the Island, so to get into the
Roade: where she met with an English ship that had
not above three cast peeces, and the Spaniards 12. They
ought a long time together, which we being in the
Island might stand and behold: whereupon the
Governour of Tercera sent two boates of Musketiers to
helpe the shippe: but before they could come at her,
he English ship had shot her under water, and we saw
her sinke into the Sea with all her sayles up, and not
any thing seene of her above the water. The Englishmen
with their boate saved the Captaine and about thirtie
others with him, but not one penie-worth of the goods,
and yet in the shippe there was at the least to the value
of two hundred thousand Duckats in Golde, Silver, and
Pearles, the rest of the men were drowned which might
be about fiftie persons, among the which were some
Fryers and women, which the Englishmen would not
save. Those that they had saved they set on land: and
then they sayled away. The seven and twentieth of
he same moneth, the sayd fourteene ships having refreshed themselves in the Island departed from Tercera
toward Sivill, and comming upon the coast of Spaine
they were taken by the English ships that lay there to
watch for them, two onely excepted which escaped away,
and the rest were wholly caried into England.

About the same time the Erle of Cumberland with one
of the Queenes ships, and five or sixe more, kept about
those Islands and came oftentimes so close under the
Island, and to the Road of Angra, that the people on
land might easily tell all his men that he had aboord, and
knewe such as walked on the Hatches: they of the Island
not once shooting at them, although they might easily
have done it, for they were within Musket shot both
of the towne and fort. In these places he continued
for the space of two moneths, and sayled round about
the Islands, and landed in Graciosa and Fayal, as in the
description of those Islands I have alreadie declared. Here
he tooke divers ships and Caravels, which he sent into

England: so that those of the Island durst not once
put foorth their heads. At the same time about three or
foure dayes after the Earle of Cumberland had beene in
the Island of Fayal, and was departed from thence, there
arrived in the said Island of Fayal sixe Indian shippes,
whose Generall was one Juan Dorives : and there they discharged in the Iland 4 millions of golde and silver. And
having with all speede refreshed their ships, fearing the
comming of the Englishmen they set sayle, and arrived
safely in S. Lucar, not meeting with the enemie, to the
great good lucke of the Spaniards and hard fortune of
the Englishmen : for that within lesse then two dayes
after the gold and silver was laden againe into the Spanish
ships, the Erle of Cumberland sayled againe by that
Island: so that it appeared that God would not let them
have it, for if they had once had sight thereof, without
doubt it had bene theirs, as the Spaniards themselves
confessed.

In the moneth of November there arrived in Tercera
two great shippes, which were the Admirall and Viceadmirall of the Fleete laden with silver, who with stormie
weather were separated from the Fleete, and had beene
in great torment and distresse, and readie to sinke : for
they were forced to use all their Pumps : so that they
wished a thousand times to have met with the Englishmen
to whom they would willingly have given their silver and
all that ever they brought with them, onely to save their
lives. And although the Erle of Cumberland lay still
[II. ii. 181.] about those Islands, yet they met not with him, so that
after much paine and labour they got into the Road before
Angra, where with all speede they unladed and discharged
above five millions of silver, all in pieces of 8 or 10
pound great: so that the whole Kay lay covered with
plates and chests of silver, full of Ryales of eight, most
wonderfull to behold, (each million being ten hundred
thousand duckats,) besides pearles, gold, and other stones,
which were not registred. The Admirall and chiefe
commaunder of those ships and Fleete called Alvaro

Flores de Quiniones was sicke of the Neapolitan disease,
and was brought to land, whereof not long after he died
in Sivillia. He brought with him the Kings broad seale
and full authoritie to be Generall and chiefe commaunder
upon the Seas, and of all Fleetes or ships, and of all
places and Islands, or lands wheresoever he came : whereupon the governour of Tercera did him great honour, and
betweene them it was concluded, perceiving the weaknesse
of their ships, and the danger of the Englishmen, that
they would send the shippes emptie with souldiers to
convey them, either to Sivill or Lisbon, where they could
first arrive, with advise unto his Majestie of all that
had past, and that he would give order to fetch the
silver with good and safe convoy. Whereupon the said
Alvaro Flores stayed there, under colour of keeping the
silver, but specially because of his disease, and for that
they were affraide of the Englishmen. This Alvaro
Flores had alone for his owne part above 50000 Duckats
in pearles which he shewed unto us, & sought to sell
them or barter them with us for spices or bils of exchange. The said two ships set sayle with 3 or 4 hundred
men, as well souldiers as others that came with them
out of India, and being at sea had a storme, wherewith
the Admiral burst and sunke in the sea, & not one
man saved. The Vice-Admirall cut downe her mast,
and ranne the ship on ground hard by Setuval, where it
burst in pieces, some of the men saving themselves by
swimming, that brought the newes, but the rest were
drowned.

In the same moneth there came two great ships out
of the Spanish Indies, and being within half a mile of
the Road of Tercera, they met with an English ship,
which, after they had fought long together, tooke them
both. About 7 or 8 moneths before, there had beene
an English shippe in Tercera, that under the name of
a Frenchman came to traffike in the Island, there to lade
woad, and being discovered was both ship and goods
confiscated to the kings use, and all the men kept

prisoners: yet went they up and downe the streetes to
get their livings, by labouring like slaves, being in deede
as safe in that Island, as if they had beene in prison.
But in the ende upon a Sunday, all the Saylers went
downe behinde the hils called Bresil: where they found
a Fisher-boat, whereinto they got and rowed into the
sea to the Erle of Cumberlands shippes, which to their
great fortune chanced at that time to come by the
Island, and ankered with his ships about halfe a mile
from the Road of Angra, hard by two small Islands,
which lie about a bases shot from the Island and are
full of Goats, Deere and Sheepe, belonging to the inhabitants of the Island of Tercera. Those Saylers knew
it well, and thereupon they rowed unto them with their
boates, and lying at anker that day, they fetched as many
Goates and sheepe as they had neede of: which those
of the towne and of the Island well saw and behelde,
yet durst not once goe foorth: so there remained no
more on land but the Master and the Marchant of the
said English ship. This Master had a brother in lawe
dwelling in England, who having newes of his brothers
imprisonment in Tercera, got licence of the Queene of
England to set forth a ship, therewith to see if he could
recover his losses of the Spaniards by taking some of
them, and so to redeeme his brother that lay prisoner
in Tercera, and he it was that tooke the two Spanish
ships before the Towne, the Master of the ship aforesaid
standing on the shore by me, and looking upon them,
for he was my great acquaintance. The ships being
taken that were worth 300 thousand duckats, he sent al
the men on land saving onely two of the principall
Gentlemen, which he kept aboord thereby to ransome
his brother: and sent the Pilot of one of the Indian
ships that were taken, with a letter to the Governor of
Tercera: wherein he wrote that he should deliver him
his brother, & he would send the 2 Gentlemen on land:
if not, he would saile with them into England, as indeed
he did, because the Governour would not doe it, saying

that the Gentlemen might make that suite to the king
of Spaine himselfe. This Spanish Pilot we bid to supper
with us, and the Englishmen likewise, where he shewed
us all the manner of their fight, much commending the
order and maner of the Englishmens fighting, as also their
courteous using of him : but in the end the English
Pilot likewise stole away in a French ship, without paying
any ransome as yet.

In the moneth of Januarie 1590 there arrived one ship
alone in Tercera, that came from the Spanish Indies,
and brought newes that there was a Fleete of a hundred
shippes which put out from the Firme land of the
Spanish Indies, and by a storme were driven upon the
coast called Florida, where they were all cast away, she
having onely escaped, wherin there were great riches,
& many men lost, as it may well be thought : so that
they made their account, that of 220 ships that for certaine were knowen to have put out of Nova Spagna,
S. Domingo, Havana, Capo verde, Brasilia, Guinea, &c. [II. ii. 182.]
in the yeere 1589. to saile for Spaine & Portugall,
there were not above 14 or 15 of them arrived there
in safetie, all the rest being either drowned, burst or
taken.

In the same moneth of January there arrived in Tercera 15 or 16 ships that came from Sivil, which were
most Flieboats of the Low countries, and some Britons
that were arrested in Spaine : these came full of souldiers,
and wel appointed with munition, to lade the silver that
lay in Tercera, and to fetch Alvares de Flores by the
kings commandement into Spaine. And because that
time of the yeere there are always stormes about those
Ilands, therefore they durst not enter into the road of
Tercera, for that as then it blew so great a storme that
some of their ships that had ankred were forced to cut
downe their mastes, and were in danger to be lost : and
among the rest a ship of Biscaie ran against the land
and was striken in pieces, but all the men saved themselves. The other ships were forced to keepe the sea

and seperate themselves one from the other, where wind and weather would drive them untill the 15 of March for that in all that time they could not have one day of faire weather to anker in, whereby they endured much miserie, cursing both the silver and the Iland. This storme being past, they chanced to meet with a small English ship of about 40 tunnes in bignesse, which by reason of the great wind could not beare all her sailes: so they set upon her and tooke her, and with the English flag in their Admirals sterne, they came as proudly into the haven as if they had conquered all the realme of England: but as the Admirall that bare the English flag upon her sterne was entring into the road, there came by chance two English ships by the Iland that paied her so well for her paines, that they were forced to cry Misericordia, and without all doubt had taken her, if she had bene but a mile further in the sea: but because she got under the Fortresse, which also began to shoot at the Englishmen, they were forced to leave her, and to put further into the sea, having slaine five or sixe of the Spaniards. The Englishmen that were taken in the small shippe were put under hatches, and coupled in bolts, and after they had bene prisoners 3 or 4 dayes, there was a Spanish Ensigne-bearer in the ship that had a brother slaine in the Fleet that came for England, who as then minding to revenge his death, and withall to shew his manhood on the English captives that were in the English ship, which they had taken, as is aforesayd, tooke a poiniard in his hand and went downe under the hatches, where finding the poore Englishmen sitting in boltes, with the same poiniard he stabbed sixe of them to the heart: which two others of them perceiving, clasped each other about the middle, because they would not be murthered by him, & threw themselves into the sea and there were drowned. This acte was of all the Spaniards much disliked and very ill taken, so that they caried the Spaniard prisoner unto Lisbon, where being arrived, the king of Spaine willed he should be sent into England, that the Queene of England might use him as she thought good: which sentence his friends by intreatie got to be reversed, notwithstanding he commanded he should without all favour be beheaded: but upon a good Friday the Cardinall going to masse, all the captaines and Commanders made so great intreaty for him, that in the end they got his pardon. This I thought good to note, that men might understand the bloody & dishonest minds of the Spaniards when they have men under their subjection.

The same two English ships which folowed the Spanish Admirall till he had got the Fort of Tercera, as I sayd before, put into the sea, where they met with another Spanish ship being of the same Fleet, that had likewise bene scattred by the storme and was onely missing, for the rest lay in the road. This small ship the Englishmen tooke, and sent all the men on shore, not hurting any of them: but if they had knowen what had bene done unto the foresayd English captives, I beleeve they would soone have revenged themselves, as afterward many an innocent soule paied for it. This ship thus taken by the Englishmen, was the same that was taken and confiscated in the Iland of Tercera by the Englishmen that got out of the Iland in a fisher boat (as I said before) and was sold unto the Spaniards that as then came from the Indies, wherewith they sayled to S. Lucar, where it was also arrested by the duke, and appointed to go in company to fetch the silver in Tercera, because it was a ship that sailed well, but among the Spaniards Fleet it was the meanest of the company. By this means it was taken from the Spaniards and caried into England, and the owners had it againe when they least thought of it.

The 19 of March the aforesayd ships being 19 in number, set saile, having laden the kings silver, and received in Alvaro Flores de Quiniones, with his company and good provision of necessaries, munition and souldiers that were fully resolved. (as they made shew) to fight valiantly to the last man before they would yeeld or lose their riches: and although they set their course for S. Lucar, the wind drave them unto Lisbon, which (as it seemed) was willing by his force to helpe them, and to bring them thither in safetie, although Alvaro de Flores, both against the wind and weather would perforce have sailed to Saint Lucar, but being constrained by the wind and importunitie of the sailers that protested they would require their losses and damages of him, he [II. ii. 183.] was content to saile to Lisbon: from whence the silver was by land caried unto Sivil. At Cape S. Vincent there lay a Fleet of 20 English ships to watch for the Armada, so that if they had put into S. Lucar, they had fallen right into their hands, which if the wind had served they had done. And therefore they may say that the wind hath lent them a happy voiage: for if the Englishmen had met with them, they had surely bene in great danger, and possibly but few of them had escaped, by reason of the feare wherewith they were possessed, because fortune or rather God was wholy against them: which is a sufficient cause to make the Spaniards out of heart, & to the contrary to give the Englishmen more courage, and to make them bolder for that they are victorious, stout and valiant: and seeing all their enterprises do take so good effect, that thereby they are become lords and masters of the sea, and need care for no man, as it wel appeareth by this briefe discourse.

The 7 of August 1590. a navie of English ships was seen before Tercera, being 20 in number, and 5 of them the Queenes ships: their Generall was one Martin Frobisher, as we after had intelligence. They came purposely to watch for the Fleet of the Spanish Indies, and for the Indian ships, and the ships of the countreys in the West: which put the Ilanders in great feare, specially those of Fayal, for that the Englishmen sent a trumpet to the Governour to aske certaine wine, flesh, and other victuals for their money and good friendship.

They of Fayal did not onely refuse to give eare unto
them, but with a shot killed their messenger or trum-
peter : which the Englishmen tooke in evill part, sending
them word that they were best to looke to themselves
and stand upon their guard, for they ment to come and
visite them whether they would or no. The Governour
made them answere, that he was there in the behalfe of
his majestie of Spaine, and that he would doe his best
to keepe them out, as he was bound : but nothing was
done, although they of Fayal were in no litle feare,
sending to Tercera for aide, from whence they had
certaine barkes with pouder and munition for warre, with
some bisket and other necessary provision.

The 30 of August we received very certaine newes
out of Portugal, that there were 80 ships put out of
the Groine laden with victuals, munition, money and
souldiours, to goe for Britaine to aide the Catholiques
and Leaguers of France against the king of Navarre. At
the same time two Netherland hulkes comming out of
Portugall to Tercera being halfe the Seas over, met with
4 of the Queenes ships, their Generall being sir John
Hawkins, that staied them, but let them go againe
without doing them any harme. The Netherlanders
reported, that each of the Queenes ships had 80 pieces
of Ordinance, and that captaine Drake lay with 40 ships
in the English chanell watching for the armie of the
Groine : and likewise that there lay at the Cape S.
Vincent ten other English ships, that if any ships escaped
from the Ilands, they might take them. These tidings
put the Ilanders in great feare, least if they failed of the
Spanish fleete and got nothing by them, that then they
would fall upon the Ilands, because they would not
returne emptie home, whereupon they held streit watch,
sending advise unto the king what newes they heard.

The first of September there came to the Iland of S.
Michael a Portugall ship out of the haven of Phernambuck in Brasile, which brought newes that the Admirall
of the Portugall Fleet that came from India, having

missed the Iland of S. Helena, was of necessitie constrained to put into Phernambuck, although the king had expresly under a great penaltie forbidden him so to doe, because of the wormes that there doe spoile the ships. The same shippe wherein Bernardin Ribero was Admirall the yeere before 1589. sailed out of Lisbon into the Indies, with 5 ships in her company, whereof but 4 got into India, the 5 was never heard of, so that it was thought to be cast away: the other foure returned safe againe into Portugall, though the Admiral was much spoiled, because he met with two English ships that fought long with him, and slew many of his men, but yet he escaped from them.

The 5 of the same moneth there arrived in Tercera a caravel of the Iland of Corvo, & brought with her 50 men that had bin spoiled by the Englishmen who had set them on shore in the Iland of Corvo, being taken out of a ship that came from the Spanish Indies, they brought tidings that the Englishmen had taken 4 more of the Indian ships, & a caravel with the king of Spaines letters of advise for the ships comming out of the Portugal Indies, & that with those which they had taken, they were at the least 40 English ships together, so y^t not one bark escaped them, but fel into their hands, & that therefore the Portugall ships comming out of India durst not put into the Ilands, but tooke their course under 40 & 42 degrees, and from thence sailed to Lisbon, shunning likewise the cape S. Vincent, otherwise they could not have had a prosperous journey of it, for that as then the sea was ful of English ships. Whereupon the king advised the fleet lying in Havana in ye Spanish Indies ready to come for Spaine, that they should stay there all that yeere till the next yeere, because of the great danger they might fal into by ye Englishmen, which was no smal charge, & hinderance to the fleet, for that the ships that lie there do consume themselves, and in a maner eat up one another, by reason of the great number of people, together with the scarcitie of al things, so that many ships chose rather one by one to adventure themselves alone to get home, then to stay there: all which fell into the Englishmens hands, wherof divers of the men were brought into Tercera, for that a whole day we could see nothing els, but spoiled men set on shore, some out of one ship, some out of another, that pitie it was to see all of them cursing the Englishmen & their owne fortunes, with those that had bene the causes to provoke the Englishmen to fight, and complaining of the small remedie and order taken therein by the king of Spaines officers.

The 19 of the same moneth there came to Tercera a Caravel of Lisbon, with one of the kings officers, to cause the goods that were saved out of the ship which came from Malacca (for ye which we staied there) to be laden and sent to Lisbon. And at the same time there put out of the Groine one Don Alonso de Baçan, with 40 great ships of warre to come unto the Ilands, there to watch for the fleet of the Spanish & Portugall Indies, and the goods of the Malacca ship being laden, they were to convoy them all together into the river of Lisbon: but being certaine daies at sea, alwaies having a contrary wind, they could not get unto the Ilands, onely two of them that were scattred from the fleet, arrived at Tercera, and not finding the fleet, they presently returned to seeke them: in the meane time the king changed his mind, & caused the fleet to stay in India, as I said before: and therefore hee sent worde unto Don Alonso de Bassan, that hee should returne againe to the Groine, which he presently did (without doing any thing, nor once approching neer the Ilands, saving onely the two foresayd ships, for he well knew that the Englishmen lay by the Iland of Corvo, but he would not visit them: and so he returned to the haven the Groine, whereby our goods that came from Malacca were yet to ship, and trussed up againe, and forced to stay a more fortunate time with patience perforce.

The 23 of October there arrived in Tercera a Caravel

with advise out of Portugall, that of 5 ships which in
the yere 1590 were laden in Lisbon for the Indies, 4 of
them were turned againe to Portin. After they had
bene 4 moneths abroad, & that the Admirall, wherein
the Viceroy called Mathias d'Albukerk sailed, had onely
gotten to India, as afterward newes thereof was brought
over-land, having bin at the least 11 moneths at sea &
never saw land, and came in great misery to Malacca.
In this ship there died by the way 280 men, according to
a note by himselfe made, and sent to the Cardinal at
Lisbon, with the names & surnames of every man,
together with a description of his voiage, & the misery
they had endured, which was onely done, because he
would not lose the government of India: and for that
cause he had sworne either to lose his life, or to arrive
in India, as in deed he did afterwards, but to the great
danger, losse and hinderance of his companie, that were
forced to buy it with their lives, & onely for want of
provision, as it may wel be thought: for he knew full
well that if he had returned backe againe into Portugal as
the other ships did, he should have bin cassiered from
his Indian regiment, because the people began already to
murmure at him for his proud & lofty mind. And
among other things that shewed his pride the more,
behind above the gallery of his ship he caused Fortune
to be painted, & his own picture w^t a staffe standing by
her, as it were threatning Fortune, with this posie, Quero
que vencas, that is, I wil have thee to overcome: which
being read by the Cardinal & other gentlemen (that to
honor him brought him aboord his ship) it was thought
to be a point of exceeding folly: but it is no strange
matter among the Portugals: for they above all others
must of force let the foole peepe out of their sleeves,
specially when they are in authoritie, for that I knew the
said Mathias d'Albukerk in India, being a souldier and a
captaine, where he was esteemed and accounted for one
of the best of them, & much honoured, and beloved of
all men, as behaving himselfe curteously to every man,

whereby they all desired that he might be Viceroy. But when he once had received his patent with full power & authoritie from the king to be Viceroy, he changed so much from his former behavior, that by reason of his pride, they all began to feare and curse him, and that before hee departed out of Lisbon, as it is often seene in many men that are advanced unto state and dignitie.

The 20 of Januarie 1591. there was newes brought out of Portugall into Tercera, that the Englishmen had taken a ship that the king had sent into the Portugal-Indies, w^t advise to the Viceroy for the returning againe of the 4 ships that should have gone to India, & because the ships were come backe againe, that ship was stuffed and laded as full of goods as possible it might be, having likewise in ready money 500 thousand duckets in roials of 8, besides other wares. It departed from Lisbon in the moneth of November 1590. & met with the Englishmen, with whom for a time it fought, but in the end it was taken and caried into England with men & all, yet when they came there, the men were set at libertie, and returned into Lisbon, where the captaine was committed prisoner; but he excused himselfe and was released, with whom I spake my selfe, & he made this report unto me. At the same time also they tooke a ship that came from the Mine laden with gold, & 2 ships laden with pepper & spices that were to saile into Italy, the pepper onely that was in them, being worth 170 thousand duckets: all these ships were caried into England, & made good prise.

In the moneth of July 1591. there hapned an earth- [II. ii. 185.] quake in the Iland of S. Michael, which continued from the 26 of July, to the 12 of August, in which time no man durst stay within his house but fled into the fields, fasting & praying with great sorow, for that many of their houses fel down, and a towne called Villa Franca, was almost cleane razed to the ground, all the cloisters & houses shaken to the earth, and therein some people slaine. The land in some places rose up, and the cliffs remooved from one place to another, and some hils were defaced and made even with the ground. The earthquake was so strong, that the ships which lay in the road and on the sea, shaked as if the world would have turned round : there sprang also a fountaine out of the earth, from whence for the space of 4 daies, there flowed a most cleare water, & after that it ceased. At the same time they heard such thunder & noise under the earth, as if all the devils in hell had bin assembled together in that place, wherewith many died for feare. The Iland of Tercera shooke 4 times together, so that it seemed to turne about, but there hapned no misfortune unto it. Earthquakes are common in those Ilands, for about 20 yeres past there hapned another earthquake, wherein a high hill that lieth by the same towne of Villa Franca, fell halfe downe, & covered all the towne with earth, and killed many men. The 25 of August the kings Armada comming out of Ferol arrived in Tercera being in all 30 ships, Biskaines, Portugals and Spaniards, and 10 dutch flieboats that were arrested in Lisbon to serve the king, besides other small ships & pataxos, that came to serve as messengers from place to place, and to discover the seas. This navie came to stay for, and convoy the ships that should come from the Spanish Indies, and the flieboats were appointed in their returne home, to take in the goods that were saved in the lost ship that came from Malacca, and to convoy them to Lisbon.

The 13 of September the said Armada arrived at the Iland of Corvo, where the Englishmen with about 16 ships as then lay, staying for the Spanish fleet, whereof some or the most part were come, and there the English were in good hope to have taken them. But when they perceived the kings army to be strong, the Admiral being the lord Thomas Howard, commanded his Fleet not to fal upon them, nor any of them once to separate their ships from him, unlesse he gave commission so to do : notwithstanding the viceadmirall sir Richard Greenvil being in the ship called the Revenge, went into the

Spanish fleet, and shot among them doing them great hurt, & thinking the rest of the company would have folowed, which they did not, but left him there, & sailed away: the cause why could not be knowen. Which the Spaniards perceiving, with 7 or 8 ships they boorded her, but she withstood them all, fighting with them at the least 12 houres together and sunke two of them, one being a new double Flieboat of 600 tunnes, and Admiral of the Flieboats, the other a Biscain: but in the end by reason of the number that came upon her, she was taken, but to their great losse: for they had lost in fighting and by drowning above 400 men, and of the English were slaine about 100, Sir Richard Greenvil himselfe being wounded in his braine, whereof afterwards he died. He was caried into the ship called S. Paul, wherein was the Admirall of the fleet Don Alonso de Baçan: there his wounds were drest by the Spanish surgeons, but Don Alonso himselfe would neither see him nor speake with him: all the rest of the captaines and gentlemen went to visite him, and to comfort him in his hard fortune, wondering at his courage and stout heart, for y^t he shewed not any signe of faintnes nor changing of colour; but feeling the houre of death to approch, he spake these words in Spanish, and said: Here die I Richard Greenvil with a joyful & quiet mind, for that I have ended my life as a true souldier ought to do, that hath fought for his countrey, Queene, religion and honor, whereby my soule most joyfull departeth out of this body, & shal alwayes leave behind it an everlasting fame of a valiant & true souldier that hath done his dutie as he was bound to doe. When he had finished these or such other like words, he gave up the Ghost, with great & stout courage, & no man could perceive any true signe of heavines in him.

This sir Rich. Greenvil was a great and a rich gentleman in England, & had great yeerely revenues of his owne inheritance, but he was a man very unquiet in his mind, and greatly affected to war; insomuch as of

his owne private motion he offred his service to the
Queene : he had performed many valiant acts, and was
greatly feared in these Ilands, and knowen of every man,
but of nature very severe, so that his owne people hated
him for his fiercenesse, & spake very hardly of him : for
when they first entred into the fleet or Armada, they
had their great saile in a readinesse, and might possibly
enough have sailed away, for it was one of the best ships
for saile in England, and the master perceiving that the
other ships had left them, & folowed not after, commanded the great saile to be cut that they might make
away : but sir Rich. Greenvil threatned both him & al the
rest that were in the ship, y^t if any man laid hand upon
it, he would cause him to be hanged, and so by that
occasion they were compelled to fight & in the end were
taken. He was of so hard a complexion, that as he continued among the Spanish captains while they were at
dinner or supper with him, he would carouse 3 or 4
glasses of wine, and in a braverie take the glasses be-
[II. ii. 186.] tweene his teeth and crash them in pieces & swalow
them downe, so that oftentimes the blood ran out of
his mouth without any harme at all unto him : & this
was told me by divers credible persons that many times
stood and beheld him. The Englishmen that were left
in the ship, as the captaine of the souldiers, the master
and others were dispersed into divers of the Spanish ships
that had taken them, where there had almost a new
fight arisen between the Biscains and the Portugals :
while each of them would have the honour to have
first boorded her, so that there grew a great noise and
quarel among them, one taking the chiefe ensigne, and
the other the flag, and the captaine and every one held his
owne. The ships that had boorded her were altogether
out of order, and broken, and many of their men hurt,
whereby they were compelled to come into the Island of
Tercera, there to repaire themselves : where being arrived,
I and my chamber-felow, to heare some newes, went
aboord one of the ships being a great Biscain, and one of

the 12 Apostles, whose captaine was called Bartandono,
that had bin General of the Biscains in the fleet that went
for England.   He seeing us called us up into the gallery,
where with great curtesie he received us, being as then
set at dinner with the English captaine that sate by him,
and had on a sute of blacke velvet, but he could not
tell us any thing, for that he could speake no other
language but English and Latine, which Bartandono also
could a litle speake.   The English captaine got licence
of the governour that he might come on land with his
weapon by his side, and was in our lodging with the
Englishman that was kept prisoner in the Iland, being of
that ship whereof the sailers got away, as I said before.
The governour of Tercera bade him to dinner, and
shewed him great curtesie.   The master likewise with
licence of Bartandono came on land and was in our
lodging, and had at the least 10 or 12 wounds, as well
in his head as on his body, whereof after that being at
sea between Lisbon & the Ilands he died.   The captaine
wrote a letter, wherein he declared all the maner of the
fight, and left it with the English marchant that lay in
our lodging, to send it to the lord Admiral of England.
This English captaine comming unto Lisbon, was there
wel received and not any hurt done unto him, but with
good convoy sent to Setuval, and from thence sailed into
England with all the rest of the Englishmen that were
taken prisoners.

The Spanish armie staied at the Iland of Corvo til
the last of September, to assemble the rest of the fleet
together, which in the ende were to the number of 140
sailes of ships partly comming from India, and partly of
the army, and being altogether ready to saile to Tercera
in good company, there suddenly rose so hard & cruell
a storme, that those of the Ilands did affirme, that in
mans memorie there was never any such seen or heard
off before: for it seemed the sea would have swalowed
up the Ilands, the water mounting higher then the cliffs,
which are so high that it amaseth a man to behold them:

but the sea reached above them, and living fishes were
throwen upon the land. This storme continued not only
a day or two with one wind, but 7 or 8 dayes continually,
the wind turning round about in al places of the compasse, at the lest twise or thrise during that time, and all
alike, with a continuall storme and tempest most terrible
to behold, even to us that were on shore, much more
then to such as were at sea : so that onely on the coasts
and cliffes of the Iland of Tercera, there were above 12
ships cast away, and not onely upon the one side, but
round about it in every corner, wherby nothing els was
heard but complaining, crying, lamenting & telling, here
is a ship broken in pieces against the cliffes, and there
another, and all the men drowned : so that for the space
of 20 dayes after the storme, they did nothing els but
fish for dead men that continually came driving on the
The wracke of shore. Among the rest was the English ship called the
the Revenge. Revenge, that was cast away upon a cliffe neere to the
Iland of Tercera, where it brake in an hundred pieces &
sunke to the ground, having in her 70 men Galegos,
Biscains, and others, with some of the captive Englishmen, whereof but one was saved that got up upon the
cliffes alive, and had his body and head all wounded, and
he being on shore brought us the newes desiring to be
shriven, & thereupon presently died. The Revenge had
in her divers faire brasse pieces that were all sunke in ye
sea, which they of the Iland were in good hope to waigh
up againe the next Sommer after. Among these ships
that were cast away about Tercera, was likewise a Flieboat, one of those that had bin arrested in Portugall to
serve the king, called the white Dove, the master of her
was one Cornelius Martenson of Schiedam in Holland,
and there were in her 100 souldiers, as in every one of
the rest there were. He being over-ruled by the captaine
that he could not be master of his owne, sayling here and
there at the mercy of God, as the storme drove him, in
the end came within the sight of the Iland of Tercera,
which the Spaniards perceiving thought all their safetie

onely to consist in putting into the road, compelling the Master and the Pilot to make towards the Iland, although the master refused to doe it, saying, that they were .most sure there to be cast away and utterly spoyled: but the captaine called him drunkard and Heretique, and striking him with a staffe, commaunded him to doe as hee would have him. The Master seeing this and being compelled to doe it, sayd: well then my Masters, seeing it is the desire of you all to bee cast away, I can but lose one life, [II. ii. 187.] and therewith desperately he sailed towards the shore, and was on that side of the Iland, where there was nothing els but hard stones and rocks, as high as mountaines, most terrible to beholde, where some of the inhabitants stood with long ropes and corke bound at the end thereof, to throw them downe unto the men, that they might lay holde upon them, and save their lives: but few of them got so neere, most of them being cast away, and smitten in pieces before they could get to the wall. The ship sailing in this maner (as I sayd before) towards the Iland, and approching to the shore, the master being an olde man, and full of yeeres, called his sonne that was in the ship with him, and having imbraced one another, and taken their last farewell, the good olde father willed his sonne not to take care for him, but seeke to save him-selfe; for (sayd he) sonne thou art yong, & mayest have some hope to save thy life, but as for me it is no great matter (I am olde) what become of me, and therewith ech of these shedding many teares, as every loving father and kinde childe may well consider, the ship fell upon the cliffes, and brake in pieces, the father on the one side, the sonne on the other side falling into the sea, ech laying holde upon that which came next to hand, but to no purpose; for the sea was so high and furious, that they were all drowned, and onely foureteene or fifteene saved themselves by swimming, with their legs and armes halfe broken and out of joynt, among which was the Masters sonne, and foure other Dutch boyes: the rest of the Spaniards and Sailers, with the Captaine and Master, were drowned. Whose heart would not melt with teares to beholde so grievous a sight, specially considering with himselfe that the greatest cause thereof was the beastlines and insolency of the Spaniards, as in this onely example may well be seene? Whereby may be considered how the other shippes sped, as we our selves did in part beholde, and by the men that were saved did heare more at large, as also some others of our countreymen that as then were in the like danger can well witnesse.

On the other Ilands the losse was no lesse then in Tercera: for on the Iland of Saint George there were two ships cast away: on the Iland of Pico two ships: on the Iland of Gratiosa three ships: and besides those there came every where round about divers pieces of broken ships, and other things fleeting towards the Ilands, wherewith the sea was all covered most pitifull to beholde. On the Iland of S. Michael there were foure ships cast away, and betweene Tercera and S. Michael three more were sunke, which were seene and heard to cry out; whereof not one man was saved. The rest put into the sea without masts, all torne and rent: so that of the *Above 100* whole fleet and armada, being 140 ships in all, there were *Spanish and* but 32 or 33 arrived in Spaine and Portugall, yea, and *Portugall* those few with so great misery, paine and labour, that *ships drowned.* not two of them arrived there together, but this day one, and to morrow another, next day the third, and so one after the other to the number aforesayd. All the rest were cast away upon the Ilands, and overwhelmed in the Sea, whereby may be considered what great losse and hindrance they received at that time: for by many mens judgements it was esteemed to be much more then was lost by their army that came for England; and it may well be thought, and presumed, that it was no other but a just plague purposely sent by God upon the Spaniards, and that it might truely be sayd, the taking of the Revenge was justly revenged upon them, and not by the might or force of man, but by the power of God, as some of them openly sayd in the Ile of Tercera, that they

beleeved verily God would consume them, and that he
tooke part with the Lutherans and heretiks: saying
further that so soone as they had throwen the dead body
of the Viceadmirall Sir Richard Greenfield over-boord,
they verily thought that as he had a divellish faith and
religion, and therefore the divels loved him, so he
presently sunke into the bottome of the sea, and downe
into hell, where he raised up all the divels to the revenge
of his death : and that they brought so great stormes and
torments upon the Spaniards, because they onely maintained the Catholike & Romish religion. Such and the
like blasphemies against God, they ceased not openly to
utter, without being reprooved of any man therein, nor
for their false opinions: but the most part of them rather
sayd and affirmed, that of trueth it must needs be so.

As one of those Indian fleets put out of Nova Spagna,
there were 35 of them by storme and tempest cast away
and drowned in the Sea, being 50 in all; so that but 15
escaped. Of the fleet that came from Santo Domingo
there were 14 cast away, comming out of the chanell of
Havana, whereof the Admirall and Viceadmirall were two
of them: and from Terra Firma in India there came
two ships laden with golde and silver, that were taken by
the Englishmen: and before the Spanish army came to
Corvo, the Englishmen at times had taken at the least
20 ships, that came from S. Domingo, India, Brasilia,
&c. and were all sent into England.

[A relation

[II. ii. 188.] A relation sent by Melchior Petoney to Nigil de Moura at Lisbon, from the Iland and Castle of Arguin, standing a little to the Southward of Cape Blanco, in the Northerly latitude of 19 degrees, concerning the rich and secret trade from the inland of Africa thither: Anno 1591.

AS concerning the trade to this Castle and Iland of Arguin, your worship is to understand, that if it would please the kings majesty to send hither two or three caravels once in a yeere with Flanders and Spanish commodities, as Bracelets of glasse, Knives, Belles, Linnen-cloth, Looking-glasses, with other kinds of small wares, his highnesse might do great good here. For 50 leagues up into the land the Moores have many exceeding rich golde mines; insomuch that they bring downe their golde to this Castle to traffique with us: and for a small trifle they will give us a great wedge of gold. And because here is no trade, the sayd Moores cary their golde to Fez being 250 leagues distant from hence, and there doe exchange the same for the foresayd kindes of commodities. By this meanes also his majesty might stop that passage, and keepe the king of Fez from so huge a masse of golde. Scarlet-clothes, and fine Purples are greatly accepted of in these parts. It is a most fertile countrey within the land, and yeeldeth great store of Wheat, flesh of all kindes, and abundance of fruits. Therefore, if it were possible, you should do well to deale with his majesty, either himselfe to send a couple of caravels, or to give your worship leave to traffique here: for here is a very good harbour where ships may ride at ancre hard by the Castle. The countrey where all the golde-mines are is called The kingdome of Darha. In this kingdome are great store

Commodities fit for Arguin.

Wedges of golde given for small trifles.

Scarlet & fine Purple cloth greatly accepted.

A good harbor before the Castle of Arguin.

of cities and townes; and in every city and towne a Captaine with certaine souldiers; which Captaines are lords and owners of the sayd townes. One city there is called Couton, another Xanigeton, as also the cities of Tubguer, Azegue, Amader, Quaherque, and the towne of Faroo. The which townes and cities are very great and fairely built, being inhabited by rich Moores, and abounding with all kinde of cattell, Barley and Dates. And here is such plenty of golde found upon the sands by the rivers side, that the sayd Moores usually carry the same Northward to Marocco, and Southward to the city of Tombuto in the land of Negros, which city standeth about 300 leagues from the kingdome of Darha; and this kingdome is but 60 leagues from this Iland and Castle of Arguin. Wherefore I beseech your worship to put his majesty in remembrance hereof; for the sayd cities and townes are but ten dayes journey from hence. I heartily wish that his majesty would send two or three marchants to see the state of the Countrey, who might travell to the aforesayd cities, to understand of their rich trade. For any man may go safe and come safe from those places. And thus without troubling of your worship any further, I humbly take my leave. From the Iland and Castle of Arguin the 20 of January 1591.

Concerning
this kingdome
reade Leo
Africanus a
little after the
beginning of
his 6 booke.

Your worships servant

Melchior Petoney.

[The voyage

The voyage of Richard Rainolds and Thomas Dassel to the rivers of Senega and Gambra adjoyning upon Guinea, 1591, with a discourse of the treasons of certain of Don Antonio his servants and followers.

Y vertue of her Majesties most gracious charter given in the yeere 1588, and in the thirtieth yeere of her Highnesse reigne, certaine English marchants are granted to trade, in and from the river of Senega to and in the river of Gambra, on the Westerne coast of Africa. The chiefest places of traffique on that coast betweene these rivers, are these:

The names of the chiefe places of traffike betweene Senega & Gambra.

1 Senega river: The commodities be hides, gumme, elephants teeth, a few graines, ostrich feathers, amber-griece, and some golde.

2 Beseguiache, a towne by Capo Verde * leagues from Senega river: The commodities be small hides, and a few teeth.

3 Refisca Viejo, a towne 4 leagues from Beseguiache: The commodities be small hides, and a few teeth now and then.

4 Palmerin, a towne 2 leagues from Refisca: The commodities be small hides, and a few elephants teeth now and then.

5 Porto d'Ally, a towne 5 leagues from Palmerin: The commodities be small hides, teeth, amber-griece, and a little golde: and many Portugals are there.

[II. ii. 189.]

6 Candimal, a towne halfe a league from Porto d'Ally: The commodities be small hides, and a few teeth now and then.

7 Palmerin, a towne 3 leagues from Candimal: The commodities be small hides, and a few teeth now and then.

8 Joala, a towne 6 leagues from Palmerin: The

commodities be hides, waxe, elephants teeth, rice, and some golde: and many Spaniards and Portugals are there.

9 Gambra river: The commodities are rice, waxe, hides, elephants teeth, and golde.

The Frenchmen of Diepe and New-haven have traded thither above thirty yeres: and commonly with foure or five ships a yere, whereof two small barks go into the river of Senega. The other were woont (untill within these foure yeres, that our ships came thither) to ride with their ships in the road of Porto d'Ally and so sent their small shaloups of sixe or eight tunnes to some of these places on the Sea coast before repeated. Where in all places generally they were well beloved and as courteously entertained of the Negros, as if they had bene naturally borne in the countrey. And very often the Negros come into France and returne againe, which is a further increasing of mutuall love and amity. Since our comming to that coast the Frenchmen ride with their shippes at Refisca Viejo, and suffer us to ancre with our shippes at Porto d'Ally. The Frenchmen never use to go into the river of Gambra: which is a river of secret trade and riches concealed by the Portugals. For long since one Frenchman entred the river with a small barke which was betrayed, surprised, and taken by two gallies of the Portugals.

Our trade hither beganne 1587.

Gambra a river of secret & rich trade concealed.

In our second voyage and second yeere there were by vile trecherous meanes of the Portugals and the king of the Negros consent in Porto d'Ally and Joala about forty Englishmen cruelly slaine and captived, and most or all of their goods confiscated: whereof there returned onely two, which were the marchants. And also by procurement of Pedro Gonsalves, one of Don Antonio the kings servants, Thomas Dassel and others had bene betrayed, if it had not pleased almighty God to reveale the same, whereby it was prevented.

The second voyage.

Forty English men traiter-ously slaine and captived.

From the South side of Senega river on the Sea coast unto about Palmerin is all one kingdome of Negros.

The kings name is Melick Zamba, who dwelleth two dayes journey within the land from Refisca.

The 12 of November 1591, I Richard Rainolds & Thomas Dassel factors in a ship called the Nightingale of London of 125 tunnes, and a pinnesse called the *Cape Verde.* Messenger of 40 tunnes arrived neere unto Capo Verde at a litle Iland called The Iland of liberty. At this Iland we set up a small pinnesse, with which we cary our marchandise on land when wee traffique. And in the meane time Thomas Dassel went with the great pinnesse to traffike with Spaniards or Portugals in Porto d'Ally or Joala. Over against the sayd Iland on the maine *Besegueache.* is an habitation of the Negros called Besegueache. The alcaide or governor thereof with a great traine came aboord in their canoas to receive the kings dueties for ankerage and permitting the quiet setting up of our pinnesse: who liked passing well that no Portugall came in the shippe, saying, we should be better thought of by the king and people, if we never did bring Portugall, but come of our selves as the Frenchmen ever did and doe. And to purchase the more love, I Richard Rainolds gave him and all his company courteous entertainment. Also upon his intreaty, having sufficient pledge aboord, I and others went on land with him. At this instant there was great warre betweene this alcaide and another governor of the next province. Neverthelesse upon our arrivall truce was taken for a space; and I with our company conducted among both enemies to the governors *Besegueache.* house in Besegueache, and were gently and friendly feasted after their maner, and with some presents returned safe aboord againe. The next day the alcaide came aboord againe, to wil me to send some yron and other commodities in the boat to traffike with the Negros, and also requested me that I would go to Refisca with the ship; which I did. And one thing I noted, that a number of Negros attended the alcaides landing in warlike maner with bowes and poisoned arrowes, darts poisoned, and swords, (because that the enemies by reason of the truce taken were there also to view the ship) who for the most part approched to him kneeling downe and kissed the backe of his hand.

The 17 of November we weyed anker; and by reason no French ship was yet come, I went to the road of Refisca: where I sent for the alcaides interpretors, who came thither aboord, and received of me the kings duties for to have free traffike with the Negros, with whom dayly I exchanged my yron & other wares for hides and some elephants teeth, finding the people very friendly and tractable. And the next day after our arrivall I went up into the land about three miles to the towne of Refisca, where I was friendly used and well entertained *Refisca.* of the alcaide, and especially of a yoong nobleman called Conde Amar Pattay, who presented me with an oxe for my company, goats and some yoong kids, assuring me that the king would be glad to heare of the arrivall of a Christians ship, whom they called Blancos, that is, [II. ii. 190.] white men: especially of an English ship. And so dayly the yong Conde came with a small company of horsemen to the sea side, feasting me very kindly and courteously. And the fift of December he with his traine came aboord to see the ship; which to them seemed woonderfull, as people that seldome had seene the like: who tolde me that his messenger from the king was returned; and the king rejoyced much to heare that English men were come with a ship to trade in his ports; and being the first Englishman that ever came with a ship, I was the better welcome; promising that I or any Englishman hereafter should be wel intreated & find good dealing at their hands. And further the Conde on the kings behalfe and his owne, earnestly requested, that before my departure off the coast I would returne againe to his road to conferre with him for the better continuance and confirming of amity betweene them and Englishmen: which I agreed unto. And so shewing him and his company the best friendship and courtesie I could, he went on shore, and should have had the honor of our ordinance but that he desired the contrary, being amazed at the sight of the ship and noise of the gunnes, which they did greatly admire.

Porto Dally.

The 13 of December at night we weighed anker, and arrived the 14 day at the road of Porto d'Ally, which is another kingdome: the king thereof is called Amar Meleck, & sonne to Meleck Zamba the other king, and dwelleth a dayes journey and an halfe from Porto d'Ally. When we had ankered, the kings kinsmen being governors, with all the officers of that towne came aboord to receive all duties for the ship & licence to traffike due to the king; who there generally seemed to be very glad that no Portugall was come in our ship out of England; saying it was the kings pleasure we should bring none hereafter; for that the king did esteeme them as people of no truth; and complained of one Francisco de Costa servant to Don Antonio, how he had often and the last yere also abused and deluded their king Amar Meleck in promising to bring him certaine things out of England, which he never performed, and deemed that to be the cause of his staying behinde this voyage, and that neither Spaniard nor Portugall could abide us, but reported very badly and gave out hard speeches tending to the defamation & great dishonor of England: and also affirmed that at the arrivall of an English ship called

The Comand a ship of Richard Kelley.
The monstrous lies of a Portugall.

The Command, of Richard Kelley of Dartmouth, one Pedro Gonsalves a Portugall that came in the sayd ship from Don Antonio reported unto them, that we were fled out of England and come away upon intent to rob and do great spoile upon this coast to the Negros and Portugals, and that Thomas Dassel had murdered Francisco de Acosta since our comming from England, who was comming to their king in our ship with great presents from Don Antonio, and desired that at our arrivall stay might be made of our goods and our selves in secret maner; which they denied, not giving credit to his report, having bene often abused by such frivolous and slanderous speeches by that nation; telling me their

king was sory for the former murder and captivity of
our nation, and would never yeeld to the like, having
the Portugals and Spaniards in generall hatred ever since,
and conceiveth much better of our countrey, and us, then
these our enemies report of. For which I yeelded them
hearty thanks, assuring them they should finde great
difference betweene the loyalty of the one and disloyalty
of the other: and so payed their dueties: and for that
it was the chiefe place of trade, I shewed them how I
was resolved to goe to their king with certaine presents
which we had brought out of England; which we determined for the more honor and credit of our countrey,
and augmenting of their better affection toward us.

*Port Dally the
chiefe place of
trade.*

All this while Thomas Dassel was with our great
pinnesse at the towne of Joala, being in the kingdome of
king Jocoel Lamiockeric, traffiking with the Spaniards &
Portugals there. And the forenamed Pedro Gonsalves,
which came out of England, was there also with other
English marchants about the busines of Rich. Kelley;
and as it should seeme, for that he could not obtaine
his mischievous pretended purpose against Thomas Dassel
and others at the towne of Porto d'Ally, where I Richard
Rainolds remained, he attempted with consent of other
Portugals which were made privy to his intent to betray
the sayd Thomas Dassel at this towne, & had with bribes
seduced the chiefe commanders and Negros to effect his
wicked & most villanous practise: which as God would,
was revealed to the sayd Thomas Dassel by Rich. Cape
an Englishman and servant to the forenamed Rich.
Kelley; to whom this sayd Pedro Gonsalves had dis-
closed his secret treachery, willing him with all expedition
to stand upon his guard. Whereupon Thomas Dassel
went aboord a small English barke called The Cherubin
of Lime, and there one John Payva a Portugall and
servant of Don Antonio declared, that if he & one Garcia
a Portugall of the sayd towne would have consented with
Pedro Gonsalves, the sayd Thomas Dassel had bene
betrayed long before. And upon this warning Thomas

Joala.

*The Cherubin
of Lime at
Joala.*

Dassel the next day having gotten three Portugals aboord, advised for our better securities to send two on land, & detained one with him called Villa nova, telling them that if the next day by eight of the clocke, they would bring [II. ii. 191.] Pedro Gonsalves aboord to him, he would release the sayd Villa nova, which they did not. And Thomas Dassel having intelligence that certaine Negros and Portugals were ridden post over-land to Porto d'Ally with intent to have Richard Rainolds and his company stayd on land, being doubtfull what friendship soever the unconstant Negros professed (by reason they be often wavering being overcome with drinking wine) how they would deale, to prevent the dangerous wiles that might be effected in the road by Portugals, and for better strength, the 24 of December he came with his pinnesse & Portugall to ride in the road of Porto d'Ally, where our great shippe the Nightingall was: who was no sooner arrived but he had newes also from the shore from John Baily Anthony Dassels servant, who was there with our goods detained by the Portugals means, that above 20 Portugals and Spaniards were come from Joala by land, and Pedro Gonsalves in their company, to take order for the releasing of Villa nova. So having had conference two or three dayes with the Commanders, the Negros, some Spaniards, and some Portugals, in the end by due examination of the matter the Negros seeing how vilely Pedro Gonsalves had delt, he being in their power, sayd he should suffer death or be tortured, for an example to others. But we in recompense of his cruelty pitied him and shewed mercy, desiring the Negros to intreat him well though undeserved: and thereupon the Commanders brought him aboord the pinnesse to Thomas Dassel to do with him what he would: where at his comming from the shore, for lavish speeches which he used of Princes, he was well buffetted by a Spaniard, and might have bene slaine, if for our sakes he had not bene rescued.

While I went on shore with Villa nova, the sayd Pedro Gonsalves confessed unto Thomas Dassel that he did

enquire of some Negros and Portugals if he might not
stay him and his goods in the land, and that he did
nothing but by commission from his king by his letters
which he received from London in Dartmouth after we
were departed from London, for that we presumed to
come to Guinea to traffike without a servant of his: and
further, that he had power or procuration from Francisco
de Costa the Portugall that stayed behinde in England
to detaine the goods of Anthony Dassel in Guinea.

By consent of M. Francis Tucker, John Browbeare,
and the rest of the factours of Richard Kelley, with whom
this Pedro Gonsalves came, for avoiding further mischiefe
that might be practised, we agreed that the sayd Pedro
Gonsalves should stay aboord our shippe, and not goe
any more on land untill they departed. So the ninth of
January he was delivered aboord to goe for England in
the same ship wherein he came: who was all the time
of his abode in our shippe both courteously and friendly
used at my hands, much against the mariners willes, who
could not abide such a wicked creature and caitive, that is
nourished and relieved in our countrey, and yet by
villanous meanes sought the destruction of us all.

The Spaniards and Portugals though they be dissem-
blers and not to be trusted, when they perceived how
king Amar Melicks Negros befriended and favored us,
and that it would be prejudiciall to their trade for divers
respects, if we should any way be injuried, renounced the
sayd practises, detesting the author, and protested to
defend us in such cases with all faithfulnesse: desiring we
would, as the king of Negros had commanded us, never
bring Portugal with us more: using this phrase in
disdaine of such as came out of England, let your
Portugals be barres of yron: for in trueth in regard of
the rich trade maintained by Frenchmen and by us of
late, they esteeme more of one barre of yron then of
twenty Portugals which we should bring out of England:
who at their comming thither very subtilly disadvantage
us, and doe great hurt to every party.

At the beginning of these broiles the king Amar Melick had sent his chiefe secretary and three horses for me Richard Rainolds: but I denied to goe by reason of the hurley burley, though I might have had Negros of account for pledges aboord: yet we sent the presents unto the king; who so soone as he understood the cause why I came not to him, being sory and offended thereat, commanded presently by proclamation, that no injury should be offered us in his dominions by his owne people, or suffered to be done by Spaniards or Portugals. And if the Negros joyning to his kingdome should confederate with the Spaniards and Portugals to molest or trouble us; that his subjects the Negros should be ready to ayde, succor and defend us. In which people appeared more confident love and goodwill towards us, then ever we shall finde either of Spaniards or Portugals, though we should relieve them of the greatest misery that can be imagined.

In the river of Senega no Spaniard or Portugall use to trade: and onely one Portugall called Ganigoga dwelleth farre within the river, who was maried to a kings daughter.

In the townes of Porto d'Ally and Joala, being townes of chiefest trade, and in the townes of Canton and Cassan in the river of Gambra are many Spaniards and Portugals resident by permission of the Negros; who have rich trades there along the coast, especially to San Domingo and Rio grande, not far distant from Gambra river; whither they transport the yron which they buy of Frenchmen and us, and exchange it for Negros; which be caried continually to the West Indies in such ships as came from Spaine. Also by the governors order and Renters of Castel de Mina and other places, where golde is, upon the coast of Guinea, they have a place limited how farre they must go to trade within the river of Gambra; and further they may not go upon paine of confiscation of their goods, and losse of life: for that the Renters themselves send at certaine times their owne

[II. ii. 192.]
San Domingo.
Rio grande.
Note this
trade.

barks within the river to such places, where as they have
great store of golde. And in all these places hereabouts, *A rich trade*
where we use to trade, they have no Fort, Castle, or *for golde in*
place of strength, but onely trading by the Negros safe- *Rio grande.*
conduct and permission. And the most part of the
Spaniards and Portugals that be resident in these places
be banished men or fugitives, for committing most
hainous crimes and incestuous acts, their life & conversation being agreeable; and they are of the basest behaviour
that we have ever seene of these nations in any other
countrey.

A briefe relation concerning the estate of the
cities and provinces of Tombuto and Gago
written in Marocco the first of August 1594,
and sent to M. Anthony Dassel marchant of
London.

Y hearty commendations premised: your
letter of late I received, and found that
you would have me discover unto you
the estate & quality of the countreyes
of Tombuto and Gago. And that you
may not thinke me to slumber in this
action, wherin you would be truely and
perfectly resolved, you shall understand, that not ten
dayes past here came a Cahaia of the Andoluzes home
from Gago, and another principall Moore, whom the
king sent thither at the first with Alcaide Hamode, and
they brought with them thirty mules laden with gold.
I saw the same come into the Alcasava with mine owne
eies: and these men themselves came not poore, but with
such wealth, that they came away without the kings
commandement: and for that cause the king will pay
them no wages for the time they have beene there. On
the other side they dare not aske the king for any wages.
And when Alcaide Hamode saw that the Cahaia of the
Andoluzes would not stay in Gago with him, he thought

good to send these thirty mules laden with golde by him, with letters of commendations, by which the king smelled their riches that they brought with them : and this was the cause of the kings displeasure towards them. So now there remaineth in Gago Alcaide Hamode, and Alcaide Jawdara, and Alcaide Bucthare. And here are in a readinesse to depart in the end of this next September Alcaide Monsor, Ben Abdrahaman Allies, Monsor Rico with five thousand men, most of the fettilase, that is *Commodities* to say, of fier-mach, & muskets. There is gone good *for Gago.* store of reds & yellowes : and this yere here was want of the same commodity; but I trust the next yere wil be no want. But in fine the king doth prosper wel in those parts, and here are many pledges come hither, and namely three of the kings sonnes of Gago and the Justice; I saw them come in with the treasure. Now when Alcaide Monsor commeth to Gago, the which will be in January next, then returneth hither Alcaide Hamode with all the treasure, and Alcaide Monsor is to keepe Gago untill the king take further order. And thus much for Gago. Thus not having any other thing to write at this present, I commend you to the mercifull tuition of the almighty. From Marocco the first of August 1594.

Your assured friend Laurence Madoc.

Another briefe relation concerning the late conquest and the exceeding great riches of the cities and provinces of Tombuto and Gago, written from Marocco the 30 August 1594, to M. Anthony Dassel marchant of London aforesayd.

Oving friend M. Dassel, two of your letters I have received, one by the shippe called The Amity, the other by The Concord: the chiefest matter therein was to be satisfied of the king of Marocco his proceedings in Guinea. Therefore these

are to let you understand that there went with Alcaide Hamode for those parts seventeene hundred
men: who passing over the sands, for want of water
perished one third part of them: and at their comming to the city of Tombuto, the Negros made some *Tombuto*
resistance; but to small purpose, for that they had no *taken.*
defence but with their asagaies or javelings poisoned.
So they tooke it, and proceeded to the city of Gago, *Gago taken.*
where the Negros were in number infinite, and meant
to stand to the uttermost for their countrey: but the
Moores slew them so fast, that they were faine to
yeeld, and do pay tribute by the yere. The rent of [II. ii. 193.]
Tombuto is 60 quintals of golde by the yeere; the goodnesse whereof you know. What rent Gago will yeeld,
you shall know at the Spring, for then Alcaide Hamode
commeth home. The rent of Tombuto is come by the
cafelow or carovan, which is, as above is mentioned, 60
quintals. The report is, that Mahomed bringeth with
him such an infinite treasure as I never heard of: it
doth appeare that they have more golde then any other
part of the world beside. The Alcaide winneth all the
countrey where he goeth without fighting, and is going
downe towards the sea coast. This king of Marocco
is like to be the greatest prince in the world for money,
if he keepe this countrey. But I make account assoone
as the king of Spaine hath quietnesse in Christendome,
he wil thrust him out: for that the kings force is not
great as yet; but he meaneth to be stronger. There
is a campe ready to go now with a viceroy: the speech is
with 3000 men: but I thinke they will be hardly 2000;
for by report, 3000 men are enough to conquer all the
countrey: for they have no defence of importance against
an enemy. I thinke Hamode will be returned home in
January or thereabout: for he stayeth but for the comming of the viceroy. Mulley Balasen the kings sonne
of Marocco was slaine in Guinea by his owne men, and
they were presently killed, because they should tell no
tales. And thus leaving to trouble you, I commit you

to God, who prosper you in all your proceedings. From
Marocco the first of August 1594.

Yours to command for ever Laurence Madoc.

Of these two rich cities and kingdomes of Tombuto
and Gago Leo Africanus writeth at large in the beginning
of his seventh booke of the description of Africa, which
worthy worke is to be annexed into· the end of this
second volume.

A briefe extract of a patent granted to M. Thomas
Gregory of Tanton, and others, for traffique
betweene the river of Nonnia and the rivers
of Madrabumba and Sierra Leona on the coast
of Guinea, in the yeere 1592.

N May the 34 yeere of our gracious
soveraigne Queene Elizabeth, a patent
of speciall licence was granted to Thomas
Gregory of Tanton in the county of
Somerset, and to Thomas Pope, and
certaine other marchants to traffique into
Guinea from the Northermost part of
the river of Nonnia to the Southermost parts of the
rivers of Madrabumba and Sierra Leona, and to other
parts aswell to the Southeast as to the Northwest, for
a certaine number of leagues therein specified which
amount to an hundred or thereabout. Which patent
was granted for the terme of ten yeeres: as appeareth at
large in the sayd patent recorded in the Rolles in her
Majesties Chancery.

The maner of the taking of two Spanish ships
laden with quicksilver & the Popes bulles,
bound for the West Indies, by M. Thomas
White in the Amity of London. 1592.

He 26 of July 1592, in my returning
out of Barbary in the ship called the
Amity of London, being in the height
of 36 degrees or thereabout, at foure
of the clocke in the morning we had
sight of two shippes, being distant from
us about three or foure leagues: by
seven of the clocke we fetched them up, and were
within gunshot: whose boldnesse, having the king of
Spaines armes displayed, did make us judge them rather
ships of warre, then laden with marchandise. And as
it appeared by their owne speeches, they made full
account to have taken us: it being a question among
them, whether it were best to cary us to S. Lucar,
or to Lisbon. We waved ech other a maine. They
having placed themselves in warlike order one a cables
length before another, we began the fight. In the which
we continued, so fast as we were able to charge and
discharge, the space of five houres, being never a cables
length distant either of us from other. In which time
we received divers shot both in the hull of our ship,
masts, and sailes, to the number of 32 great, besides
500 musket shot and harquebuzes a crocke at the least,
which we tolde after the fight. And because we perceived them to be stout, we thought good to boord
the Biscaine, which was on head the other: where lying
aboord about an houre, and plying our ordinance and
small shot; in the end we stowed all his men. Now
the other in the flieboat, thinking we had entred our
men in their fellow, bare roome with us, meaning to have
layed us aboord, and so to have intrapped us betwixt
them both: which we perceiving, fitted our ordinance

so for him, as we quitted our selves of him, and he boorded his fellow : by which meanes they both fell from us. Then presently we kept our loofe, hoised our top-sailes, and weathered them, and came hard aboord [II. ii. 194.] the flieboat with our ordinance prepared, and gave her our whole broad side, with the which we slew divers of their men ; so as we might see the blood run out at the scupper holes. After that we cast about, and new charged all our ordinance, and came upon them againe, willing them to yeeld, or els we would sinke them : wherupon the one would have yeelded, which was shot betweene winde and water; but the other called him traitor. Unto whom we made answere, that if he would not yeeld presently also, we would sinke him first. And thereupon he understanding our determination, presently put out a white flag, and yeelded, and yet refused to

Marke this othe.

strike their own sailes, for that they were sworne never to strike to any Englishman. We then commanded their captaines and masters to come aboord us; which they did. And after examination & stowing them, we sent certaine of our owne men aboord them, and strook their sailes, and manned their ships : finding in them both 126 persons living, & 8 dead, besides those which they themselves had cast overboord. So it pleased God to give us the victory being but 42 men and a boy, whereof 2 were killed and 3 wounded : for the which good successe we give God the only praise. These two rich prizes laden with 1400 chests of quicksilver with the armes of Castile and Leon fastened upon them, and with a great quantity of bulles or indulgences, and guilded Missals or Service books, with an hundred tunnes of excellent wines, we brought shortly after into the river of Thames up to Blacke-wall.

By the taking of this quicksilver, about 1400 chests, the king of Spaine loseth for every quintall of the same a quintall of silver, that should have beene delivered him by the masters of the mines there, which amounteth to 600000 pounds.

More by taking of his bulles, to wit, two millions and 72 thousand for living and dead persons for the provinces of Nova Hispania, Iucatan, Guatimala, the Honduras, and the Phillipinas, taxed at two reals the piece. And more for eighteene thousand bulles taxed at foure reals, amounteth all to 107700 pounds. Summa totalis 707700 li.

More there were taken ten fardels of gilt missals and breviaries sent for the kings account.

So the hinderance that the king receiveth by the losse of his bulles and quicksilver amounteth as is abovesaid: besides the lacking of his wines, about 100 tunnes, whereby his fleet is disappointed of a great part of their provision.

A true report of the honourable service at Sea perfourmed by Sir John Burrough Knight, Lieutenant generall of the fleet prepared by the honor. Sir Walter Ralegh Knight, Lord warden of the Stanneries of Cornwall and Devon. Wherin chiefly the Santa Clara of Biscay, a ship of 600 tunnes was taken, and the two East Indian caraks, the Santa Cruz and the Madre de Dios were forced, the one burnt, and the other taken and brought into Dartmouth the seventh of September, 1592.

Ir Walter Ralegh upon commission received from her Majesty for an expedition to be made to the West Indies, slacked not his uttermost diligence to make full provision of all things necessary, as both in his choise of good ships, and sufficient men to performe the action evidently appeared. For his shippes which were in number 14 or 15, those two of her Majesties, the Garland & the Foresight were the chiefest; the rest

either his owne or his good friends or adventurers of London. For the gentlemen his consorts and officers, to give them their right, they were so well qualited in courage, experience, & discretion, as the greatest prince might repute himselfe happy to be served with their like. The honor of Lieutenant generall was imposed upon sir John Burrough, a gentleman, for his manifold good and heroicall parts, thought every way worthy of that commandement: with whom after sir W. R. returned was joyned in commission sir Martin Frobisher, who for his speciall skill & knowledge in marine causes had formerly caried imploiments of like or greater place. The rest of the captaines, souldiers, and sailers were men of notable resolution, and for the most part such as heretofore had given to the world sufficient proofe of their valour in divers services of the like nature. With these ships thus manned sir Walter Ralegh departed towards the West countrey, there to store himselfe with such further necessaries as the state of his voyage did needfully require: where the Westerly windes blowing for a long time contrary to his course, bound and constrained him to keepe harborough so many weeks, that the fittest season for his purpose was gone, the mindes of his people much altered, his victuals consumed; and withall, her Majesty understanding how crosly all this sorted, began to call the proceeding of this preparation into question: insomuch that, whereas the sixt of May was first come before sir Walter could put to sea, the very next day sir Martin Frobisher in a pinnesse of my lord Admirals called The Disdaine, met him, and brought to him from her Majesty letters of revocation, with commandement to relinquish (for his owne part) the [II. ii. 195.] intended attempt, and to leave the charge and conduct of all things in the hands of sir John Burrough and sir Martin Frobisher. But sir Walter finding his honor so farre engaged in the undertaking of this voyage, as without proceeding he saw no remedy either to salve his reputation, or to content those his friends which had put

in adventures of great summes with him; and making
construction of the Queenes letters in such sort as if
her commandement had bene propounded in indifferent
termes, either to advance forward or to retire, at his owne
discretion; would in no case yeeld to leave his fleet
now under saile. Wherefore continuing his course into
the sea, he met within a day or two, with certaine sailes
lately come from Spaine: among which was a ship appertaining to Monsieur Gourdon governor of Caleis, and
found aboord her one M. Nevel Davies an Englishman,
who having indured a long and miserable captivity for
the space of twelve yeeres, partly in the inquisition in
Spaine, was now by good fortune escaped, and upon
returne to his countrey. This man, among other things,
reported for certaine, that there was little hope of any
good this yeere to be done in the West India; considering that the king of Spaine had sent expresse order to
all the ports both of the Ilands and of Terra firma, that
no ship should stirre that yeere, nor any treasure be layed
aboord for Spaine. But neither this unpleasant relation
nor ought els could stay his proceedings, untill a
tempest of strange and uncouth violence arising upon
Thursday the 11 of May, when he was athwart the Cape
Finister, had so scattered the greater part of the fleet,
and sunke his boats and pinnesses, that as the rest were
driven and severed, some this way and some that, sir
Walter himselfe being in the Garland of her Majesty was
in danger to be swallowed up of the Sea. Whereupon
sir W. Ralegh finding that the season of the yere was
too farre gone to proceed with the enterprise which he
had upon Panama, having bene held on the English coast
from February till May, and thereby spent three moneths
victuals; and considering withall, that to lie upon the
Spanish coast or at the Ilands to attend the returne of
the East or West Indian fleets was rather a worke of
patience then ought els: he gave directions to sir John
Burgh and sir M. Frobisher to divide the fleet in two
parts; sir M. with the Garland, cap. George Gifford,

cap. Henry Thin, cap. Grenvile and others to lie off the South cape, thereby to amaze the Spanish fleet, and to holde them on their owne coast; while sir J. Burgh, capt. Robert Crosse, capt. Tomson, & others should attend at the Ilands for the caraks or any other Spanish ships comming from Mexico or other parts of the West Indies. Which direction tooke effect accordingly; for the king of Spaines Admirall receiving intelligence that the English fleet was come on the coast, attended to defend the South parts of Spaine, & to keepe himselfe as nere sir Mart. Frobisher as he could, to impeach him in all things which he might undertake; and thereby neglected the safeconduct of the caraks, with whom it fared as hereafter shall appeare. Before the fleet severed themselves they mette with a great Biscain on the Spanish coast called Santa Clara a ship of 600 tunnes.

The Santa Clara a Biscain ship of 600 tunnes taken.

The noise of the artillery on both sides being heard, immediatly they drew to their fleet; where after a reasonable hot fight, the ship was entred and mastered, which they found fraighted with all sorts of small yron-worke, as horse-shoes, nailes, plough-shares, yron barres, spikes, boults, locks, gimbols, & such like, valued by us at 6000 or 7000 li. but woorth to them treble the value. This Biscain was sailing towards S. Lucar, there to take in some further provision for the West India. This ship being first roomaged, and after sent for England, our fleet coasted along towards the Southcape of S. Vincent, and by the way, about the Rocke nere Lisbon, sir John Burrough in the Robucke spying a saile afarre off, gave her present chase; which being a flieboat and of good saile, drew him farre Southwards before he could fetch her; but at last she came under his lee and strooke saile. The master of which flieboat comming aboord him, confessed that the king indeed had prepared a great fleet in S. Lucar and Cadiz, and (as the report in Spaine was currant) for the West Indies. But in deed the Spanish king had provided this fleet upon this counsell. He received intelligence, that sir Walter Ralegh was to put

out strong for the West India: to impeach him, and
to ranconter his force he appointed this fleet; although
looking for the arrivall of his East Indian caraks, he first
ordained those ships to waft them from the Açores. But
perswading himselfe, that if the fleet of sir Walter Ralegh
did go for the West India, then the Ilands should have
none to infest them but small men of warre, which the
caraks of themselves would be well able to match; his
order was to Don Alonso de Baçan brother to the
Marques of Santa Cruz, and Generall of his armada, to
pursue sir Walters fleet, and to confront him, what
course soever he held. And that this was true, our men
in short time by proofe understood: for sir John
Burrough, not long after the taking of his last prize
the flieboat, as he sailed backe againe towards the rest
of his company, discovered the Spanish fleet to sea-ward
of him: which having likewise espied him betwixt them
and the shore, made full account to bring him safe into
Spanish harbour; and therefore spred themselves in such
sort before him, that indeed his danger was very great:
for both the liberty of the sea was brought into a narrow
straight, and the shore being enemy could give him no [II. ii. 196.]
comfort of reliefe: so that trusting to Gods helpe onely
and his good saile, he thrust out from among them in
spight of all their force, and to the notable illusion of all
their cunning, which they shewed to the uttermost, in
laying the way for his apprehension. But now sir John   *Sir John Bur-*
Burrough having happily escaped their clouches, finding   *rough in great*
danger of the
the coast guarded by this fleet, and knowing it was but   *Spanish fleet.*
folly to expect a meeting there with sir Martin Frobisher
(who understanding of this armada aswell as himselfe,
would be sure not to come that way) beganne to shape
his course to the Açores according to sir W. Raleghs   *The Ile of S.*
direction, and came in sight of S. Michael, running so   *Michael.*
neere by Villa Franca, that he might easily discerne the
shippes lying there at anker. Divers small caravels both   *Divers small*
ships taken.
here and betweene S. Georges and the Pike in his course
toward Flores he intercepted; of which no great intelli-

gence for his affaires could be understood. Arriving before Flores upon Thursday the 21 of June, towards evening, accompanied onely with captaine Caufield and the Master of his shippe, the rest not being yet arrived, he made towards the shore with his boat, finding all the people of Santa Cruz, a village of that Iland, in armes, fearing their landing, and ready marshalled to defend their towne from spoile. Sir John contrariwise made signes of amity unto them by advancing a white flagge, a common token of peace, which was answered againe of them with the like: whereupon ensued entercourses of good friendship ; and pledges were taken on both sides, the captaine of the towne for them, and captaine Caufield for ours: so that whatsoever our men wanted, which that place could supply either in fresh water, victuals, or the like, was very willingly granted by the inhabitants : and good leave had they to refresh themselves on shore as much and as oft as they would without restraint. At this Santa Cruz sir John Burrough was informed, that indeed there was among them no expectation of any fleet to come from the West, but from the East, that no longer since then three dayes before his arrivall a carak was passed by for Lisbon, and that there were foure caraks more behinde, of one consort. Sir John being very glad of this newes, stayed no longer on shore, but presently imbarqued himselfe, having onely in company a small barke of threescore tunnes belonging to one M. Hopkins of Bristoll. In the meane while that these things thus passed at Flores, part of the rest of the English fleet, which sir John Burrough had left upon the coast of Spaine, drew also towards the Açores : and whereas he quickly at sea had discovered one of the caraks, the same evening he might descry two or three of the Earle of Cumberlands ships (whereof one M. Norton was captaine) which having in like sort kenned the carak, pursued her by that course which they saw her to runne towards the Ilands. But on no side was there any way made by reason of a great calme which yeelded

Santa Cruz a village in the Ile of Flores.

Newes of the East Indian caraks.

no breath to spread a saile. Insomuch that fitly to discover her what she was, of what burthen, force, and countenance, sir John Burrough tooke his boat, and rowed the space of three miles, to make her exactly: and being returned, he consulted with the better sort of the company then present, upon the boording her in the morning. But a very mighty storme arising in the night, the extremity thereof forced them all to wey ankers, yet their care was such in wrestling with the weather not to lose the carak, that in the morning, the tempest being qualified, and our men bearing againe with the shore, they might perceive the carak very neere the land, and the Portugals confusedly carrying on shore such things as they could any maner of way convey out of her; and seeing the haste our men made to come upon them, forsooke her: but first, that nothing might be left commodious to our men, set fire to that which they could not cary with them, intending by that meanes wholly to consume her; that neither glory of victory nor benefit of shippe might remaine to ours. And least the approch and industry of the English should bring meanes to extinguish the flame, thereby to preserve the residue of that which the fire had not destroyed; being foure hundred of them in number and well armed, they intrenched themselves on land so neere to the carak, that she being by their forces protected, and our men kept aloofe off, the fire might continue to the consumption of the whole. This being noted by sir John Burrough he soone provided a present remedy for this mischiefe. For landing one hundred of his men, whereof many did swim and wade more then brest high to shore, and easily scattering those that presented themselves to guard the coast, he no sooner drew toward their new trenches, but they fled immediatly, leaving as much as the fire had spared to be the reward of our mens paines. Here was taken among others one Vincent Fonseca a Portugall, Purser of the carak, with two others, one an Almaine and the second a Low-dutchman, canoniers: who refusing

A carak called The Santa Cruz set on fire.

An hundred of our men land.

to make any voluntary report of those things which were demanded of them, had the torture threatened, the feare whereof at the last wrested from them this intelligence, that within fifteene dayes three other greater caraks then that lately fired would arrive at the same Iland: and that being five caraks in the fleet at their departure from Goa, to wit, the Buen Jesus admirall, the Madre de Dios, the S Bernardo, the S. Christophoro, and the S. Cruz, (whose fortune you have already heard) they had received speciall commandement from the king not to

[II. ii. 197.] touch in any case at the Iland of S. Helena, where the Portugall caraks in their returne from the East India were alwayes till now woont to arrive to refresh themselves with water and victuals. And the kings reason was; because of the English men of warre, who (as he was informed) lay there in wait to intercept them. If therefore their necessity of water should drive them to

Angola a new watering place for the caraks. seeke supply any where, he appointed them Angola in the maine of Africa, with order there to stay onely the taking in of water to avoid the inconvenice of infections, wherunto that hot latitude is dangerously subject. The last rendevous for them all was the Iland of Flores, where the king assured them not to misse of his armada thither sent of purpose for their wafting to Lisbon. Upon this information sir John drew to counsel, meeting there captaine Norton, captaine Dounton, captaine Abraham Cocke, captaines of three ships of the Earle of Cumberland, M. Tomson of Harwich cap. of the Dainty of sir John Haukins, one of sir W. Raleghs fleet, and M. Christopher Newport cap. of the Golden dragon newly returned from the West India, and others. These being assembled, he communicated with them what he had understood of the foresaid examinates, and what great presumptions of trueth their relation did cary: wishing that forasmuch as God & good fortune had brought them together in so good a season, they would shew the uttermost of their indevors to bring these Easterlings under the lee of the English obedience. Hereupon a present accord on all sides followed not to part company or leave of those seas till time should present cause to put their consultations in execution. The next day her Majesties good ship the Foresight commanded by sir Rob. Crosse came in to the rest: and he likewise informed of the matter was soone drawen into this service. Thus sir John with al these ships departing thence 6 or 7 leagues to the West of Flores, they spread themselves abroad from the North to the South, ech ship two leagues at the least distant from another. By which order of extension they were able to discover the space of two whole degrees at sea. In this sort they lay from the 29 of June to the third of August, what time cap. Thomson in the Dainty had first sight of the huge carak called the Madre de Dios, one of the greatest receit belonging to the crowne of Portugall. The Dainty being of excellent saile got the start of the rest of our fleet, and began the conflict somewhat to her cost, with the slaughter and hurt of divers of her men. Within a while after, sir John Burrough in the Robucke of sir W. Raleghs, was at hand to second her, who saluted her with shot of great ordinance, and continued the fight within musket shot assisted by cap. Tomson and cap. Newport till sir R. Crosse viceadmirall of the fleet came up being to leeward, at whose arrival sir J. Burgh demanded of him what was best to be done, who answered, that if the carak were not boorded she would recover the shore and fire herselfe as the other had done. Wherupon sir J. Burgh concluded to intangle her; and sir R. Crosse promised also to fasten himselfe to her together at the instant; which was performed: but after a while sir John Burgh receiving a shot with a canon perier under water, and ready to sinke, desired sir R. C. to fall off, that he might also cleere himselfe, and save his ship from sinking, which with difficulty he did: for both the Roebucke and the Foresight were so intangled, as with much adoe could they cleere themselves.

The same evening sir R. Crosse finding the carak then

sure & drawing nere the Iland perswaded his company
to boord her againe, or els there was no hope to recover
her : who after many excuses & feares, were by him
incouraged, and so fell athwart her foreships all alone;
and so hindered her sailing that the rest had time to
come up to his succour, & to recover the carak yer she
recovered the land : and so toward the evening after
he had fought with her alone three houres single, my
lord of Cumberlands two ships came up, & with very
litle losse entred with sir R. Crosse, who had in that time
broken their courages, and made the assault easie for
the rest.

The generall having disarmed the Portugals, and
stowed them for better security on all sides, first had
presented to his eyes the true proportion of the vast body
of this carak, which did then and may still justly provoke
the admiration of all men not formerly acquainted with
such a sight. But albeit this first apparance of the
hugenesse thereof yeelded sights enough to entertaine
our mens eyes ; yet the pitifull object of so many bodies
slaine and dismembred could not but draw ech mans eye
to see, and heart to lament, and hands to helpe those
miserable people, whose limnes were so torne with the
violence of shot, and paine made grievous with the multitude of woundes. No man could almost steppe but
upon a dead carkase or a bloody floore, but specially
about the helme, where very many of them fell suddenly
from stirring to dying. For the greatnesse of the stirrage
requiring the labour of twelve or foureteene men at once,
and some of our shippes beating her in at the sterne with
their ordinance often times with one shot slew foure or
five labouring on either side of the helme ; whose roomes
being still furnished with fresh supplies, and our artillery
still playing upon them with continuall volleys, it could
not be but that much bloud should be shed in that place.
Whereupon our Generall moved with singular commiser-
ation of their misery, sent them his owne chyrurgions,
denying them no possible helpe or reliefe that he or any

of his company could affoord them.   Among the rest of
those, whose state this chance had made very deplorable,
was Don Fernando de Mendoça Grand captaine and
Commander of this Carake : who indeed was descended
of the house of Mendoça in Spaine; but being married
into Portugall, lived there as one of that nation; a
gentleman well stricken in yeeres, well spoken, of comely
personage, of good stature, but of hard fortune.   In his
severall services against the Moores he was twise taken
prisoner, and both times ransomed by the king.   In a
former voyage of returne from the East India he was
driven upon the Baxos or sands of Juda nere the coast
of Cephala, being then also captaine of a caracke which
was there lost, and himselfe, though escaping the sea-
danger, yet fell into the hands of infidels on land; who
kept him under long and grievous servitude.   Once more
the king carying a loving respect to the man, and desirous to better his condition, was content to let him try
his fortune in this Easterly navigation, and committed
unto him the conduct of this caracke, wherein he went
from Lisbon Generall of the whole fleet, and in that
degree had returned, if the Vice-rey of Goa embarked for
Portugall in the Bon Jesus had not, by reason of his late
office, bene preferred.   Sir John intending not to adde
too much affliction to the afflicted, mooved with pity and
compassion of humane misery, in the end resolved freely
to dismisse this captaine & the most part of his followers
to their owne countrey, and for the same purpose bestowed them in certaine vessels furnished with all kindes
of necessary provision.   This businesse thus dispatched,
good leasure had he to take such view of the goods as
conveniency might affoord.   And having very prudently
(to cut off the unprofitable spoile & pillage whereunto
he saw the minds of many inclined) seised upon the
whole to her Majesties use, after a short & slender
romaging & searching of such things as first came to
hand, he perceived that ye wealth would arise nothing
disanswerable to expectation; but that the variety and

grandure of all rich commodities would be more then sufficient to content both the adventurers desire & the souldiers travell. And here I cannot but enter into the consideration and acknowledgement of Gods great favor towards our nation, who by putting this purchase into our hands hath manifestly discovered those secret trades & Indian riches, which hitherto lay strangely hidden, and cunningly concealed from us; whereof there was among some few of us some small and unperfect glimse onely, which now is turned into the broad light of full and perfect knowledge. Whereby it should seeme that the will of God for our good is (if our weaknesse could apprehend it) to have us communicate with them in those East Indian treasures, & by the erection of a lawfull traffike to better our meanes to advance true religion and his holy service. The caracke being in burden by the estimation of the wise and experienced no lesse then 1600 tunnes had full 900 of those stowed with the grosse bulke of marchandise, the rest of the tunnage being allowed, partly to the ordinance which were 32 pieces of brasse of all sorts, partly to the passengers and the victuals, which could not be any small quantity, considering the number of the persons betwixt 600 and 700,

A briefe cata-logue of ye sundry rich commodities of ye Madre de Dios. and the length of the navigation. To give you a taste (as it were) of the commodities, it shall suffice to deliver you a generall particularity of them, according to the catalogue taken at Leaden hall the 15 of September 1592. Where upon good view it was found, that the principall wares after the jewels (which were no doubt of great value, though they never came to light) consisted of spices, drugges, silks, calicos, quilts, carpets and colours, &c. The spices were pepper, cloves, maces, nutmegs, cinamom, greene ginger: the drugs were benjamim, frank-incense, galingale, mirobolans, aloes zocotrina, camphire: the silks, damasks, taffatas, sarcenets, altobassos, that is, counterfeit cloth of gold, unwrought China silke, sleaved silke, white twisted sike, curled cypresse. The calicos were book-calicos, calico-launes, broad white calicos, fine

116

starched calicos, course white calicos, browne broad calicos,
browne course calicos.   There were also canopies, and
course diaper-towels, quilts of course sarcenet and of
calico, carpets like those of Turky; wherunto are to be
added the pearle, muske, civet, and amber-griece.   The
rest of the wares were many in number, but lesse in
value; as elephants teeth, porcellan vessels of China,
coco-nuts, hides, eben-wood as blacke as jet, bedsteds of
the same, cloth of the rindes of trees very strange for the
matter, and artificiall in workemanship.   All which piles
of commodities being by men of approved judgement
rated but in reasonable sort amounted to no lesse then
150000 li. sterling, which being divided among the adventurers (whereof her Majesty was the chiefe) was
sufficient to yeeld contentment to all parties.   The
cargazon being taken out, and the goods fraighted in
tenne of our ships sent for London, to the end that the
bignesse, heigth, length, bredth, and other dimensions of
so huge a vessell might by the exact rules of Geometricall
observations be truly taken, both for present knowledge,
and derivation also of the same unto posterity, one M.
Robert Adams, a man in his faculty of excellent skill, *The capacity
omitted nothing in the description, which either his arte *and dimensions
could demonstrate, or any mans judgement thinke woorthy *de Dios.*
the memory.   After an exquisite survey of the whole
frame he found the length from the beak-head to the
sterne (whereupon was erected a lanterne) to containe 165
foote.   The breadth in the second close decke whereof [II. ii. 199.]
she had three, this being the place where there was most
extension of bredth, was 46 foot and 10 inches.   She
drew in water 31 foot at her departure from Cochin in
India, but not above 26 at her arrivall in Dartmouth,
being lightened in her voyage by divers meanes, some
5 foote.   She caried in height 7 severall stories, one maine
Orlop, three close decks, one fore-castle, and a spar-decke
of two floores a piece.   The length of the keele was 100
foote, of the maine-mast 121 foot, and the circuite about
at the partners 10 foote 7 inches, the maine-yard was 106

foote long. By which perfect commensuration of the parts appeareth the hugenesse of the whole, farre beyond the mould of the biggest shipping used among us either for warre or receit.

Don Alonso de Baçan having a great Fleet and suffering these two caraks, the Santa Cruz to be burnt, and the Madre de Dios to be taken, was disgraced by his prince for this negligence.

The firing and sinking of the stout and warre-like Carack called Las Cinque Llaguas, or, The five Wounds, by three tall Ships set foorth at the charges of the right honorable the Erle of Cumberland and his friends : Written by the discreet and valiant captaine M. Nicholas Downton.

I N the latter ende of the yeere 1593. the right honourable Erle of Cumberland, at his owne charges and his friends, prepared 3 ships all at equall rate, and either of them had like quantitie of victuals, and like numbers of men, there being embarked in all 3 ships 420 men of al sorts. The Roial Exchange went as Admirall, wherein M. George Cave was captaine. The May-flower Viceadmirall under the conduct of William Anthonie : and the Sampson, the charge whereof it pleased his honour to commit unto me Nicholas Dounton. Our directions were sent us to Plimmouth, and we were to open them at sea.

Besides these 3 ships there was a pinnas called the Violet, or the Why not I.

The sixt of Aprill 1594 we set sayle in the sound of Plimmouth, directing our course toward the coast of Spaine.

The 24 of the sayd moneth at the Admirals direction wee divided our selves East and West from ech other, being then in the heigth of 43 degrees, with commaundement at night to come together againe.

The 27 day in the morning we descried the May-
flower and the litle Pinnasse with a Prise that they had
taken, being of Viana in Portugall, and bound for Angola
in Africa. This Barke was of 28 tunnes, having some
17 persons in the same. There were in her some 12   *Commodities*
Buts of Galicia wine, whereof we tooke into every shippe   *fit for Angola.*
a like part, with some Ruske in chests and barrels, with
5 buts of blew course cloth, and certaine course linnen-
cloth for Negros shirts, which goods were divided among
our fleet.

The 4 of May we had sight of our Pinnasse, and the
Admirals Shallop which had taken three Portugall
Caravels, whereof they had sent two away and kept the
third.

The second of June we had sight of S. Michael. The
third day in the morning wee sent our small pinnasse,
which was of some 24 tunnes, with the small Caravell
which we had taken at the Burlings to range the road
of all the Ilands, to see if they could get any thing in the
same: appointing them to meet us W. S. W. 12 leagues
from Faiall. Their going from us was to no purpose.
They missed comming to us when we appointed, as also
we missed them, when we had great cause to have used
them.

The 13 of June we met with a mightie Carack of the
East Indies, called Las cinque Llagas, or The five wounds.
The May-flower was in fight with her before night. I,
in the Sampson, fetched her up in the evening, and as I
commanded to give her the broad side, as we terme it,
while I stood very heedfully prying to discover her
strength: and where I might give counsel to boord her
in the night when the Admirall came up to us, and as
I remember at the very first shot she discharged at us, I
was shot in a litle above the belly, whereby I was made
unserviceable for a good while after, without touching
any other for that night. Yet by meanes of an honest
truehearted man which I had with me, one captaine
Grant, nothing was neglected: untill midnight when

the Admirall came up, the May-flower, and the Sampson never left by turnes to ply her with their great ordinance; but then captaine Cave wished us to stay till morning, at what time each one of us should give her three bouts with our great ordinance, & so should clap her a boord: but indeed it was long lingered in the morning untill 10 of the clocke before wee attempted to boord her. The Admirall laid her a boord in the mid ship: the May-flower comming up in the quarter, as it should seeme, to lie at the sterne of the Admirall on the larboord side. The captaine of the sayd May-flower was slaine at the first comming up: whereby the ship fell to
[II. ii. 200.] the sterne of the out-licar of the Carack, which (being a piece of timber) so wounded her foresaile, that they sayd they could come no more to fight, I am sure they did not, but kept aloofe from us. The Sampson went aboord on the bow, but having not rome enough, our quarter lay on the Exchanges bow, and our bowe on the Caracks bowe. The Exchange also at the first comming had her captaine M. Cave shot into both the legs, the one whereof he never recovered, so he for that present was not able to doe his office, and in his absence he had not any that would undertake to lead out his company to enter upon the enemie. My friend captaine Grant did lead my men on the Caracks side, which being not manfully backed by the Exchanges men, his forces being smal, made the enemie bolder then he would have bene, whereby I had six men presently slaine and many more hurt, which made them that remained unhurt to returne aboord, and would never more give the assault. I say not but some of the Exchanges men did very well, and many more (no doubt) would have done the like, if there had bene any principall man to have put them forward, and to have brought all the company to the fight, and not to have run into corners themselves. But I must needs say, that their ship was as well provided for defence, as any that I have seene. And the Portugals peradventure encouraged by our slacke working, plaied

the men and had Barricados made, where they might stand without any danger of our shot. They plied us also very much with fire, so that most of our men were burnt in some place or other: & while our men were putting out of the fire, they would ever be plying them with small shot or darts. This unusuall casting of fire did much dismay many of our men and made them draw backe as they did. When we had not men to enter, we plied our great ordinance much at them as high up as they might be mounted, for otherwise we did them litle harme, and by shooting a piece out of our forecastle being close by her, we fired a mat on her beak-head, which more and more kindled, and ran from thence to the mat on the bow-sprit, and from the mat up to the wood of the bow-sprit, and thence to the top-saile yard, which fire made the Portugals abaft in the ship to stagger, and to make shew of parle. But they that had the charge before encouraged them, making shew, that it might easily be put out, and that it was nothing. Whereupon againe they stood stifly to their defence. Anone the fire grew so strong, that I saw it beyond all helpe, although she had bene already yeelded to us. Then we desired to be off from her, but had litle hope to obtaine our desire; neverthelesse we plied water very much to keep our ship well. In deed I made litle other reckoning for the ship, my selfe, and divers hurt men, then to have ended there with the Carack, but most of our people might have saved themselves in boats. And when my care was most, by Gods providence onely, by the burning asunder of our spritsaile-yard with ropes and saile, and the ropes about the spritsaile-yard of the Carack, whereby we were fast intangled, we fell apart, with burning of some of our sailes which we had then on boord. The Exchange also being farther from the fire, afterward was more easily cleared, and fell off from abaft. And as soone as God had put us out of danger, the fire got into the fore-castle, where, I thinke, was store of Benjamin, and such other like combustible matter, for it flamed and ran over all the Carack at an instant in a maner. The Portugals lept over-boord in great numbers. Then sent I captaine Grant with the boat, with leave to use his owne discretion in saving of them. So he brought me aboord two gentlemen, the one an old man called Nuno Velio Pereira, which (as appeareth by the 4 chapter in the first booke of the woorthy history of Huighen de Linschoten) was governour of Moçambique and Cefala, in the yeere 1582. and since that time had bene likewise a governour in a place of importance in the East Indies. And the shippe wherein he was comming home was cast away a litle to the East of the Cape of Buona Speranza, and from thence he travelled over-land to Moçambique, and came as a passenger in this Carack. The other was called Bras Carrero, and was captaine of a Carack which was cast away neere Moçambique, and came likewise in this ship for a passenger. Also three men of the inferior sort we saved in our boat, onely these two we clothed and brought into England. The rest which were taken up by the other ship boats, we set all on shore in the Ile of Flores, except some two or three Negros, whereof one was borne in Moçambique, and another in the East Indies. This fight was open off the Sound betweene Faial and Pico 6 leagues to the Southward. The people which we saved told us that the cause why they would not yeeld, was, because this Carack was for the king, and that she had all the goods belonging to the king in the countrey for that yeere in her, and that the captaine of her was in favour with the king, and at his returne into the Indies should have bene Viceroy there. And withall this ship was nothing at all pestered neither within boord nor without, and was more like a ship of warre then otherwise: moreover, she had the ordinance of a Carak that was cast away at Moçambique, and the company of her, together with the company of another Carack that was cast away a litle to the Eastwards of the Cape of Buona Speranza. Yet through sicknesse which they caught at Angola, where they watered, they

say, they had not now above 150 white men, but Negros
a great many.   They likewise affirmed that they had [II. ii. 201.]
three noblemen and three ladies in her, but we found
them to differ in most of their talke.   All this day and
all the night she burned, but the next morning her
poulder which was lowest being 60 barrels blew her
abroad, so that most of the ship did swim in parts above
the water.   Some of them say, that she was bigger then
the Madre de Dios, and some, that she was lesse : but
she was much undermasted, and undersailed, yet she
went well for a ship that was so foule.   The shot which
wee made at her in great Ordinance before we layde her
aboord might be at seven bouts which we had, and sixe
or 7 shot at a bout, one with another, some 49 shot : the
time we lay aboord might be two houres.   The shot
which we discharged aboord the Carack might be some
twentie Sacars.   And thus much may suffice concerning
our daungerous conflict with that unfortunate Carack.

The last of June after long traversing of the seas we
had sight of another mightie Carack which diverse of our
company at the first tooke to be the great S. Philip the
Admirall of Spaine, but the next day being the first of
July fetching her up we perceived her indeede to be a
Carack, which after some few shot bestowed upon her
we summoned to yeeld ; but they standing stoutly to
their defence utterly refused the same.   Wherefore seeing
no good could be done without boording her I consulted
what course we should take in the boording.   But by
reason that wee which were the chiefe captaines were
partly slaine and partly wounded in the former conflict,
and because of the murmuring of some disordered and
cowardly companions, our valiant and resolute determinations were crossed : and to conclude a long discourse in
few wordes, the Carack escaped our hands.   After this
attending about Corvo & Flores for some West Indian
purchase, and being disappointed of our expectation, and
victuals growing short, we returned for England, where
I arrived at Portesmouth the 28 of August.

The casting away of the Tobie neere Cape Espartel corruptly called Cape Sprat without the Straight of Gibraltar on the coast of Barbarie. 1593.

He Tobie of London a ship of 250 tunnes manned with fiftie men, the owner whereof was the worshipfull M. Richard Staper, being bound for Livorno, Zante and Patras in Morea, being laden with marchandize to the value of 11 or 12 thousand pounds sterling, set sayle from Black-wall the 16 day of August 1593, and we went thence to Portesmouth where we tooke in great quantitie of wheate, and set sayle foorth of Stokes bay in the Isle of Wight, the 6. day of October, the winde being faire: and the 16 of the same moneth we were in the heigth of Cape S. Vincent, where on the next morning we descried a sayle which lay in try right a head off us, to which we gave chase with very much winde, the sayle being a Spaniard, which wee found in fine so good of sayle that we were faine to leave her and give her over. Two dayes after this we had sight of mount Chiego, which is the first high-land which we descrie on the Spanish coast at the entrance of the Straight of Gibraltar, where we had very foule weather and the winde scant two dayes together. Here we lay off to the sea. The Master, whose name was George Goodlay, being a young man, and one which never tooke charge before for those parts, was very proud of that charge which he was litle able to discharge, neither would take any counsel of any of his company, but did as he thought best himselfe, & in the end of the two dayes of foule weather cast about, and the winde being faire, bare in with the straights mouth. The 19 day at night he thinking that he was farther off the land then he was, bare sayle all that night, & an houre and

an halfe before day had ranne our shippe upon the ground on the coast of Barbarie without the straight foure leagues to the South of Cape Espartel. Whereupon being all not a litle astonied, the Master said unto us, I pray you forgive me; for this is my fault and no mans else. The company asked him whether they should cut off the maine maste: no sayd the Master we will hoyse out our boate. But one of our men comming speedily up, sayd, Sirs, the ship is full of water, well sayd the Master, then cut the maynemast over boord: which thing we did with all speede. But the after part suddenly split a sunder in such sort that no man was able to stand upon it, but all fled upon the foremast up into the shrouds thereof; and hung there for a time: but seeing nothing but present death approch (being so suddenly taken that we could not make a raft which we had determined) we committed our selves unto the Lord and beganne with dolefull tune and heavy hearts to sing the 12 Psalme. Helpe Lord for good and godly men &c. Howbeit before we had finished foure verses the waves of the sea had stopped the breathes of most of our men. For the foremast with the weight of our men & the force of the sea fell downe into the water, and upon the fall thereof there were 38 drowned, and onely 12 by Gods providence partly by swimming and other meanes of chests gote on shoare, which was about a quarter of a mile from the wracke of the ship. The [II. ii. 202.] master called George Goodley, and William Palmer his mate, both perished. M. Cæsar also being captaine and owner was likewise drowned: none of the officers were saved but the carpenter.

We twelve which the Lord had delivered from extreme danger of the Sea, at our comming ashore fell in a maner into as great distresse. At our first comming on shore we all fell downe on our knees, praying the Lord most humbly for his mercifull goodnesse. Our prayers being done, we consulted together what course

to take, seeing we were fallen into a desert place, &
we travelled all that day untill night, sometimes one
way and sometimes another, and could finde no kinde
of inhabitants; onely we saw where wilde beasts had
bene, and places where there had bene houses, which
after we perceived to have bene burnt by the Portugals.
So at night falling into certaine groves of olive trees,
we climed up and sate in them to avoid the danger of
lions and other wilde beasts, whereof we saw many the
next morning. The next day we travelled untill three
of the clocke in the afternoone without any food, but
water and wilde date roots: then going over a mountaine, we had sight of Cape Espartel; whereby we knew
somewhat better which way to travell, and then we went
forward untill we came to an hedgerow made with
great long canes; we spied and looked over it, and
beheld a number of men aswell horsemen as footmen,
to the number of some five thousand in skirmish
together with small shot and other weapons. And after
consultation what we were best to do, we concluded to
yeeld our selves unto them, being destitute of all meanes
of resistance. So rising up we marched toward them,
who espying us, foorthwith some hundred of them with
their javelings in their hands came running towards us
as though they would have run us thorow: howbeit
they onely strooke us flatling with their weapons, and
said that we were Spaniards: and we tolde them that we
were Englishmen; which they would not beleeve yet.
By and by the conflict being ended, and night approching, the captaine of the Moores, a man of some 56
yeres olde, came himselfe unto us, and by his inter-
pretor which spake Italian, asked what we were, and
from whence we came. One Thomas Henmer of our
company which could speake Italian, declared unto him
that we were marchants, and how by great misfortune
our ship, marchandise, & the greatest part of our company were pitifully cast away upon their coast. But he
void of humainity & all manhood, for all this, caused

his men to strip us out of our apparell even to our
shirts to see what money and jewels we had about us:
which when they had found to the value of some 200
pounds in golde and pearles they gave us some of our
apparel againe, and bread and water onely to comfort
us. The next morning they carried us downe to the
shore where our shippe was cast away, which was some
sixteene miles from that place. In which journey they
used us like their slaves, making us (being extreame
weake,) to carry their stuffe, and offering to beat us
if we went not so fast as they. We asked them why
they used us so, and they replied, that we were their
captives: we sayd we were their friends, and that there
was never Englishman captive to the king of Marocco.
So we came downe to the ship, and lay there with
them seven dayes, while they had gotten all the goods
they could, and then they parted it amongst them.
After the end of these seven dayes the captaine appointed twenty of his men wel armed, to bring us up
into ye countrey: and the first night we came to the
side of a river called Alarach, where we lay on the
grasse all that night: so the next day we went over
the river in a frigate of nine oares on a side, the river
being in that place above a quarter of a mile broad:
and that day we went to a towne of thirty houses,
called Totteon: there we lay foure dayes having nothing
to feed on but bread and water; and then we went to
a towne called Cassuri, and there we were delivered by
those twenty souldiers unto the Alcaide, which examined
us what we were: and we tolde him. He gave us a
goode answere, and sent us to the Jewes house, where
we lay seven dayes. In the meane while that we lay
here, there were brought thither twenty Spaniards and
twenty Frenchmen, which Spaniards were taken in a
conflict on land, but the Frenchmen were by foule
weather cast on land within the Straights about Cape
de Gate, and so made captives. Thus at the seven
dayes end we twelve Englishmen, the twelve French,

and the twenty Spaniards were all conducted toward
Marocco with nine hundred souldiers, horsemen and
fotmen, and in two dayes journey we came to the river
of Fez, where we lodged all night, being provided of
tents. The next day we went to a towne called Salle,
and lay without the towne in tents. From thence we
travelled almost an hundred miles without finding any
towne, but every night we came to fresh water, which
was partly running water and sometime raine water.
So we came at last within three miles of the city of
Marocco, where we pitched our tents: and there we
mette with a carrier which did travell in the countrey
for the English marchants: and by him we sent word
unto them of our estate: and they returned the next
day unto us a Moore, which brought us victuals, being
at that instant very feeble and hungry; and withall
sent us a letter with pen, inke, and paper, willing us
[II. ii 203.] to write unto them what ship it was that was cast
away, and how many and what men there were alive.
For said they we would knowe with speed, for to
morow is the kings court: and therefore we would
know, for that you should come into the citie like
captives. But for all that we were carried in as captives
and with ropes about our neckes as well English as
the French and Spaniards. And so we were carried
before the king: and when we came before him he did
commit us all to ward, where wee lay 15 dayes in close
prison: and in the end we were cleared by the English
Marchants to their great charges: for our deliverance
cost them 700 ounces, every ounce in that country contayning two shillings. And when we came out of prison
we went to the Alfandica, where we continued eight
weekes with the English marchants. At the end of which
time being well apparelled by the bountie of our marchants we were conveyed downe by the space of eight
dayes journey to S. Cruz, where the English ships road:
where we tooke shipping about the 20 of March, two in
the Anne Francis of London, and five more of us five

dayes after in the Expedition of London, and two more
in a Flemish flie-boat, and one in the Mary Edward also
of London, other two of our number died in the countrey
of the bloodie-fluxe: the one at our first imprisonment
at Marocco, whose name was George Hancock, and the
other at S. Cruz, whose name was Robert Swancon, whose
death was hastened by eating of rootes and other unnaturall things to slake their raging hunger in our
travaile, and by our hard and cold lodging in the open
fields without tents. Thus of fiftie persons through the
rashnesse of an unskilfull Master ten onely survived of
us, and after a thousand miseries returned home poore,
sicke, and feeble into our countrey.

Richard Johnson.	Thomas Henmore.
William Williams Carpenter.	John Silvester.
John Durham.	Thomas Whiting.
Abraham Rouse.	William Church.
John Matthewes.	John Fox.

The letters of the Queenes most excellent Majestie
sent by one Laurence Aldersey unto the Emperour of Aethiopia, 1597.

Invictissimo potentissimóque Abassenorum regi,
magnóque utriusque Aethiopiæ imperatori &c.

Lizabetha dei gratia Angliæ, Franciæ, &
Hiberniæ regina, fidei defensor &c. summo
ac potentissimo Æthiopiæ imperatori
salutem. Quod ab omnibus qui ubivìs
terrarum ac gentium sunt regibus princi-
píbusque præstari par & æquum est, ut
quanquàm maximo locorum intervallo
dissiti, & moribus ac legibus discrepantes, communem
tamen generis humani societatem tueri & conservare,
mutuáque ut occasio ferret, charitatis & benevolentiæ
officia velint exercere: in eo nos de vestra fide atque
humanitate spem certissimam concipientes, huic subito

nostro Laurentio Alderseio in regnum vestrum proficiscenti, hasce literas nostras, quibus & nostra erga vos benevolentia testata sit, & illum hinc profectum esse constet, potissimùm vobis indicandas dedimus. Qui cùm orbis terrarum perscrutandi cognoscendíque studio permotus, multis antehàc regionibus peragratis, jam tandem in eas regiones, quæ vestræ ditionis sunt, longum, periculosúmque iter instituat: cùm ipse existimavit, tum nos etiam sumus in eadem opinione, ad incolumitatem suam, atque etiam ad gratiam apud vos, plurimum illi profuturum, si diplomate nostro munitus, benevolentiæ nostræ & profectionis hinc suæ testimonium ad vos deferret. Nam cum summus ille mundi conditor rectórque præpotens deus, regibus principibúsque qui suam vicem gerunt, orbem terrarum, suis cuique finibus pro rata portione designatis, regendum atque administrandum dederit; eóque munere jus quoddam inter eos fraternæ necessitudinis, æternúmque fœdus ab illis colendum sanxerit: non erit (ut arbitramur) ingratum vobis, cùm benevolentiæ nostræ significationem, tàm immensa maris ac terrarum spatia transgressam, ab ultima Britannia ad vos in Aethiopiam perferri intellexeritis. Nobísque rursùs erit jucundum, cùm subditorum nostrorum prædicatione, ab ipsis Nili fontibus, & ab iis regionibus quæ solis cursum definiunt, fama vestri nominis ad nos recurret. Erit igitur humanitatis vestræ huic subdito nostro eam largiri gratiam, ut in ditionem vestram sub præsidio ac tutela vestri nominis intrare, ibique salvus & incolumis manere possit: quod ipsum etiam ab aliis principibus, per quorum regiones illi transeundum erit, magnoperè petimus, nobísque ipsis illud honoris causa tributum existimabimus: néque tamèn majorem hac in re gratiam postulamus, quàm vicissìm omnium principum subditis, omniúmque gentium hominibus ad nos commeantibus liberrimè concedimus. Datum Londini quinto die Novembris: anno regni nostri tricesimo nono: annóque Dom. 1597.

The same in English.

To the most invincible and puissant king of the
Abassens, the mightie Emperour of Aethiopia
the higher and the lower.

ELizabeth by the grace of God Queene of England,
France and Ireland, defender of the faith, &c. To
the most high and mightie Emperour of Aethiopia
greeting. Whereas it is a matter requisite and well be-
seeming all kings and princes of what lands or nations
soever, be they never so much dissevered in place or
differing in customes and lawes, to maintaine and preserve
the common societie of mankinde, and, as occasion shall
be offered, to performe mutuall duties of charitie and
benevolence : we for that cause conceiving most un-
doubted hope of your princely fidelity and courtesie,
have given unto this our subject Laurence Aldersey
intending to travell into your dominions, these our
letters to be delivered without faile unto your Highnesse,
to the end they may be a testimony of our good will
towards you and of our saide subject his departure from
England. Who, after his travels in many forren
countreys, being as yet enflamed with a desire more
throughly to surveigh and contemplate the world, and
now at length to undertake a long and daungerous
journey into your territories and regions : both the sayd
Laurence thought, and our selves also deemed, that it
would very much availe him, as well for his owne safetie
as for the attayning of your favour, if, being protected
with our broad seale, hee might transport unto your
Highnesse a testimony of our loving affection & of his
departure from hence. For sithence almightie God the
highest creatour and governour of the world hath allotted
unto kings and princes his vicegerents over the face
of the whole earth, their designed portions and limits
to be ruled and administred by them ; and by this his
gift hath established among them a certaine law of

brotherly kindnesse, and an eternall league by them to be observed : it will not (we hope) seeme unpleasant unto your highnesse, when you shall have intelligence of our loving letters sent so huge a distance over sea and land, even from the farthest realme of England unto you in Aethiopia. On the other side our selves shall take great solace and delight, when as by the relation of our owne subjects, the renowme of your name shall be brought unto us from the fountains of Nilus, and from those regions which are situate under the Southerne Tropike. May it please you therefore of your princely clemencie to vouchsafe so much favour on this our subject, that he may, under the safeguard and protection of your name, enter into your highnesse dominions, and there remaine safe and free from danger. Which favour and courtesie wee doe likewise most earnestly request at the hands of other princes, through whose Seigniories our said subject is to passe ; and we shall esteeme it as done unto our selfe and for our honours sake.

Neither do we require any. greater favour in this behalfe, then we are upon the like occasion most ready to graunt unto the subjects of all princes and the people of all Nations, traveiling into our dominions.

Given at London the fift day of November,
in the thirtie and ninth yeere of
our reigne : and in the
yeare of our Lorde
1597.

THE THIRD AND LAST VOLUME

of the

Principall Navigations, Voyages, Traffiques and Discoveries of the English Nation

made to the Northwest, West, and Southwest parts of
the world, with the Letters, Privileges, Discourses,
Observations, and other necessary things
concerning the same

The most ancient Discovery of the West Indies [III. 1.]
by Madoc the sonne of Owen Guyneth Prince
of North-wales, in the yeere 1170: taken
out of the history of Wales, lately published
by M. David Powel Doctor of Divinity.

Fter the death of Owen Guyneth, his
sonnes fell at debate who should inherit
after him: for the eldest sonne borne
in matrimony, Edward or Jorweth Drwy-
dion, was counted unmeet to governe,
because of the maime upon his face:
and Howell that tooke upon him all the
rule was a base sonne, begotten upon an Irish woman.
Therefore David gathered all the power he could, and
came against Howel, and fighting with him, slew him;
and afterwards injoyed quietly the whole land of North-
wales, until his brother Jorwerths sonne came to age. *Madoc the son*
Madoc another of Owen Guyneth his sonnes left the *of Owen*
land in contention betwixt his brethren, & prepared *Guyneth.*

133

certaine ships, with men and munition, and sought adven
tures by Seas, sailing West, and leaving the coast o
Ireland so farre North, that he came unto a land un
knowen, where he saw many strange things.

Humf. Lloyd. This land must needs be some part of that Countrey
of which the Spanyards affirme themselves to be the
first finders since Hannos time. Whereupon it i
manifest that that countrey was by Britaines discovered
long before Columbus led any Spanyards thither.

Of the voyage and returne of this Madoc there be
many fables fained, as the common people doe use in
distance of place and length of time rather to augment
then to diminish : but sure it is there he was. And after
he had returned home, and declared the pleasant and
fruitfull countreys that he had seene without inhabitants
and upon the contrary part, for what barren & wild
The second ground his brethren and nephewes did murther one
voyage of Ma- another, he prepared a number of ships, and got with
doc the sonne of him such men and women as were desirous to live in
Owen quietnesse : and taking leave of his friends, tooke his
Guyneth. journey thitherward againe. Therefore it is to be supposed that he and his people inhabited part of those
Gomara. lib. countreys : for it appeareth by Francis Lopez de Gomara,
2. cap. 16. that in Acuzamil and other places the people honored
the crosse. Wherby it may be gathered that Christians
had bene there before the comming of the Spanyards.
But because this people were not many, they followed the
maners of the land which they came unto, & used the
language they found there.

M. Powels This Madoc arriving in the Westerne country, unto
addition. the which he came in the yere 1170, left most of his
people there, and returning backe for more of his owne
nation, acquaintance & friends to inhabit that faire &
large countrey, went thither againe with ten sailes, as
Gutyn Owen. I find noted by Gutyn Owen. I am of opinion that the
land whereunto he came was some part of the West
Indies.

Carmina Meredith filii Rhesi mentionem facientia de Madoco filio Oweni Guynedd, & de sua navigatione in terras incognitas. Vixit hic Meredith circiter annum Domini 1477.

M Adoc wyf, mwyedic wedd,
   Iawn genau, Owyn Guynedd:
Ni fynnum dir, fy enaid oedd
Na da mawr, ond y moroedd,

These verses I received of my learned friend M. William Camden.

The same in English.

Madoc I am the sonne of Owen Gwynedd
With stature large, and comely grace adorned:
No lands at home nor store of wealth me please,
My minde was whole to search the Ocean seas.

The offer of the discovery of the West Indies [III. 2.] by Christopher Columbus to king Henry the seventh in the yeere 1488 the 13 of February: with the kings acceptation of the offer, & the cause whereupon hee was deprived of the same: recorded in the thirteenth chapter of the history of Don Fernand Columbus of the life and deeds of his father Christopher Columbus.

Hristophoro Colon temendo, se parimente i Re di Castiglia non assentissero alla sua impresa, non gli bisognasse proporla di nuovo à qualche altro principe, & cosi in cio passasse lungo tempo; mando in Inghilterra un suo fratello, che haveva appresso di se, chiamato Bartholomeo Colon: il qual, quantunque non havesse lettere Latine, erà però huomo prattico, & giudicioso nelle cose del mare, & sapea molto bene far carte da navigare, & sphere, & altri instrumenti di quella professione, come dal suo fratello era instrutto. Partito adunque Bartholomeo Colon per Inghilterra, volle la sua sorte, che desse in man di cor sali, i quali lo spogliarono insieme con gli altri della sua nave. Per la qual cosa, & per la sua povertà & infirmità, che in cosi diverse terre lo assalirono crudelmente, prolungo per gran tempo la sua ambasciata, fin che, aquistata un poco di faculta con le carte, ch' ei fabricava, cominció a far pratiche co' il Re Enrico settimo, padre de Enrico ottavo, che al presente regna: a cui appresentò un mappamondo, nel quale erano scritti questi versi, che fra le sue scriture Io trovai, & da me saranno qui posti piu tosto per l' antichità, che per la loro eleganza.

Terrarum quicunque cupis fœliciter oras
Noscere, cuncta decens doctè pictura docebit,
Quam Strabo affirmat, Ptolomæus, Plinius, atque
Isidorus: non una tamen sententia cuique.
Pingitur hîc etiam nuper sulcata carinis
Hispanis Zona illa, priùs incognita genti
Torrida, quæ tandem nunc est notissima multis.

Et piu di sotto diceva.

Pro Authore sive Pictore.

Janua cui patriæ est nomen, cui Bartholomæus
Columbus de Terra Rubra, opus edidit istud,
Londoniis anno Domini 1480 atque insuper anno
Octavo, decimáque die cùm tertia mensis
Februarii. Laudes Christo cantentur abundè.

Et, percioche avvertirà alcuno, che dice Columbus de Terra Rubra, dico, che medesimamente Io viddi alcune sotto scritioni dell' Ammiraglio, primo che acquistasse lo stato, ou' egli si sotto scriveva, Columbus de Terra Rubra. Ma, tornando al Re d' Inghilterra, dico, che, da lui il mappamondo veduto, & cio che l' Ammiraglio gli offeriva, con allegro volto accettò la sua offerta, & mandolo a chiamare. Ma, percioche Dio l' haveva per Castiglia serbata, gia l' Ammiraglio in quel tempo era

andato, & tornato con la vittoria della sua impresa,
secondo che per ordine si racconterà. Lasciarò hora di
raccontar ciò, che Bartolomeo Colon haveva negociato in
Inghilterra, & tornarò all' Ammiraglio, &c.

The same in English.

CHristopher Columbus fearing least if the king of
Castile in like maner (as the king of Portugall had
done) should not condescend unto his enterprise, he
should be inforced to offer the same againe to some other
prince, & so much time should be spent therein, sent
into England a certaine brother of his which he had
with him, whose name was Bartholomew Columbus, who,
albeit he had not the Latine tongue, yet neverthelesse
was a man of experience and skilfull in Sea causes, and
could very wel make sea cards & globes, and other
instruments belonging to that profession, as he was
instructed by his brother. Wherfore after that Bartholomew Columbus was departed for England, his lucke was
to fall into the hands of pirats, which spoiled him with
the rest of them which were in the ship which he went
in. Upon which occasion, and by reason of his poverty [III. 3.]
and sicknesse which cruelly assaulted him in a countrey *The occasion
so farre distant from his friends, he deferred his am- *why the West*
bassage for a long while, untill such time as he had *not discovered*
gotten somewhat handsome about him with making of Sea *for England.*
cards. At length he began to deale with king Henry
the seventh the father of Henry the eight, which reigneth
at this present: unto whom he presented a mappe of the
world, wherein these verses were written, which I found
among his papers: and I will here set them downe, rather
for their antiquity then for their goodnesse.

Thou which desirest easily the coasts of lands to know,
This comely mappe right learnedly the same to thee
    will shew:
Which Strabo, Plinie, Ptolomew and Isodore maintaine:
Yet for all that they do not all in one accord remaine.

Here also is set downe the late discovered burning
Zone
By Portingals, unto the world which whilom was un-
knowen,
Whereof the knowledge now at length thorow all the
world is blowen.

And a little under he added:

For the Authour or the Drawer.

He, whose deare native soile hight stately Genua,
Even he whose name is Bartholomew Colon de Terra
Rubra,
The yeere of Grace a thousand and foure hundred and
fourescore
And eight, and on the thirteenth day of February
more,
In London published this worke. To Christ all laud
therefore.

And because some peradventure may observe that he
calleth himselfe Columbus de Terra Rubra, I say, that
in like maner I have seene some subscriptions of my
father Christopher Columbus, before he had the degree
of Admirall, wherein he signed his name thus, Columbus
King Henry de Terra Rubra. But to returne to the king of England,
the seventh his I say, that after he had seene the map, and that which
acceptation of my father Christopher Columbus offered unto him, he
Columbus accepted the offer with joyfull countenance, and sent to
offer. call him into England. But because God had reserved
the sayd offer for Castile, Columbus was gone in the
meane space, and also returned with the performance of
his enterprise, as hereafter in order shall be rehearsed.
Now will I leave off from making any farther mention
of that which Bartholomew Colon had negotiated in
England, and I will returne unto the Admirall, &c.

Another testimony taken out of the 60 chàpter
of the foresayd history of Ferdinando
Columbus, concerning the offer that Bartholomew Colombus made to king Henry the
seventh on the behalfe of his brother Christopher.

Ornato adunque l' Ammiraglio dallo
scoprimento di Cuba & di Giamaica,
tronò nella Spagnuola Bartolomeo Colon
suo fratello, quello, che era già andato a
trattare accordo col Re d' Inghilterra
sopra lo scoprimento delle Indie, come
di sopra habiam detto. Questo poi,
ritornando sene verso Castiglia con capitoli conceduti,
haveva inteso a Parigi dal re Carlo di Francia l' Ammiraglio suo fratello haver gia scoperte l' Indie : per che
gli sovenne per poter far il Viaggio di cento scudi. Et,
Avenga che per cotal nuova egli si fosse molto affrettato,
per arrivar l' Ammiraglio in Spagna, quando non dimeno
giunse a Siviglia, egli era gia tornato alle Indie co' 17
navigli. Perche, per asseguir quanto ei gli havea lasciato,
di subito al principio dell' anno del 1494 sen' andò a i
Re Catholici, menando seco Don Diego Colon, mio
fratello, & me ancora, accioche servissimo di paggi al
serenissimo principe Don Giovanni, il qual viva in gloria,
si come havea commandato la Catholica Reina donna
Isabella, che alhora era in Vagliadolid. Tosto adunque
che noi giungemmo, i Re chiamarono Don Bartolomeo,
& mandaronlo alla Spagnuola contre navi, &c.

The same in English.

CHristopher Columbus the Admirall being returned
from the discovery of Cuba and Jamayca, found in
Hispaniola his brother Bartholomew Columbus, who
before had beene sent to intreat of an agreement with the
king of England for the discovery of the Indies, as we

[III. 4.] have sayd before. This Bartholomew therefore returning unto Castile, with the capitulations granted by the king of England to his brother, understood at Paris by Charles the king of France, that the Admirall his brother had already performed that discovery : whereupon the French king gave unto the sayd Bartholomew an hundred French crownes to beare his charges into Spaine. And albeit he made great haste upon this good newes to meet with the Admirall in Spaine, yet at his comming to Sivil his brother was already returned to the Indies with seventeene saile of shipps. Wherefore to fulfill that which he had left him in charge in the beginning of the yeere 1494 he repaired to the Catholike princes, taking with him Diego Colon my brother and me also, which were to be preferred as Pages to the most excellent Prince Don John, who now is with God, according to the commandement of the Catholike Queene Lady Isabell, which was then in Validolid. Assoone therefore as we came to the Court, the princes called for Don Bartholomew, and sent him to Hispaniola with three ships, &c.

The English Voyages, Navigations, and Discoveries (intended for the finding of a Northwest passage) to the North parts of America, to Meta incognita, and the backeside of Gronland, as farre as 72 degrees and 12 minuts: performed first by Sebastian Cabota, and since by Sir Martin Frobisher, and M. John Davis, with the Patents, Discourses, and Advertisements thereto belonging.

The Letters patents of King Henry the seventh granted unto John Cabot and his three sonnes, Lewis, Sebastian, and Sancius for the discoverie of new and unknowen lands.

Enricus Dei gratia rex Angliæ, & Franciæ, & Dominus Hiberniæ, omnibus, ad quos præsentes literæ nostræ pervenerint, salutem. Notum sit & manifestum, quòd dedimus & concessimus, ac per præsentes damus & concedimus pro nobis & hæredibus nostris, dilectis nobis Joanni Caboto civi Venetiarum, Lodovico, Sebastiano, & Sancio, filiis dicti Joannis, & eorum ac cujuslibet eorum hæredibus & deputatis, plenam ac liberam authoritatem, facultatem & potestatem navigandi ad omnes partes, regiones, & sinus maris orientalis, occidentalis, & septentrionalis, sub banneris, vexillis, & insigniis nostris, cum quinque navibus sive navigiis, cujuscúnque portituræ & qualitatis existant, & cum tot & tantis nautis & hominibus, quot & quantos in dictis navibus secum ducere voluerint, suis & eorum propriis sumptibus & expensis, ad inveniendum, discooperiendum, & investigandum quascunque insulas, patrias, regiones sive provincias gentilium & infidelium quorumcúnque, in quacunque parte mundi positas, quæ Christianis omnibus ante hæc tempora fuerint incognitæ.

141

Concessimus etiam eisdem & eorum cuilibet, eorúmque
& cujuslibet eorum hæredibus & deputatis, ac licentiam
dedimus ad affigendum prædictas banneras nostras &
insignia in quacunque villa, oppido, castro, insula seu
terra firma à se noviter inventis. Et quòd prænominatus
Joannes, & filii ejusdem, seu hæredes & eorum deputati,
quascunque hujusmodi villas, castra, oppida, & insulas à
se inventas, quæ subjugari, occupari, possideri possint,
subjugare, occupare, possidere valeant tanquam vasalli
nostri, & gubernatores, locatenentes, & deputati eorun-
dem, dominium, titulum & jurisdictionem earundem
villarum, castrorum, oppidorum, insularum, ac terræ
firmæ sic inventorum nobis acquirendo. Ita tamen, ut
ex omnibus fructibus, proficuis, emolumentis, commodis,
lucris, & obventionibus ex hujusmodi navigatione pro-
venientibus, præfatus Johannes, & filii ac hæredes, &
eorum deputati, teneantur & sint obligati nobis pro omni
viagio suo, toties quoties ad portum nostrum Bristolliæ
applicuerint (ad quem omnino applicare teneantur & sint
astricti) deductis omnibus sumptibus & impensis neces-
sariis per eosdem factis, quintam partem capitalis lucri
facti, sive in mercibus, sive in pecuniis persolvere:
Dantes nos & concedentes eisdem suisque hæredibus
& deputatis, ut ab omni solutione custumarum omnium
& singulorum bonorum & mercium, quas secum re-
portarint ab illis locis sic noviter inventis, liberi sint &
immunes. Et insuper dedimus & concessimus eisdem ac
suis hæredibus & deputatis, quòd terræ omnes firmæ,
insulæ, villæ, oppida, castra, & loca quæcunque a se
[III. 5.] inventa, quotquot ab eis inveniri contigerit, non possint
ab aliis quibusvis nostris subditis frequentari seu visitari,
absque licentia prædictorum Joannis & ejus filiorum,
suorúmque deputatorum, sub pœna amissionis tam
navium quàm bonorum omnium quorumcúnque ad ea
loca sic inventa navigare præsumentium. Volentes &
strictissimè mandantes omnibus & singulis nostris subditis, tam in terra quàm in mari constitutis, ut præfato
Joanni, & ejus filiis ac deputatis, bonam assistentiam

faciant, & tam in armandis navibus seu navigiis, quàm
in provisione commeatus & victualium pro sua pecunia
emendorum, atque aliarum omnium rerum sibi provi-
dendarum pro dicta navigatione sumenda suos omnes
favores & auxilia impertiant. In cujus rei testimonium   *Ann. Dom.*
has literas nostras fieri fecimus patentes. Teste meipso   *1495.*
apud Westmonasterium quinto die Martii anno regni
nostri undecimo.

The same in English.

HEnry by the grace of God, king of England and
France, and lord of Ireland, to all to whom these
presents shall come, Greeting.

Be it knowen that we have given and granted, and by
these presents do give and grant for us and our heires,
to our welbeloved John Cabot citizen of Venice, to
Lewis, Sebastian, and Santius, sonnes of the sayd John,
and to the heires of them, and every of them, and their
deputies, full and free authority, leave, and power to
saile to all parts, countreys, and seas of the East, of the
West, and of the North, under our banners and ensignes,
with five ships of what burthen or quantity soever they
be, and as many mariners or men as they will have with
them in the sayd ships, upon their owne proper costs
and charges, to seeke out, discover, and finde whatsoever
isles, countreys, regions or provinces of the heathen and
infidels whatsoever they be, and in what part of the world
soever they be, which before this time have bene unknowen to all Christians : we have granted to them, and
also to every of them, the heires of them, and every of
them, and their deputies, and have given them licence
to set up our banners and ensignes in every village,
towne, castle, isle, or maine land of them, newly found.
And that the aforesayd John and his sonnes, or their
heires and assignes may subdue, occupy and possesse all
such townes, cities, castles and isles of them found, which
they can subdue, occupy and possesse, as our vassals, and
lieutenants, getting unto us the rule, title, and jurisdic-

tion of the same villages, townes, castles, & firme land so found. Yet so that the aforesayd John, and his sonnes and heires, and their deputies, be holden and bounden of all the fruits, profits, gaines, and commodities growing of such navigation, for every their voyage, as *Bristol thought* often as they shall arrive at our port of Bristoll (at the *ye meetest port* which port they shall be bound and holden onely to *for Westerne* arrive) all maner of necessary costs and charges by them *discoveries.* made, being deducted, to pay unto us in wares or money the fift part of the capitall gaine so gotten. We giving and granting unto them and to their heires and deputies, *Freedome from* that they shall be free from all paying of customes of *custome.* all and singular such merchandize as they shall bring with them from those places so newly found. And moreover, we have given and granted to them, their heires and deputies, that all the firme lands, isles, villages, townes, castles and places whatsoever they be that they shall chance to finde, may not of any other of our subjects be frequented or visited without the licence of the foresayd John and his sonnes, and their deputies, under paine of forfeiture aswell of their shippes as of all and singuler goods of all them that shall presume to saile to those places so found. Willing, and most straightly commanding all and singuler our subjects aswell on land as on sea, to give good assistance to the aforesayd John and his sonnes and deputies, and that as well in arming and furnishing their ships or vessels, as in provision of food, and in buying of victuals for their money, and all other things by them to be provided necessary for the sayd navigation, they do give them all their helpe and favour. In witnesse whereof we have caused to be made these our Letters patents. Witnesse our selfe at Westminster the fift day of March, in the eleventh yeere of our reigne.

Billa signata anno 13 Henrici septimi.

A record of the rolls touching the voyage of John Cabot and Sebastian his sonne.

Ex tertio die Februarii, anno 13, licentiam dedit Joanni Caboto, quod ipse capere possit sex naves Anglicanas, in aliquo portu, sive portibus regni Angliæ, ita quod sint de portagio 200. doliorum, vel subtùs, cum apparatu requisito, & quod recipere possit in dictas naves omnes tales magistros, marinarios, & subditos regis, qui cum eo exire voluerint, &c.

The same in English.

[III. 6.]

THe king upon the third day of February, in the 13 yeere of his reigne, gave licence to John Cabot to take sixe English ships in any haven or havens of the realme of England, being of the burden of 200 tunnes, or under, with all necessary furniture, and to take also into the said ships all such masters, mariners, and subjects of the king as willingly will go with him, &c.

An extract taken out of the map of Sebastian Cabot, cut by Clement Adams, concerning his discovery of the West Indies, which is to be seene in her Majesties privie gallerie at Westminster, and in many other ancient merchants houses.

Nno Domini 1497 Joannes Cabotus Venetus, & Sebastianus illius filius eam terram fecerunt perviam, quam nullus priùs adire ausus fuit, die 24 Junii, circiter horam quintam bene manè. Hanc autem appellavit Terram primùm visam, credo quod ex mari in eam partem primùm oculos injecerat. Nam quæ ex adverso sita est insula, eam appellavit insulam Divi Joannis, hac opinor ratione, quòd aperta fuit eo die qui est sacer Divo Joanni Baptistæ: Hujus incolæ pelles animalium, exuviásque ferarum pro indumentis habent, easque tanti faciunt, quanti nos vestes preciosissimas. Cùm bellum gerunt, utuntur arcu, sagittis, hastis, spiculis, clavis ligneis & fundis. Tellus sterilis est, neque ullos fructus affert, ex quo fit, ut ursis albo colore, & cervis inusitatæ apud nos magnitudinis referta sit: piscibus abundat, iisque sane magnis, quales sunt lupi marini, & quos salmones vulgus appellat; soleæ autem reperiuntur tam longæ, ut ulnæ mensuram excedant. Imprimis autem magna est copia eorum piscium, quos vulgari sermone vocant Bacallaos. Gignuntur in ea insula accipitres ita nigri, ut corvorum similitudinem mirum in modum exprimant, perdices autem & aquilæ sunt nigri coloris.

The same in English.

IN the yere of our Lord 1497 John Cabot a Venetian, and his sonne Sebastian (with an English fleet set out from Bristoll) discovered that land which no man before that time had attempted, on the 24 of June, about five of the clocke early in the morning. This land he called Prima vista, that is to say, First seene, because as I suppose it was that part whereof they had the first sight from sea. That Island which lieth out before the land, he called the Island of S. John upon this occasion, as I thinke, because it was discovered upon the day of John the Baptist. The inhabitants of this Island use to weare beasts skinnes, and have them in as great estimation as we have our finest garments. In their warres they use bowes, arrowes, pikes, darts, woodden clubs, and slings. The soile is barren in some places, & yeeldeth litle fruit, but it is full of white beares, and stagges farre greater then ours. It yeeldeth plenty of fish, and those very great, as seales, and those which commonly we call salmons: there are soles also above a yard in length: but especially there is great abundance of that kinde of fish which the Savages call baccalaos. In the same Island also there breed hauks, but they are so blacke that they are very like to ravens, as also their partridges, and egles, which are in like sort blacke.

A discourse of Sebastian Cabot touching his discovery of part of the West India out of England
in the time of king Henry the seventh, used
to Galeacius Butrigarius the Popes Legate in
Spaine, and reported by the sayd Legate in
this sort.

Oe you not understand sayd he (speaking
to certaine Gentlemen of Venice) how to
passe to India toward the Northwest, as
did of late a citizen of Venice, so valiant
a man, and so well practised in all things
pertaining to navigations, and the science
of Cosmographie, that at this present he
hath not his like in Spaine, insomuch that for his vertues
he is preferred above all other pilots that saile to the
West Indies, who may not passe thither without his
licence, and is therefore called Piloto mayor, that is, the
grand Pilot. And when we sayd that we knew him not,
he proceeded, saying, that being certaine yeres in the city
of Sivil, and desirous to have some knowledge of the
navigations of the Spanyards, it was tolde him that there
was in the city a valiant man, a Venetian borne named
Sebastian Cabot, who had the charge of those things,
being an expert man in that science, and one that coulde
make Cardes for the Sea with his owne hand, and that
by this report, seeking his acquaintance, hee found him
a very gentle person, who intertained him friendly, and
shewed him many things, and among other a large Mappe
of the world, with certaine particuler Navigations, as well
of the Portugals, as of the Spaniards, and that he spake
further unto him to this effect.

When my father departed from Venice many yeeres
since to dwell in England, to follow the trade of mar-
chandises, hee tooke mee with him to the citie of London,
while I was very yong, yet having neverthelesse some
knowledge of letters of humanitie, and of the Sphere.

*This discourse
is taken out of
the second
volume of ye
voyages of
Baptista
Ramusius.*

*Sebastian
Cabota
Pilot mayor
of Spaine.*

[III. 7.]

And when my father died in that time when newes were brought that Don Christopher Colonus Genuese had discovered the coasts of India, whereof was great talke in all the Court of king Henry the 7. who then raigned, insomuch that all men with great admiration affirmed it to be a thing more divine then humane, to saile by the West into the East where spices growe, by a way that was never knowen before, by this fame and report there increased in my heart a great flame of desire to attempt some notable thing. And understanding by reason of the Sphere, that if I should saile by way of the North-west, I should by a shorter tract come into India, I thereupon caused the King to be advertised of my devise, who immediatly commanded two Carvels to bee furnished with all things appertayning to the voyage, which was as farre as I remember in the yeere 1496. in the beginning of Sommer. I began therefore to saile toward the North-west, not thinking to finde any other land then that of Cathay, & from thence to turne toward India, but after certaine dayes I found that the land ranne towards the North, which was to mee a great displeasure. Never-thelesse, sayling along by the coast to see if I could finde any gulfe that turned, I found the lande still continent to the 56. degree under our Pole. And seeing that there the coast turned toward the East, despairing to finde the passage, I turned backe againe, and sailed downe by the coast of that land toward the Equinoctiall (ever with intent to finde the saide passage to India) and came to that part of this firme lande which is nowe called Florida, where my victuals failing, I departed from thence and returned into England, where I found great tumults among the people, and preparation for warres in Scot-land : by reason whereof there was no more consideration had to this voyage.

Whereupon I went into Spaine to the Catholique king, and Queene Elizabeth, which being advertised what I had done, intertained me, and at their charges furnished certaine ships, wherewith they caused me to saile to discover the coastes of Brasile, where I found an exceeding great and large river named at this present Rio de la plata, that is, the river of silver, into the which I sailed and followed it into the firme land, more then sixe score leagues, finding it every where very faire, and inhabited with infinite people, which with admiration came running dayly to our ships. Into this River runne so many other rivers, that it is in maner incredible.

After this I made many other voyages, which I nowe pretermit, and waxing olde, I give my selfe to rest from such travels, because there are nowe many yong and lustie Pilots and Mariners of good experience, by whose for- *The office of* wardnesse I doe rejoyce in the fruit of my labours, and *Pilote maior.* rest with the charge of this office, as you see.

The foresaide Baptista Ramusius in his preface to the thirde volume of the Navigations, writeth thus of Sebastian Cabot.

N the latter part of this volume are put certaine relations of John de Vararzana, Florentine, and of a great captaine a Frenchman, and the two voyages of Jaques Cartier a Briton, who sailed unto the land situate in 50. degrees of Latitude to the North, which is called New France, which landes hitherto are not throughly knowen, whether they doe joyne with the firme land of Florida and Nova Hispania, or whether they bee separated and devided all by the Sea as Ilands : and whether that by that way one may goe by Sea unto the countrey of Cathaia. As many yeeres past it was written unto mee by Sebastian Cabota our Countrey man a Venetian, a man of great experience, and very rare in the art of Navigation, and the knowledge of Cosmographie, who sailed along and beyond this lande of New France, at the charges of King *The great pro-* Henry the seventh king of England : and he advertised *babilitie of this* mee, that having sailed a long time West and by North, *Northwest passage.*

beyond those Ilands unto the Latitude of 67. degrees
and an halfe, under the North pole, and at the 11. day
of June finding still the open Sea without any maner of
impediment, he thought verily by that way to have passed
on still the way to Cathaia, which is in the East, and
[III. 8.] would have done it, if the mutinie of the shipmaster and
Mariners had not hindered him and made him to returne
homewards from that place. But it seemeth that God
doeth yet still reserve this great enterprise for some great
prince to discover this voyage of Cathaia by this way,
which for the bringing of the Spiceries from India into
Europe, were the most easie and shortest of all other
wayes hitherto found out. And surely this enterprise
would be the most glorious, and of most importance
of all other that can be imagined to make his name great,
and fame immortall, to all ages to come, farre more then
can be done by any of all these great troubles and warres
which dayly are used in Europe among the miserable
Christian people.

Another testimonie of the voyage of Sebastian
    Cabot to the West and Northwest, taken out
    of the sixt Chapter of the third Decade of
    Peter Martyr of Angleria.

Crutatus est oras glaciales Sebastianus
quidam Cabotus genere Venetus, sed à
parentibus in Britanniam insulam ten-
dentibus (uti moris est Venetorum, qui
commercii causa terrarum omnium sunt
hospites) transportatus penè infans. Duo
is sibi navigia, propria pecunia in Britannia ipsa instruxit, & primò tendens cum hominibus
tercentum ad Septentrionem donec etiam Julio mense
vastas repererit glaciales moles pelago natantes, & lucem
ferè perpetuam, tellure tamen libera, gelu liquefacto:
quare coactus fuit, uti ait, vela vertere & occidentem
sequi: tetendítque tantum ad meridiem littore sese in-

curvante, ut Herculei freti latitudinis fere gradus æquarit:
ad occidentémque profectus tantum est ut Cubam Insulam
à læva, longitudine graduum penè parem, habuerit. Is
ea littora percurrens, quæ Baccalaos appelavit, eosdem se
reperisse aquarum, sed lenes delapsus ad Occidentem ait,
quos Castellani, meridionales suas regiones adnavigantes,
inveniunt. Ergò non modò verisimilius, sed necessario
concludendum est, vastos inter utrámque ignotam hac-
tenus tellurem jacere hiatus, qui viam præbeant aquis
ab oriente cadentibus in Occidentem. Quas arbitror
impulsu cœlorum circulariter agi in gyrum circa terræ
globum, non autem Demogorgone anhelante vomi,
absorberíque ut nonnulli senserunt, quod influxu, & re-
fluxu forsan assentire daretur. Baccalaos, Cabotus ipse
terras illas appellavit, eò quod in earum pelago tantam
reperierit magnorum quorundam piscium, tynnos æmu-
lantium, sic vocatorum ab indigenis, multitudinem, ut
etiam illi interdum navigia detardarent. Earum Regionum
homines pellibus tantum coopertos reperiebat, rationis
haudquaquam expertes. Ursorum inesse regionibus
copiam ingentem refert, qui & ipsi piscibus vescantur.
Inter densa namque piscium illorum agmina sese im-
mergunt ursi, & singulos singuli complexos, unguibúsque
inter squammas immissis in terram raptant & comedunt.
Propterea minimè noxios hominibus visos esse ait.
Orichalcum in plerisque locis se vidisse apud incolas
prædicat. Familiarem habeo domi Cobotum ipsum, &
contubernalem interdum. Vocatus namque ex Britannia
à Rege nostro Catholico, post Henrici Majoris Britanniæ
Regis mortem, concurialis noster est, expectátque indies,
ut navigia sibi parentur, quibus arcanum hoc naturæ
latens jam tándem detegatur.

The same in English.

THese North Seas have bene searched by one Sebastian Cabot, a Venetian borne, whom being yet but
in maner an infant, his parents caried with them into
England, having occasion to resort thither for trade of mar-

chandise, as is the maner of the Venetians to leave no part
of the world unsearched to obtaine riches. Hee therefore
furnished two ships in England at his owne charges, and
first with 300 men directed his course so farre towards
the North pole, that even in the moneth of July he
found monstrous heapes of ice swimming on the sea, and
in maner continuall day light, yet saw he the land in that
tract free from ice, which had bene molten by the heat
of the Sunne. Thus seeing such heapes of yce before
him, hee was enforced to turne his sailes and follow
the West, so coasting still by the shore, that he was
thereby brought so farre into the South, by reason of
the land bending so much Southwards, that it was there
almost equall in latitude, with the sea Fretum Herculeum,
having the Northpole elevate in maner in the same degree.
He sailed likewise in this tract so farre towards the West,
that hee had the Island of Cuba on his left hand, in
maner in the same degree of longitude. As hee traveiled
by the coastes of this great land, (which he named Baccalaos) he saith that hee found the like course of the
waters toward the West, but the same to runne more
softly and gently then the swift waters which the Spaniards
found in their Navigations Southward. Wherfore it is
not onely more like to be true, but ought also of
necessitie to be concluded that betweene both the lands
hitherto unknowen, there should be certaine great open
places whereby the waters should thus continually passe
from the East unto the West: which waters I suppose
to be driven about the globe of the earth by the un-
cessant moving and impulsion of the heavens, and not
to bee swallowed up and cast up againe by the breathing
of Demogorgon, as some have imagined, because they
see the seas by increase and decrease to ebbe and flowe.
Sebastian Cabot himselfe named those lands Baccalaos,
because that in the Seas thereabout hee found so great
multitudes of certaine bigge fishes much like unto Tunies,
(which the inhabitants call Baccalaos) that they sometime
stayed his shippes. He found also the people of those

*A current
toward the
West.*

*The people of
Island say the
Sea and yce
setteth also
West.
Jonas Arn-
grimus.*

regions covered with beastes skinnes, yet not without the use of reason. He also saith there is great plentie of Beares in those regions which use to eate fish : for plunging themselves into ye water, where they perceive a multitude of these fishes to lie, they fasten their clawes in their scales, and so draw them to land and eate them, so (as he saith) the Beares being thus satisfied with fish, are not noisome to men. Hee declareth further, that in many places of these Regions he saw great plentie of Copper among the inhabitants. Cabot is my very friend, whom I use familiarly, and delight to have him sometimes keepe mee company in mine owne house. For being called out of England by the commandement of the Catholique King of Castile, after the death of King Henry the seventh of that name King of England, he was made one of our councill and Assistants, as touching the affaires of the new Indies, looking for ships dayly to be furnished for him to discover this hid secret of Nature.

Copper found in many places by Cabote.

The testimonie of Francis Lopez de Gomara a Spaniard, in the fourth Chapter of the second Booke of his generall history of the West Indies concerning the first discoverie of a great part of the West Indies, to wit, from 58. to 38. degrees of latitude, by Sebastian Cabota out of England.

E which brought most certaine newes of the countrey & people of Baccalaos, saith Gomara, was Sebastian Cabote a Venetian, which rigged up two ships at the cost of K. Henry the 7. of England, having great desire to traffique for the spices as the Portingals did. He caried with him 300. men, and tooke the way towards Island from beyond the Cape of Labrador, untill he found himselfe in 58. degrees and better. He made relation

153

that in the moneth of July it was so cold, and the ice so great, that hee durst not passe any further: that the dayes were very long, in a maner without any night, and for that short night that they had, it was very cleare. Cabot feeling the cold, turned towards the West, refreshing himselfe at Baccalaos: and afterwards he sayled along the coast unto 38. degrees, and from thence he shaped his course to returne into England.

A note of Sebastian Cabots first discoverie of part of the Indies taken out of the latter part of Robert Fabians Chronicle not hitherto printed, which is in the custodie of M. John Stow a diligent preserver of Antiquities.

Cabots voyage from Bristol wherein he discovered Newfound land, & the Northerne parts of that land, and from thence as farre almost as Florida.

IN. the 13. yeere of K. Henry the 7. (by meanes of one John Cabot a Venetian which made himselfe very expert and cunning in knowledge of the circuit of the world and Ilands of the same, as by a Sea card and other demonstrations reasonable he shewed) the king caused to man and victuall a ship at Bristow, to search for an Island, which he said hee knew well was rich, and replenished with great commodities: Which shippe thus manned and victualled at the kings cost, divers Marchants of London ventured in her small stocks, being in her as chiefe patron the said Venetian. And in the company of the said ship, sailed also out of Bristow three or foure small ships fraught with sleight and grosse marchandizes, as course cloth, caps, laces, points & other trifles. And so departed from Bristow in the beginning of May, of whom in this Maiors time returned no tidings.

Of three Savages which Cabot brought home and presented unto the King in the foureteenth yere of his raigne, mentioned by the foresaid Robert Fabian.

His yeere also were brought unto the king three men taken in the Newfound Island that before I spake of, in William Purchas time being Maior: These were clothed in beasts skins, & did eate raw flesh, and spake such speech that no man could understand them, and in their [III. 10.] demeanour like to bruite beastes, whom the King kept a time after. Of the which upon two yeeres after, I saw two apparelled after the maner of Englishmen in Westminster pallace, which that time I could not discerne from Englishmen, til I was learned what they were, but as for speach, I heard none of them utter one word.

A briefe extract concerning the discoverie of Newfound-land, taken out of the booke of M. Robert Thorne, to doctor Leigh, &c.

Reason, that as some sickenesses are hereditarie, so this inclination or desire of this discovery I inherited from my father, which with another marchant of Bristol named Hugh Eliot, were the discoverers of the Newfound-lands; of the which there is no doubt (as nowe plainely appeareth) if the Mariners would then have bene ruled, and followed their Pilots minde, but the lands of the West Indies, from whence all the golde commeth, had bene ours; for all is one coast as by the Card appeareth, and is aforesaid.

[The large

The large pension granted by K. Edward the 6. to Sebastian Cabota, constituting him grand Pilot of England.

Dwardus sextus Dei gratia Angliæ, Franciæ, & Hiberniæ rex, omnibus Christi fidelibus, ad quos præsentes hæ literæ nostræ pervenerint, salutem. Sciatis quod nos in consideratione boni & acceptabilis servitii, nobis per dilectum servientem nostrum Sebastianum Cabotam impensi atque impendendi, de gratia nostra speciali, ac ex certa scientia, & mero motu nostro, nec non de advisamento, & consensu præclarissimi avunculi nostri Edwardi Ducis Somerseti personæ nostræ Gubernatoris, ac Regnorum, dominiorum, subditorúmque nostrorum protectoris, & cæterorum consiliariorum nostrorum, dedimus & concessimus, ac per præsentes damus, & concedimus eidem Sebastiano Cabotæ, quandam annuitatem sive annualem reditum, centum sexaginta & sex librarum, tresdecim solidorum, & quatuor denariorum sterlingorum, habendam, gaudendam, & annuatìm percipiendam prædictam annuitatem, sive annalem reditum eidem Sebastiano Cabotæ, durante vita sua naturali, de thesauro nostro ad receptum scacarii nostri Westmonasterii per manus thesaurariorum, & Camerariorum nostrorum, ibidem pro tempore existentium, ad festa annuntiationis beatæ Mariæ Virginis, nativitatis sancti Joannis Baptistæ, Sancti Michaelis Archangeli, & Natalis Domini per æquales portiones solvendam. Et ulteriùs de uberiori gratia nostra, ac de advisamento, & consensu prædictis damus, & per præsentes concedimus præfato Sebastiano Cabotæ, tot & tantas Denariorum summas, ad quot & quantas dicta annuitas sive annalis reditus centum sexaginta sex librarum, tresdecim solidorum, & quatuor denariorum, à festo sancti Michaelis Archangeli ultimò præterito huc usque se extendit, & attingit, habendas

& recipiendas præfato Sebastiano Cabotæ & assignatis
suis de thesauro nostro prædicto per manus prædictorum Thesaurariorum, & Camerariorum nostrorum de
dono nostro absque computo, seu aliquo alio nobis,
hæredibus, vel successoribus nostris proinde reddendo,
solvendo, vel faciendo: eo quòd expressa mentio, &c.
In cujus rei testimonium, &c. Teste Rege, apud Westmonasterium 6. die Januarii, Anno 2. Regis Edwardi *Anno D.*
sexti.   *1549.*

The same in English.

EDward the sixt by the grace of God, King of
England, France and Ireland, defender of the faith,
to all Christian people to whom these presents shall
come, sendeth greeting. Know yee that we, in consideration of the good and acceptable service done, and
to be done, unto us by our beloved servant Sebastian
Cabota, of our speciall grace, certaine knowledge, meere
motion, and by the advice and counsel of our most
honourable uncle Edward duke of Somerset governour
of our person, and Protector of our kingdomes,
dominions, and subjects, and of the rest of our Counsaile, have given & granted, and by these presents do
give and graunt to the said Sebastian Cabota, a certaine
annuitie, or yerely revenue of one hundreth, threescore
& sixe pounds, thirteene shillings foure pence sterling,
to have, enjoy, and yerely receive the foresaid annuitie,
or yerely revenue, to the foresaid Sebastian Cabota
during his natural life, out of our Treasurie at the
receit of our Exchequer at Westminster, at the hands
of our Treasurers & paymasters, there remayning for
the time being, at the feasts of the Annuntiation of the
blessed Virgin Mary, the Nativitie of S. John Baptist,
S. Michael ye Archangel, & the Nativitie of our Lord,
to be paid by equal portions.

And further, of our more speciall grace, and by the [III. 11.]
advise and consent aforesaide wee doe give, and by
these presents doe graunt unto the aforesaide Sebastian

157

Cabota, so many, and so great summes of money as the saide annuitie or yeerely revenue of an hundreth, threescore and sixe pounds, thirteene shillings 4. pence, doeth amount and rise unto from the feast of S. Michael the Archangel last past unto this present time, to be had and received by the aforesaid Sebastian Cabota, and his assignes out of our aforesaid Treasurie, at the handes of our aforesaide Treasurers, and officers of our Exchequer of our free gift without accompt, or any thing else therefore to be yeelded, payed, or made, to us, our heires or successours, forasmuch as herein expresse mention is made to the contrary.

In witnesse whereof we have caused these our Letters to be made. patents : Witnesse the King at Westminster the sixt day of Januarie, in the second yeere of his raigne. The yeere of our Lord 1548.

A discourse written by Sir Humphrey Gilbert Knight, to prove a passage by the Northwest to Cathaia, and the East Indies.

¶ The Table of the matters in every Chapter of this discourse.

Capitulo 1.

O prove by authoritie a passage to be on the North side of America, to goe to Cataia, China, and to the East India.

Capitulo 2.

To prove by reason a passage to be on the North side of America, to goe to Cataia, Moluccæ, &c.

Capitulo 3.

To prove by experience of sundry mens travailes the opening of this Northwest passage, whereby good hope remaineth of the rest.

Capitulo 4.

To prove by circumstance, that the Northwest passage hath bene sailed throughout.

Capitulo 5.

To proove that such Indians as have bene driven upon the coastes of Germanie came not thither by the Southeast, and Southwest, nor from any part of Afrike or America.

Capitulo 6.

To proove that the Indians aforenamed came not by the Northeast, and that there is no thorow passage navigable that way.

Capitulo 7.

To prove that these Indians came by the Northwest, which induceth a certaintie of this passage by experience.

Capitulo 8.

What several reasons were alleaged before the Queenes Majestie, and certaine Lords of her Highnesse privie Council, by M. Anth. Jenkinson a Gentleman of great travaile and experience, to prove this passage by the Northeast, with my severall answeres then alleaged to the same.

Capitulo 9.

How that this passage by the Northwest is more commodious for our traffike, then the other by the Northeast, if there were any such.

Capitulo 10.

What commodities would ensue, this passage being once discovered.

[To prove

To prove by authoritie a passage to be on the Northside of America, to goe to Cathaia, and the East India.

Chapter 1.

WHen I gave my selfe to the studie of Geographie, after I had perused and diligently scanned the descriptions of Europe, Asia & Afrike, and conferred them with the Mappes and Globes both Antique and Moderne: I came in fine to the fourth part of the world, commonly called America, which by all descriptions I found to bee an Iland environed round about with Sea, having on the Southside of it the frete or straight of Magellan, on the West side Mar del Sur, which Sea runneth towards the North, separating it from the East parts of Asia, where the Dominions of the Cathaians are: On the East part our West Ocean, and on the North side the sea that severeth it from Groneland, thorow which Northren Seas the Passage lyeth, which I take now in hand to discover.

Plato in Timæo, and in the Dialogue called Critias, discourseth of an incomparable great Iland then called Atlantis, being greater then all Affrike and Asia, which lay Westward from the Straights of Gibraltar, navigable round about: affirming also that the Princes of Atlantis did aswell enjoy the governance of all Affrike, and the most part of Europe, as of Atlantis it selfe.

Also to prove Platos opinion of this Iland, and the inhabiting of it in ancient time by them of Europe, to be of the more credite; Marinæus Siculus in his Chronicle of Spaine, reporteth that there have bene found by the Spaniards in the gold Mines of America, certaine pieces of Money ingraved with the Image of Augustus Cæsar: which pieces were sent to the Pope for a testimonie of the matter, by John Rufus Archbishop of Consentinum.

Moreover, this was not only thought of Plato, but by Marsilius Ficinus, and excellent Florentine Philosopher,

Crantor the Græcian, and Proclus, and Philo the famous *Proclus pag.* Jew (as appeareth in his booke De Mundo, and in the *24.* Commentaries upon Plato) to be overflowen and swallowed up with water, by reason of a mightie earthquake, and streaming downe of the heavenly Fludgates. The like whereof happened unto some part of Italy, when by the forciblenes of the Sea, called Superum, it cut off Sicilia from the Continent of Calabria, as appeareth in Justine, in the beginning of his fourth booke. Also *Justine Lib. 4.* there chanced the like in Zetland a part of Flanders.

And also the Cities of Pyrrha and Antissa, about *Plinie.* Meotis palus: and also the Citie Burys, in the Corynthian bosome, commonly called Sinus Corinthiacus, have bene swallowed up with the Sea, and are not at this day to be discerned: By which accident America grew to be unknowen of long time, unto us of the later ages, and was lately discovered againe, by Americus Vespucius, in the yeere of our Lord 1497. which some say to have bene first discovered by Christophorus Columbus a Genuois, Anno 1492.

The same calamitie happened unto this Isle of Atlantis 600. and odde yeres before Plato his time, which some of the people of the Southeast parts of the world accompted as 9000. yeeres: for the maner then was to reckon the Moone her Period of the Zodiak for a yeere, which is our usual moneth, depending à Luminari minori.

So that in these our dayes there can no other mayne or Islande be found or judged to bee parcell of this Atlantis, then those Westerne Islands, which beare now the name of America: countervailing thereby the name of Atlantis, in the knowledge of our age.

Then, if when no part of the sayd Atlantis was oppressed by water, and earthquake, the coasts round about the same were navigable: a farre greater hope now remaineth of the same by the Northwest, seeing the most part of it was (since that time) swallowed up with *A minore ad* water, which could not utterly take away the olde deeps *majus.* and chanels, but rather, be an occasion of the inlarging

of the olde, and also an inforcing of a great many new:
why then should we now doubt of our Northwest passage
and navigation from England to India? &c. seeing that
Atlantis now called America, was ever knowen to be an
Island, and in those dayes navigable round about, which
by accesse of more water could not be diminished.

Also Aristotle in his booke De Mundo, and the
learned Germaine Simon Gryneus in his annotations
upon the same, saith that the whole earth (meaning
thereby, as manifestly doth appeare, Asia, Africk, and
Europe, being all the countreys then knowen) is but
one Island, compassed about with the reach of the sea
Atlantine: which likewise prooveth America to be an
Island, and in no part adjoyning to Asia, or the rest.

Strabo lib. 15. Also many ancient writers, as Strabo and others, called
both the Ocean sea, (which lieth East of India) Atlanti-
cum pelagus, and that sea also on the West coasts of
Spaine and Africk, Mare Atlanticum: the distance betweene the two coasts is almost halfe the compasse of
the earth.

So that it is incredible, as by Plato appeareth manifestly, that the East Indian Sea had the name Atlanticum
pelagus of the mountaine Atlas in Afrik, or yet the
sea adjoining to Africk, had the name Oceanus Atlanticus
*Valerius
Anselmus in
Catalogo anno-
rum & prin-
cipium. fol.* 6.
Gen. 9. 10. of the same mountaine: but that those seas and the
mountaine Atlas were so called of this great Island
Atlantis, and that the one and the other had their names
for a memorial of the mighty prince Atlas, sometime king
thereof, who was Japhet yongest sonne to Noah, in
whose time the whole earth was divided between the
three brethren, Sem, Cam, and Japhet.

Wherefore I am of opinion that America by the
Northwest will be found favourable to this our enterprise, and am the rather imboldened to beleeve the same,
for that I finde it not onely confirmed by Plato, Aristotle,
and other ancient Phylosophers: but also by all the best
[II moderne Geographers, as Gemma Frisius, Munsterus,
Appianus, Hunterus, Gastaldus, Guyccardinus, Michael

Tramasinus, Franciscus Demongenitus, Bernardus Pute-
anus, Andreas Vavasor, Tramontanus, Petrus Martyr,
and also Ortelius, who doth coast out in his generall
Mappe set out Anno 1569, all the countreys and Capes,
on the Northwest side of America, from Hochelaga to
Cape de Paramantia: describing likewise the sea coastes
of Cataia and Gronland, towards any part of America,
making both Gronland and America, Islands disjoyned
by a great sea, from any part of Asia.

All which learned men and painefull travellers have
affirmed with one consent and voice, that America was an
Island: and that there lyeth a great Sea betweene it,
Cataia, and Grondland, by the which any man of our
countrey, that will give the attempt, may with small
danger passe to Cataia, the Moluccæ, India, and all other
places in the East, in much shorter time, then either
the Spaniard, or Portugal doeth, or may doe, from the
neerest parte of any of their countreys within Europe.

What moved these learned men to affirme thus much,
I know not, or to what ende so many and sundry
travellers of both ages have allowed the same: But I
conjecture that they would never have so constantly
affirmed, or notified their opinions therein to the world,
if they had not had great good cause, and many probable
reasons, to have lead them thereunto.

We ought by reasons right to have a reverent opinion of worthy men.

Now least you should make small accompt of ancient
writers or of their experiences which travelled long before
our times, reckoning their authority amongst fables of
no importance: I have for the better assurance of those
proofes, set downe some part of a discourse, written in
the Saxon tongue, and translated into English by M.
Nowel servant to Sir William Cecil, lord Burleigh, and
lord high treasurer of England, wherein there is described
a Navigation, which one Ochther made, in the time of
king Alfred, king of Westsaxe Anno 871. the words of
which discourse were these: Hee sailed right North,
having alwaies the desert land on the Starborde, and on
the Larbord the maine sea, continuing his course, untill

A Navigation of one Ochther made in king Alfreds time.

*A perfect de-
scription of our
Moscovia voy-
age.*

hee perceived that the coast bowed directly towards the
East, or else the Sea opened into the land he could not
tell how farre, where he was compelled to stay until he
had a westerne winde, or somewhat upon the North, and
sayled thence directly East alongst the coast, so farre as
hee was able in foure dayes, where he was againe inforced
to tary untill hee had a North winde, because the coast
there bowed directly towards the South, or at least
opened he knew not howe farre into the land, so that he
sayled thence along the coast continually full South, so
farre as he could travell in the space of five dayes, where
hee discovered a mighty river, which opened farre into
the land, and in the entrie of this river he turned
backe againe.

Whereby it appeareth that he went the very same way,
that we now doe yerely trade by S. Nicholas into Moscovia, which way no man in our age knew for certaintie
to be by sea, until it was since discovered by our English
men, in the time of King Edward the sixt; but thought
before that time that Groneland had joyned to Normoria
Byarmia, &c. and therefore was accompted a new discovery, being nothing so indeede, as by this discourse
of Ochther it appeareth.

*By Sir Hugh
Willoughbie
knight, Chan-
cellor and
Borough.*

Neverthelesse if any man should have taken this
voyage in hand by the encouragement of this onely
author, he should have bene thought but simple: considering that this Navigation was written so many yeres
past, in so barbarous a tongue by one onely obscure
author, and yet we in these our dayes finde by our owne
experiences his former reports to be true.

How much more then ought we to beleeve this
passage to Cataia to bee, being verified by the opinions
of all the best, both Antique, and Moderne Geographers,
and plainely set out in the best and most allowed
Mappes, Charts, Globes, Cosmographical tables & discourses of this our age, and by the rest not denied, but
left as a matter doubtfull.

To proove by reason, a passage to be on the
Northside of America, to goe to Cataia, &c.

Chap. 3.

Flrst, all seas are maintained by the abundance of *Experimented*
water, so that the neerer the end any River, Bay *by our English*
fishers.
or Haven is, the shallower it waxeth, (although by some
accidentall barre, it is sometime found otherwise) But
the farther you sayle West from Island towards the place,
where this fret is thought to be, the more deepe are the
seas: which giveth us good hope of continuance of the
same Sea with Mar del Sur, by some fret that lyeth
betweene America, Groneland and Cataia.

2 Also if that America were not an Island, but a part
of ye continent adjoyning to Asia, either the people [III. 14.]
which inhabite Mangia, Anian, & Quinzay, &c. being
borderers upon it, would before this time have made
some road into it, hoping to have found some like commodities to their owne.

3 Or els the Scythians and Tartarians (which often
times heretofore have sought farre and neere for new
seats, driven thereunto through the necessitie of their *Neede makes*
the old wife to
cold and miserable countreys) would in all this time have *trotte.*
found the way to America, and entred the same, had the
passages bene never so straite or difficult; the countrey
being so temperate, pleasant and fruitfull, in comparison
of their owne. But there was never any such people
found there by any of the Spaniards, Portugals, or
Frenchmen, who first discovered the Inland of that
countrey: which Spaniards, or Frenchmen must then of
necessitie have seene some one civil man in America,
considering how full of civill people Asia is: But they
never saw so much as one token or signe, that ever
any man of the knowen part of the world had bene
there.

4 Furthermore it is to be thought, that if by reason
of mountaines, or other craggy places, the people neither

of Cataia or Tartarie could enter the countrey of America, or they of America have entred Asia if it were so joyned: yet some one savage or wandring beast would in so many yeres have passed into it: but there hath not any time bene found any of the beasts proper to Cataia, or Tartarie &c. in America: nor of those proper to America, in Tartarie, Cataia, &c. or any part of Asia. Which thing proveth America, not onely to be one Island, and in no part adjoyning to Asia: But also that the people of those Countreys, have not had any traffique with each other.

5 Moreover at the least some one of those painefull travellers, which of purpose have passed the confines of both countreys, with intent only to discover, would as it is most likely have gone from the one to the other: if there had bene any piece of land, or Isthmos, to have joyned them together, or els have declared some cause to the contrary.

6 But neither Paulus Venetus, who lived and dwelt a long time in Cataia, ever came into America, and yet was at the sea coastes of Mangia, over against it where he was embarked, and perfourmed a great Navigation along those seas: Neither yet Verarzanus, or Franciscus Vasques de Coronado, who travelled the North part of America by land, ever found entry from thence by land to Cataia, or any part of Asia.

The Sea hath
three motions.
1 Motum ab
oriente in occi-
dentem.
2 Motum
fluxus & re-
fluxus.
3 Motum cir-
cularem.
Ad cœli
motum ele-
menta omnia
(excepta
terra) moven-
tur.

7 Also it appeareth to be an Island, insomuch as the Sea runneth by nature circularly from the East to the West, following the diurnal motion of Primum Mobile, which carieth with it all inferiour bodies moveable, aswel celestiall as elemental: which motion of the waters is most evidently seene in the Sea, which lieth on the Southside of Afrike, where the current that runneth from the East to the West is so strong (by reason of such motion) that the Portugals in their voyages Eastward to Calicut, in passing by Cap. de buona Sperança are inforced to make divers courses, the current there being so swift as it striketh from thence all along Westward

upon the fret of Magellan, being distant from thence, neere the fourth part of the longitude of the earth : and not having free passage and entrance thorow the fret towards the West, by reason of the narrownesse of the sayd Straite of Magellan, it runneth to salve this wrong (Nature not yeelding to accidentall restraints) all along the Easterne coastes of America, Northwards so far as Cape Fredo, being the farthest knowne place of the same continent towards the North : which is about 4800 leagues, reckoning therewithall the trending of the land.

8 So that this current being continually maintained with such force, as Jaques Cartier affirmeth it to be, who met with the same being at Baccalaos, as he sayled along the coastes of America, then either it must of necessitie have way to passe from Cape Fredo, thorow this fret, Westward towards Cataia, being knowen to come so farre, onely to salve his former wrongs, by the authority before named : or els it must needes strike over, upon the coast of Island, Norway, Finmarke, and Lappia, (which are East from the sayd place about 360 leagues) with greater force then it did from Cape de *Posita causa,* buona Sperança, upon the fret of Magellan, or from *ponitur effec-* the fret of Magellan to Cape Fredo, upon which coastes *tus.* Jaques Cartier met with the same, considering the shortnesse of the Cut from the sayd Cape Fredo, to Island, Lappia, &c. And so the cause Efficient remaining, it would have continually followed along our coasts, through the narrow seas, which it doth not, but is disgested about the North of Labrador, by some through passage there thorow this fret.

The like course of the water in some respect happeneth in the Mediterrane sea (as affirmeth Conterenus) wheras *Conterenus.* the current which commeth from Tanais, & Pontus Euxinus, running along all the coasts of Greece, Italy, France, and Spaine, and not finding sufficient way out through Gibraltar, by meanes of the straitnesse of the fret it runneth backe againe along the coastes of Barbary, by Alexandria, Natolia, &c.

*An objection
answered.
The sea doth
evermore per-
forme this cir-
cular motion,
either in
Suprema, or
concava super-
ficie aquæ.*

*The yce set
westward
every yeere
from Island.
Auth. Jona
Arngrimo.*

It may (peradventure) bee thought that this course of
the sea doth sometime surcease, and thereby impugne
this principle, because it is not discerned all along the
coast of America, in such sort as Jaques Cartier found
it: Whereunto I answere this: that albeit, in every part
of the Coast of America, or elswhere this current is not
sensibly perceived, yet it hath evermore such like motion,
either in the uppermost or nethermost part of the sea:
as it may be proved true, if ye sinke a sayle by a couple
of ropes, neere the ground, fastening to the nethermost
corners two gunne chambers or other weights: by the
driving whereof you shall plainely perceive, the course
of the water, and current, running with such course in
the bottome.

By the like experiment, you may finde the ordinary
motion of the sea, in the Ocean: howe farre soever you
be off the land.

9 Also there commeth another current from out the
Northeast from the Scythian Sea (as M. Jenkinson a man
of rare vertue, great travaile and experience, told me)
which runneth Westward towardes Labrador, as the other
did, which commeth from the South: so that both these
currents, must have way thorow this our fret, or else
encounter together and runne contrarie courses, in one
line, but no such conflicts of streames, or contrary courses
are found about any part of Labrodor, or Terra nova, as
witnesse our yeerely fishers, and other saylers that way,
but is there disgested, as aforesayd, and found by experience of Barnard de la Torre, to fall into Mar del Sur.

10 Furthermore, the current in the great Ocean, could
not have beene maintained to runne continually one way,
from the beginning of the world unto this day, had there
not beene some thorow passage by the fret aforesayd, and
so by circular motion bee brought againe to maintaine it
selfe: For the Tides and courses of the sea are main-
tayned by their interchangeable motions: as fresh rivers
are by springs, by ebbing and flowing, by rarefaction and
condensation.

So that it resteth not possible (so farre as my simple reason can comprehend) that this perpetuall current can by any meanes be maintained, but onely by continuall reaccesse of the same water, which passeth thorow the fret, and is brought about thither againe, by such circular motion as aforesayd. And the certaine falling thereof by this fret into Mar del Sur is prooved by the testimonie and experience, of Bernard de la Torre, who was sent from P. de la Natividad to the Moluccæ, Anno domini 1542. by commandement of Anthony Mendoza, then Viceroy of Nova Hispania, which Bernard sayled 750. Leagues, on the Northside of the Aequator, and there met with a current, which came from the Northeast the which drove him backe againe to Tidore.

The flowing is occasioned by reason that the heate of the moone boyleth, and maketh the water thinne by way of rarefaction. An experience to proove the falling of this current into Mar del Sur.

Wherfore, this current being proved to come from C. de buona Sperança to the fret of Magellan, and wanting sufficient entrance there, by narrownes of the straite, is by the necessitie of natures force, brought to Terra de Labrador, where Jaques Cartier met the same, and thence certainly knowen, not to strike over upon Island, Lappia, &c. and found by Bernard de la Torre in Mar del Sur, on the backeside of America: therefore this current (having none other passage) must of necessity, fall out thorow this our fret into Mar del Sur, and so trending by the Moluccæ, China, and C. de buona Sperança, maintaineth it selfe by circular motion, which is all one in nature, with Motus ab Oriente in Occidentem.

Cinian

So that it seemeth, we have now more occasion to doubt of our returne, then whether there be a passage that way, yea or no: which' doubt, hereafter shall be sufficiently remooved. Wherefore, in mine opinion, reason it self, grounded upon experience, assureth us of this passage, if there were nothing els to put us in hope thereof. But least these might not suffice, I have added in this chapter following, some further proofe hereof, by the experience of such as have passed some part of this discoverie: and in the next adjoining to that the authority of those, which have sailed wholy, thorow every part thereof.

To prove by experience of sundry mens travels, the opening of some part of this Northwest passage: wherby good hope remaineth of the rest.

Chap. 3.

PAulus Venetus, who dwelt many yeres in Cataia, affirmed that hee sayled 1500 miles upon the coastes of Mangia, and Anian, towards the Northeast: alwayes finding the Seas open before him, not onely as farre as he went, but also as farre as he could discerne.

2 Also Franciscus Vasques de Coronado passing from Mexico by Cevola, through the countrey of Quivira, to Siera Nevada, found there a great sea, where were certaine ships laden with Merchandise, carrying on their prowes the pictures of certaine birds called Alcatrarzi, part whereof were made of golde, and part of silver, who signified by signes, that they were thirty dayes comming thither: which likewise proveth America by experience to be disjoyned from Cataia, on that part by a great Sea, because they could not come from any part of America, as Natives thereof: for that, so farre as is discovered, there hath not bene found there any one Shippe of that countrey.

[III. 16.]
Alcatrarzi be Pellicanes.

Baros lib. 9. Of his first Decas cap. 1. 3 In like maner, John Baros testifieth that the Cosmographers of China (where he himselfe had bene) affirme that the Sea coast trendeth from thence Northeast, to 50 degrees of Septentrional latitude, being the furthest part that way which the Portugals had then knowledge of: And that the said Cosmographers knew no cause to the contrary, but that it might continue further.

By whose experiences America is prooved to be separate from those parts of Asia, directly against the same. And not contented with the judgements of these learned men only, I have searched what might be further sayd for the confirmation hereof.

4 And I found that Franciscus Lopez de Gomara affirmeth America to be an Island, and likewise Gronland: and that Gronland is distant from Lappia 40 leagues, and from Terra de Labrador, 50.

5 Moreover, Alvarus Nunnius a Spaniard, and learned Cosmographer, and Jacobus Cartier, who made two voyages into those parts, and sayled 900 miles upon the Northeast coastes of America doe in part confirme the same.

6 Likewise Hieronymus Fracastorius, a learned Italian, and travailer in the North parts of the same land.

7 Also Jaques Cartier having done the like, heard say at Hochelaga in Nova Francia, how that there was a great Sea at Saguinay, whereof the end was not knowen: which they presupposed to be the passage to Cataia.

Furthermore, Sebastian Cabota by his personal experience and travel hath set foorth, and described this passage in his Charts, which are yet to be seene in the Queens Majesties privie Gallerie at Whitehall, who was sent to make this discovery by king Henrie the seventh, and entred the same fret: affirming that he sayled very farre Westward, with a quarter of the North, on the Northside of Terra de Labrador the eleventh of June, untill he came to the Septentrionall latitude of 67 degrees and a halfe, and finding the Seas still open, sayd, that he might, & would have gone to Cataia, if the mutinie of the Master and Mariners had not bene. *Written in the discourses of Navigation.*

Now as these mens experience hath proved some part of this passage: so the chapter following shal put you in full assurance of the rest, by their experiences which have passed through every part thereof.

[To proove

To proove by circumstance that the Northwest passage hath bene sayled throughout.

Chap. 4.

THe diversitie betweene bruite beastes and men, or betweene the wise and the simple is, that the one judgeth by sense onely, and gathereth no surety of any thing that he hath not seene, felt, heard, tasted, or smelled: And the other not so onely, but also findeth the certaintie of things by reason, before they happen to be tryed. Wherefore I have added proofes of both sorts, that the one and the other might thereby be satisfied.

1 First, as Gemma Frisius reciteth, there went from Europe three brethren through this passage: whereof it tooke the name of Fretum trium fratrum.

2 Also Plinie affirmeth out of Cornelius Nepos, (who wrote 57 yeeres before Christ) that there were certaine Indians driven by tempest, upon the coast of Germanie which were presented by the king of Suevia, unto Quintus Metellus Celer, the Proconsull of France.

3 And Plinie upon the same sayth, that it is no marvell though there be Sea by the North, where there is such abundance of moisture: which argueth that hee doubted not of a navigable passage that way, through which those Indians came.

4 And for the better proofe that the same authoritie of Cornelius Nepos is not by me wrested, to prove my opinion of the Northwest passage: you shall finde the same affirmed more plainly in that behalfe, by the excellent Geographer Dominicus Marius Niger, who
sheweth how many wayes the Indian sea stretcheth it selfe, making in that place recital of certaine Indians, that were likewise driven through the North Seas from
India, upon the coastes of Germany, by great tempest, as they were sayling in trade of marchandize.

5 Also while Frederic Barbarossa reigned Emperour, *Avouched by* Anno Do. 1160. there came certaine other Indians upon *Franciscus Lo-* the coast of Germanie. *pes de Gomara in his historie*

6 Likewise Othon in the storie of the Gothes affirmeth, *of India, lib.* that in the time of the Germane Emperours, there were 1. *cap.* 10. also certaine Indians cast by force of weather, upon the coast of the sayd countrey, which foresaid Indians could not possibly have come by the Southeast, Southwest, nor from any part of Afrike or America, nor yet by the Northeast: therefore they came of necessitie by this our Northwest passage.

To proove that these Indians aforenamed came not by the Southeast, Southwest, nor from any other part of Afrike, or America.

Cap. 5.

FIrst, they could not come from the Southeast by the Cape de bona Sperança, because the roughnes of the Seas there is such (occasioned by the currents and great winds in that part) that the greatest Armadas the king of Portugal hath, cannot without great difficultie passe that way, much lesse then a Canoa of India could live in those outragious seas without shipwracke (being a vessell of very small burden) and have conducted themselves to the place aforesayd, being men unexpert in the Arte of navigation.

2 Also, it appeareth plainely that they were not able to come from alongst the coast of Afrike aforesayd, to those parts of Europe, because the winds doe (for the most part) blow there Easterly off from the shore, and the current running that way in like sort, should have driven them Westward upon some part of America: for such winds and tides could never have led them from thence to the said place where they were found, nor yet could they have come from any of the countries afore- sayd, keeping the seas alwayes, without skilful mariners

to have conducted them such like courses as were necessary to performe such a voiage.

3 Presupposing also, if they had bene driven to the West (as they must have bene, comming that way) then they should have perished, wanting supplie of victuals, not having any place (once leaving the coast of Afrike) untill they came to America, nor from America untill they arrived upon some part of Europe, or the Islands adjoyning to it, to have refreshed themselves.

4 Also, if (notwithstanding such impossibilities) they might have recovered Germanie by comming from India by the Southeast, yet must they without all doubt have striken upon some other part of Europe before their arrivall there, as the Isles of the Açores, Portugal, Spaine, France, England, Ireland, &c. which if they had done, it is not credible that they should or would have departed undiscovered of the inhabitants: but there was never found in those dayes any such ship or men but only upon the coasts of Germanie, where they have bene sundry times and in sundry ages cast aland: neither is it like that they would have committed themselves againe to sea, if they had so arrived, not knowing where they were, nor whither to have gone.

This fift reason by later experience is proved utterly untrue.

5 And by the Southwest it is unpossible, because the current aforesayd which commeth from the East, striketh with such force upon the fret of Magellan, and falleth with such swiftnesse and furie into Mar del Zur, that hardly any ship (but not possibly a Canoa, with such unskilfull mariners) can come into our Westerne Ocean through that fret, from the West seas of America, as Magellans experience hath partly taught us.

6 And further, to proove that these people so arriving upon the coast of Germany, were Indians, & not inhabiters of any part either of Africa or America, it is

That the Indians could not be natives either of Africa, or of America.

manifest, because the natives both of Africa and America neither had, or have at this day (as is reported) other kind of boates then such as do beare neither mastes nor sailes, (except onely upon the coasts of Barbarie and the

Turkes ships) but do carie themselves from place to place neere the shore by the ore onely.

To proove that those Indians came not by the Northeast, and that there is no thorow navigable passage that way.

Cap. 6.

IT is likely that there should be no thorow passage by the Northeast, whereby to goe round about the world, because all Seas (as aforesayd) are maintained by the abundance of water, waxing more shallow and shelffie towards the ende, as we find it doeth by experience in Mare Glaciali, towards the East, which breedeth small hope of any great continuance of that sea, to be navigable towards the East, sufficient to saile thereby round about the world.

2 Also, it standeth scarcely with reason, that the Indians dwelling under Torrida Zona, could endure the injurie of the cold ayre, about the Septentrional latitude of 80. degrees, under which elevation the passage by the Northeast cannot bee (as the often experience had of all the South parts of it sheweth) seeing that some of the inhabitants of this cold climate (whose Summer is to them an extreme Winter) have bene stroken to death with the cold damps of the aire about 72 degrees, by an accidental mishap, and yet the aire in such like Elevation is alwaies cold, and too cold for such as the Indians are.

3 Furthermore, the piercing cold of the grosse thicke aire so neere the Pole wil so stiffen and furre the sailes and ship tackling, that no mariner can either hoise or strike them (as our experience farre neerer the South, then this passage is presupposed to be, hath taught us) without the use whereof no voiage can be performed.

4 Also, the aire is so darkened with continuall mists and fogs so neere the Pole, that no man can well see, either to guide his ship, or direct his course.

5 Also the compasse at such elevation doth very

[III. 18.]
Quicquid naturali loco privatur, quam citissimè corrumpitur.

Qualis causa talis effectus.

suddenly vary, which things must of force have bene their destructions, although they had bene men of much more skill then the Indians are.

Similium
similis est
ratio.

6 Moreover, all baies, gulfes, and rivers doe receive their increase upon the flood, sensibly to be discerned on the one side of the shore or the other, as many waies as they be open to any main sea, as Mare Mediterraneum, Mare Rubrum, Sinus Persicus, Sinus Bodicus, Thamesis, and all other knowen havens or rivers in any part of the world, and each of them opening but on one part to the maine sea, doe likewise receive their increase upon the flood the same way, and none other, which Mare Glaciale doeth, onely by the West; as M. Jenkinson affirmed unto me: and therfore it followeth that this Northeast sea, receiving increase but onely from the West, cannot possibly open to the maine Ocean by the East.

7 Moreover, the farther you passe into any sea towards the end of it, on that part which is shut up from the maine sea (as in all those above mentioned) the lesse and lesse the tides rise and fall. The like whereof also happeneth in Mare Glaciale, which proveth but small continuance of that Sea toward the East.

8 Also, the further yee goe toward the East in Mare Glaciale, the lesse salt the water is: which could not

Quicquid cor-
rumpitur à
contrario cor-
rumpitur.

happen, if it were open to the salt Sea towards the East, as it is to the West only, seeing Every thing naturally ingendreth his like: and then must it be like salt throughout, as all the seas are, in such like climate and elevation.

And therefore it seemeth that this Northeast sea is maintained by the river Ob, and such like fresshets, as

Omne simile
gignit sui
simile.

Mare Goticum, and Mare Mediterraneum, in the uppermost parts thereof by the rivers Nilus, Danubius, Neper, Tanais, &c.

9 Furthermore, if there were any such sea at that elevation, of like it should be alwaies frozen throughout (there being no tides to hinder it) because the extreme coldnes of the aire being in the uppermost part, and the extreme coldnesse of the earth in the bottome, the sea

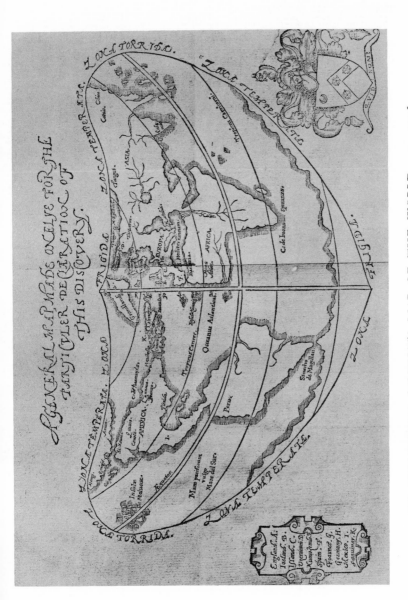

SIR HUMPHREY GILBERT'S MAP OF THE WORLD, A.D. 1576

there being but of small depth, whereby the one accidentall coldnesse doth meet with the other, and the Sunne not having his reflection so neere the Pole, but at very blunt angels, it can never be dissolved after it is frozen, notwithstanding the great length of their day: for that the sunne hath no heate at all in his light or beames, but proceeding onely by an accidentall reflection, which there wanteth in effect.

10 And yet if the Sunne were of sufficient force in that elevation, to prevaile against this ice, yet must it be broken before it can be dissolved, which cannot be but through the long continuance of the sunne above their Horizon, and by that time the Sommer would be so farre spent, and so great darkenes and cold ensue, that no man could be able to endure so cold, darke, and discomfortable a navigation, if it were possible for him then, and there to live.

11 Further, the ice being once broken, it must of force so drive with the windes and tides, that no ship can saile in those seas, seeing our Fishers of Island, and the New found land, are subject to danger through the great Islands of Ice which fleete in the Seas (to the sailers great danger) farre to the South of that presupposed passage.

12 And it cannot be that this Northeast passage should be any neerer the South, then before recited, for then it should cut off Ciremissi, & Turbi Tartari, with Uzesucani, Chisani, and others from the Continent of Asia, which are knowen to be adjoyning to Scythia, Tartaria, &c. with the other part of the same Continent.

And if there were any thorowe passage by the Northeast, yet were it to small ende and purpose for our traffique, because no shippe of great burden can Navigate in so shallow a Sea: and ships of small burden [III. 19.] are very unfit & unprofitable, especially towards the blustering North, to performe such a voyage.

[To proove

To proove that the Indians aforenamed, came only by the Northwest, which induceth a certaintie of our passage by experience.

Cap. 7.

IT is as likely that they came by the Northwest, as it is unlikely that they should come either by the Southeast, Southwest, Northeast, or from any other part of Africa or America, and therefore this Northwest passage having bene alreadie so many wayes proved, by disprooving of the others, &c. I shall the lesse neede in this place, to use many words otherwise then to conclude in this sort, That they came onely by the Northwest from England, having these many reasons to leade me thereunto.

1 First, the one halfe of the windes of the compasse might bring them by the Northwest, bearing alwayes betweene two sheats, with which kind of sayling the Indians are onely acquainted, not having any use of a bow line, or quarter winde, without the which no ship can possibly come either by the Southeast, Southwest or Northeast, having so many sundry Capes to double, whereunto are required such change and shift of windes.

True, both in ventis oblique flantibus, as also in ventis ex diametro spirantibus.

2 And it seemeth likely that they should come by the Northwest, because the coast whereon they were driven, lay East from this our passage, And all windes doe naturally drive a ship to an opposite point from whence it bloweth, not being otherwise guided by Arte, which the Indians do utterly want, & therefore it seemeth that they came directly through this our fret, which they might doe with one wind.

3 For if they had come by the Cape de buona Sperança, then must they (as aforesaid) have fallen upon the South parts of America.

4 And if by the fret of Magellan, then upon the coasts of Afrike, Spaine, Portugall, France, Ireland or England.

5 And if by the Northeast, then upon the coasts of Ceremissi, Tartarii, Lappia, Island, Terra de Labrador, &c. and upon these coasts (as aforesaid) they have never bene found.

So that by all likelihood they could never have come without shipwracke upon the coastes of Germanie, if they had first striken upon the coastes of so many countries, wanting both Arte and shipping to make orderly discovery, and altogether ignorant both in the Arte of Navigation, and also of the Rockes, Flats, Sands or Havens of those parts of the world, which in most of these places are plentifull.

6 And further it. seemeth very likely, that the inhabitants of the most part of those countries, by which they must have come any other way besides by the Northwest, being for the most part Anthropophagi, or men eaters, would have devoured them, slaine them, or (at the least wise) kept them as wonders for the gaze.

So that it plainely appeareth that those Indians (which as you have heard in sundry ages were driven by tempest upon the shore of Germanie) came onely through our Northwest passage. ·

7 Moreover, the passage is certainely prooved by a Navigation that a Portugall made, who passed through this fret, giving name to a Promontorie farre within the same, calling it after his owne name, Promontorium Corterialis, neere adjoyning unto Polisacus fluvius.

8 Also one Scolmus a Dane entred and passed a great part thereof.

9 Also there was one Salvaterra, a Gentleman of Victoria in Spaine, that came by chance out of the West Indias into Ireland, Anno 1568. who affirmed the Northwest passage from us to Cataia, constantly to be beleeved in America navigable. And further said in the presence of sir Henry Sidney (then lord Deputie of Ireland) in my hearing, that a Frier of Mexico, called Andrew Urdaneta, more then eight yeeres before

his then comming into Ireland, told him there, that he came from Mar del Sur into Germany through this Northwest passage, & shewed Salvaterra (at that time being then with him in Mexico) a Sea Card made by his owne experience and travell in that voyage, wherein was plainly set downe and described this Northwest passage, agreeing in all points with Ortelius mappe.

And further, this Frier tolde the king of Portugall (as he returned by that countrey homeward) that there was (of certainty) such a passage Northwest from England, and that he meant to publish the same: which done, the king most earnestly desired him not in any wise to disclose or make the passage knowen to any

[III. 20.]
The words of the king of Portugall, to Andro Urda- neta a Frier, touching the concealing of this Northwest passage from England to Cataia.

nation: For that (said the king) if England had knowledge and experience thereof, it would greatly hinder both the king of Spaine and me. This Frier (as Salvaterra reported) was the greatest Discoverer by sea, that hath bene in our age. Also Salvaterra being perswaded of this passage by the frier Urdaneta, and by the common opinion of the Spaniards inhabiting America, offered most willingly to accompanie me in this Discovery, which of like he would not have done if he had stood in doubt thereof.

And now as these moderne experiences cannot be impugned, so, least it might be objected that these things (gathered out of ancient writers, which wrote so many yeeres past) might serve litle to proove this

An objection.

Aristotle lib. de mundo, cap. 2. Berosus lib. 5.

passage by the North of America, because both America and India were to them then utterly unknowen: to remoove this doubt, let this suffise: That Aristotle (who was 300. yeeres before Christ) named Mare Indicum. Also Berosus (who lived 330 yeres before Christ) hath these words, Ganges in India. Also in the first chapter of Hester be these wordes, In the dayes of Assuerus which ruled from India to Aethiopia, which Assuerus lived 580 yeeres before Christ. Also Quintus Curtius (where he speaketh of the conquests of Alexander) mentioneth India. Also, Arianus, Philostratus, and Sidrach in his discourses of the warres of the king of Bactria, and of Garaab, who had the most part of India under his government. All which assureth us, that both India and Indians were knowen in those days.

These things considered, we may (in my opinion) not only assure our selves of this passage by the Northwest, but also that it is navigable both to come and go, as hath bene prooved in part and in all, by the experience of divers, as Sebastian Cabota, Corterialis, the three brethren above named, the Indians, and Urdaneta the Frier of Mexico, &c.

And yet notwithstanding all this, there be some that have a better hope of this passage to Cataia by the Northeast then by the West, whose reasons with my severall answeres ensue in the chapter following.

Certaine reasons alleaged for the prooving of a passage by the Northeast, before the Queenes Majestie, and certaine Lords of the Counsell, by Master Anthonie Jenkinson, with my severall answeres then used to the same.

Cap. 8.

BEcause you may understand as well those things alleaged against me, as what doth serve for my purpose, I have here added the reasons of Master Anthony Jenkinson a worthy gentleman, and a great traveller, who conceived a better hope of the passage to Cataia from us, to be by the Northeast, then by the Northwest.

He first said that he thought not to the contrary, but that there was a passage by the Northwest, according to mine opinion: but assured he was, that there might be found a navigable passage by the Northeast from England, to goe to all the East parts of the world, which he endevoured to proove three wayes.

The first was that he heard a Fisherman of Tartaria say in hunting the Morce, that he sayled very farre

The North-west passage assented unto.

The first reason.

towards the Southeast, finding no end of the Sea :
whereby he hoped a thorow passage to be that way.

The answer or resolution.

Whereunto I answered, that the Tartarians were a
barbarous people, and utterly ignorant in the Arte of
Navigation, not knowing the use of the Sea Card,
Compasse or Starre, which he confessed to be true : and
therfore they could not (said I) certainly know the
Southeast from the Northeast, in a wide sea, and a place
unknowen from the sight of the land.

Or if he sailed any thing neere the shore, yet he
(being ignorant) might be deceived by the doubling of
many points and Capes, and by the trending of the
land, albeit he kept continually alongst the shore.

And further, it might be that the poore Fisherman
through simplicitie thought that there was nothing that

Visus nonnunquam fallitur in suo objecto.

way but sea, because he saw no land : which proofe
(under correction) giveth small assurance of a Navigable
sea by the Northeast, to goe round about the world.
For that he judged by the eye onely, seeing we in this
our cleare aire doe account twentie miles a ken at Sea.

The second reason or allegation.

His second reason is, that there was an Unicornes
horne found upon the coast of Tartaria, which could
not come (said he) thither by any other meanes then
with the tides, through some fret in the Northeast of
Mare Glaciale, there being no Unicorne in any part of
Asia, saving in India and Cataia : which reason (in my
simple judgement) forceth as litle.

The answer or resolution.

First, it is doubtfull whether those barbarous Tartarians do know an Unicornes horne, yea, or no : and
if it were one, yet it is not credible that the Sea could
have driven it so farre, being of such nature that it will
not swimme.

[III. 21.]

Also the tides running too and fro, would have driven
it as farre backe with the ebbe, as it brought it forward
with the flood.

There is also a beast called Asinus Indicus (whose
horne most like it was) which hath but one horne like
an Unicorne in his forehead, whereof there is great

plenty in all the North parts therunto adjoyning, as in
Lappia, Noruegia, Finmarke, &c. as Jacobus Zieglerus
writeth in his historie of Scondia.

And as Albertus saieth, there is a fish which hath but
one horne in his forehead like to an Unicorne, and
therefore it seemeth very doubtfull both from whence
it came, and whether it were an Unicornes horne, yea,
or no.

His third and last reason was, that there came a con- *The third and*
tinuall streame or current through Mare Glaciale, of such *last reason or*
swiftnesse (as a Colmax told him) that if you cast any *assertion.*
thing therein, it would presently be carried out of sight
towards the West.

Whereunto I answered, that there doth the like from *The answer or*
Mæotis Palus, by Pontus Euxinus, Sinus Bosphorus, *resolution.*
and along the coast of Græcia, &c. As it is affirmed by
Contarenus, and divers others that have had experience
of the same: and yet that Sea lieth not open to any
maine Sea that way, but is maintained by freshets as by
Tanais, Danubius, &c.

In like maner is this current in Mare Glaciale increased and maintained by the Dwina, the river Ob, &c.

Now as I have here briefly recited the reasons alleaged,
to proove a passage to Cataia by the Northeast, with
my severall answeres thereunto: so will I leave it to
your judgement, to hope or dispaire of either at your
pleasure.

How that the passage by the Northwest is more
commodious for our traffique, then the other
by the East, if there were any such.

Cap. 9.

First, by the Northeast (if your windes doe not give
you a marvelous speedie & luckie passage) you are
in danger (being so neere the Pole) to be benighted
almost the one halfe of the yeere, and what danger that
were, to live so long comfortlesse, voide of light, (if the

cold killed you not) each man of reason or understanding may judge.

Some doubt of this.

2 Also Mangia, Quinzai, and the Moluccæ are neerer unto us by the Northwest, then by the Northeast, more then two five parts, which is almost by the halfe.

3 Also we may have by the West a yerely returne, it being at all times navigable, whereas you have but 4. moneths in the whole yeere to goe by the Northeast: the passage being at such elevation as it is formerly expressed, for it cannot be any neerer the South.

4 Furthermore, it cannot be finished without divers wintrings by the way, having no havens in any temperate climate to harbour in there: for it is as much as we can well saile from hence to S. Nicholas, in the trade of Moscovia, and returne in the navigable season of the yeere, & from S. Nicholas to Cerimissi Tartari, which stande at 80 degrees of the Septentrionall latitude, it is at the least 400 leagues, which amounteth scarce to the third part of the way, to the end of your voyage by the Northeast.

5 And yet after you have doubled this Cape, if then there might be found a navigable Sea to carie you Southeast according to your desire, yet can you not winter conveniently, until you come to 60 degrees, and to take up one degree running Southeast, you must saile 24 leagues and three foure parts, which amounteth to 495 leagues.

6 Furthermore, you may by the Northwest saile thither with all Easterly windes, and returne with any Westerly windes, whereas you must have by the Northeast sundry windes, and those proper, according to the lying of the coast and Capes, you shalbe inforced to double, which windes are not alwaies to be had, when they are looked for: whereby your journey should be greatly prolonged, and hardly endured so neere the Pole. As we are taught by sir Hugh Willoughbie, who was frozen to death farre neerer the South.

7 Moreover, it is very doubtfull, whether we should

long injoy that trade by the Northeast, if there were
any such passage that way, the commodities thereof once
knowen to the Moscovite, what privilege soever hee hath
granted, seeing pollicy with the masse of excessive gaine,
to the inriching (so greatly) of himselfe and all his
dominions would perswade him to presume the same,
having so great opportunitie to utter the commodities of
those countries by the Narve.

But by the Northwest, we may safely trade without
danger or annoyance of any prince living, Christian or
Heathen, it being out of all their trades.

8 Also the Queenes Majesties dominions are neerer [III. 22.]
the Northwest passage then any other great princes that
might passe that way, and both in their going and
returne, they must of necessitie succour themselves and
their ships upon some part of the same, if any tempestuous weather should happen.

Further, no princes navie of the world is able to in-
counter the Queenes Majesties navie, as it is at this present : and yet it should be greatly increased by the
traffike insuing upon this discoverie, for it is the long
voyages that increase and maintaine great shipping.

Now it seemeth necessarie to declare what commodities
would growe thereby, if all these things were, as we have
heretofore presupposed, and thought them to be : which
next adjoyning are briefly declared.

What commodities would ensue, this passage once discovered.

Cap. 10.

FIrst, it were the onely way for our princes, to possesse
the wealth of all the East parts (as they terme them)
of the world, which is infinite : as appeareth by the
experience of Alexander the great, in the time of his conquest of India, and other the East parts of the world,
alleaged by Quintus Curtius, which would be a great
advancement to our countrey, a wonderfull inriching to

our prince, and an unspeakable commoditie to all the inhabitants of Europe.

2 For through the shortnesse of the voyage, we should be able to sell all maner of merchandize, brought from thence, farre better cheape then either the Portugall or Spaniard doth or may do. And further, we should share with the Portugall in the East, & the Spaniard in the West, by trading to any part of America, thorow Mar del Sur, where they can no maner of way offend us.

3 Also we might sayle to divers very rich countreys, both civill and others, out of both their jurisdictions, trades and traffikes, where there is to be found great abundance of golde, silver, precious stones, cloth of gold, silkes, all maner of spices, grocery wares, and other kinds of merchandize of an inestimable price, which both the Spaniard and Portugall, through the length of their journies, cannot well attaine unto.

4 Also we might inhabite some part of those countryes, and settle there such needy people of our countrey, which now trouble the common wealth, and through want here at home are inforced to commit outragious offences, whereby they are dayly consumed with the gallowes.

5 Moreover, we might from all the aforesaid places have a yeerely returne, inhabiting for our staple some convenient place of America, about Sierra Nevada, or some other part, whereas it shal seeme best for the shortning of the voyage.

6 Beside uttering of our countrey commodities, which the Indians, &c. much esteeme : as appeareth in Hester, where the pompe is expressed of the great king of India, Assuerus, who matched the coloured clothes, wherewith his houses and tents were apparelled, with gold and silver, as part of his greatest treasure : not mentioning either velvets, silkes, cloth of gold, cloth of silver, or such like, being in those countreyes most plentifull : whereby it plainly appeareth in what great estimation they would have the clothes of this our countrey, so

that there would be found a farre better vent for them by this meanes, then yet this realme ever had: and that without depending either upon France, Spaine, Flanders, Portugall, Hamborow, Emden, or any other part of Europe.

7 Also, here we shall increase both our ships and mariners, without burthening of the state.

8 And also have occasion to set poore mens children to learne handie craftes, and thereby to make trifles and such like, which the Indians and those people do much esteeme: by reason whereof, there should be none occasion to have our countrey combred with loiterers, vagabonds, and such like idle persons.

All these commodities would grow by following this our discovery, without injury done to any Christian prince, by crossing them in any of their used trades, whereby they might take any just occasion of offence.

Thus have I briefly shewed you some part of the grounds of mine opinion, trusting that you will no longer judge me fantasticke in this matter: seeing I have conceived no vaine hope of this voyage, but am perswaded thereunto by the best Cosmographers of our age, the same being confirmed both by reason and certaine experiences.

Also this discovery hath bene divers times heretofore by others both offered, attempted, and performed.

It hath bene offered by Stephan Gomes unto Carolus the fift Emperour, in the yeere of our Lord God 1527, [III. 23.] as Alphonso Ullva testifieth in the story of Carolus life: who would have set him forth in it (as the story mentioneth) if the great want of money, by reason of his long warres had not caused him to surcease the same.

And the king of Portugall fearing least the Emperour would have persevered in this his enterprise, gave him to leave the matter unattempted, the summe of 350000 crownes: and it is to be thought that the king of Portugall would not have given to the Emperour such summes of money for egges in mooneshine.

This discovery offered.

*This discovery
attempted.*

It hath bene attempted by Sebastian Cabota in the time of king Henry the seventh, by Corterialis the Portugall, and Scolmus the Dane.

*This discovery
performed.*

And it hath bene performed by three brethren, the Indians aforesaid, and by Urdaneta the Frier of Mexico.

Also divers have offered the like unto the French king, who hath sent two or three times to have discovered the same: The discoverers spending and consuming their victuals in searching the gulfes and bayes betweene Florida and Terra de Labrador, whereby the yce is broken to the after commers.

So that the right way may now easily be found out in short time: and that with litle jeoperdie and lesse expences.

For America is discovered so farre towardes the North as Cape Frio, which is at 62 degrees, and that part of Grondland next adjoyning is known to stand but at 72 degrees. So that wee have but 10 degrees to saile North & South, to put the world out of doubt hereof: and it is likely that the king of Spaine, and the king of Portugall would not have sit out all this while, but that they are sure to possesse to themselves all that trade they now use, and feare to deale in this discovery, least the Queenes Majestie having so good opportunitie, and finding the commoditie which thereby might ensue to the common wealth, would cut them off, and enjoy the whole traffique to her selfe, and thereby the Spaniards and Portugals, with their great charges, should beate the bush, and other men catch the birds: which thing they foreseeing, have commanded that no pilot of theirs upon paine of death, should seeke to discover to the Northwest, or plat out in any Sea card any thorow passage that way by the Northwest.

*The labour of
this discoverie
shortned by
other mens
travell.*

*Why ye kings
of Spaine and
Portugal
would not
persever in
this discovery.*

Now, and if you will indifferently compare the hope that remaineth, to animate me to this enterprise, with those likelihoods which Columbus alleaged before Ferdinando the king of Castilia, to proove that there were such Islands in the West Ocean, as were after by him and others discovered to the great commodity of Spaine and all the world: you will thinke then this Northwest passage to be most worthy travell therein.

For Columbus had none of the West Islands set foorth unto him, either in globe or card, neither yet once mentioned of any writer (Plato excepted, and the commentaries upon the same) from 942 yeeres before Christ, untill that day.

Moreover, Columbus himselfe had neither seene America nor any other of the Islands about it, neither, understood he of them by the report of any other that had seene them, but only comforted himselfe with this hope, that the land had a beginning where the Sea had an ending: for as touching that which the Spaniards doe write of a Biscaine, which should have taught him the way thither, it is thought to be imagined of them, to deprive Columbus of his honour, being none of their countrey man, but a stranger borne.

And if it were true of the Biscaine, yet did he but rove at the matter, or (at the least) gathered the knowledge of it, by conjectures onely.

And albeit my selfe have not seene this passage or any part thereof, but am ignorant of it as touching experience (as Columbus was before his attempt made) yet have I both the report, relation, and authoritie of divers most credible men, which have both seene and passed through some and every part of this discovery, besides sundry reasons for my assurance thereof: all which Columbus wanted.

These things considered, & indifferently weighed togither, with the wonderfull commodities which this discovery may bring, especially to this realme of England: I must needes conclude with learned Baptista Ramusius, and divers other learned men, who said, that this discovery hath bene reserved for some noble prince or woorthie man, thereby to make himselfe rich, and the world happie: desiring you to accept in good part this briefe and simple discourse, written in haste, which if

I may perceive that it shall not sufficiently satisfie you in this behalfe, I will then impart unto you a large discourse, which I have written onely of this discovery.

And further, because it sufficeth not only to know that such a thing there is, without abilitie to performe the same, I wil at leasure make you partaker of another simple discourse of navigation, wherein I have not a litle travelled, to make my selfe as sufficient to bring these things to effect, as I have bene readie to offer my selfe therein.

And therein I have devised to amend the errors of usuall sea cards, whose common fault is, to make the degrees of longitude in every latitude of one like bignesse.

And have also devised therein a Spherical instrument, with a compasse of variation for the perfect knowing of the longitude.

And a precise order to pricke the sea card, together with certaine infallible rules for the shortning of any discovery, to know at the first entring of any fret, whether it lie open to the Ocean more wayes then one, how farre soever the sea stretcheth it selfe into the land.

Desiring you hereafter never to mislike with me, for the taking in hande of any laudable and honest enterprise: for if through pleasure or idlenesse we purchase shame, the pleasure vanisheth, but the shame remaineth for ever.

And therefore to give me leave without offence, alwayes to live and die in this mind, That he is not worthy to live at all, that for feare, or danger of death, shunneth his countries service, and his owne honour: seeing death is inevitable, and the fame of vertue immortall. Wherefore in this behalfe, Mutare vel timere sperno.

[III. 24.] (margin)

Pereas qui umbras times. (margin)

Certaine other reasons, or arguments to proove
a passage by the Northwest, learnedly written
by M. Richard Willes Gentleman.

FOure famous wayes there be spoken of to those
fruitfull and wealthie Islands, which wee doe usually
call Moluccaes, continually haunted for gaine, and dayly
travelled for riches therein growing. These Islands,
although they stand East from the Meridian, distant
almost halfe the length of the worlde, in extreame heate,
under the Equinoctiall line, possessed of Infidels and
Barbarians : yet by our neighbours great abundance of
wealth there is painefully sought in respect of the voyage
deerely bought, and from thence dangerously brought
home unto us. Our neighbours I call the Portugals in
comparison of the Molucchians for neerenesse unto us,
for like situation Westward as we have, for their usuall
trade with us, for that the farre Southeasterlings doe
knowe this part of Europe by no other name then
Portugall, not greatly acquainted as yet with the other
Nations thereof. Their voyage is very well understood
of all men, and the Southeasterne way round about *1 By the Southeast.*
Afrike by the Cape of Good hope more spoken of, better
knowen and travelled, then that it may seeme needfull
to discourse thereof any further.

The second way lyeth Southwest, betweene the West *2 By the Southwest.*
India or South America, and the South continent, through
that narrow straight where Magellan first of all men that
ever we doe read of, passed these latter yeeres, leaving
thereunto therefore his name. The way no doubt the
Spaniardes would commodiously take, for that it lyeth
neere unto their dominions there, could the Easterne
current and levant windes as easily suffer them to returne, *This is an er-*
as speedily therwith they may be carried thither : for *rour.*
the which difficultie, or rather impossibility of striving
against the force both of winde and streame, this passage
is litle or nothing used, although it be very well knowen.

A.D.
1576.

3 By the Northeast.

   The third way by the Northeast, beyond all Europe and Asia, that worthy and renowmed knight sir Hugh Willoughbie sought to his perill, enforced there to ende his life for colde, congealed and frozen to death. And truely this way consisteth rather in the imagination of Geographers, then allowable either in reason, or approved by experience, as well it may appeare by the dangerous

Ortel. tab. Asiæ 3.

trending of the Scythish Cape set by Ortelius under the 80 degree North, by the unlikely sailing in that Northerne sea alwayes clad with yce and snow, or at the least continually pestred therewith, if happily it be at any time dissolved: besides bayes and shelfes, the water waxing more shallow toward the East, that we say nothing of the foule mists and darke fogs in the cold clime, of the litle power of the Sunne to cleare the aire, of the uncomfortable nights, so neere the Pole, five moneths long.

4 By the Northeast.

   A fourth way to go unto these aforesaid happy Islands Moluccæ sir Humphrey Gilbert a learned and valiant knight discourseth of at large in his new passage to Cathayo. The enterprise of it selfe being vertuous, the fact must doubtlesse deserve high praise, and whensoever it shal be finished, the fruits thereof cannot be smal: where vertue is guide, there is fame a follower, & fortune a companion. But the way is dangerous, the passage doubtfull, the voiage not throughly knowen, and therefore gainesaid by many, after this maner.

Ob. 1.
[III. 25.]

   First, who can assure us of any passage rather by the Northwest, then by the Northeast? doe not both wayes lye in equall distance from the North Pole? Stand not the North Capes of eyther continent under like elevation? Is not the Ocean sea beyond America farther distant from our Meridian by 30. or 40. degrees West, then the extreame poyntes of Cathayo Eastward, if Ortelius

In Theatro.

generall Carde of the world be true? In the Northeast that noble Knight Syr Hugh Willoughbie perished for colde: and can you then promise a passenger any better happe by the Northwest? Who hath gone for triall sake at any time this way out of Europe to Cathayo?

Ob. 2.

If you seeke the advise herein of such as make profession in Cosmographie, Ptolome the father of Geographie, and his eldest children, will answere by their
mappes with a negative, concluding most of the Sea
within the land, and making an ende of the world Northward, neere the 63. degree. The same opinion, when
learning chiefly florished, was received in the Romanes
time, as by their Poets writings it may appeare : tibi
serviat ultima Thyle, said Virgil, being of opinion, that
Island was the extreme part of the world habitable toward
the North. Joseph Moletius an Italian, and Mercator
a Germaine, for knowledge men able to be compared with
the best Geographers of our time, the one in his halfe
Spheres of the whole world, the other in some of his
great globes, have continued the West Indies land, even
to the North Pole, and consequently, cut off all passage
by sea that way.

The same doctors, Mercator in other of his globes
and mappes, Moletius in his sea Carde, neverthelesse
doubting of so great continuance of the former continent,
have opened a gulfe betwixt the West Indies and the
extreame Northerne land : but such a one, that either
is not to be travelled for the causes in the first objection
alledged, or cleane shut up from us in Europe by
Groenland : the South ende whereof Moletius maketh
firme land with America, the North part continent with
Lappeland and Norway.

Thirdly, the greatest favourers of this voyage can not *Ob.* 3.
denie, but that if any such passage be, it lieth subject
unto yce and snow for the most part of the yeere,
whereas it standeth in the edge of the frostie Zone.
Before the Sunne hath warmed the ayre, and dissolved
the yce, eche one well knoweth that there can be no
sailing : the yce once broken through the continuall
abode the sunne maketh a certaine season in those parts,
how shall it be possible for so weake a vessel as a shippe
is, to holde out amid whole Islands, as it were of yce
continually beating on eche side, and at the mouth of

that gulfe, issuing downe furiously from the north, and safely to passe, when whole mountaines of yce and snow shall be tumbled downe upon her?

Well, graunt the West Indies not to continue continent unto the Pole, grant there be a passage betweene these two lands, let the gulfe lie neerer us then commonly in cardes we finde it set, namely, betweene the 61. and 64. degrees north, as Gemma Frisius in his mappes and globes imagineth it, and so left by our countryman Sebastian Cabot in his table which the Earle of Bedford hath at Cheinies: Let the way be voyde of all difficulties, yet doeth it not follow that wee have free passage to Cathayo. For examples sake: You may trend all Norway, Finmarke, and Lappeland, and then bowe Southward to Saint Nicholas in Moscovia: you may likewise in the Mediterranean Sea fetch Constantinople, and the mouth of Tanais: yet is there no passage by Sea through Moscovia into Pont Euxine, now called Mare Maggiore. Againe, in the aforesaid Mediterranean sea, we saile to Alexandria in Egypt, the Barbarians bring their pearle and spices from the Moluccaes up the Red sea or Arabian gulph to Sues, scarcely three dayes journey from the aforesayd haven: yet have wee no way by sea from Alexandria to the Moluccaes, for that Isthmos or litle straight of land betweene the two seas. In like maner although the Northerne passage be free at 61 degrees of latitude, and the West Ocean beyond America, usually called Mar del Zur, knowen to be open at 40. degrees elevation from the Island Japan, yea three hundred leagues Northerly above Japan: yet may there be land to hinder the thorow passage that way by Sea, as in the examples aforesaid it falleth out, Asia and America there being joyned together in one continent. Ne can this opinion seeme altogether frivolous unto any one that diligently peruseth our Cosmographers doings. Josephus Moletius is of that minde, not onely in his plaine Hemispheres of the world, but also in his Sea card. The French Geographers in like maner be of the same opinion, as by their Mappe cut out in forme of a Hart you may perceive: as though the West Indies were part of Asia. Which sentence well agreeth with that old conclusion in the Schooles: Quicquid præter Africam & Europam est, Asia est, Whatsoever land doeth neither apperteine unto Afrike nor to Europe, is part of Asia.

Furthermore it were to small purpose to make so long, *Ob. 5.* so painefull, so doubtfull a voyage by such a new found way, if in Cathayo you should neither bee suffered to land for silkes and silver, nor able to fetch the Molucca spices and pearle for piracie in those Seas. Of a law denying all Aliens to enter into China, and forbidding all the inhabiters under a great penaltie to let in any stranger into those countryes, shall you reade in [III. 26.] the report of Galeotto Perera there imprisoned with other Portugals: as also in the Japonish letters, how for that cause the worthy traveller Xavierus bargained with a Barbarian Merchant for a great summe of pepper to be brought into Canton, a port in China. The great and dangerous piracie used in those Seas no man can be ignorant of, that listeth to reade the Japonish and East Indian historie.

Finally, all this great labour would be lost, all these *Ob. 6.* charges spent in vaine, if in the ende our travellers might not be able to returne againe, and bring safely home into their owne native countrey that wealth & riches, which they in forrein regions with adventure of goods, & danger of their lives have sought for. By the Northeast there is no way, the Southeast passage the Portugals doe hold as the Lords of those Seas. At ye Southwest Magellans experience hath partly taught us, and partly we are persuaded by reason, how the Easterne current striketh so furiously on that straight, and falleth with such force into that narrow gulph, that hardly any ship can returne that way into our West Ocean out of Mar del Zur. The which if it be true, as truely it is, then wee may say that the aforesayd Easterne current or levant course of waters continually following after the heavenly motions, looseth not altogether his force, but is doubled rather by an other current from out the Northeast, in the passage betweene America and the North land, whither it is of necessity caryed: having none other way to maintaine it selfe in circular motion, & consequently the force and fury thereof to be no lesse in the straight of Anian, where it striketh South into Mar del Zur, beyond America (if any such straight of Sea there be) then in Magellans fret, both straights being of like bredth: as in Belognine Zalterius table of new France, and in Don Diego Hermano de Toledo his Card for navigation in that region we doe finde precisely set downe.

Neverthelesse to approove that there lyeth a way to Cathayo at the Northwest from out of Europe, we have experience, namely of three brethren that went that journey, as Gemma Frisius recordeth, and left a name unto that straight, whereby now it is called Fretum trium fratrum. We doe reade againe of a Portugall that passed this straight, of whom Master Frobisher speaketh, that was imprisoned therefore many yeeres in Lisbone, to verifie the olde Spanish proverbe, I suffer for doing well. Likewise Andrew Urdaneta a Fryer of Mexico came out of Mar del Zur this way into Germanie: his Carde (for he was a great Discoverer) made by his owne experience and travell in that voyage, hath bene seene by Gentlemen of good credite.

Cic. 1. de
orat. Arist.
pri. Metaph.

Now if the observation and remembrance of things breedeth experience, and of experience proceedeth arte, and the certaine knowledge we have in all faculties, as the best Philosophers that ever were doe affirme: truely the voyage of these aforesayd travellers that have gone out of Europe into Mar del Zur, and returned thence at the Northwest, do most evidently conclude that way to be navigable, and that passage free. So much the

Lib. 1. Geog.
Cap. 2.

more we are so to thinke, for that the first principle and chiefe ground in all Geographie, as Ptolome saith, is the history of travell, that is, reports made by travellers skilful in Geometrie and Astronomie, of all such things in their journey as to Geographie doe belong. It onely then remaineth, that we now answere to those arguments that seemed to make against this former conclusion.

The first objection is of no force, that generall table *Sol.* 1. of the world set forth by Orteli̯us or Mercator, for it greatly skilleth not, being unskilfully drawen for that point: as manifestly it may appeare unto any one that conferreth the same with Gemma Frisius his universall Mappe, with his round quartered carde, with his globe, with Sebastian Cabota his table, and Ortelius his generall mappe alone, worthily preferred in this case before all Mercator & Ortelius other doings: for that Cabota was not onely a skilful Sea man, but a long traveller, and such a one as entred personally that straight, sent by king Henry the seventh to make this aforesayd Discoverie, as in his owne discourse of navigation you may reade in his carde drawen with his owne hand, that the mouth of the Northwesterne straight lyeth neere the 318. Meridian, betweene 61. and 64. degrees in the elevation, continuing the same bredth about 10. degrees West, where it openeth Southerly more and more, untill it come under the tropicke of Cancer, and so runneth into Mar del Zur, at the least 18. degrees more in bredth there, then it was where it first began: otherwise I could as well imagine this passage to be more unlikely then the voyage to Moscovia, and more impossible then it for the farre situation and continuance thereof in the frostie clime: as now I can affirme it to be very possible and most likely in comparison thereof, for that it neither coasteth so farre North as the Moscovian passage doeth, neither is this straight so long as that, before it bow downe Southerly towardes the Sunne againe.

The second argument concludeth nothing. Ptolome *Sol.* 2. knew not what was above sixteene degrees South beyond the Equinoctiall line, he was ignorant of all passages Northward from the elevation of 63. degrees: he knewe no Ocean sea beyond Asia, yet have the [III. 27.] Portugals trended the cape of Good hope at the South point of Afrike, and travelled to Japan an Island in the East Ocean, betweene Asia & America: our merchants in the time of king Edward the sixt discovered the Moscovian passage farther North then Thyle, & shewed Groenland not to be continent with Lappeland & Norway: the like our Northwesterne travellers have done, declaring by their navigation that way, the ignorance of all Cosmographers that either doe joyne Groenland with America, or continue the West Indies with that frosty region under the north pole. As for Virgil he sang according to the knowledge of men in his time, as an other Poet did of the hot Zone.

Ovid. 1.
Meta.

Quarum quæ media est, non est habitabilis æstu. Imagining, as most men then did, Zonam torridam, the hot Zone to be altogether dishabited for heat, though presently wee know many famous and woorthy kingdomes and cities in that part of the earth, and the Island of S. Thomas neere Æthiopia, & the wealthy Islands for the which chiefly all these voyages are taken in hand, to be inhabited even under the equinoctiall line.

Sol. 3.

To answere the third objection, besides Cabota and all other travellers navigations, the onely credit of M. Frobisher may suffice, who lately through all these Islands of ice, and mountaines of snow, passed that way, even beyond the gulfe that tumbleth downe from the North, and in some places though he drewe one inch thicke ice, as he returning in August did, yet came he home safely againe.

Sol 4.

The fourth argument is altogether frivolous & vaine, for neither is there any isthmos or strait of land betweene America and Asia, ne can these two landes joyntly be one continent. The first part of my answere is manifestly allowed of by Homer, whom that excellent

Geographer Strabo followeth, yeelding him in this facultie the price. The authour of that booke likewise περὶ κόσμου to Alexander, attributed unto Aristotle, is of the same opinion that Homer and Strabo be of, in two or three places. Dionisius in ὀικουμένης περιήγησι hath this verse ὧτως ὠκεανός περιδέδρομε γαἰαν ἅπασαν. So doth the Ocean Sea runne round about the worlde : speaking onely of Europe, Afrike and Asia, as then Asia was travelled and knowen. With these Doctours may *Note.* you joyne Pomponius Mela. cap. 2. lib. I. Plinius lib. 2. cap. 67. and Pius 2. cap. 2. in his description of Asia. All the which writers doe no lesse confirme the whole Easterne side of Asia to be compassed about with the sea, then Plato doeth affirme in Timæo, under the name Atlantis, the West Indies to be an Island, as in a special discourse thereof R. Eden writeth, agreeable *RichardEden.* unto the sentence of Proclus, Marsilius Ficinus, and others. Out of Plato it is gathered that America is an Island. Homer, Strabo, Aristotle, Dionysius, Mela, Plinie, Pius 2. affirme the continent of Asia, Afrike, & Europe, to be environed with the Ocean. I may therfore boldly say (though later intelligences therof had we none at all) that Asia & the West Indies be not tied together by any Isthmos or straight of land, contrary to the opinion of some new Cosmographers, by whom doubtfully this matter hath bin brought in controversie. And thus much for the first part of my answere unto the fourth objection.

The second part, namely that America and Asia cannot be one continent, may thus be proved, κατα *Lib. 2. Me-* τὴν τῆς γῆς κοιλότητα ῥἐι καὶ τῶν ποτάμων τὸ πλῆθος. The *teor. cap. 1.* most Rivers take downe that way their course, where the earth is most hollow and deepe, writeth Aristotle : and the Sea (sayth he in the same place) as it goeth further, so is it found deeper. Into what gulfe doe the Moscovian rivers Onega, Duina, Ob, powre out their streames Northward out of Moscovia into the sea ? Which way doeth that sea strike ? The South is maine

land, the Easterne coast waxeth more and more shalow:
from the North, either naturally, because that part of the
earth is higher Aristot. 2 Met. cap. 1. or of necessitie,
for that the forcible influence of some Northerne starres
causeth the earth there to shake off the Sea, as some
Philosophers doe thinke: or finally for the great store
of waters engendred in that frostie and colde climate, that
the bankes are not able to holde them. Alber. in 2.
Meteor. cap. 6. From the North, I say, continually
falleth downe great abundance of water. So that this
Northeasterne currant must at the length abruptly bow
toward us South on the West side of Finmarke and
Norway: or else strike downe Southwest above Groneland, or betwixt Groneland and Iseland, into the Northwest straight we speake of, as of congruence it doeth,
if you marke the situation of that Region, and by the
report of M. Frobisher experience teacheth us. And M.
Frobisher the further he travailed in the former passage,
as he tolde me, the deeper alwayes he found the Sea.
Lay you now the summe hereof together. The rivers
runne where the chanels are most hollow, the sea in
taking his course waxeth deeper, the Sea waters fall continually from the North Southward, the Northeasterne
current striketh downe into the straight we speake of,
and is there augmented with whole mountaines of yce
and snowe falling downe furiously out from the land

*Plin. lib. 2.
cap. 67.*

under the North pole. Where store of water is, there
is it a thing impossible to want Sea, where Sea not onely
doeth not want, but waxeth deeper, there can be discovered no land. Finally, whence I pray you came the

[III 28.]

contrary tide, that M. Frobisher mette withall after that
he had sailed no small way in that passage, if there bee
any Isthmos or straight of land betwixt the aforesayd
Northwesterne gulfe, and Mar del Zur, to joyne Asia
and America together? That conclusion frequented in
scholes Quicquid præter, &c. was meant of the partes
of the world then knowen, and so is it of right to be
understood.

The fift objection requireth for answere wisedome and
policie in the travailer, to winne the Barbarians favour
by some good meanes: and so to arme and strengthen
himselfe, that when he shal have the repulse in one coast,
he may safely travaile to an other, commodiously taking
his convenient times, and discreetely making choise of
them with whom hee will throughly deale. To force a
violent entry, would for us Englishmen be very hard,
considering the strength and valour of so great a Nation,
farre distant from us, and the attempt thereof might be
most perillous unto the doers, unlesse their part were
very good.

Touching their lawes against strangers, you shall reade
neverthelesse in the same relations of Galeotto Perera,
that the Cathaian king is woont to graunt free accesse
unto all forreiners that trade into his Countrey for Marchandise, and a place of libertie for them to remaine in:
as the Moores had, untill such time as they had brought
the Loutea or Lieutenant of that coast to bee a circum-
cised Saracene: wherefore some of them were put to the
sword, the rest were scattered abroad: at Fuquien a great
citie in China, certaine of them are yet this day to be
seene. As for the Japans they be most desirous to be
acquainted with strangers. The Portingals though they
were straitly handled there at the first, yet in the ende
they found great favour at the Prince his hands, insomuch
that the Loutea or president that misused them was therefore put to death. The rude Indian Canoa halleth those
seas, the Portingals, the Saracenes, and Moores travaile
continually up and downe that reach from Japan to China,
from China to Malacca, from Malacca to the Moluccaes:
and shall an Englishman, better appointed then any of
them all (that I say no more of our Navie) feare to saile
in that Ocean? What seas at all doe want piracie?
what Navigation is there voyde of perill?

To the last argument. Our travailers neede not to
seeke their returne by the Northeast, neither shall they
be constrained, except they list, either to attempt

Magellans straight at the Southwest, or to be in danger
of the Portingals for the Southeast: they may returne
by the Northwest, that same way they doe goe foorth,
as experience hath shewed.

The reason alleadged for proofe of the contrary may
be disproved after this maner. And first it may be called
in controversie, whether any current continually be forced
by the motion of Primum mobile, round about the world,
or no ? For learned men doe diversly handle that question. The naturall course of all waters is downeward,
wherefore of congruence they fall that way where they
finde the earth most lowe and deepe: in respect whereof,

it was erst sayd, the seas doe strike from the Northren
landes Southerly. Violently the seas are tossed and
troubled divers wayes with the windes, encreased and
diminished by the course of the Moone, hoised up &
downe through the sundry operations of the Sunne and
the starres: finally, some be of opinion, that the seas be
caried in part violently about the world, after the dayly
motion of the highest moveable heaven, in like maner as

the elements of ayre and fire, with the rest of the heavenly
spheres, are from the East unto the West. And this
they doe call their Easterne current, or levant streame.
Some such current may not be denied to be of great force
in the hot Zone, for the neerenesse thereof unto the
centre of the Sunne, and blustring Easterne windes
violently driving the seas Westward: howbeit, in the
temperate climes, the Sunne being further off, & the
windes more divers, blowing as much from the North,
the West and South, as from the East, this rule doeth
not effectually withholde us from travailing Eastward,
neither be we kept ever backe by the aforesaid Levant
windes and streame. But in Magellans streight wee are
violently driven backe Westward: Ergo, through the
Northwesterne straight or Anian frette shall we not be
able to returne Eastward ? It followeth not. The first,
for that the northwesterne straight hath more sea roome
at the least by one hundreth English myles, then

Magellans frette hath, the onely want whereof causeth all narrow passages generally to be most violent. So would I say in the Anian gulfe, if it were so narrow as Don Diego and Zalterius have painted it out, any returne that way to bee full of difficulties, in respect of such streightnesse thereof, not for the neerenesse of the Sunne, or Easterne windes, violently forcing that way any levant streame: But in that place there is more sea roome by many degrees, if the Cardes of Cabota, and Gemma Frisius, and that which Tramezine imprinted, be true.

And hitherto reason see I none at all, but that I may as well give credite unto their doings, as to any of the rest. It must be Peregrinationis historia, that is, true *Lib.* 1. *Geog.* reportes of skilfull travailers, as Ptolome writeth, that in *Cap.* 2. such controversies of Geographie must put us out of doubt. Ortelius in his universall tables, in his particular [III. 29.] Mappes of the West Indies, of all Asia, of the Northren kingdomes, of the East Indies, Mercator in some of his globes, and generall Mappes of the world, Moletius in his universall table of the Globe divided, in his sea Carde, and particuler tables of the East Indies, Zalterius, and Don Diego, with Ferdinando Bertely, and others, doe so much differ from Gemma Frisius and Cabota, among themselves, and in divers places from themselves, concerning the divers situation and sundry limits of America, that one may not so rashly, as truely surmise, these men either to be ignorant in those points touching the aforesaid region, or that the Mappes they have given out unto the world, were collected onely by them, and never of their owne drawing.

[The first

The first Voyage of M. Martine Frobisher, to the Northwest, for the search of the straight or passage to China, written by Christopher Hall, Master in the Gabriel, and made in the yeere of our Lord 1576.

He 7. of June being Thursday, the two Barks, viz. the Gabriel, and the ‖ Michael & our Pinnesse set saile at Ratcliffe, and bare down to Detford, and there we ancred: the cause was, that our Pinnesse burst her boultsprit, and foremast aboard of a ship that rode at Detford, else wee meant to have past that day by the Court then at Grenewich.

The 8. day being Friday, about 12 of the clocke we wayed at Detford, and set saile all three of us, and bare downe by the Court, where we shotte off our ordinance and made the best shew we could: Her Majestie beholding the same, commended it, and bade us farewell, with shaking her hand at us out of the window. Afterward shee sent a Gentleman aboord of us, who declared that her Majestie had good liking of our doings, and thanked us for it, and also willed our Captaine to come the next day to the Court to take his leave of her.

The same day towards night M. Secretarie Woolly came aboorde of us, and declared to the company, that her Majestie had appointed him to give them charge to be obedient, and diligent to their Captaine, and governours in all things, and wished us happie successe.

The 12. day being over against Gravesend, by the castle or blockehouse, we observed the latitude, which was 51. degrees 33. min. And in that place the variation of the Compasse is 11. degrees and a halfe.

Faire Island. The 24. day at 2. of the clocke after noone, I had sight of Faire yle, being from us 6. leagues North and by East, and when I brought it Northwest and by North, it did rise at the Southermost ende with a litle hommocke, and swampe in the middes.

The 25. day from 4. to 8. a clocke in the forenoone, the winde at Northwest and by North a fresh gale, I cast about to the Westward, the Southermost head of Shot- *Shotland.* land called Swinborne head Northnorthwest from me, and the land of Faire yle, West Southwest from me. I sailed directly to the North head of that said land, sounding as I ranne in, having 60. 50. and 40. fathoms, and gray redde shels: and within halfe a mile of that Island, there are 36. fathoms, for I sailed to that Island to see whether there were any roadesteede for a Northwest winde, and I found by my sounding hard rockes, and foule ground, and deepe water, within two cables length of the shoare, 28. fathome, and so did not ancre but plied to and fro with my foresaile, and mizen till it was a high water under the Island. The tide setteth there Northwest and Southeast: the flood setteth Southeast, and the ebbe Northwest.

The 26. day having the winde at South a faire gale, sayling from Faire yle to Swinborne head, I did observe the latitude, the Island of Fowlay being West Northwest from me 6. leagues, and Swinborne head East southeast from me, I found my *elevation to be 37. degr. and my ** By elevation* declination 22. degr. 46. min. So that my latitude was *he meaneth* 59. degr. 46. min. At that present being neere to *the sunne from* Swinborne head, having a leake which did trouble us, as *the zenith.* also to take in fresh water, I plyed roome with a sound, which is called S. Tronions, and there did ancre in seven *S. Tronions.* fathoms water, and faire sande. You have comming in the sounds mouth in the entring 17. 15. 12. 10. 9. 8. and 7. fathoms, and the sound lyeth in North northwest, and there we roade to a West sunne, & stopped our leake, and having refreshed our selves with water, at a North northwest sunne, I set saile from S. Tronions the winde at South Southest, and turned out till wee were cleare of the sound, and so sailed West to go cleare of the Island of Fowlay. And running off toward Fowlay, *Fowlay Island.*

[III. 30.]

I sounded, having fiftie fathome, and streamie ground, and also I sounded Fowlay being North from mee one league off that Islande, having fiftie fathome at the South head, and streamie ground, like broken otmell, and one shell being redde and white like mackerell.

Latitude 59. *deg.* 59. *min. Here they begin to saile West and by North.*

The 27. day at a South sunne I did observe the latitude, the Island of Fowlay being from me two leagues East Northeast: I found my selfe to be in latitude 59. degrees, 59. min. truly observed, the winde at South Southwest: I sailed West and by North.

From 12. to foure a clocke afternoone, the wind at South, a faire gale the shippe sailed West and by North 6. leagues, and at the ende of this watch, I sounded having 60. fathome, with little stones and shels, the Island from us 8. leagues East.

July the first.

The first of July, from 4. to 8. a clocke, wee sailed West 4. glasses 4. leagues, and at that present we had so much winde that we spooned afore the sea Southwest 2. leagues.

3.

The 3. day we found our Compasse to bee varied one point to the Westwards: this day from 4. to 8. a clocke we sailed West and by North 6. leagues.

The Compasse varying Westwards one point.

From 8. to 12. a clocke at noone West and by North 4. leagues. At that present I found our Compasse to be varied 11. deg. and one 4. part to the Westwards, which is one point.

11.

The Island of Friseland.

The 11 day at a Southeast sunne we had sight of the land of Friseland bearing from us West northwest 16. leagues, and rising like pinacles of steeples, and all covered with snowe. I found my selfe in 61. degr. of latitude. Wee sailed to the shoare and could finde no ground at 150. fathoms, we hoised out our boate, and the Captaine with 4. men rowed to the shoare to get on land, but the land lying full of yce, they could not get on land, and so they came aboord againe: We had much adoe to get cleare of the yce by reason of the fogge. Yet from Thursday 8. a clocke in the morning to Friday at noone we sailed Southwest 20. leagues.

The 18. day at a Southwest sunne I found the sunne
to be elevated 33. deg. And at a Southsoutheast sunne
40. deg. So I observed it till I found it at the highest,
and then it was elevated 52. deg. I judged the variation
of the Compasse to be 2. points and a halfe to the
Westward.

The variation of the needle, two points and a halfe to the West.

The 21. day we had sight of a great drift of yce,
seeming a firme lande, and we cast Westward to be
cleare of it.

A great drift of yce.

The 26. we had sight of a land of yce: the latitude
was 62. degrees, and two minutes.

The latitude of 62. degrees 2. min.

The 28. day in the morning was very foggie: but at
the clearing up of the fogge, wee had sight of lande,
which I supposed to be Labrador, with great store of
yce about the land: I ranne in towards it, and sownded,
but could get no ground at 100. fathom, and the yce
being so thicke, I could not get to the shoare, and so
lay off, and came cleare of the yce. Upon Munday
we came within a mile of the shoare, and sought a
harborowe: all the sownd was full of yce, and our boate
rowing a shoare, could get no ground at 100. fathom,
within a Cables length of the shoare: then we sailed
Eastnortheast along the shoare, for so the lande lyeth,
and the currant is there great, setting Northeast, and
Southwest: and if we could have gotten anker ground,
wee would have seene with what force it had runne, but
I judge a ship may drive a league and a halfe, in one
houre, with that tide.

Sight of land supposed to have bene Labrador.

30.

This day at 4. of the cloke in the morning, being
faire and cleere, we had sight of a head land, as we
judged, bearing from us north, and by East, and we
sailed Northeast, and by North to that land, and when
we came thither, wee could not get to the lande for yce:
for the yce stretched along the coast, so that we could
not come to the land, by five leagues.

31.

Wednesday the first of August it calmed, and in the
after noone I caused my boate to be hoysed out, being
hard by a great Island of yce, and I and foure men rowed

August.

1.
2.

to that yce, and sownded within two Cables length of it, and had sixteene fathome, and little stones, and after that sownded againe within a Minion shot, and had ground at an hundreth fathome, and faire sand: we sownded the next day a quarter of a myle from it, and had sixtie fathome rough ground, and at that present being aboord, that great Island of yce fell one part from another, making a noyse as if a great cliffe had fallen into the Sea. And at foure of the clocke I sownded againe, and had 90. fathome, and small blacke stones, and little white stones, like pearles. The tide here did set to the shoare.

10. The tenth I tooke foure men, and my selfe, and rowed to shoare to an Island one league from the maine, and there the flood setteth Southwest alongest the shoare, and it floweth as neere as I could judge so too, I could not tarry to proove it, because the ship was a great way from me, and I feared a fogge: but when I came a shoare, it was a low water. I went to ye top of the Island, and before I came backe, it was hied a foote water, and so without tarrying I came aboord.

11. The 11. we found our latitude to be 63. degr. and
They enter the eight minutes, and this day we entred the streight.
Streit in the
latitude of 63. The 12. wee set saile towardes an Island, called the
deg.and8.min. Gabriels Island, which was 10. leagues then from us.

12. We espied a sound, and bare with it, and came to a
13. sandie Baye, where we came to an anker, the land bearing
[III. 31.] East southeast off us, and there we rode al night in 8. fathome water. It floweth there at a Southeast Moone. We called it Priors sownd, being from the Gabriels Island, tenne leagues.

14. The 14. we waied, and ranne into another sownde, where wee ankered in 8. fathome water, faire sand, and blacke oaze, and there calked our ship, being weake from the wales upward, and tooke in fresh water.

15. The 15. day we waied, and sailed to Priors Bay, being a mile from thence.

16. The 16. day was calme, and we rode still, without yce,

HERUSF auratus MARTINUS FROBISHER

FORBISHERUS ouans NEPTUNIA regna frequentat
Pre patria at tandem glande peremptus obit

but presently within two houres it was frozen round about the ship, a quarter of an ynch thicke, and that day very faire, and calme.

The 17. day we waied, and came to Thomas Williams Island.

The 18. day we sailed North northwest, and ankered againe in 23. fathome, and tough oaze, under Burchers Island, which is from the former Island, ten leagues.

The 19. day in the morning, being calme, and no winde, the Captaine and I tooke our boate, with eight men in her, to rowe us a shoare, to see if there were there any people, or no, and going to the toppe of the Island, we had sight of seven boates, which came rowing from the East side, toward that Island: whereupon we returned aboord againe: at length we sent our boate with five men in her, to see whither they rowed, and so with a white cloth brought one of their boates with their men along the shoare, rowing after our boate, till such time as they sawe our ship, and then they rowed a shoare: then I went on shoare my selfe, and gave every of them a threadden point, and brought one of them aboord of me, where hee did eate and drinke, and then carried him on shoare againe. Whereupon all the rest came aboord with their boates, being nineteene persons, and they spake, but we understoode them not. They bee like to Tartars, with long blacke haire, broad faces, and flatte noses, and tawnie in colour, wearing Seale skinnes, and so doe the women, not differing in the fashion, but the women are marked in the face with blewe streekes downe the cheekes, and round about the eyes. Their boates are made all of Seales skinnes, with a keele of wood within the skin: the proportion of them is like a Spanish shallop, save only they be flat in the bottome, and sharpe at both ends.

19

Sigh of the Countrey people.

The description of the people.

The twentieth day wee wayed, and went to the East-side of this Island, and I and the Captaine, with foure men more went on shoare, and there we sawe their houses, and the people espying us, came rowing towards our boate: whereupon we plied toward our boate: and wee being in our boate and they ashoare, they called to us, and we rowed to them, and one of their company came into our boate, and we carried him a boord, and gave him a Bell, and a knife: so the Captaine and I

willed five of our men to set him a shoare at a rocke, and not among the company, which they came from, but their wilfulnesse was such, that they would goe to them, and so were taken themselves, and our boate lost.

21. The next day in the morning, we stoode in neere the shoare, and shotte off a fauconet, and sounded our trumpet, but we could heare nothing of our men: this sound wee called the five mens sound, and plyed out of it, but ankered againe in thirtie fathome, and oaze: and riding there all night, in the morning, the snow lay a foote thicke upon our hatches.

22. The 22. day in the morning we wayed, and went againe to the place where we lost our men, and our boate. We had sight of foureteene boates, and some came neere to us, but wee could learne nothing of our men: among the rest, we intised one boate to our ships side, with a Bell, and in giving him the Bell, we tooke him, and his boate, and so kept him, and so rowed downe to Thomas Williams Island, and there ankered all night.

26. The 26. day we waied, to come homeward, and by 12. of the clocke at noone, we were thwart of Trumpets Island.

27. The next day we came thwart of Gabriels Island, and at 8. of the clocke at night we had the Cape Labrador as we supposed West from us, ten leagues.

28. The 28. day we went our course Southeast.

29. We sailed Southeast, and by East, 22. leagues.

1. The first day of September in the morning we had sight of the land of Friseland, being eight leagues from us, but we could not come neerer it, for the monstrous yce that lay about it. From this day, till the sixth of this Moneth, we ranne along Island, and had the South part of it at eight of the clocke, East from us ten leagues.

The seventh day of this moneth we had a very terrible 7.
storme, by force whereof, one of our men was blowen
into the sea out of our waste, but he caught hold of
the foresaile sheate, and there held till the Captaine
pluckt him againe into the ship.

The 25. day of this moneth we had sight of the [III. 32.]
Island of Orkney, which was then East from us.

The first day of October we had sight of the Sheld, *The Sheld.*
and so sailed about the coast, and ankered at Yarmouth,
and the next day we came into Harwich.

The language of the people of Meta incognita.

Argoteyt, a hand.	Attegay, a coate.
Cangnawe, a nose.	Pollevetagay, a knife.
Arered, an eye.	Accaskay, a shippe.
Keiotot, a tooth.	Coblone, a thumbe.
Mutchatet, the head.	Teckkere, the foremost
Chewat, an eare.	finger.
Comagaye, a legge.	Ketteckle, the middle finger.
Atoniagay, a foote.	Mekellacane, the fourth
Callagay, a paire of	finger.
breeches.	Yacketrone, the litle finger.

The second voyage of Master Martin Frobisher,
made to the West and Northwest Regions,
in the yeere 1577. with a description of the
Countrey, and people: Written by Master
Dionise Settle.

N Whitsunday, being the sixe and twentieth of May, in the yeere of our Lord
God 1577. Captaine Frobisher departed
from Blacke Wall, with one of the
Queenes Majesties ships, called The
Aide, of nine score tunnes, or thereabouts: and two other little Barkes like-
wise, the one called The Gabriel, whereof Master Fenton,
a Gentleman of my Lord of Warwikes, was Captaine:

and the other, The Michael, whereof Master Yorke, a Gentleman of my Lord Admirals was Captaine, accompanied with seven score Gentlemen, souldiers, and sailers, well furnished with victuals, and other provision necessarie for one halfe yeere, on this his second voyage, for the further discovering of the passage to Cathay, and other Countreys, thereunto adjacent, by West and Northwest navigations: which passage or way, is supposed to bee on the North and Northwest part of America: and the said America to be an Island invironed with the sea, where through our Merchants may have course and recourse with their merchandize, from these our Northernmost parts of Europe, to those Orientall coasts of Asia, in much shorter time, and with greater benefite then any others, to their no little commoditie and profite that do or shall frequent the same. Our said Captaine and General of this present voyage and company having the yeere before, with two little pinnesses, to his great danger, and no small commendations, given a worthy attempt towards the performance thereof, is also prest, when occasion shall be ministred (to the benefite of his Prince, and native Countrey) to adventure himselfe further therein. As for this second voyage, it seemeth sufficient, that he hath better explored and searched the commodities of those people and Countreys, which in his first voyage the yeere before he had found out.

Upon which considerations, the day and yeere before expressed, we departed from Blacke Wall to Harwich, where making an accomplishment of things necessary, the last of May we hoised up sailes, and with a merrie wind the 7. of June we arrived at the Islands called Orcades, or vulgarly Orkney, being in number 30. subject and adjacent to Scotland, where we made provision of fresh water; in the doing whereof our Generall licensed the Gentlemen and souldiers for their recreation, to goe on shore. At our landing, the people fled from their poore cottages, with shrikes and alarms, to warne their neighbours of enemies, but by gentle perswasions we reclamed

*The Islands
Orcades, or
Orkney.*

*The Orcadians
upon smal occa-
sion flee their
home.*

them to their houses. It seemeth they are often frighted with Pirats, or some other enemies, that moove them to such sudden feare. Their houses are very simply builded with Pibble stone, without any chimneis, the fire being made in the middest thereof. The good man, wife, children, and other of their family eate and sleepe on the one side of the house, and the cattell on the other, very beastly and rudely, in respect of civilitie. They are destitute of wood, their fire is turffes, and Cowshards. *No wood in Orkney.* They have corne, bigge, and oates, with which they pay their Kings rent, to the maintenance of his house. They take great quantitie of fish, which they dry in the wind and Sunne. They dresse their meat very filthily, and eate it without salt. Their apparell is after the rudest sort of Scotland. Their money is all base. Their Church and religion is reformed according to the Scots. The fisher men of England can better declare the dispositions *Fisher men of England have daily traffike to Orkney.* of those people then I: wherefore I remit other their usages to their reports, as yeerely repaires thither, in their course to and from Island for fish.

We departed herehence the 8. of June, and followed [III. 33.] *In June and July no night in those West and Northwest regions.* our course betweene West and Northwest, untill the 4. of July: all which time we had no night, but that easily, and without any impediment we had when we were so disposed, the fruition of our bookes, and other pleasures to passe away the time: a thing of no small moment, to such as wander in unknowen seas, and long navigations, especially, when both the winds and raging surges do passe their common and wonted course. This benefite endureth in those parts not 6. weekes, while the sunne is neere the Tropike of Cancer: but where the pole is raised to 70. or 80. degrees, it continueth much longer.

All along these seas, after we were six dayes sailing *Great abundance of Firre trees floting in the sea.* from Orkney, we met floting in the sea, great Firre trees, which as we judged, were with the furie of great floods rooted up, and so driven into the sea. Island hath almost no other wood nor fuell, but such as they take up upon their coastes. It seemeth, that these trees are

Inquire further of this current.

driven from some part of the New found land, with the current that setteth from the West to the East.

The 4. of July we came within the making of Frisland. From this shoare 10. or 12. leagues, we met great Islands of yce, of halfe a mile, some more, some lesse in compasse, shewing above the sea, 30. or 40. fathoms, and as we supposed fast on ground, where with our lead we could scarse sound the bottome for depth.

Here, in place of odoriferous and fragrant smels of sweete gums, & pleasant notes of musicall birdes, which other Countreys in more temperate Zones do yeeld, wee *Yce, snow, and* tasted the most boisterous Boreal blasts mixt with snow *haile in June and July.* and haile, in the moneths of June and July, nothing inferior to our untemperate winter: a sudden alteration, and especially in a place or Parallele, where the Pole is not elevate above 61. degrees: at which height other Countreys more to the North, yea unto 70. degrees, shew themselves more temperate then this doth.

All along this coast yce lieth, as a continuall bulwarke, & so defendeth the Countrey, that those that would land there, incur great danger. Our Generall 3. dayes together attempted with the ship boate to have gone on shoare, which for that without great danger he could not accomplish, he deferred it untill a more convenient time. All along the coast lie very high mountaines covered with snow, except in such places, where through the steepenes of the mountaines of force it must needs fall. Foure dayes coasting along this land, we found no signe of habitation. Little birds, whiche we judged to have lost *Friseland subject to fogge.* the shore, by reason of thicke fogges which that Countrey is much subject unto, came flying into our ships, which causeth us to suppose, that the Countrey is both more tollerable, and also habitable within, then the outward shore maketh shew or signification.

From hence we departed the eight of July: and the 16. of the same, we came with the making of land, which land our Generall the yeere before had named The Queenes foreland, being an Island as we judge, lying neere the supposed continent with America: and on the other side, opposite to the same, one other Island called Halles Isle, after the name of the Master of the ship, neere adjacent to the firme land, supposed continent with Asia. Betweene the which two Islands there is a large entrance or streight, called Frobishers streight, after *Frobishers* the name of our Generall, the first finder thereof. This *streight.* said streight is supposed to have passage into the sea of Sur, which I leave unknowen as yet.

It seemeth that either here, or not farre hence, the sea should have more large entrance, then in other parts within the frozen or untemperate Zone: and that some contrary tide, either from the East or West, with maine force casteth out that great quantity of yce, which commeth floting from this coast, even unto Friseland, causing that Countrey to seeme more untemperate then others, much more Northerly then the same.

I cannot judge that any temperature under the Pole, the time of the Sunnes Northerne declination being halfe a yere together, and one whole day, (considering that the Sunnes elevation surmounteth not 23. degrees and 30. minuts) can have power to dissolve such monstrous and huge yce, comparable to great mountaines, except by *Islands of yce* some other force, as by swift currents and tides, with *comparable to mountaines.* the helpe of the said day of halfe a yeere.

Before we came within the making of these lands we tasted cold stormes, in so much that it seemed we had changed summer with winter, if the length of the dayes had not remooved us from that opinion.

At our first comming, the streights seemed to be shut up with a long mure of yce, which gave no litle cause of discomfort unto us all: but our Generall, (to whose *Captaine Fro-* diligence imminent dangers, and difficult attempts seemed *bisher his spe-* nothing, in respect of his willing mind, for the com- *ciall care and* moditie of his Prince and Countrey,) with two little *the benefite of* Pinnesses prepared of purpose, passed twise thorow *his Prince and* them to the East shore, and the Islands thereunto *Countrey.* adjacent: and the ship, with the two Barks lay off and

[III. 34.]
*The order of
the people ap-
pearing on
shoare.*

on something further into the sea, from the danger of
the yce.

Whilest he was searching the Countrey neere the
shoare, some of the people of the Countrey shewed
themselves leaping and dauncing, with strange shrikes
and cries, which gave no little admiration to our men.
Our Generall desirous to allure them unto him by faire
meanes, caused knives, and other things to be profered
unto them, which they would not take at our hands: but
being laid on the ground, and the party going away, they
came and tooke up, leaving some thing of theirs to
countervaile the same. At the length two of them leaving their weapons, came downe to our Generall and
Master, who did the like to them, commanding the
company to stay, and went unto them: who after certaine dumbe signes, and mute congratulations, began to
lay handes upon them, but they deliverly escaped, and

ranne to their bowes and arrowes, and came fiercely upon
them, (not respecting the rest of our companie which
were ready for their defence) but with their arrowes hurt
divers of them: we tooke the one, and the other
escaped.

Whilest our Generall was busied in searching the
Countrey, and those Islands adjacent on the Eastshoare,
the ship and barkes having great care, not to put farre
into the sea from him, for that he had small store of
victuals, were forced to abide in a cruell tempest, chanc-
ing in the night, amongst and in the thickest of the yce,
which was so monstrous, that even the least of a thousand
had bene of force sufficient, to have shivered our ship
and barks into small portions, if God (who in all necessities, hath care upon the infirmitie of man) had not
provided for this our extremitie a sufficient remedie
through the light of the night, whereby we might well
discerne to flee from such imminent dangers, which we
avoyded with 14. Bourdes in one watch the space of 4
houres. If we had not incurred this danger amongst
these monstrous Islands of yce, we should have lost our

Generall and Master, and the most of our best sailers, which were on the shoare destitute of victuals: but by the valure of our Master Gunner, Master Jackman, and Andrew Dier, the Masters Mates, men expert both in navigation, and other good qualities, wee were all content to incurre the dangers aforerehearsed, before we would with our owne safetie, runne into the seas, to the destruction of our sayd Generall, and his company.

Richard Cox, Master gunner. Master Jackman. Andrew Dier.

The day following, being the 19. of Julie, our captaine returned to the ship, with report of supposed riches, which shewed it selfe in the bowels of those barren mountaines, wherewith wee were all satisfied.

Within foure daies after we had bene at the entrance of the streights, the Northwest and West winds dispersed the yce into the sea, & made us a large entrance into the streights, so that without any impediment, on the 19. of Julie we entred them, and the 20. thereof, our Generall and Master with great diligence, sought out and sounded the West shoare, and found out a faire Harborough for the ship and barkes to ride in, and named it after our Masters mate, Jackmans sound, and brought the ship, barkes, and all their company to safe anker, except one man, which died by Gods visitation.

Jackmans sound.

At our first arrivall, after the ship rode at anker, our generall, with such company as could well be spared from the ships, in marching order entred the lande, having speciall care by exhortations, that at our entrance thereinto, wee should all with one voyce, kneeling upon our knees, chiefly thanke God for our safe arrivall: secondly beseech him, that it would please his divine Majestie, long to continue our Queene, for whom he, and all the rest of our company in this order tooke possession of the Countrey: and thirdly, that by our Christian studie and endevour, those barbarous people trained up in Paganisme, and infidelitie, might be reduced to the knowledge of true religion, and to the hope of salvation in Christ our Redeemer. With other words very apt to signifie his willing mind, and affection toward his Prince and

Possession taken.

Countrey : whereby all suspicion of an undutifull subject, may credibly be judged to be utterly exempted from his mind. All the rest of the Gentlemen and other deserve worthily herein, their due praise and commendation.

These things in this order accomplished, our Generall commanded all the company to be obedient in things needfull for our owne safegard, to Master Fenton, Master Yorke, and Master Beast his Lieutenant, while he was occupied in other necessarie affaires, concerning our comming thither.

After this order we marched through the Countrey, with Ensigne displaied, so farre as was thought needfull, and now and then heaped up stones on high mountaines, and other places in token of possession, as likewise to signifie unto such as hereafter may chance to arrive there, that possession is taken in the behalfe of some other Prince, by those who first found out the Countrey.

Whoso maketh navigations to those Countreys, hath not onely extreme winds, and furious seas to encounter withall, but also many monstrous and great Islands of yce : a thing both rare, wonderfull, and greatly to be regarded.

We were forced sundry times, while the ship did ride here at anker, to have continuall watch, with boats & men ready with halsers to knit fast unto such yce, as with the ebbe & flood were tossed to and fro in the harborough, & with force of oares to hale them away, for endangering the ship.

[III. 35.]

Our Generall certaine dayes searched this supposed continent with America, and not finding the commodity to answere his expectation, after he had made triall thereof he departed thence with two little barks, and men sufficient to the East shore being the supposed continent of Asia, and left the ship with most of the Gentlemen, souldiers, and sailers, untill such time as he either thought good to send or come for them.

The stones of this supposed continent with America be altogether sparkled, and glister in the Sunne like

218

gold: so likewise doth the sand in the bright water, yet they verifie the old Proverb: All is not gold that glistereth.

A common proverbe.

On this West shore we found a dead fish floating, which had in his nose a horne streight and torquet, of length two yards lacking two ynches, being broken in the top, where we might perceive it hollow, into the which some of our sailers putting spiders they presently died. I saw not the triall hereof, but it was reported unto me of a trueth: by the vertue whereof we supposed it to be the sea Unicorne.

The sea Unicorne.

After our Generall had found out good harborough for the ship and barks to anker in, and also such store of supposed gold ore as he thought himselfe satisfied withall, he returned to the Michael, whereof Master Yorke aforesaid was Captaine, accompanied with our master and his Mate: who coasting along the West shore not farre from whence the ship rode, they perceived a faire harborough, and willing to sound the same, at the entrance thereof they espied two tents of Seale skins, unto which the Captaine, our said Master, and other company resorted. At the sight of our men the people fled into the mountaines: neverthelesse they went to their tents, where leaving certaine trifles of ours, as glasses, bels, knives, and such like things they departed, not taking any thing of theirs except one dogge. They did in like maner leave behind them a letter, pen, yncke, and paper, whereby our men whom the Captaine lost the yere before, and in that peoples custody, might (if any of them were alive) be advertised of our presence and being there.

The people fled at the sight of our men.

On the same day after consultation had, all the Gentlemen, and others likewise that could be spared from the ship, under the conduct and leading of Master Philpot, (unto whom in our Generall his absence, and his Lieutenant Master Beast, al the rest were obedient) went a shore, determining to see, if by faire means we could either allure them to familiarity, or otherwise take some of

Master Philpot.

Master Beast.

them, and so attaine to some knowledge of those men whom our Generall lost the yeere before.

At our comming backe againe to the place where their tents were before, they had remooved their tents further into the said Bay or Sound, where they might if they were driven from the land, flee with their boates into the sea. We parting our selves into two companies, and compassing a mountaine came suddenly upon them by land, who espying us, without any tarying fled to their boates, leaving the most part of their oares behind them for haste, and rowed downe the bay, where our two Pinnesses met them and drove them to shore: but if they had had all their oares, so swift are they in rowing, it had bene lost time to have chased them.

When they were landed they fiercely assaulted our men with their bowes and arrowes, who wounded three of them with our arrowes: and perceiving themselves thus hurt, they desperatly leapt off the Rocks into the Sea, and drowned themselves: which if they had not done, but had submitted themselves, or if by any meanes we could have taken them alive (being their enemies as they judged) we would both have saved them, & also have sought remedy to cure their wounds received at our hands. But they altogether voyd of humanity, and ignorant what mercy meaneth, in extremities looke for no other then death: and perceiving they should fall into our hands, thus miserably by drowning rather desired death then otherwise to be saved by us: the rest perceiving their fellowes in this distresse, fled into the high mountaines. Two women not being so apt to escape as the men were, the one for her age, and the other being incombred with a yong child, we tooke. The old wretch, whom divers of our Saylers supposed to be eyther a devill, or a witch, had her buskins plucked off, to see if she were cloven footed, and for her ougly hew and deformity we let her goe: the yong woman and the child we brought away. We named the place where they were slaine, Bloodie point: and the Bay or Harborough, Yorks sound, after the name of one of the Captaines of the two Barks.

Having this knowledge both of their fiercenesse and cruelty, and perceiving that faire meanes as yet is not able to allure them to familiarity, we disposed our selves, contrary to our inclination, something to be cruel, returned to their tents and made a spoyle of the same: where we found an old shirt, a doublet, a girdle, and also shooes of our men, whom we lost the yeere before: on nothing else unto them belonging could we set our eyes. *Faire meanes not able to allure them to familiarity.*

Their riches are not gold, silver or precious Drapery, but their said tents and botes, made of the skins of red Deare and Seale skins: also dogges like unto woolves, but for the most part black, with other trifles, more to be wondred at for their strangenesse, then for any other commoditie needefull for our use. *[III. 36.] Boates of skinnes.*

Thus returning to our ship the 3. of August, we departed from the West shore supposed firme with America, after we had ankered there 13. dayes: and so the 4. thereof we came to our Generall on the East shore, and ankered in a faire Harborough named Anne Warwickes sound, unto which is annexed an Island both named after the Countesse of Warwicke, Anne Warwickes sound and Isle. *Our departure from the West shore.*

In this Isle our Generall thought good for this voyage, to fraight both the ship and barkes, with such stone or supposed gold minerall, as he judged to countervaile the charges of his first, and this his second navigation to these Countreys.

In the meane time of our abode here some of the countrey people came to shew themselves unto us, sundry times on the maine shore, neere adjacent to the said Isle. Our Generall desirous to have some newes of his men, whom he lost the yeere before, with some company with him repaired with the ship boat to common, or signe with them for familiaritie, whereunto he is perswaded to bring them. They at the first shew made tokens, that three of his five men were alive, and desired *The countrey people shew themselves unto us.*

221

penne, ynck, and paper, and that within three or foure dayes they would returne, and (as we judged) bring those of our men which were living, with them.

They also made signes or tokens of their King, whom they called Cacough, & how he was carried on mens shoulders, and a man farre surmounting any of our company, in bignesse and stature.

With these tokens and signes of writing, penne, yncke, and paper was delivered them, which they would not take at our hands, but being laid upon the shore, and *Their usage* the partie gone away, they tooke up: which likewise *in traffique or* they do when they desire any thing for change of theirs, *exchange.* laying for that which is left so much as they thinke will countervaile the same, and not comming neere together. It seemeth they have bene used to this trade or traffique, with some other people adjoyning, or not farre distant from their Countrey.

The people After 4. dayes some of them shewed themselves upon *shew them-* the firme land, but not where they were before. Our *selves the* General very glad thereof, supposing to heare of our *third time.* men, went from the Island, with the boat, and sufficient company with him. They seemed very glad, and allured him about a certaine point of the land: behind which they might perceive a company of the crafty villaines to lye lurking, whom our Generall would not deale withall, for that he knew not what company they were, and so with few signes dismissed them and returned to his company.

The people An other time as our said Generall was coasting the *shew them-* Countrey with two little Pinnesses, whereby at our returne *selves againe* he might make the better relation thereof, three of the *on firme land.* crafty villains, with a white skin allured us to them. Once againe our generall, for that he hoped to heare of his men, went towards them: at our comming neere the shore whereon they were, we might perceive a number of them lie hidden behind great stones, & those 3. in sight labouring by al meanes possible that some would come on land: and perceiving we made no hast

by words nor friendly signes, which they used by clapping *Their first*
of their hands, and being without weapon, and but 3. *meanes to*
in sight, they sought further meanes to provoke us *shore.*
thereunto. One alone laid flesh on the shore, which *Their second*
we tooke up with the Boat hooke, as necessary victuals *meanes.*
for the relieving of the man, woman, and child, whom
we had taken: for that as yet they could not digest our
meat: whereby they perceived themselves deceived of.
their expectation, for all their crafty allurements. Yet
once againe to make (as it were) a full shew of their *Their third*
craftie natures, and subtile sleights, to the intent thereby *and craftiest*
to have intrapped and taken some of our men, one of *allurement.*
them counterfeited himselfe impotent and lame of his
legs, who seemed to descend to the water side, with
great difficulty: and to cover his craft the more, one
of his fellowes came downe with him, and in such places
where he seemed unable to passe, he tooke him on his
shoulders, set him by the water side, and departed from
him, leaving him (as it should seeme) all alone, who
playing his counterfait pageant very well, thought thereby
to provoke some of us to come on shore, not fearing,
but that one of us might make our party good with a
lame man.

Our Generall having compassion of his impotency, *Compassion to*
thought good (if it were possible) to cure him thereof: *cure a crafty*
wherefore he caused a souldier to shoote at him with *lame man.*
his Caleever, which grased before his face. The counterfeit villeine deliverly fled, without any impediment at
all, and got him to his bow and arrowes, and the rest
from their lurking holes, with their weapons, bowes,
arrowes, slings, and darts. Our Generall caused some
caleevers to be shot off at them, wherby some being
hurt, they might hereafter stand in more feare of us.

This was all the answere for this time we could have [III. 37.]
of our men, or of our Generals letter. Their crafty
dealing at these three severall times being thus manifest
unto us, may plainely shew their disposition in other
things to be correspondent. We judged that they used

these stratagemes, thereby to have caught some of us, for the delivering of the man, woman and child whom we had taken.

They are men of a large corporature, and good proportion : their colour is not much unlike the Sunne burnt Countrey man, who laboureth daily in the Sunne for his living.

They weare their haire something long, and cut before either with stone or knife, very disorderly. Their women weare their haire long, and knit up with two loupes, shewing forth on either side of their faces, and the rest foltred upon a knot. Also some of their women race their faces proportionally, as chinne, cheekes, and forehead, and the wrists of their hands, whereupon they lay a colour which continueth darke azurine.

They eate their meat all raw, both flesh, fish, and foule, or something per boyled with blood and a little water which they drinke. For lacke of water they wil eate yce, that is hard frosen, as pleasantly as we will do Sugar Candie, or other Sugar.

If they for necessities sake stand in need of the premisses, such grasse as the Countrey yeeldeth they plucke up and eate, not deintily, or salletwise to allure their stomacks to appetite : but for necessities sake without either salt, oyles or washing, like brute beasts devouring the same. They neither use table, stoole, or table cloth for comlines : but when they are imbrued with blood knuckle deepe, and their knives in like sort, they use their tongues as apt instruments to lick them cleane in doing whereof they are assured to loose none of their victuals.

Dogges like unto wolves. They frank or keepe certaine dogs not much unlike Wolves, which they yoke togither, as we do oxen & horses, to a sled or traile : and so carry their necessarie over the yce and snow from place to place : as the captive, whom we have, made perfect signes. And when those dogs are not apt for the same use : or when with hunger they are constrained for lacke of other victuals

they eate them: so that they are as needfull for them *They eate dogs flesh.*
in respect of their bignesse, as our oxen are for us.

They apparell themselves in the skins of such beasts as they kill, sewed together with the sinewes of them. All the foule which they kill, they skin, and make thereof one kind of garment or other, to defend them from the cold.

They make their apparel with hoods and tailes, which *Hoods and tailes to their apparell.*
tailes they give when they thinke to gratifie any friend-ship shewed unto them: a great signe of friendship with them. The men have them not so side as the women.

The men and women weare their hose close to their legges, from the wast to the knee without any open before, as well the one kind as the other. Upon their legges they weare hose of leather, with the furre side inward two or three paire on at once, and especially the women. In those hose they put their knives, needles, and other things needfull to beare about. They put a bone within their hose, which reacheth from the foote to the knee, whereupon they draw their said hose, and so in place of garters they are holden from falling downe about their feete.

They dresse their skinnes very soft and souple with the haire on. In cold weather or Winter they weare the furre side inward: and in Summer outward. Other apparell they have none but the said skinnes.

Those beasts, fishes, and foules, which they kill, are their meat, drinke, apparell, houses, bedding, hose, shooes, threed, and sailes for their boates, with many other necessaries whereof they stand in need, and almost all their riches.

Their houses are tents made of Seale skins, pitched *Their houses of Seale skins and Firre.*
up with 4. Firre quarters foure square meeting at the top, and the skins sewed together with sinewes, and laid thereupon: they are so pitched up, that the entrance into them is always South or against the Sunne.

They have other sorts of houses which we found not

to be inhabited, which are raised with stones and **Whale** bones, and a skinne layd over them, to withstand the raine, or other weather: the entrance of them being not much unlike an Ovens mouth, whereto I thinke they resort for a time to fish, hunt, and foule, and so leave them untill the next time they come thither againe.

Their weapons of defence.

Their weapons are bowes, arrowes, darts, and slings. Their bowes are of wood of a yard long, sinewed at the back with strong sinewes, not glued too, but fast girded and tyed on. Their bow strings are likewise sinewes. Their arrowes are three pieces nocked with bone, and ended with bone, with those two ends, and the wood in the midst, they passe not in length halfe a yard or little more. They are fethered with two fethers the penne end being cut away, and the fethers layd upon the arrow with the broad side to the wood; insomuch

[III. 38.]
Three sorts of heads to their arrowes.

that they seeme when they are tyed on, to have foure fethers. They have also three sorts of heads to those arrowes: one sort of stone or yron, proportioned like to a heart: the second sort of bone, much like unto a stopt head, with a hooke on the same: the third sort of bone likewise made sharpe at both sides, and sharpe pointed. They are not made very fast but lightly tyed to, or else set in a nocke, that upon small occasion the arrowes leave these heads behind them: and they are of small force, except they be very neere when they shoote.

Two sorts of darts.

Their Darts are made of two sorts: the one with many forkes of bones in the fore end and likewise in the midst: their proportions are not much unlike our toasting yrons but longer: these they cast out of an instrument of wood, very readily. The other sort is greater then the first aforesayd, with a long bone made sharpe on both sides not much unlike a Rapier, which I take to bee their most hurtfull weapon.

Two sorts of boates made of leather.

They have two sorts of boats made of leather, set out on the inner side with quarters of wood, artificially tyed together with thongs of the same: the greater sort are not much unlike our wherries, wherein sixteene or twenty men may sit: they have for a sayle drest the guts of such beasts as they kill very fine and thinne, which they sew together: the other boate is but for one man to sit and row in with one oare.

Their order of fishing, hunting, and fouling are with these said weapons: but in what sort, or how they use them we have no perfect knowledge as yet.

They use to foule, fish, and hunt.

I can suppose their abode or habitation not to be here, for that neither their houses or apparell, are of such force to withstand the extremity of cold, that the Countrey seemeth to be infected with all: neither do I see any signe likely to performe the same.

It is to be supposed that their inhabiting is elsewhere.

Those houses or rather dennes which stand there, have no signe of footway, or any thing else troden, which is one of the chiefest tokens of habitation. And those tents which they bring with them, when they have sufficiently hunted and fished, they remove to other places: and when they have sufficiently stored them of such victuals, as the Countrey yeeldeth or bringeth forth, they returne to their winter stations or habitations. This conjecture do I make, for the infertility which I conjecture to be in that Countrey.

They have some yron whereof they make arrow heads, knives, and other little instruments, to worke their boates, bowes, arrowes, and darts withall, which are very unapt to doe any thing withall but with great labour.

Their use of yron.

It seemeth that they have conversation with some other people, of whom for exchange they should receive the same. They are greatly delighted with any thing that is bright, or giveth a sound.

What knowledge they have of God, or what Idoll they adore, we have no perfect intelligence, I thinke them rather Anthropophagi, or devourers of mans flesh then otherwise: for that there is no flesh or fish which they find dead (smell it never so filthily) but they will eate it, as they finde it without any other dressing. A loathsome thing, either to the beholders or hearers.

Anthropophagi.

There is no maner of creeping beast hurtfull, except

some Spiders (which as many affirme, are signes of great store of gold) and also certaine stinging Gnattes, which bite so fiercely, that the place where they bite shortly after swelleth and itcheth very sore.

They make signes of certaine people that weare bright plates of gold in their foreheads, and other places of their bodies.

The Countreys on both sides the streights lye very high with rough stony mountaines, and great quantitie of snow thereon. There is very little plaine ground and no grasse, except a little which is much like unto mosse that groweth on soft ground, such as we get Turffes in. There is no wood at all. To be briefe there is nothing fit or profitable for the use of man, which that Countrey with roote yeeldeth or bringeth forth : Howbeit there is great quantity of Deere, whose skins are like unto Asses, there heads or hornes doe farre exceede, as well in length as also in breadth, any in these our parts or Countreys : their feete likewise are as great as our oxens, which we measured to be seven or eight ynches in breadth. There are also hares, wolves, fishing beares, and sea foule of sundry sorts.

As the Countrey is barren and unfertile, so are they rude and of no capacitie to culture the same to any perfection : but are contented by their hunting, fishing, and fouling, with raw flesh and warme blood to satisfie their greedy panches, which is their only glory.

There is great likelihood of Earthquakes or thunder : for that there are huge and monstrous mountaines, whose greatest substance are stones, and those stones so shaken with some extraordinarie meanes that one is separated from another, which is discordant from all other Quarries.

[III. 39.]
No rivers, but
such as the
Sunne doth
cause to come
of snow.

There are no rivers or running springs, but such as through the heate of the Sunne, with such water as discendeth from the mountaines and hilles, whereon great drifts of snow do lie, are ingendred.

It argueth also that there should be none : for that the earth, which with the extremitie of the Winter is so frosen within, that that water which should have recourse *A probability that there should be neither spring or rivers in the ground.* within the same to maintaine springs, hath not his motion, whereof great waters have their originall, as by experience is seene otherwhere. Such valleis as are capable to receive the water, that in the Summer time by the operation of the Sunne descendeth from great abundance of snowe, which continually lyeth on the mountaines and hath no passage, sinketh into the earth and so vanisheth away, without any runnell above the earth, by which occasion or continuall standing of the said water, the earth is opened, and the great frost yeeldeth to the force thereof, which in other places foure or five fathoms within the ground for lacke of the said moisture, the earth (even in the very Summer time) is frosen, and so combineth the stones together, that scarcely instruments with great force can unknit them.

Also where the water in those valleis can have no such passage away, by the continuance of time in such order as is before rehearsed, the yeerely descent from the mountaines filleth them full, that at the lowest banke of the same, they fall into the valley, and so continue as fishing Ponds or Stagnes in Summer time full of water, and in the Winter hard frosen: as by skarres that remaine thereof in Summer may easily be perceived: so that the heat of Summer is nothing comparable or of force to dissolve the extremitie of cold that commeth in Winter.

Neverthelesse I am assured that below the force of the frost within the earth, the waters have recourse, and emptie themselves out of sight into the sea, which through the extremitie of the frost are constrained to doe the same: by which occasion the earth within is kept the warmer, and springs have their recourse, which is the *Springs nourish gold.* onely nutriment of golde and Minerals within the same.

There is much to be sayd of the commodities of these Countreys, which are couched within the bowels of the earth, which I let passe till more perfect triall be made thereof.

THE ENGLISH VOYAGES

The 24. of August, after we had satisfied our minds with fraight sufficient for our vessels, though not our covetous desires with such knowledge of the Countrey, people, and other commodities as are before rehearsed,

Our departure from those Countreys. we departed therehence. The 17. of September we fell with the lands end of England, and so sailed to Milford Haven, from whence our Generall rode to the Court for order, to what Port or Haven to conduct the ship.

How & when we lost our 2. Barks, which God neverthe-lesse restored. We lost our two Barkes in the way homeward, the one the 29. of August, the other the 31. of the same moneth, by occasion of great tempest and fogge. Howbeit God restored the one to Bristowe, and the other made his course by Scotland to Yermouth. In this voyage we lost two men, one in the way by Gods visitation, and the other homeward cast over borde with a surge of the sea.

The conclusion. I Could declare unto the Readers, the latitude and longitude of such places and regions as we have bene at, but not altogether so perfectly as our masters and others, with many circumstances of tempests and other accidents incident to Sea faring men, which seeme not altogether strange, but I let them passe to their reports as men most apt to set forth and declare the same. I have also left the names of the Countreys on both the shores untouched, for lacke of understanding the peoples language: as also for sundry respects, not needfull as yet to be declared.

Countreys new discovered where commoditie is to be looked for, doe better accord with a new name given by the discoverers, then an uncertaine name by a doubtfull Authour.

Our general named sundry Islands, Mountaines, Capes, and Harboroughs after the names of divers Noble men and other gentlemen his friends, aswel on the one shore as also on the other.

The third and last voyage unto Meta Incognita, made by M. Martin Frobisher, in the yeere 1578. Written by Thomas Ellis.

Hese are to let you know, that upon the 25. of May, the Thomas Allen being Viceadmirall whose Captaine was M. Yorke, M. Gibbes Master, Christopher Hall Pilot, accompanied with the Reareadmiral named the Hopewel, whose Captaine was M. Henrie Carewe, the M. Andrewe Dier, and certaine other ships came to Gravesend, where wee ankred and abode the comming of certaine of our Fleete which were not yet come. *Master Yorke.* *Christopher Hall.* *The Hopewel.* *Captaine Carew.* *Andrew Dier.*

The 27. of the same moneth our Fleete being nowe come together, and all things prest in a readinesse, the wind favouring, and tide serving, we being of sailes in number eight, waied ankers and hoised our sailes toward Harwich to meete with our Admirall, and the residue which then and there abode our arrivall: where we safely arrived the 28. thereof, finding there our Admirall, whom we with the discharge of certaine pieces saluted, acording to order and duety, and were welcommed with the like courtesie: which being finished we landed: where our Generall continued mustering his souldiers and Miners, and setting things in order appertaining to the voyage untill the last of the said moneth of May, which day we hoised our sailes, and committing our selves to the conducting of Almightie God, we set forward toward the west Countrey in such luckie wise and good successe, that by the fift of June we passed the Dursies, being the utmost part of Ireland to the Westward. *Dursies.* *Ireland.*

[III. 40.] *Harwich.*

And here it were not much amisse nor farre from our purpose, if I should a little discourse and speake of our adventures and chances by the way, as our landing at Plimmouth, as also the meeting certaine poore men, which were robbed and spoyled of all that they had by *Plimmouth.*

Pirates and Rovers: amongst whom was a man of Bristow, on whom our Generall used his liberality, and sent him away with letters into England.

But because such things are impertinent to the matter, I will returne (without any more mentioning of the same) to that from the which I have digressed and swarved, I meane our ships now sailing on the surging seas, sometime passing at pleasure with a wished Easterne wind, sometime hindered of our course againe by the Westerne blasts, untill the 20. day of the foresayd moneth of June,

on which day in the morning we fell with Frizeland, which is a very hie and cragged land and was almost cleane covered with snow, so that we might see nought but craggie rockes and the tops of high and huge hilles, sometimes (and for the most part) all covered with foggie mists. There might we also perceive the great Isles of yce lying on the seas, like mountaines, some small, some big, of sundry kinds of shapes, and such a number of them, that wee could not come neere the shore for them.

Thus sailing alongst the coast, at the last we saw a place somewhat voyd of yce, where our Generall (accompanied with certaine other) went a shore, where they sawe certaine tents made of beasts skinnes, and boates much the like unto theirs of Meta Incognita. The tents were furnished with flesh, fish, skins, and other trifles: amongst the which was found a boxe of nailes: whereby we did conjecture, that they had either Artificers amongst them, or els a traffike with some other nation. The men ran away, so that wee could have no conference or communication with them. Our Generall (because hee would have them no more to flee, but rather incouraged

to stay through his courteous dealing) gave commaundement that his men should take nothing away with them, saving only a couple of white dogs, for the which he left pinnes, poynts, knives, and other trifling things, and departed without taking or hurting any thing, and so came abord, and hoysed sailes, and passed forwards.

But being scarce out of the sight thereof, there fell such a fogge and hidious mist that we could not see one another: whereupon we stroke our drums, and sounded our trumpets, to the ende we might keepe together: and so continued all that day and night till the next day that the mist brake up: so that we might easily perceive all the ships thus sailing together all that day, until the next day, being the 22. of the same: on which day wee sawe an infinite number of yce, from the which we cast about to shun the danger thereof.

But one of our small Barkes named the Michael, whose Captaine was Master Kinderslie, the Master Bartholomew Bull, lost our company, insomuch that we could not obteine the sight of her many dayes after, of whom I meane to speake further anon when occasion shall be ministred, and opportunitie serve. Thus we continued in our course untill the second of July, on which day we fell with the Queenes foreland, where we saw so much yce, that we thought it unpossible to get into the Straights: yet at the last we gave the adventure and entred the yce.

Master Kinderslie. Bartholomew Bull.

Being amongst it wee sawe the Michael, of whom I spake before, accompanied with the Judith, whose Captaine was Master Fenton, the Master Charles Jackman, bearing into the foresayd yce, farre distant from us, who in a storme that fell that present night, (whereof I will at large God willing, discourse hereafter) were severed from us, and being in, wandred up and downe the Straights amongst the yce many dayes in great perill, till at the last, (by the providence of God) they came safely to harbor in their wished Port. In the Countesse of Warwicks sound, the 20. of July aforesayd, tenne dayes before any of the other shippes: who going on shore found where the people of the Countrey had bene, and had hid their provision in great heapes of stones being both of flesh and fish, which they had killed; whereof wee also found great store in other places after our arrival. They found also divers engins, as bowes,

The Michael. The Judith. M. Fenton. Charles Jackman.

The Countesse of Warwicks sound.

[III. 41.]

slings, and darts. They found likewise certaine pieces of the Pinnesse which our Generall left there the yeere before, which Pinnesse he had sunke, minding to have it againe the next yeere.

Now seeing I have entreated so much of the Judith and the Michael: I will returne to the rest of the other ships, and will speake a little of the storme which fell, with the mishaps that we had, the night 'that we put into the yce: whereof I made mention before.

At the first entring into the yce in the mouth of the Straights, our passage was very narrow, and difficult but being once gotten in, we had a faire open place without any yce for the most part, being a league in compasse, the yce being round about us and inclosing us, as it were, within the pales of a parke. In which place, (because it was almost night) we minded to take in our sailes, and lie a hull all that night. But the storme so increased, and the waves began to mount aloft, which brought the yce so neere us, and comming on so fast upon us, that we were faine to beare in and out, where we might espie an open place. Thus the yce comming on us so fast, we were in great danger, looking every houre for death. And thus passed we on in that great danger, seeing both our selves and the rest of our ships so troubled and tossed amongst the yce, that it would make the strongest heart to relent.

At the last the Barke Dionyse being but a weake ship, and bruised afore amongst the yce, being so leake that no longer she could tarry above the water, sanke without saving any of the goods which were within her: which sight so abashed the whole Fleete, that we thought verily we should have tasted of the same sauce. But neverthelesse we seeing them in such danger, manned our boates and saved all the men in such wise, that not one perished: God be thanked.

The storme still increased and the yce inclosed us, so that we were faine to take downe top and top mastes: for the yce had so invironed us, that we could see neither land nor sea, as farre as we could kenne: so that we were faine to cut our cables to hang over boord for fenders, somewhat to ease the ships sides from the great and driry strokes of the yce: some with Capstan barres, some fending off with oares, some with plancks of two ynches thicke, which were broken immediatly with the force of the yce, some going out upon the yce to beare it off with their shoulders from the ships. But the rigorousnes of the tempest was such, and the force of the yce so great, that not onely they burst and spoyled the foresaid provision, but likewise so rased the sides of the ships, that it was pitifull to behold, and caused the hearts of many to faint.

Thus we continued all that dismall and lamentable night plunged in this perplexity, looking for instant death: but our God (who never leaveth them destitute *Gods provi-* which faithfully call upon him, although he often punisheth *dence.* for amendements sake) in the morning caused the winds to cease, and the fogge which all that night lay on the face of the water to cleare: so that we might perceive about a mile from us, a certaine place cleare from any yce, to the which with an easie breath of wind which our God sent us, we bent our selves. And furthermore, hee provided better for us then we deserved or hoped for: for when we were in the foresaid cleare place, he sent us a fresh gale at West or at West Southwest, which set us cleare without all the yce. And further he added more: for he sent us so pleasant a day as the like we had not of a long time before, as after punishment consolation.

Thus we joyfull wights being at libertie, tooke in all our sailes and lay a hull, praysing God for our deliverance, and stayed to gather together our Fleete: which once being done, we seeing that none of them had any great hurt, neither any of them wanted, saving onely they of whom I spake before and the ship which was lost, then at the last wee hoised our sailes, and lay bulting off and on, till such time as it would please God to take away the yce that wee might get into the Straights.

A mountaine of yce appearing in sundry figures.

And as we thus lay off and on we came by a marveilous huge mountaine of yce, which surpassed all the rest that ever we saw: for we judged it to be neere fourescore fathomes above water, and we thought it to be a ground for any thing that we could perceive, being there nine score fathoms deepe, and of compasse about halfe a mile.

A fog of long continuance.

Also the fift of July there fell a hidious fogge and mist, that continued till the nineteenth of the same: so that one shippe could not see another. Therefore we were faine to beare a small sayle and to observe the time: but there ran such a current of a tide, that it set us to the Northwest of the Queenes foreland the backside of all the Straights: where (through the contagious fogge having no sight either of Sunne or Starre) we scarce knew where we were. In this fogge the tenth of July we lost the company of the Viceadmirall, the Anne Francis, the Busse of Bridgewater, and the Francis of Foy.

A current to the Northwest.

The 16. day one of our small Barkes named the Gabriel was sent by our Generall to beare in with the land to descrie it, where being on land, they met with the people of the Countrey, which seemed very humane and civill, and offered to traffike with our men, profering them foules and skins for knives, and other trifles: whose courtesie caused us to thinke, that they had small conversation with other of the Straights.

The Gabriel.

[III. 42.]
The people offer to traffike with us.

Then we bare backe againe to goe with the Queenes foreland: and the eighteenth day wee came by two Islands whereon we went on shore, and found where the people had bene: but we saw none of them. This day wee were againe in the yce, and like to be in as great perill as we were at the first. For through the darknesse and obscuritie of the foggie mist, we were almost run on rocks and Islands before we saw them: But God (even miraculously) provided for us, opening the fogges that we might see clearely, both where and in what danger we presently were, and also the way to escape: or els without faile we had ruinously runne upon the rocks.

When we knew perfectly our instant case, wee cast about to get againe on Sea-bord, which (God be thanked) by night we obtained and praised God. The cleare continued scarce an houre, but the fogge fell againe as thicke as ever it was.

Then the Rearadmirall and the Beare got themselves cleare without danger of yce and rocks, strooke their sailes and lay a hull, staying to have the rest of the Fleete come forth: which as yet had not found the right way to cleare themselves from the danger of rockes and yce, untill the next morning, at what time the Rearadmirall discharged certaine warning pieces to give notice that she had escaped, and that the rest (by following of her) might set themselves free, which they did that day.

Warning pieces of safe passage discharged.

Then having gathered our selves togither we proceeded on our purposed voyage, bearing off, and keeping our selves distant from the coast till the 19. day of July: at which time the fogges brake up and dispersed, so that we might plainely and clearely behold the pleasant ayre, which so long had bene taken from us, by the obscuritie of the foggie mists: and after that time we were not much encombred therewith untill we had left the confines of the Countrey.

Then we espying a fayre sound, supposed it to goe into the Straights betweene the Queenes foreland and Jackmans sound, which proved as we imagined. For our Generall sent forth againe the Gabriel to discover it, who passed through with much difficulty: for there ran such an extreme current of a tide, with such a horrible gulfe, that with a fresh gale of wind they were scarce able to stemme it: yet at the length with great travaile they passed it, and came to the Straights, where they met with the Thomas Allen, the Thomas of Ipswich, and the Busse of Bridgewater: who altogether adventured to beare into the yce againe, to see if they could obtaine their wished Port. But they were so incombred that with much difficultie they were able to get out againe, yet at the last they escaping, the Thomas Allen, and the Gabriel

A faire sound betweene the Queenes foreland and Jackmans sound.

bare in with the Westerne shore, where they found harbour, and there moared their ships untill the fourth of August, at which time they came to us in the Countesse of Warwicks sound. The Thomas of Ipswich caught a great leake which caused her to cast againe to Seabord and so was mended.

We sailed along still by the coast untill we came to the Queenes foreland, at the point whereof we met with part of the gulfe aforesayd, which place or gulfe (as some of our Masters doe credibly report) doeth flow nine houres, and ebs but three. At that point wee discovered certaine lands Southward, which neither time nor opportunitie would serve to search. Then being come to the mouth of the Straights we met with the Anne Francis, who had laine bulting up and downe ever since her departure alone, never finding any of her company. We met then also the Francis of Foy, with whom againe we intended to venture and get in : but the yce was yet so thicke, that we were compelled againe to retyre and get us on Sea-bord.

*An horrible
snowe fell in
July.*

There fell also the same day being the 26. of July, such an horrible snow, that it lay a foot thick upon the hatches which frose as it fell.

We had also at other times divers cruell stormes both of snow and haile, which manifestly declared the distemperature of the Countrey : yet for all that wee were so many times repulsed and put backe from our purpose, knowing that lingering delay was not profitable for us, but hurtfull to our voyage, we mutually consented to our valiant Generall once againe, to give the onset.

The 28. day therefore of the same July we assayed, and with little trouble (God be praysed) we passed the dangers by day light. Then night falling on the face of the earth, wee hulled in the cleare, til the chearefull light of the day had chased away the noysome darkenesse

*The time of
our setting for-
ward, &c.*

of the night : at which time we set forward towards our wished Port : by the 30. day wee obteined our expected desire, where we found the Judith, and the Michael :

which brought no smal joy unto the General, and great consolation to the heavie hearts of those wearied wights. The 30. day of July we brought our ships into the Countesse of Warwicks sound, and moared them, namely these ships, The Admirall, the Rearadmiral, the Francis of Foy, the Beare Armenel, the Salomon, and the Busse of Bridgewater : which being done, our Generall commaunded us all to come a shore upon the Countesses Iland, where he set his Miners to worke upon the Mine, giving charge with expedition to dispatch with their lading.

[III. 43.]

Our Generall himselfe, accompanied with his Gentlemen, divers times made rodes into sundry partes of the Countrey, as well to finde new Mines, as also to finde out and see the people of the Countrey. He found out one Mine upon an Island by Beares sound, and named it the Countesse of Sussex Island. One other was found in Winters Fornace, with divers others, to which the ships were sent sunderly to be laden. In the same rodes he mette with divers of the people of the Countrey at sundry times, as once at a place called Davids sound : who shot at our men, and very desperately gave them the onset, being not above three or foure in number, there being of our Countrey men above a dosen : but seeing themselves not able to prevaile, they tooke themselves to flight : whom our men pursued, but being not used to such craggie cliffes, they soone lost the sight of them, and so in vaine returned.

The Countesse of Sussex Iland.
Winters Fornace.
Davids Sound.

We also saw of them at Beares sound, both by Sea and land in great companies : but they would at all times keepe the water betweene them and us. And if any of our ships chanced to be in the sound (as they came divers times, because the Harbor was not very good) the ship laded, and departed againe : then so long as any ships were in sight, the people would not be seene. But when as they perceived the ships to be gone, they would not only shew themselves standing upon high cliffes, and call us to come over unto them : but also

The policie of the people for safetie of themselves.

would come in their Botes very neere to us, as it were to brag at us: whereof our Generall having advertisement, sent for the Captaines and Gentlemen of the Ships, to accompany and attend upon him, with the Captaine also of the Anne Francis, who was but the night before come unto us. For they, and the Fleebote having lost us the 26. day in the great snowe, put into an harbour in the Queenes foreland, where they found good Oare, wherewith they laded themselves, and came to seeke the Generall: so that now we had all our Shippes, saving one Barke, which was lost, and the Thomas of Ipswich, who (compelled by what furie I knowe not) forsooke our company, and returned home without lading.

Their speedie flight at our Generals arrivall.

Our Generall accompanied with his Gentlemen, (of whom I spake) came all together to the Countesse of Sussex Island, neere to Beares sound: where he manned out certaine Pinnisses, and went over to the people: who perceiving his arrivall, fledde away with all speede, and in haste left certaine dartes and other engines behinde them, which we found: but the people we could not finde.

The next morning our Generall perceiving certaine of them in botes upon the Sea, gave chase to them in a Pinnesse under saile, with a fresh gale of winde, but could by no meanes come neere unto them: for the longer he sailed, the further off he was from them: which well shewed their cunning and activitie. Thus time wearing away, and the day of our departure approching, our Generall commaunded us to lade with all expedition, that we might be againe on Seaboard with our ships: for whilest we were in the Countrey, we were in continual danger of freezing in: for often snow and haile often falling, the water was so much frosen and congealed in the night, that in the morning we could scarce rowe our botes or Pinnesses, especially in Diers sound, which is a calme and still water: which caused our Generall to make the more haste, so that by the 30. day of August we were all laden, and made all things ready to depart.

But before I proceede any further herein, to shew what *Gentlemen should have inhabited the Countrey.* fortune befell at our departure, I will turne my penne a litle to M. Captaine Fenton, and those Gentlemen which should have inhabited all the yeere in those Countries, whose valiant mindes were much to be commended: For doubtlesse they had done as they intended, if lucke had not withstoode their willingnesse.

For the Barke Dionyse which was lost, had in her much of their house which was prepared and should have bene builded for them, with many other implements. Also the Thomas of Ipswich which had most of their provision in her, came not into the Streights at all: neither did we see her since the day we were separated in the great snow, of which I spake before. For these causes, having not their house, nor yet provision, they were disappointed of their pretence to tarie, and therefore laded their ships, and so came away with us.

But before we tooke shipping, we builded a litle house *An house tricked and garnished with divers trinkets.* in the Countesse of Warwicks Island, and garnished it with many kinds of trifles, as Pinnes, Points, Laces, Glasses, Kombes, Babes on horsebacke and on foote, with innumerable other such fansies and toyes: thereby to allure and entice the people to some familiaritie against other yeeres.

Thus having finished all things we departed the [III. 44.] Countrey, as I sayd before: but because the Busse had not lading enough in her, she put into Beares sound to take in a little more. In the meane while the Admirall, and the rest without at Sea stayed for her. And that night fell such an outragious tempest, beating *An outragious tempest.* on our ships with such vehement rigor, that anchor and cable availed nought: for we were driven on rockes and Islands of yce, insomuch that (had not the great goodnesse of God bene miraculously shewed to us) we had bene cast away every man. This danger was more doubtfull and terrible, then any that preceded or went before: for there was not any one shippe (I thinke) that escaped without damage. Some lost anchor and also cables, some botes, some Pinnisses: some anchor, cables, boates and Pinnisses.

This boystrous storme so severed us from one another, that one shippe knewe not what was become of another. The Admirall knewe not where to finde the Viceadmirall or Rearadmirall, or any other ship of our company. Our Generall being on land in Beares sound could not come to his Shippe, but was compelled to goe aboord the Gabriel where he continued all the way homeward: for the boystrous blasts continued so extreamely and so long a time, that they sent us homewarde (which was Gods favour towardes us) will we, nill we, in such haste, as not any one of us were able to keepe in company with other, but were separated. And if by chance any one Shippe did overtake other, by swiftnesse of sayle, or mette, as they often did: yet was the rigour of the wind so hidious, that they could not continue company together the space of one whole night.

*Our entring
the coastes
dangerous.*

Thus our journey outward was not so pleasant, but our comming thither, entering the coasts and countrey, by narrow Streights, pèrillous yce, and swift tides, our times of aboade there in snowe and stormes, and our departure from thence the 31. of August with dangerous blustering windes and tempests, which that night arose, was as uncomfortable: separating us so as wee sayled, that not any of us mette together, untill the 28. of September, which day we fell on the English coastes, betweene Sylley and the landes ende, and passed the channell, untill our arrivall in the river of Thames.

The report of Thomas Wiars passenger in the Emanuel, otherwise called the Busse of Bridgewater, wherein James Leech was Master, one of the ships in the last Voyage of Master Martin Frobisher 1578. concerning the discoverie of a great Island in their way homeward the 12. of September.

He Busse of Bridgewater was left in Beares sound at Meta incognita, the second day of September behinde the Fleete in some distresse, through much winde, ryding neere the Lee shoare, and forced there to ride it out upon the hazard of her cables and anchors, which were all aground but two. The third of September being fayre weather, and the winde North northwest she set sayle, and departed thence, and fell with Frisland on the 8. day of September at sixe of the clocke at night, and then they set off from the Southwest point of Frisland, the wind being at East, and East Southeast, but that night the winde veared Southerly, and shifted oftentimes that night: but on the tenth day in the morning, the wind at West northwest faire weather, they steered Southeast, and by south, and continued that course until the 12. day of September, when about 11. a clocke before noone, they descryed a lande, which was from them about five leagues, and the Southermost part of it was Southeast by East from them, and the Northermost next, North Northeast, or Northeast. The master accompted that the Southeast poynt of Frisland was from him at that instant when hee first descryed this new Islande, Northwest by North, 50. leagues. They account this Island to be 25. leagues long, and the longest way of it Southeast, and Northwest. The Southerne part of it is in the latitude of 57. degrees and 1. second part, or there about. They continued in sight of it, from the 12. day at a 11. of the clocke, till the

The Island in length 25. leagues. This Iland is in the latitude of 57. degrees and 1 second pars.

13. day three of the clocke in the after noone, when they left it: and the last part they saw of it, bare from them Northwest by North. There appeared two Harboroughs upon that coast: the greatest of them seven leagues to the Northwards of the Southermost poynt, the other but foure leagues. There was very much yce neere the same land, and also twentie or thirty leagues from it, for they were not cleare of yce, till the 15. day of September after noone. They plyed their Voyage homewards, and fell with the West part of Ireland about Galway, and had first sight of it on the 25. day of September.

[III. 45.] Notes framed by M. Richard Hakluyt of the middle Temple Esquire, given to certaine Gentlemen that went with M. Frobisher in his Northwest discoverie, for their directions: And not unfit to be committed to print, considering the same may stirre up considerations of these and of such other things, not unmeete in such new voyages as may be attempted hereafter.

Hat the first Seate be chosen on the seaside, so as (if it may be) you may have your owne Navie within Bay, river or lake, within your Seate safe from the enemie: and so as the enemie shalbe forced to lie in open rode abroad without, to be dispersed with all windes and tempests that shall arise. Thus seated you shall be least subject to annoy of the enemie, so may you by your Navie within passe out to all parts of the world, and so may the Shippes of England have access to you to supply all wants, so may your commodities be caryed away also. This seat is to be chosen in a temperate Climat, in sweete ayre, where you may possesse always sweete water, wood, seacoles or turfe, with

fish, flesh, graine, fruites, herbes and rootes, or so many of those as may suffice very necessitie for the life of such as shall plant there. And for the possessing of mines of golde, of silver, copper, quicksilver, or of any such precious thing, the wants of those needfull things may be supplyed from some other place by sea, &c.

Stone to make Lyme of,
Slate stone to tyle withall, or
   such clay as maketh tyle,
Stone to wall withall, if
   Brycke may not bee made,
Timber for buylding easely to
   be conveied to the place,
Reede to cover houses or
   such like, if tyle or slate
   be not.

are to be looked for as things without which no Citie may be made nor people in civil sort be kept together.

The people there to plant and to continue are eyther to live without traffique, or by traffique and by trade of marchandise. If they shall live without sea traffique, at the first they become naked by want of linnen and woollen, and very miserable by infinite wants that will otherwise ensue, and so will they be forced of themselves to depart, or else easely they will be consumed by the Spanyards, by the Frenchmen, or by the naturall inhabitants of the countrey, and so the enterprize becomes reprochfull to our Nation, and a let to many other good purposes that may be taken in hand.

And by trade of marchandise they can not live, except the Sea or the Land there may yeelde commoditie. And therefore you ought to have most speciall regard of that poynt, and so to plant, that the naturall commodities of the place and seate may draw to you accesse of Navigation for the same, or that by your owne Navigation you may cary the same out, and fetch home the supply of the wants of the seate.

Such Navigation so to be employed shall, besides the supply of wants, be able to encounter with forreine force.

And for that in the ample vent of such things as are brought to you out of England by Sea, standeth a matter of great consequence, it behoveth that all humanitie and curtesie and much forbearing of revenge to the Inland people be used: so shall you have firme amitie with your neighbours, so shall you have their inland commodities to mainteine traffique, and so shall you waxe rich and strong in force. Divers and severall commodities of the inland are not in great plenty to be brought to your hands, without the ayde of some portable or Navigable river, or ample lake, and therefore to have the helpe of such a one is most requisite: And so is it of effect for the dispersing of your owne commodities in exchange into the inlands.

Nothing is more to be indevoured with the Inland people then familiarity. For so may you best discover all the natural commodities of their countrey, & also all their wants, al their strengths, all their weaknesse, and with whom they are in warre, and with whom confederate in peace and amitie, &c. which knowen you may worke many great effects of greatest consequence.

And in your planting the consideration of the clymate and of the soyle be matters that are to be respected. For if it be so that you may let in the salt sea water, not mixed with the fresh into flats, where the sunne is of the heate that it is at Rochel, in the Bay of Portugal, or in Spaine, then may you procure a man of skill, and so you have wonne one noble commoditie for the fishing, and for trade of marchandize by making of Salt.

[III. 46.]   Or if the soyle and clymate be such as may yeeld you the Grape as good as that at Burdeaux, as that in Portugal, or as that about Sivil in Spaine, or that in the Islands of the Canaries, then there resteth but a workeman to put in execution to make Wines, and to dresse Resigns of the sunne and other, &c.

Or if ye finde a soyle of the temperature of the South part of Spaine or Barbarie in the which you finde the Olive tree to growe: Then you may be assured of a noble marchandize for this Realme, considering that our great trade of clothing doeth require oyle, and weying how deere of late it is become by the vent they have of that commoditie in the West Indies, and if you finde the wilde Olive there it may be graffed.

Or if you can find the berrie of Cochenile with which we colour Stammelles, or any Roote, Berrie, Fruite, wood or earth fitte for dying, you winne a notable thing fitte for our state of clothing. This Cochenile is naturall in the West Indies on that firme.

Or if you have Hides of beasts fitte for sole Lether, &c. It will be a marchandize right good, and the Savages there yet can not tanne Lether after our kinde, yet excellently after their owne manner.

Or if the soyle shall yeeld Figges, Almonds, Sugar Canes, Quinces, Orenges, Lemonds, Potatos, &c. there may arise some trade and traffique by Figs, Almonds, Sugar, Marmelade, Sucket, &c.

Or if great woods be found, if they be of Cypres, chests may be made, if they be of some kinde of trees, Pitch and Tarre may be made, if they be of some other, then they may yeeld Rosin, Turpentine, &c. and all for trade and traffique, and Caskes for wine and oyle may be made, likewise ships and houses, &c.

And because traffique is a thing so materiall, I wish that great observation be taken what every soyle yeeldeth naturally, in what commoditie soever, and what it may be made to yeelde by indevour, and to send us notice home, that thereupon we may devise what meanes may be thought of to raise trades.

Now admit that we might not be suffered by the Savages to enjoy any whole country or any more then the scope of a citie, yet if we might enjoy traffique, and be assured of the same, we might be much inriched, our Navie might be increased, and a place of safetie might there be found, if change of religion or civil warres should happen in this realme, which are things of great benefit. But if we may enjoy any large territorie of apt soyle, we might so use the matter, as we should not depend upon Spaine for oyles, sacks, resignes, orenges, lemonds, Spanish skins, &c. Nor upon France for woad, baysalt, and Gascoyne wines, nor on Eastland for flaxe, pitch, tarre, mastes, &c. So we should not so exhaust our treasure, and so exceedingly inrich our doubtfull friends, as we doe, but should purchase the commodities that we want for halfe the treasure that now wee doe : and should by our owne industries and the benefites of the soyle there cheaply purchase oyles, wines, salt, fruits, pitch, tarre, flaxe, hempe, mastes, boords, fish, golde, silver, copper, tallow, hides and many commodities : besides if there be no flatts to make salt on, if you have plentie of wood you may make it in sufficient quantitie for common uses at home there.

If you can keepe a safe Haven, although you have not the friendship of the neere neighbours, yet you may have traffique by sea upon one shore or other, upon that firme in time to come, if not present.

If you find great plentie of tymber on the shore side or upon any portable river, you were best to cut downe of the same the first winter, to be seasoned for ships, barks, boates and houses.

And if neere such wood there be any river or brooke upon the which a sawing mill may be placed, it would doe great service, and therefore consideration would be had of such places.

And if such port & chosen place of setling were in possession and after fortified by arte, although by the land side our Englishmen were kept in, and might not enjoy any traffique with the next neighbours, nor any victuals : yet might they victuall themselves of fish to serve very necessitie, and enter into amitie with the enemies of their next neighbours, and so have vent of their marchandize of England & also have victual, or by meanes hereupon to be used, to force the next neighbours to amitie. And keeping a navy at the setling place, they should find out along the tract of the land to have traffique, and at divers Islands also. And so this first seat might in time become a stapling place of the commodities of many countreys and territories, and in time this place might become of all the provinces round about the only governour. And if the place first chosen should not so well please our people, as some other more lately found out : There might be an easie remove, and that might be rased, or rather kept for others of our nation to avoyd an ill neighbour.

If the soyles adjoyning to such convenient Haven and setling places be found marshie and boggie, then men [III. 47.] skilful in drayning are to be caryed thither. For arte may worke wonderful effects therein, and make the soyle rich for many uses.

To plant upon an Island in the mouth of some notable river, or upon the point of the land entring into the river, if no such Island be, were to great end. For if such river were navigable or portable farre into the land, then would arise great hope of planting in fertil soyles, and traffike on the one or on the other side of the river, or on both, or the linking in amitie with one or other pettie king contending there for dominion.

Such rivers found, both Barges and Boates may be made for the safe passage of such as shall pierce the same. These are to be covered with doubles of course linnen artificially wrought, to defend the arrow or the dart of the savage from the rower.

Since every soile of the world by arte may be made to yeeld things to feede and to clothe man, bring in your returne a perfect note of the soile without and within, and we shall devise if neede require to amend the same, and to draw it to more perfection. And if you finde not fruites in your planting place to your liking, we shall in five drifats furnish you with such kindes of plants to be carryed thither the winter after your planting, as shall the very next summer following yeeld you some fruite, and the yeere next following, as much as shall suffice a towne as bigge as Calice, and that shortly after shall be able to yeeld you great store of strong durable good sider to drinke, and these trees shall be able to encrease you within lesse then seven yeeres as many trees presently to beare, as may suffice the people of divers parishes, which at the first setling may stand you in great stead, if the soile have not the commoditie of fruites of goodnesse already. And because you ought greedily to hunt after things that yeeld present reliefe, without trouble of carriage thither, therefore I make mention of these thus specially, to the end you may have it specially in minde.

A true discourse of the three Voyages of discoverie, for the finding of a passage to Cathaya, by the Northwest, under the conduct of Martin Frobisher Generall: Before which, as a necessary Preface is prefixed a twofolde discourse, conteining certaine reasons to prove all partes of the World habitable. Penned by Master George Best, a Gentleman employed in the same voyages.

What commodities and instructions may be reaped by diligent reading this Discourse.

1 FIrst, by example may be gathered, how a Discoverer of new Countries is to proceede in his first attempt of any Discoverie.

2 Item, how he should be provided of shipping, victuals, munition, and choice of men.

3 How to proceede and deale with strange people, be they never so barbarous, cruell and fierce, either by lenitie or otherwise.

4 How trade of Merchandize may be made without money.

5 How a Pilot may deale, being invironed with mountaines of yce in the frozen Sea.

6 How length of dayes, change of seasons, Summers and Winters doe differ in sundry regions.

7 How dangerous it is to attempt new Discoveries, either for the length of the voyage, or the ignorance of the language, the want of Interpretors, new and unaccustomed Elements and ayres, strange and unsavoury meates, danger of theeves and robbers, fiercenesse of wilde beastes and fishes, hugenesse of woods, dangerousnesse of Seas, dread of tempestes, feare of hidden rockes, steepnesse of mountaines, darkenesse of sudden falling fogges, continuall paines taking without any rest, and infinite others.

8 How pleasant and profitable it is to attempt new Discoveries, either for the sundry sights and shapes of strange beastes and fishes, the wonderfull workes of nature, the different maners and fashions of divers nations, the sundry sortes of government, the sight of strange trees, fruite, foules, and beastes, the infinite treasure of Pearle, Golde and Silver, the newes of newe found landes, the sundry positions of the Sphere, and many others.

9 How valiant Captaines use to deale upon extremitie, and otherwise.

10 How trustie souldiers dutifully use to serve.

11 Also here may bee seene a good example to be observed of any private person, in taking notes, and making observations of all such things as are requisite for a Discoverer of newe Countries.

12 Lastly, the Reader here may see a good paterne of [III. 48.] a well governed service, sundry instructions of matters of Cosmographie, Geographie, and Navigation, as in reading more at large may be seene.

[Experiences

Experiences and reasons of the Sphere, to proove
all partes of the worlde habitable, and thereby
to confute the position of the five Zones.

Irst, it may be gathered by experience of
our Englishmen in Anno 1553. For
Captaine Windam made a Voyage with
Merchandise to Guinea, and entred so
farre within the Torrida Zona, that he
was within three or foure degrees of the
Equinoctiall, and his company abiding
there certaine Moneths, returned, with gaine.

Also the Englishmen made another Voyage very prosperous and gainefull, An. 1554. to the coasts of Guinea,
within 3. degrees of the Equinoctiall. And yet it is
reported of a trueth, that all the tract from Cape de
las Palmas trending by C. de tres puntas alongst by
Benin, unto the Ile of S. Thomas (which is perpendi-
culer under the Equinoctial) all that whole Bay is more
subject to many blooming and smoothering heates, with
infectious and contagious ayres, then any other place in
all Torrida Zona: and the cause thereof is some accidents
in the land. For it is most certaine, that mountaines,
Seas, woods and lakes &c. may cause through their
sundry kinde of situation, sundry strange and extraor-
dinary effects, which the reason of the clyme otherwise
would not give. I mention these Voyages of our
Englishmen, not so much to proove that Torrida Zona
may bee, and is inhabited, as to shew their readinesse
in attempting long and dangerous Navigations. Wee
also among us in England have blacke Moores, Æthio-
pians, out of all partes of Torrida Zona, which after a
small continuance, can well endure the colde of our
Countrey, and why should not we as well abide the
heate of their Countrey? But what should I name
any more experiences, seeing that all the coastes of
Guinea and Benin are inhabited of Portugals, Span-

yardes, French, and some Englishmen, who there have built Castles and Townes. Onely this I will say to the Merchants of London, that trade yeerely to Marochus, it is very certaine, that the greatest part of the burning Zone is farre more temperate and coole in June, then the Countrey of Marochus, as shall appeare by these reasons and experiences following. For let us first consider the breadth and bignesse of this burning Zone (which as every man knoweth, is 47. degrees) each Tropicke, which are the bounders thereof, being 23. degrees and a halfe distant from the Equinoctiall. Imagine againe two other Parallels, on each side the Equinoctiall one, eyther of them distant from the Equinoctial about 20. degrees, which Paralels may be described either of them twice a yeere by the Sunne, being in the first degrees of Gemini the 11. of May, and in Leo the 13. of July, having North latitude. And againe, the Sunne being in the first degrees of Sagittarius, the 12. of November, and in Aquarius the 9. of January, having South latitude, I am to proove by experience and reason, that all that distance included betweene these two Paralels last named (conteyning 40. degrees in latitude, going round about the earth, according to longitude) is not onely habitable, but the same most fruitfull and delectable, and that if any extremitie of heate bee, the same not to be within the space of twenty degrees of the Equinoctiall on either side, but onely under and about the two Tropickes, and so proportionally the neerer you doe approch to eyther Tropicke, the more you are subject to extremitie of heate (if any such be) and so Marochus being situate but sixe or seven degrees from the Tropicke of Cancer, shall be more subject to heate, then any place under or neere the Equinoctiall line.

And first by the experience of sundry men, yea thousands, Travailers and Merchants, to the East and West Indies in many places both directly under, and hard by the Equinoctiall, they with one consent affirme, that it aboundeth in the middest of Torrida Zona with all

Marochus more hote then about the Equi-noctiall.

manner of Graine, Hearbes, grasse, fruite, wood and
cattell, that we have heere, and thousandes other sortes,
farre more wholesome, delectable and precious, then any
wee have in these Northerne climates, as very well shall
appeare to him that will reade the Histories and Navigations of such as have traveiled Arabia, India intra
& extra Gangem, the Islands Moluccæ, America, &c.
which all lye about the middle of the burning Zone,
where it is truely reported, that the great hearbes, as
are Radish, Lettuce, Colewortes, Borage, and such like,
doe waxe ripe, greater, more savourie and delectable in
taste then ours, within sixteene dayes after the seede is
sowen. Wheate being sowed the first of Februarie, was
found ripe the first of May, and generally, where it is
lesse fruitfull, the wheate will be ripe the fourth moneth
after the seed is sowne, and in some places will bring
foorth an eare as bigge as the wrist of a man's arme
containing 1000. graines; Beanes, peace, &c. are there
ripe twice a yeere. Also grasse being cut downe, will
grow up in sixe dayes above one foote high. If our
cattell be transported thither, within a small time their
young ones become of bigger stature, and more fat then
ever they would have bene in these countreys. There
are found in every wood in great numbers, such timber
trees as twelve men holding handes together are not able
to fathome. And to be short, all they that have bene
there with one consent affirme, that there are the goodliest
greene medowes and plaines, the fairest mountaines
covered with all sorts of trees and fruites, the fairest
valleys, the goodliest pleasant fresh rivers, stored with
infinite kinde of fishes, the thickest woods, greene and
bearing fruite all the whole yeere, that are in all the
world. And as for gold, silver, and all other kinde of
Metals, all kinde of spices and delectable fruites, both
for delicacie and health, are there in such abundance,
as hitherto they have bene thought to have beene bred
no where else but there. And in conclusion, it is nowe
thought that no where else but under the Equinoctiall,

Marveilous
fruitfull soile
under the
Equinoctiall.

[III. 49.]

Great trees.

Commodities
and pleasures
under the
Equinoctiall.

or not farre from thence, is the earthly Paradise, and the onely place of perfection in this worlde. And that these things may seeme the lesse strange, because it hath bene accompted of the olde Philosophers, that there coulde nothing prosper for the extreme heat of the Sunne continually going over their heades in the Zodiacke, I thought good here to alleadge such naturall causes as to me seeme very substantiall and sure reasons.

First you are to understand that the Sunne doeth worke his more or lesse heat in these lower parts by two meanes, the one is by the kinde of Angle that the Sunne beames doe make with the earth, as in all Torrida Zona it maketh perpendicularly right Angles in some place or other at noone, and towards the two Poles very oblique and uneven Angles. And the other meane is the longer or shorter continuance of the Sunne above the Horizon. So that wheresoever these two causes do most concurre, there is most excesse of heat: and when the one is wanting, the rigor of the heat is lesse. For though the Sunne beames do beat perpendicularly upon any region subject unto it, if it hath no continuance or abode above the Horizon, to worke his operation in, there can no hote effect proceed. For nothing can be done in a moment. And this second cause *mora Solis supra Horizontem*, the time of the sunnes abiding above the Horizon, the old Philosophers never remembred, but regarded onely the maner of Angles that the Sunne beames made with the Horizon, which if they were equall and right, the heat was the greater, as in Torrida Zona: if they were unequall and oblique, the heat was the lesse, as towards both Poles, which reason is very good and substantiall: for the perpendicular beames reflect and reverberate in themselves, so that the heat is doubled, every beame striking twice, & by uniting are multiplied, and continue strong in forme of a Columne. But in our Latitude of 50. and 60. degrees, the Sunne beames descend oblique and slanting wise, and so strike but once and depart, and therefore our

Heat is caused by two meanes that is by his maner of Angle and by his continuance.

Note this reason.

heat is the lesse for any effect that the Angle of the
Sunne beames make. Yet because wee have a longer
continuance of the Sunnes presence above our Horizon
then they have under the Equinoctial; by this continuance the heat is increased, for it shineth to us 16.
or 18. houres sometime, when it continueth with them
but twelve houres alwayes.

And againe, our night is very short wherein cold
vapours use to abound, being but sixe or eight houres
long, whereas theirs is alwayes twelve houres long, by
which two advantages of long dayes and short nights,
though we want the equalitie of Angle, it commeth to
passe that in Sommer our heat here is as great as theirs
is there, as hath bene proved by experience, and is
nothing dissonant from good reason. Therefore whosoever will rightly way the force of colde and heat in
any region, must not onely consider the Angle that the
Sunne beames make, but also the continuance of the same
above the Horizon. As first to them under the Equinoctiall the Sunne is twice a yeere at noone in their
Zenith perpendicular over their heads, and therefore
during the two houres of those two dayes the heat is
very urgent, and so perhaps it will be in foure or five
dayes more an houre every day, untill the Sunne in
his proper motion have crossed the Equinoctiall; so that
this extreme heat caused by the perpendicular Angle of
the Sunne beames, endureth but two houres of two
dayes in a yeere. But if any man say the Sunne may
scalde a good while before and after it come to the
Meridian, so farre foorth as reason leadeth, I am content
to allow it, and therefore I will measure and proportion
the Sunnes heat, by comparing the Angles there, with
the Angles made here in England, because this temperature is best knowen unto us. As for example, the
11. day of March, when under the Equinoctiall it is
halfe houre past eight of the clocke in the morning,
the Sunne will be in the East about 38. degrees above
the Horizon, because there it riseth alwayes at sixe

of the clocke, and mooveth every houre 15. degrees,
and so high very neere will it be with us at London [III. 50.]
the said eleventh day of March at noone. And therefore
looke what force the Sunne hath with us at noone, the
eleventh of March, the same force it seemeth to have
under the Equinoctial at half an houre past eight in
the morning, or rather lesse force under the Equinoctiall.
For with us the Sunne had bene already sixe houres
above the horizon, and so had purified and clensed all
the vapours, and thereby his force encreased at noone;
but under the Equinoctiall, the Sunne having bene up
but two houres and an halfe, had sufficient to doe, to
purge and consume the cold and moyst vapours of the
long night past, and as yet had wrought no effect of
heate. And therefore I may boldly pronounce, that
there is much lesse heate at halfe an houre past eight
under the Equinoctiall, then is with us at noone: à
fortiori. But in March we are not onely contented to
have the Sunne shining, but we greatly desire the same.
Likewise the 11 of June, the Sunne in our Meridian
is 62 degrees high at London: and under the Equinoctiall
it is so high after 10 of the clocke, and seeing then it is
beneficial with us; à fortiori it is beneficiall to them after
10 of the clocke.

And thus have wee measured the force of the Sunnes
greatest heate, the hottest dayes in the yeere, under the
Equinoctiall, that is in March and September, from sixe
till after tenne of the clocke in the morning, and from
two untill Sunne set. And this is concluded, by respecting onely the first cause of heate, which is the
consideration of the Angle of the Sunne beames, by a
certaine similitude, that whereas the Sunne shineth never
above twelve houres, more then eight of them would bee
coole and pleasant even to us, much more to them
that are acquainted alwayes with such warme places. So
there remaineth lesse then foure houres of any excessive
heate, and that onely in the two Sommer dayes of the
yeere, that is the eleventh day of March, and the foure-

teenth of September: for under the Equinoctiall they have two Sommers, the one in March, and the other in September, which are our Spring and Autumne: and likewise two Winters, in June and December, which are our Sommer and Winter, as may well appeare to him that hath onely tasted the principles of the Sphere. But if the Sunne bee in either Tropicke, or approching neere thereunto, then may wee more easily measure the force of his Meridian altitude, that it striketh upon the Equinoctiall. As for example, the twelfth of June the Sunne will be in the first degree of Cancer. Then looke what force the heate of the Sunne hath under the Equinoctiall, the same force and greater it hath in all that Parallel, where the Pole is elevated betweene fourtie and seven, and fourtie and eight degrees. And therefore Paris in France the twelfth day of June sustaineth more heate of the Sunne, then Saint Thomas Iland lying neere the same Meridian doeth likewise at noone, or the Ilands Taprobana, Moluccæ, or the firme lande of Peru in America, which all lye underneath the Equinoctiall. For upon the twelfth day of June aforesaide, the Sunne beames at noone doe make an Isoscheles Triangle, whose Vertex is the Center of the Sunne, the Basis a line extended from Saint Thomas Iland under the Equinoctiall, unto Paris in France neere the same Meridian: therefore the two Angles of the Base must needs be equal per 5. primi, Ergo the force of the heat equal, if there were no other cause then the reason of the Angle, as the olde Philosophers have appointed. But because at Paris the Sunne riseth two houres before it riseth to them under the Equinoctiall, and setteth likewise two houres after them, by meanes of the obliquitie of the Horizon, in which time of the Sunnes presence foure houres in one place more then the other, it worketh some effect more in one place then in the other, and being of equall height at noone, it must then needs follow to be more hote in the Parallel of Paris, then it is under the Equinoctiall.

Paris in France is as hote as under the Equinoctiall in June.

In June is greater heat at Paris then under the Equinoctial,

Also this is an other reason, that when the Sunne setteth to them under the Equinoctiall, it goeth very deepe and lowe under their Horizon, almost even to their Antipodes, whereby their twilights are very short, and their nights are made very extreme darke and long, and so the moysture and coldnesse of the long nights wonderfully encreaseth, so that at length the Sunne rising can hardly in many houres consume and drive away the colde humours and moyst vapours of the night past, which is cleane contrary in the Parallel of Paris: for the Sunne goeth under their Horizon but very little, after a sloping sort, whereby their nights are not very darke, but lightsome, as looking into the North in a cleare night without cloudes it doeth manifestly appeare, their twilights are long: for the Parallel of Cancer cutteth not the Horizon of Paris at right Angles, but at Angles very uneven, and unlike as it doeth the Horizon of the Equinoctiall. Also the Sommer day at Paris is sixteene houres long, and the night but eight: where contrarywise under the Equinoctiall the day is but twelve houres long, and so long is also the night, in whatsoever Parallel the Sunne be: and therefore looke what oddes and difference of proportion there is betweene the Sunnes abode above the Horizon in Paris, and the abode it hath under the Equinoctiall, (it being in Cancer) the same proportion would seeme to be betweene the heate of the one place, and heate of the other: [III. 51.] for other things (as the Angle of the whole arke of the Sunnes progresse that day in both places) are equall.

But under the Equinoctiall the presence and abode of the Sunne above the Horizon is equall to his absence, and abode under the Horizon, eche being twelve houres. And at Paris the continuance and abode of the Sunne is above the Horizon sixteene houres long, and but eight houres absence, which proportion is double, from which if the proportion of the equalitie be subtracted to finde the difference, there will remaine still a double propor-

The twilights are shorter, and the nights darker under the Equinoctial then at Paris.

tion, whereby it seemeth to follow, that in June the heate at Paris were double to the heate under the equinoctiall. For (as I have said) the Angles of the Sunne beames are in all points equall, and the cause of difference is, Mora Solis supra Horizontem, the stay of the Sunne in the one Horizon more then in the other. Therefore, whosoever could finde out in what proportion the Angle of the Sunne beames heateth, and what encrease the Sunnes continuance doeth adde thereunto, it might expresly be set downe, what force of heat and cold is in all regions.

Thus you partly see by comparing a Climate to us well knowen, and familiarly acquainted by like height of the Sunne in both places, that under the Equinoctiall in June is no excessive heat, but a temperate aire rather tending to cold. For as they have there for the most part a continuall moderate heat, so yet sometime they are a little pinched with colde, and use the benefite of fire as well as we, especially in the evening when they goe to bed, for as they lye in hanging beds tied fast in the upper part of the house, so will they have fires made on both sides their bed, of which two fires, the one they devise superstitiously to drive away spirits, and the other to keepe away from them the coldnesse of the nights.

Also in many places of Torrida Zona, especially in the higher landes somewhat mountainous, the people a litle shrincke at the cold, and are often forced to provide themselves clothing, so that the Spaniards have found in the West Indies many people clothed, especially in Winter, whereby appeareth, that with their heat there is colde intermingled, else would they never provide this remedy of clothing, which to them is rather a griefe and trouble then otherwise. For when they goe to warres, they will put off all their apparell, thinking it to be combersome, and will alwayes goe naked, that they thereby might be more nimble in their fight.

Some there be that thinke the middle Zone extreme hot, because the people of the countrey can, and doe live without clothing, wherein they childishly are deceived: for our Clime rather tendeth to extremitie of colde, because wee cannot live without clothing: for this our double lining, furring, and wearing so many clothes, is a remedy against extremitie, and argueth not the goodnesse of the habitation, but inconvenience and injury of colde: and that is rather the moderate, temperate, and delectable habitation, where none of these troublesome things are required, but that we may live naked and bare, as nature bringeth us foorth.

Others againe imagine the middle Zone to be extreme hot, because the people of Africa, especially the Ethiopians, are so cole blacke, and their haire like wooll curled short, which blacknesse and curled haire they suppose to come onely by the parching heat of the Sunne, which how it should be possible I cannot see: for even under the Equinoctiall in America, and in the East Indies, and in the Ilands Moluccæ the people are not blacke, but tauney and white, with long haire uncurled as wee have, so that if the Ethiopians blacknesse came by the heat of the Sunne, why should not those Americans and Indians also be as blacke as they, seeing the Sunne is equally distant from them both, they abiding in one Parallel: for the concave and convexe Superficies of the Orbe of the Sunne is concentrike, and equidistant to the earth; except any man should imagine somewhat of Aux Solis, and Oppositum, which indifferently may be applied aswel to the one place as to the other. But the Sunne is thought to give no otherwise heat, but by way of Angle in reflection, and not by his neerenesse to the earth: for throughout all Africa, yea in the middest of the middle Zone, and in all other places upon the tops of mountaines there lyeth continuall snow, which is neerer to the Orbe of the Sunne, then the people are in the valley, by so much as the height of these mountaines amount unto, and yet the Sunne notwithstanding his neerenesse, can not melt the snow for want of convenient place of reflections. Also

Ethiopians blacke, with curled haire.

The Sunne heateth not by his neerenesse, but onely by reflection.

the middle region of the aire where all the haile, frost, and snow is engendred, is neerer unto the Sunne then the earth is, and yet there continueth perpetuall cold, because there is nothing that the Sunne beames may reflect against, whereby appeareth that the neerenesse of the body of the Sunne worketh nothing.

Therefore to returne againe to the blacke Moores. I my selfe have seene an Ethiopian as blacke as a cole brought into England, who taking a faire English woman to wife, begat a sonne in all respects as blacke as the father was, although England were his native countrey, and an English woman his mother: whereby it seemeth this blacknes proceedeth rather of some natural infection of that man, which was so strong, that neither the nature of the Clime, neither the good complexion of the mother concurring, coulde any thing alter, and therefore, wee cannot impute it to the nature of the Clime. And for a more fresh example, our people of Meta Incognita (of whom and for whom this discourse is taken in hande) that were brought this last yeere into England, were all generally of the same colour that many nations be, lying in the middest of the middle Zone. And this their colour was not onely in the face which was subject to Sunne and aire, but also in their bodies, which were stil covered with garments as ours are, yea the very sucking childe of twelve moneths age had his skinne of the very same colour that most have under the Equinoctiall, which thing cannot proceed by reason of the Clime, for that they are at least ten degrees more towardes the North then wee in England are, No, the Sunne never commeth neere their Zenith by fourtie degrees: for in effect, they are within three or foure degrees of that which they call the frosen Zone, and as I saide, fourtie degrees from the burning Zone, whereby it followeth, that there is some other cause then the Climate or the Sonnes perpendicular reflexion, that should cause the Ethiopians great blacknesse. And the most probable cause to my judgement is, that this blackenesse proceedeth of some

A black
Moores sonne
borne in Eng-
land.
[III. 52.]

The colour of
the people in
Meta Incog-
nita. The
complexion of
the people of
Meta incog-
nita.

naturall infection of the first inhabitants of that Countrey, and so all the whole progenie of them descended, are still polluted with the same blot of infection. Therefore it shall not bee farre from our purpose, to examine the first originall of these blacke men, and howe by a lineall discent they have hitherto continued thus blacke.

It manifestly and plainely appeareth by holy Scripture, *The cause of the Ethiopians blacknesse.* that after the generall inundation and overflowing of the earth, there remained no moe men alive but Noe and his three sonnes, Sem, Cham, and Japhet, who onely were left to possesse and inhabite the whole face of the earth : therefore all the sundry discents that until this present day have inhabited the whole earth, must needes come of the off-spring either of Sem, Cham, or Japhet, as the onely sonnes of Noe, who all three being white, and their wives also, by course of nature should have begotten and brought foorth white children. But the envie of our great and continuall enemie the wicked Spirite is such, that as hee coulde not suffer our olde father Adam to live in the felicitie and Angelike state wherein hee was first created, but tempting him, sought and procured his ruine and fall : so againe, finding at this flood none but a father and three sonnes living, hee so caused one of them to transgresse and disobey his fathers commaundement, that after him all his posteritie shoulde bee accursed. The fact of disobedience was this : When *The Arke of Noe.* Noe at the commandement of God had made the Arke and entred therein, and the floud-gates of heaven were opened, so that the whole face of the earth, every tree and mountaine was covered with abundance of water, hee straitely commaunded his sonnes and their wives, that they should with reverence and feare beholde the justice and mighty power of God, and that during the time of the floud while they remained in the Arke, they should use continencie, and abstaine from carnall copulation with their wives : and many other precepts hee gave unto them, and admonitions touching the justice of God, in revenging sinne, and his mercie in delivering them,

*Chus the sonne
of Cham ac-
cursed.*

who nothing deserved it. Which good instructions and exhortations notwithstanding his wicked sonne Cham disobeyed, and being perswaded that the first childe borne after the flood (by right and Lawe of nature) should inherite and possesse all the dominions of the earth, hee contrary to his fathers commandement while they were yet in the Arke, used company with his wife, and craftily went about thereby to dis-inherite the off-spring of his other two brethren: for the which wicked and detestable fact, as an example for contempt of Almightie God, and disobedience of parents, God would a sonne should bee borne whose name was Chus, who not onely it selfe, but all his posteritie after him should bee so blacke and lothsome, that it might remaine a spectacle of disobedience to all the worlde. And of this blacke and cursed Chus

came all these blacke Moores which are in Africa, for after the water was vanished from off the face of the earth, and that the lande was dry, Sem chose that part of the land to inhabite in, which nowe is called Asia, and Japhet had that which now is called Europa, wherein wee dwell, and Africa remained for Cham and his blacke sonne Chus, and was called Chamesis after the fathers name, being perhaps a cursed, dry, sandy, and unfruitfull ground, fit for such a generation to inhabite in.

Thus you see, that the cause of the Ethiopians blacknesse is the curse and naturall infection of blood, and not the distemperature of the Climate; Which also may bee prooved by this example, that these blacke men are found in all parts of Africa, as well without the Tropickes, as within, even unto Capo de buona Speranza Southward, where, by reason of the Sphere, should be the same temperature that is in Sicilia, Morea and Candie, where al be of very good complexions. Wherefore I conclude, that the

blacknesse proceedeth not of the hotenesse of the Clime, but as I saide, of the infection of blood, and therefore this their argument gathered of the Africans blacknesse is not able to destroy the temperature of the middle Zone. Wee may therefore very well bee assertained,

that under the Equinoctiall is the most pleasant and
delectable place of the worlde to dwell in; where although
the Sunne for two houres in a yeere be direct over
their heades, and therefore the heate at that time somewhat of force, yet because it commeth so seldome, and
continueth so small a time, when it commeth, it is not
to bee wayed, but rather the moderate heate of other *Greatest tem-*
times in all the yeere to be remembred. And if the *perature under*
heate at any time should in the short day waxe somewhat *the Equinoc-*
urgent, the coldnesse of the long night there would easily *tial.*
refresh it, according as Honterus sayeth, speaking of
the temperature under the Equinoctiall.

> Quódque die solis violento incanduit æstu,
> Humida nox reficit, paribusque refrigerat horis.

If the heate of the Sunne in the day time doe burne
or parch any thing, the moysture of the night doeth
coole and refresh the same againe, the Sunne being as
long absent in the night, as it was present in the day.

Also our Aucthour of the Sphere, Johannes de Sacro
Bosco, in the Chapter of the Zodiacke, deriveth the
Etymologie of Zodiacus, of the Greeke word Zoe, which
in Latine signifieth Vita, life; for out of Aristotle hee
alleadgeth, that Secundum accessum & recessum solis in
Zodiaco, fiunt generationes & corruptiones in rebus
inferioribus: according to the Sunnes going to and fro in
the Zodiake, the inferiour bodies take their causes of
generation and corruption. Then it followeth, that where
there is most going too and fro, there is most generation
and corruption: which must needes be betweene the two
Tropickes; for there the Sunne goeth too and fro most,
and no where else but there. Therefore betweene the *Under the*
two Tropikes, that is, in the middle Zone, is greatest *Equinoctiall is*
increase, multiplication, generation, and corruption of *greatest gene-*
things, which also wee finde by experience; for there is *ration.*
Sommer twice in the yeere, and twice Winter, so that
they have two Harvests in the yeere, and continuall
Spring. Seeing then the middle Zone falleth out so

temperate, it resteth to declare where the hottest part of the world should bee, for we finde some places more hote then others.

Greatest heate under the Tropicks. To answere this doubt, reason perswadeth, the hotest place in the world to bee under and about the two Tropickes; for there more then in any other place doe both the causes of heate concurre, that is, the perpendicular falling of the Sunne beames, at right angles, and a greater continuance of the Sunne above the Horizon, the Pole there being elevated three or foure and twentie degrees. And as before I concluded, that though the Sunne were perpendicular to them under the Equinoctiall, yet because the same continued but a small time, (their dayes being short, and their nights long) and the speedie departure of the Sunne from their Zenith, because of the suddeine crossing of the Zodiake with the Equinoctiall, and that by such continuall course and recourse of hote and colde, the temperature grew moderate, and very well able to bee endured: so nowe to them under the two Tropickes, the Sunne having once by his proper motion declined twentie degrees from the Equinoctial, beginneth to draw neere their Zenith, which may bee (as before) about the eleventh day of May, and then beginneth to sende his beames almost at right Angles, about which time the Sunne entreth into the first degree of Gemini, and with this almost right Angle the Sunne beames will continue untill it bee past Cancer, that is, the space of two moneths every day at noone, almost perpendicular over their heades, being then the time of Solstitium Aestivale: which so long continuance of the Sunne about their Zenith may cause an extreme heate (if any be in the world) but of necessitie farre more heate then can bee under the Equinoctiall, where the Sunne hath no such long abode in the Zenith, but passeth away therehence very quickly. Also under the Tropickes, the day is longer by an houre and a halfe, then it is under the Equinoctiall; wherefore the heate of the Sunne having a longer time of operation, must needes be encreased, especially seeing the night wherein colde and moysture doe abound under the Tropickes, is lesse then it is under the Equinoctiall. Therefore I gather, that under the Tropickes is the hotest place, not onely of Torrida Zona, but of any other part of the world, especially because there both causes of heate doe concurre, that is, the perpendicular falling of the Sunne beames two monethes together, and the longer abode of the Sunnes presence above the Horison. And by this meanes more at large is prooved, that Marochus in Sommer is farré more hote, then at any time under the Equinoctiall, because it is situate so neere the Tropick of Cancer, and also for the length of their dayes. Neither yet do I thinke, that the Regions situate under the Tropicks are not habitable, for they are found to be very fruitfull also; although Marochus and some other parts of Afrike neere the Tropike for the drinesse of the native sandie soile, and [III. 54.] some accidents may seeme to some to be intemperate for over much heat. For Ferdinandus Oviedus speaking of Cuba and Hispaniola, Ilands of America, lying hard *Cuba.* under, or by the Tropike of Cancer, saith, that these *Hispaniola.* Ilands have as good pasture for cattell, as any other countrey in the world.

Also, they have most holesome and cleare water, and temperate aire, by reason whereof the heards of beastes are much bigger, fatter, and of better taste, then any in Spaine, because of the ranke pasture, whose moysture is better digested in the hearbe or grasse, by continuall and temperate heate of the Sunne, whereby being made more fat and unctious, it is of better and more stedfast nourishment: For continuall and temperate heate doeth not onely drawe much moysture out of the earth to the nourishment of such things as growe, and are engendred in that Clime, but doeth also by moderation preserve the same from putrifying, digesting also, and condensating or thickning the said moyst nourishment into a gumme and *Under the* unctious substance, whereby appeareth also, that under *Tropickes is* the Tropikes is both holesome, fruitefull, and pleasant *moderate temperature.*

267

habitation, whereby lastly it followeth, that all the middle Zone, which untill of late dayes hath bene compted and called the burning, broyling, and parched Zone, is now found to be the most delicate, temperate, commodious, pleasant, and delectable part of the world, and especially under the Equinoctiall.

Having now sufficiently at large declared the temperature of the middle Zone, it remaineth to speake somewhat also of the moderate and continuall heate in colde Regions, as well in the night as in the day all the Sommer long, and also how these Regions are habitable to the inhabitants of the same, contrary to the opinion of the olde writers.

Of the temperature of colde Regions all the Sommer long, and also how in Winter the same is habitable, especially to the inhabitants thereof.

He colde Regions of the world are those, which tending toward the Poles Arctike, and Antarctike, are without the circuite or boundes of the seven Climates: which assertion agreeable to the opinion of the olde Writers, is found and set out in our authour of the Sphere, Johannes de Sacrobosco, where hee plainely saith, that without the seventh Climate, which is bounded by a Parallel passing at *Nine Climates.* fiftie degrees in Latitude, all the habitation beyonde is discommodious and intollerable. But Gemma Frisius a late writer finding England and Scotland to be without the compasse of those Climates, wherein hee knewe to bee very temperate and good habitation, added thereunto two other Climates, the uttermost Parallel whereof passeth by 56. degrees in Latitude, and therein comprehendeth over and above the first computation, England, Scotland, Denmarke, Moscovia, &c. which all are rich and mightie kingdomes.

The olde writers perswaded by bare conjecture, went about to determine of those places, by comparing them to their owne complexions, because they felt them to bee hardly tollerable to themselves, and so took thereby an argument of the whole habitable earth; as if a man borne in Marochus, or some other part of Barbarie, should at the latter end of Sommer upon the suddeine, either naked, or with his thinne vesture, bee brought into England, hee would judge this Region presently not to bee habitable, because hee being brought up in so warme a Countrey, is not able here to live, for so suddeine an alteration of the colde aire: but if the same man had come at the beginning of Sommer, and so afterward by little and little by certaine degrees, had felt and acquainted himselfe with the frost of Autumne, it would have seemed by degrees to harden him, and so to make it farre more tollerable, and by use after one yeere or two, the aire would seeme to him more temperate. It was compted a great matter in the olde time, that there was a brasse pot broken in sunder with frosen water in Pontus, which after was brought and shewed in Delphis, in token of a miraculous colde region and winter, and therefore consecrated to the Temple of Apollo.

A comparison betweene Marochus and England.

This effect being wrought in the Parallel of fouretie three degrees in Latitude, it was presently counted a place very hardly and uneasily to be inhabited for the great colde. And how then can such men define upon other Regions very farre without that Parallel, whether they were inhabited or not, seeing that in so neere a place they so grossely mistooke the matter, and others their followers being contented with the inventions of the olde Authors, have persisted willingly in the same opinion, with more confidence then consideration of the cause: so lightly was that opinion received, as touching the unhabitable Clime neere and under the Poles.

Therefore I am at this present to prove, that all the land lying betweene the last climate even unto the point directly under either poles, is or may be inhabited,

[III. 55.]
All the North regions are habitable.

especially of such creatures as are ingendred and bred therein. For indeed it is to be confessed, that some particular living creature cannot live in every particular place or region, especially with the same joy and felicitie, as it did where it was first bred, for the certeine agreement of nature that is betweene the place and the thing

bred in that place; as appeareth by the Elephant, which being translated and brought out of the second or third climat, though they may live, yet will they never ingender or bring forth yong. Also we see the like in many kinds

of plants and herbs; for example, the Orange trees, although in Naples they bring forth fruit abundantly, in Rome and Florence they will beare onely faire greene leaves, but not any fruit: and translated into England, they will hardly beare either flowers, fruit, or leaves, but are the next Winter pinched and withered with colde: yet it followeth not for this, that England, Rome, and Florence should not be habitable.

In the proving of these colde regions habitable, I shalbe very short, because the same reasons serve for this purpose, which were alleged before in the proving the middle Zone to be temperate, especially seeing all heat and colde proceed from the Sunne, by the meanes either of the Angle which his beames do make with the Horizon, or els by the long or short continuance of the Suns presence above ground: so that if the Sunnes beames do beat perpendicularly at right Angles, then there is one cause of heat, and if the Sunne do also long continue above the Horizon, then the heat thereby is much increased by accesse of this other cause, & so groweth to a kinde of extremity. And these two causes, as I sayd before, do most concurre under the two Tropicks, and therefore there is the greatest heat of the world. And likewise, where both these causes are most absent, there is greatest want of heat, and increase of colde (seeing that colde is nothing but the privation and absence of heat) and if one cause be wanting, and the other present, the effect will grow indifferent. Therefore this is to be

understood, that the neerer any region is to the Equinoctiall, the higher the Sunne doth rise over their heads
at noone, and so maketh either right or neere right
Angles, but the Sunne tarieth with them so much the
shorter time, and causeth shorter dayes, with longer
and colder nights, to restore the domage of the day past,
by reason of the moisture consumed by vapour. But in
such regions, over the which the Sunne riseth lower
(as in regions extended towards either pole) it maketh
there unequall Angles, but the Sunne continueth longer,
and maketh longer dayes, and causeth so much shorter
and warmer nights, as retaining warme vapours of the
day past. For there are found by experience Summer
nights in Scotland and Gothland very hot, when under
the Equinoctiall they are found very cold. This benefit
of the Sunnes long continuance & increase of the day,
doth augment so much the more in colde regions as
they are nerer the poles, and ceaseth not increasing untill
it come directly under the point of the pole Arcticke,
where the Sunne continueth above ground the space of
sixe moneths or halfe a yere together, and so the day
is halfe a yere long, that is the time of the Sunnes being
in the North signes, from the first degree of Aries untill
the last of Virgo, that is all the time from our 10 day
of March untill the 14 of September. The Sunne therfore during the time of these sixe moneths without any
offence or hindrance of the night, giveth his influence
upon those lands with heat that never ceaseth during
that time, which maketh to the great increase of Summer,
by reason of the Sunnes continuance. Therefore it
followeth, that though the Sunne be not there very high
over their heads, to cause right angle beames, and to
give great heat, yet the Sun being there sometime almost
24 degrees high doth cast a convenient and meane heate,
which there continueth without hindrance of the night
the space of sixe moneths (as is before sayd) during which
time there followeth to be a convenient, moderate and
temperate heat: or els rather it is to be suspected the

Hote nights nere the pole.

Colde nights under the Equinoctiall.

One day of sixe moneths.

Moderate hea under ye pole

heat there to be very great, both for continuance, and also, Quia virtus unita crescit, the vertue and strength of heat united in one increaseth. If then there be such a moderate heat under the poles, and the same to continue so long time; what should moove the olde writers to say there cannot be place for habitation. And that the certainty of this temperate heat under both the poles might more manifestly appeare, let us consider the position & quality of the sphere, the length of the day, and so gather the height of the Sunne at all times, and by consequent the quantity of his angle, and so lastly the strength of his heat.

Those lands and regions lying under the pole, and having the pole for their Zenith, must needs have the Equinoctial circle for their Horizon: therefore the Sun entring into the North signes, and describing every 24 houres a parallel to the Equinoctiall by the diurnall motion of Primum mobile, the same parallels must needs be wholly above the Horizon: and so looke how many degrees there are from the first of Aries to the last of Virgo, so many whole revolutions there are above their Horizon that dwell under the pole, which amount to 182, and so many of our dayes the Sunne continueth with them. During which time they have there continuall day and light, without any hindrance of moist nights. Yet it is to be noted, that the Sunne being in the first degree of Aries, and last degree of Virgo, maketh his revolution in the very horizon, so that in these 24 houres halfe the body of the Sunne is above the horizon, and the other halfe is under his only center, describing both the horizon and the equinoctiall circle.

The Sunne never setteth in 182 dayes.

[III. 56.]

Horizon and Equinoctiall all one under the pole.

And therefore seeing the greatest declination of the Sunne is almost 24 degrees, it followeth, his greatest height in those countreys to be almost 24 degrees. And so high is the Sun at noone to us in London about the 29 of October, being in the 15 degree of Scorpio, and likewise the 21 of January being in the 15 of Aquarius. Therefore looke what force the Sun at noone hath in

London the 29 of October, the same force of heat it London.
hath, to them that dwell under the pole, the space almost
of two moneths, during the time of the Summer solstitium, and that without intermingling of any colde
night; so that if the heat of the Sunne at noone could
be well measured in London (which is very hard to do,
because of the long nights which ingender great moisture
and cold) then would manifestly appeare by expresse
numbers the maner of the heat under the poles, which
certainly must needs be to the inhabitants very commodious and profitable, if it incline not to overmuch
heat, and if moisture do not want.

For as in October in England we finde temperate aire,
and have in our gardens hearbs and floures notwithstanding our cold nights, how much more should they
have the same good aire, being continuall without night.
This heat of ours continueth but one houre, while the
Sun is in that meridian, but theirs continueth a long
time in one height. This our heat is weake, and by
the coolenesse of the night vanisheth, that heat is
strong, and by continuall accesse is still increased and
strengthened. And thus by a similitude of the equall
height of the Sun in both places appeareth the com- Commodious
modious and moderate heat of the regions under the dwellingunder
poles.   the poles.

And surely I cannot thinke that the divine providence
hath made any thing uncommunicable, but to have given
such order to all things, that one way or other the same
should be imployed, and that every thing and place
should be tollerable to the next: but especially all things
in this lower world be given to man to have dominion
and use thereof. Therefore we need no longer to doubt
of the temperate and commodious habitation under the
poles during the time of Summer.

But all the controversie consisteth in the Winter, for
then the Sunne leaveth those regions, and is no more
seene for the space of other sixe moneths, in the which
time all the Sunnes course is under their horizon for

THE ENGLISH VOYAGES

the space of halfe a yere, and then those regions (say some) must needs be deformed with horrible darknesse, and continuall night, which may be the cause that beasts can not seeke their food, and that also the colde should then be intollerable. By which double evils all living creatures should be constrained to die, and were not able to indure the extremity and injury of Winter, and famine insuing thereof, but that all things should perish before the Summer following, when they should bring foorth their brood and yoong, and that for these causes the sayd Clime about the pole should be desolate and not habitable. To all which objections may be answered in this maner: First, that though the Sunne be absent from them those six moneths, yet it followeth not that there should be such extreme darknesse; for as the Sunne is departed under their horizon, so is it not farre from them: and not so soone as the Sunne falleth so suddenly commeth the darke night; but the evening doth substitute and prolong the day a good while after by twilight. After which time the residue of the night receiveth light of the Moone and Starres, untill the breake of the day, which giveth also a certaine light before the Sunnes rising; so that by these meanes the nights are seldome darke; which is verified in all parts of the world, but least in the middle Zone under the Equinoctiall, where the twilights are short, and the nights darker then in any other place, because the Sunne goeth under their horizon so deepe, even to their antipodes. We see in England in the Summer nights, when the Sunne goeth not farre under the horizon, that by the light of the Moone & Starres we may travell all night, and if occasion were, do some other labour also. And there is no man that doubteth whether our cattell can see to feed in the nights, seeing we are so well certified therof by our experience: and by reason of the sphere our nights should be darker then any time under the poles.

The Astronomers consent that the Sunne descending

A.D.
1578.

from our upper hemisphere at the 18 parallel under the
horizon maketh an end of twilight, so that at length
the darke night insueth, and that afterward in the morning the Sun approching againe within as many parallels,
doth drive away the night by accesse of the twilight.
Againe, by the position of the sphere under the pole,
the horizon, and the equinoctiall are all one. These
revolutions therefore that are parallel to the equinoctiall
are also parallel to the horizon, so that the Sunne descending under that horizon, and there describing certaine
parallels not farre distant, doth not bring darke nights to
those regions untill it come to the parallels distant 18 [III. 57.]
degrees from the equinoctiall, that is, about the 21 degree
of Scorpio, which will be about the 4 day of our
November, and after the Winter solstitium, the Sunne
returning backe againe to the 9 degree of Aquarius,
which will be about the 19 of January; during which
time onely, that is, from the 4 day of November untill
the 19 day of January, which is about six weeks space,
those regions do want the commodity of twilights:
therefore, during the time of these sayd six moneths of
darknesse under the poles, the night is destitute of the
benefit of the Sunne and the sayd twilights onely for the *The regions*
space of six weeks or thereabout. And yet neither this *under the poles*
time of six weeks is without remedy from heaven; for *want twilights*
the Moone with her increased light hath accesse at that *but sixe weeks.*
time, and illuminateth the moneths lacking light every
one of themselves severally halfe the course of that
moneth, by whose benefit it commeth to passe that the
night named extreame darke possesseth those regions no
longer then one moneth, neither that continually, or all
at one time, but this also divided into two sorts of shorter
nights, of the which either of them indureth for the space
of 15 dayes, and are illuminate of the Moone accordingly.
And this reason is gathered out of the sphere, whereby
we may testifie that the Summers are warme and fruitfull,
and the Winters nights under the pole are tolerable to
living creatures. And if it be so that the Winter and

THE ENGLISH VOYAGES

time of darknesse there be very colde, yet hath not nature left them unprovided therefore: for there the beasts are covered with haire so much the thicker in how much the vehemency of colde is greater; by reason whereof the best and richest furres are brought out of the coldest regions. Also the fowles of these colde countreys have thicker skinnes, thicker feathers, and more stored of downe then in other hot places. Our English men that travell to S. Nicholas, and go a fishing to Wardhouse, enter farre within the circle Arctike, and so are in the frozen Zone, and yet there, aswell as in Island and all along those Northerne Seas, they finde the greatest store of the greatest fishes that are; as Whales, &c. and also abundance of meane fishes; as Herrings, Cods, Haddocks, Brets, &c. which argueth that the sea as well as the land may be and is well frequented and inhabited in the colde countreys.

But some perhaps will marvell there should be such temperate places in the regions about the poles, when at under 62 degrees in latitude our captaine Frobisher & his company were troubled with so many and so great mountaines of fleeting ice, with so great stormes of colde, with such continuall snow on tops of mountaines, and with such barren soile, there being neither wood nor trees, but low shrubs, and such like. To all which objections may be answered thus: First, those infinite Islands of ice were ingendred and congealed in time of Winter, and now by the great heat of Summer were thawed, and then by ebs, flouds, winds, and currents, were driven to and fro, and troubled the fleet; so that this is an argument to prove the heat in Summer there to be great, that was able to thaw so monstrous mountaines of ice. As for continuall snow on tops of mountaines, it is there no otherwise then is in the hotest part of the middle Zone, where also lieth great snow all the Summer long upon tops of mountaines, because there is not sufficient space for the Sunnes reflection, whereby the snow should be molten. Touching the colde stormy winds and the barrennesse of the country, it is there as it is in Cornwall and Devonshire in England, which parts though we know to be fruitfull and fertile, yet on the North side thereof all alongst the coast within seven or eight miles off the sea there can neither hedge nor tree grow, although they be diligently by arte husbanded and seene unto: and the cause thereof are the Northerne driving winds, which comming from the sea are so bitter and sharpe that they kill all the yoong & tender plants, and suffer scarse any thing to grow; and so is it in the Islands of Meta incognita, which are subject most to East & Northeastern winds, which the last yere choaked up the passage so with ice that the fleet could hardly recover their port. Yet notwithstanding all the objections that may be, the countrey is habitable; for there are men, women, children, & sundry kind of beasts in great plenty, as beares, deere, hares, foxes and dogs: all kinde of flying fowles, as ducks, seamewes, wilmots, partridges, larks, crowes, hawks, and such like, as in the third booke you shall understand more at large. Then it appeareth that not onely the middle Zone but also the Zones about the poles are habitable.

Which thing being well considered, and familiarly knowen to our Generall captaine Frobisher, aswell for that he is thorowly furnished of the knowledge of the sphere and all other skilles appertaining to the arte of navigation, as also for the confirmation he hath of the same by many yeres experience both by sea and land, and being persuaded of a new and nerer passage to Cataya then by Capo de buona Sperança, which the Portugals yerely use: he began first with himselfe to devise, and then with his friends to conferre, and layed a plaine plat unto them that that voyage was not onely possible by the Northwest, but also he could prove easie to be performed. And further, he determined and resolved with himselfe to go make full proofe thereof, and to accomplish or bring true certificate of the truth, or els never to returne againe, knowing this to be the only thing of

[III. 58.]

the world that was left yet undone, whereby a notable minde might be made famous and fortunate. But although his will were great to performe this notable voyage, whereof he had conceived in his minde a great hope by sundry sure reasons and secret intelligence, which here for sundry causes I leave untouched, yet he wanted altogether meanes and ability to set forward, and performe the same. Long time he conferred with his private friends of these secrets, and made also many offers for the performing of the same in effect unto sundry merchants of our countrey above 15 yeres before he attempted the same, as by good witnesse shall well appeare (albeit some evill willers which challenge to themselves the fruits of other mens labours have greatly injured him in the reports of the same, saying that they have bene the first authours of that action, and that they have learned him the way, which themselves as yet have never gone) but perceiving that hardly he was hearkened unto of the merchants, which never regard vertue without sure, certaine, and present gaines, he repaired to the Court (from whence, as from the fountaine of our Common wealth, all good causes have their chiefe increase and maintenance) and there layed open to many great estates and learned men the plot and summe of his device. And amongst many honourable minds which favoured his honest and commendable enterprise, he was specially bound and beholding to the right honourable Ambrose Dudley earle of Warwicke, whose favourable minde and good disposition hath alwayes bene ready to countenance and advance all honest actions with the authours and executers of the same : and so by meanes of my lord his honourable countenance he received some comfort of his cause, and by litle and litle, with no small expense and paine brought his cause to some perfection, and had drawen together so many adventurers and such summes of money as might well defray a reasonable charge to furnish himselfe to sea withall.

He prepared two small barks of twenty and five and

twenty tunne a piece, wherein he intended to accomplish his pretended voyage. Wherefore, being furnished with the foresayd two barks, and one small pinnesse of ten tun burthen, having therein victuals and other necessaries for twelve moneths provision, he departed upon the sayd voyage from Blacke-wall the 15 of June anno Domini 1576.

One of the barks wherein he went was named The Gabriel, and the other The Michael; and sailing Northwest from England upon the 11 of July he had sight of an high and ragged land, which he judged to be Frisland (whereof some authors have made mention) but durst not approch the same by reason of the great store of ice that lay alongst the coast, and the great mists that troubled them not a litle. Not farre from thence he lost company of his small pinnesse, which by meanes of the great storme he supposed to be swallowed up of the Sea, wherein he lost onely foure men.

Also the other barke named The Michael mistrusting the matter, conveyed themselves privily away from him, and returned home, with great report that he was cast away.

The Michael returned home.

The worthy captaine notwithstanding these discomforts, although his mast was sprung, and his toppe mast blowen overboord with extreame foule weather, continued his course towards the Northwest, knowing that the sea at length must needs have an ending, & that some land should have a beginning that way; and determined therefore at the least to bring true proofe what land and sea the same might be so farre to the Northwestwards, beyond any man that hath heretofore discovered. And the twentieth of July he had sight of an high land, which he called Queene Elizabeths Forland, after her Majesties name. And sailing more Northerly alongst that coast, he descried another forland with a great gut, bay, or passage, divided as it were two maine lands or continents asunder. There he met with store of exceeding great ice all this coast along, and coveting still to continue his course to the Northwards, was alwayes by contrary winde deteined overthwart these straights, and could not get beyond. Within few dayes after he perceived the ice to be well consumed and gone, either there ingulfed in by some swift currents or indrafts, carried more to the Southwards of the same straights, or els conveyed some other way : wherefore he determined to make proofe of this place, to see how farre that gut had continuance, and whether he might carry himselfe thorow the same into some open sea on the backe side, whereof he conceived no small hope, and so entred the same the one and twentieth of July, and passed above fifty leagues therein, as he reported, having upon either hand a great maine or continent. And that land upon his right hand as he sailed Westward he judged to be the continent of Asia, and there to be divided from the firme of America, which lieth upon the left hand over against the same.

This place he named after his name, Frobishers streights, like as Magellanus at ye Southwest end of the world, having discovered the passage to the South sea (where America is divided from the continent of that land, which lieth under the South pole) and called the same straights, Magellanes straits.

After he had passed 60 leagues into this foresayd straight, he went ashore, and found signes where fire had bene made.

He saw mighty deere that seemed to be mankinde, which ranne at him, and hardly he escaped with his life in a narrow way, where he was faine to use defence and policy to save his life.

In this place he saw and perceived sundry tokens of the peoples resorting thither. And being ashore upon the top of a hill, he perceived a number of small things fleeting in the sea afarre off, which he supposed to be porposes or seales, or some kinde of strange fish; but comming neerer, he discovered them to be men in small boats made of leather. And before he could descend downe from the hill, certaine of those people had almost cut off his boat from him, having stollen secretly behinde the rocks for that purpose, where he speedily hasted to his boat, and bent himselfe to his halberd, and narrowly escaped the danger, and saved his boat. Afterwards he had sundry conferences with them, and they came aboord his ship, and brought him salmon and raw flesh and fish, and greedily devoured the same before our mens faces. And to shew their agility, they tried many masteries upon the ropes of the ship after our mariners fashion, and appeared to be very strong of their armes, and nimble of their bodies. They exchanged coats of seales, and beares skinnes, and such like, with our men; and received belles, looking glasses, and other toyes, in recompense thereof againe. After great curtesie, and many meetings, our mariners, contrary to their captaines direction, began more easily to trust them; and five of our men going ashore were by them intercepted with their boat, and were never since heard of to this day againe: so that the captaine being destitute of boat, barke, and all company, had scarsely sufficient number to conduct backe his barke againe. He could now neither convey himselfe ashore to rescue his men (if he had bene able) for want of a boat; and againe the subtile traitours were so wary, as they would after that never come within our mens danger. The captaine notwithstanding desirous to bring some token from thence of his being there, was greatly discontented that he had not before apprehended some of them: and therefore to deceive the deceivers he wrought a prety policy; for knowing wel how they greatly delighted in our toyes, and specially in belles, he rang a prety lowbell, making signes that he would give him the same that would come and fetch it. And because they would not come within his danger for feare, he flung one bell unto them, which of purpose he threw short, that it might fall into the sea and be lost. And to make them more greedy of the matter he rang a louder bell, so that in the end one of them came nere the ship

Salmon.

Five English-men intercepted and taken.

Taking of the first Savage.

side to receive the bel; which when he thought to take at the captaines hand, he was thereby taken himselfe: for the captaine being readily provided let the bell fall, and caught the man fast, and plucked him with maine force boat and all into his barke out of the sea. Whereupon when he found himselfe in captivity, for very choler and disdaine he bit his tongue in twaine within his mouth: notwithstanding, he died not thereof, but lived untill he came in England, and then he died of cold which he had taken at sea.

Now with this new pray (which was a sufficient witnesse of the captaines farre and tedious travell towards the unknowen parts of the world, as did well appeare by this strange infidell, whose like was never seene, read, nor heard of before, and whose language was neither knowen nor understood of any) the sayd captaine *Frobisher* returned homeward, and arrived in England in Harwich the 2 of October following, and thence came to London 1576, where he was highly commended of all men for his great and notable attempt, but specially famous for the great hope he brought of the passage to Cataya.

Frobishers returne.

And it is especially to be remembred that at their first arrivall in those parts there lay so great store of ice all the coast along so thicke together, that hardly his boat could passe unto the shore. At length, after divers attempts he commanded his company, if by any possible meanes they could get ashore, to bring him whatsoever thing they could first finde, whether it were living or dead, stocke or stone, in token of Christian possession, which thereby he tooke in behalfe of the Queenes most excellent Majesty, thinking that thereby he might justify the having and injoying of the same things that grew in these unknowen parts.

The taking possession of Meta incognita.

Some of his company brought floures, some greene grasse; and one brought a piece of blacke stone much like to a sea cole in colour, which by the waight seemed to be some kinde of metall or minerall. This

How the ore was found by chance.

was a thing of no account in the judgement of the captaine at the first sight; and yet for novelty it was kept in respect of the place from whence it came.

After his arrivall in London, being demanded of sundry his friends what thing he had brought them home out of that countrey, he had nothing left to present them withall but a piece of this blacke stone. [III. 60.] And it fortuned a gentlewoman one of the adventurers wives to have a piece therof, which by chance she threw and burned in the fire, so long, that at the length being taken forth, and quenched in a litle vineger, it glistered with a bright marquesset of golde. Whereupon the matter being called in some question, it was brought to certaine Goldfiners in London to make assay thereof, who gave out that it held golde, and that very richly for the quantity. Afterwards, the same Goldfiners pro-*Many adven-*mised great matters thereof if there were any store to *turers.* be found, and offered themselves to adventure for the searching of those parts from whence the same was brought. Some that had great hope of the matter sought secretly to have a lease at her Majesties hands of those places, whereby to injoy the masse of so great a publike profit unto their owne private gaines.

In conclusion, the hope of more of the same golde ore to be found kindled a greater opinion in the hearts of many to advance the voyage againe. Whereupon preparation was made for a new voyage against the yere following, and the captaine more specially directed by commission for the searching more of this golde ore *In the second* then for the searching any further discovery of the *voyage com-* passage. And being well accompanied with divers resolute *mission was* and forward gentlemen, her Majesty then lying at the *for the bring-* right honourable the lord of Warwicks house in Essex, *ing of ore.* he came to take his leave, and kissing her hignesse hands, with gracious countenance & comfortable words departed toward his charge.

[A true

A true report of such things as happened in the
second voyage of captaine Frobisher, pretended
for the discovery of a new passage to Cataya,
China and the East India, by the Northwest.
Ann. Dom. 1577.

Eing furnished with one tall ship of her
Majesties, named The Ayde, of two
hundred tunne, and two other small
barks, the one named The Gabriel, the
other The Michael, about thirty tun a
piece, being fitly appointed with men,
munition, victuals, and all things necessary for the voyage, the sayd captaine Frobisher, with
the rest of his company came aboord his ships riding at
Blackwall, intending (with Gods helpe) to take the first
winde and tide serving him, the 25 day of May, in the
yere of our Lord God 1577.

The names of such gentlemen as attempted this discovery, and the number of souldiers and mariners in
ech ship, as followeth.

A Boord the Ayd being Admirall were the number of
100 men of all sorts, whereof 30 or moe were
Gentlemen and Souldiers, the rest sufficient and tall
Sailers.

Aboord the Gabriel being Viceadmirall, were in
all 18 persons, whereof sixe were Souldiers, the rest
Mariners.

Aboord the Michael were 16 persons, whereof five
were Souldiers, the rest Mariners.

	Generall of the whole company for her Majesty	Martin Frobisher.
Aboord the Ayde was	His Lieutenant His Ensigne	George Best. Richard Philpot.
	Corporall of the shot	Francis Forder.
	The rest of the gentlemen	Henry Carew. Edmund Stafford. John Lee. M. Harvie. Mathew Kinersley. Abraham Lins. Robert Kinersley. Francis Brakenbury. William Armshow.
	The Master The Mate The Pilot	Christopher Hall. Charles Jackman. Andrew Dier.
	The Master gunner	Richard Cox.
Aboord the Gabriell was	Captaine One Gentleman The Maister	Edward Fenton. William Tamfield. William Smyth.
Aboord the Michaell was	Captaine One Gentleman The Maister	Gilbert Yorke. Thomas Chamberlaine. James Beare.

[III. 61.]

ON Whitsunday being the 26 of May, Anno 1577, early in the morning, we weighed anker at Blackwall, and fell that tyde downe to Gravesend, where we remained untill Monday at night.

On munday morning the 27 of May, aboord the Ayde we received all the Communion by the Minister of

They received the communion

Gravesend, and prepared us as good Christians towards God, and resolute men for all fortunes: and towards night we departed to Tilbery Hope.

Tuesday the eight and twenty of May, about nine of the clocke at night, we arrived at Harwitch in Essex and there stayed for the taking in of certaine victuals, untill Friday being the thirtieth of May, during which time came letters from the Lordes of the Councell, straightly commanding our Generall, not to exceede his complement *The number of* and number appointed him, which was, one hundred and *men in this* twentie persons: whereupon he discharged many proper *voyage.* men which with unwilling mindes departed.

The con- He also dismissed all his condemned men, which he *demned men* thought for some purposes very needefull for the voyage, *discharged.* and towards night upon Friday the one and thirtieth of May we set saile, and put to the Seas againe. And sayling Northward alongst the East coasts of England *The first arri-* and Scotland, the seventh day of June we arrived in Saint *vall after our* Magnus sound in Orkney Ilands, called in latine Orcades, *departing from* and came to ancker on the South side of the Bay, and *England.* this place is reckoned from Blackwall where we set saile first   leagues.

Here our companie going on lande, the Inhabitants of these Ilandes beganne to flee as from the enemie, whereupon the Lieutenant willed every man to stay togither, and went himselfe unto their houses to declare what we were and the cause of our comming thither, which being understood, after their poore maner they friendly entreated us, and brought us for our money such things as *A Mine of sil-* they had. And here our Goldfiners found a Mine of silver. *ver found in* Orkney is the principall of the Isles of the Orcades, *Orkney.* and standeth in the latitude of fiftie nine degrees and a halfe. The countrey is much subject to colde, answerable for such a climate, and yet yeeldeth some fruites, and sufficient maintenance for the people contented so poorely to live.

There is plentie ynough of Poultrey, store of egges, fish, and foule.

For their bread they have Oaten Cakes, and their drinke is Ewes milke, and in some partes Ale.

Their houses are but poore without and sluttish ynough within, and the people in nature thereunto agreeable.

For their fire they burne heath and turffe, the Countrey in most parts being voide of wood.

They have great want of Leather, and desire our old shoes, apparell, and old ropes (before money) for their victuals, and yet are they not ignorant of the value of our coine. The chiefe towne is called Kyrway.

In this Island hath bene sometime an Abbey or a religious house called Saint Magnus, being on the West side of the Ile, whereof this sound beareth name, through which we passed. Their Governour or chiefe Lord is called the Lord Robert Steward, who at our being there, as we understood, was in durance at Edenburgh, by the Regents commandement of Scotland.

After we had provided us here of matter sufficient for our voyage the eight of June wee set sayle againe, and passing through Saint Magnus sound having a merrie winde by night, came cleare and lost sight of all the land, and keeping our course West Northwest by the space of two dayes, the winde shifted upon us so that we lay in traverse on the Seas, with contrary windes, making good (as neere as we could) our course to the westward, and sometime to the Northward, as the winde shifted. And hereabout we met with 3 saile of English fishermen from Iseland, bound homeward, by whom we wrote our letters unto our friends in England. We traversed these Seas by the space of 26 dayes without sight of any land, and met with much drift wood, & whole bodies of trees. We sawe many monsterous fishes and strange foules, which seemed to live onely by the Sea, being there so farre distant from any land. At length God favoured us with more prosperous windes, and after wee had sayled foure dayes with good winde in the Poop, the fourth of July the Michaell being formost a head shot off a peece

Kyrway the chiefe towne of Orkney.
S. Magnus sound why so called.

Great bodies of trees driving in the seas.
[III. 62.]
Monstrous fish & strange foule living onely by the Sea.

287

of Ordinance, and stroke all her sayles, supposing that they descryed land which by reason of the thicke mistes they could not make perfit: howbeit, as well our account *Water being* as also the great alteration of the water, which became *blacke and* more blacke and smooth, did plainely declare we were *smooth signifi-* not farre off the coast. Our Generall sent his Master *eth land to be neere.* aboord the Michaell (who had beene with him the yeere *Ilands of yce.* before) to beare in with the place to make proofe thereof, who descryed not the land perfect, but sawe sundry huge Ilands of yce, which we deemed to be not past twelve leagues from the shore, for about tenne of the clocke at *The first sight* night being the fourth of July, the weather being more *of Frisland the 4. of July.* cleare, we made the land perfect and knew it to be Frislande. And the heigth being taken here, we found our selves to be in the latitude of 60 degrees and a halfe, and were fallen with the Southermost part of this land. Betweene Orkney and Frisland are reckoned leagues.

Frisland de-scribed. This Frislande sheweth a ragged and high lande, having the mountaines almost covered over with snow alongst the coast full of drift yce, and seemeth almost inaccessible, and is thought to be an Iland in bignesse not inferiour to England, and is called of some Authors, West Frislande, I thinke because it lyeth more West then any part of Europe. It extendeth in latitude to the Northward very farre as seemed to us, and appeareth by a description set out by two brethren Venetians, Nicholaus and Antonius Zeni, who being driven off from Ireland with a violent tempest made shipwracke here, and were the first knowen Christians that discovered this land about two hundred yeares sithence, and they have in their Sea-cardes set out every part thereof and described the condition of the inhabitants, declaring them to be as civill and religious people as we. And for so much of this land as we have sayled alongst, comparing their Carde with the coast, we finde it very agreeable. *An easie kind* This coast seemeth to have good fishing, for we lying *of Fishing.* becalmed let fall a hooke without any bayte and presently caught a great fish called a Hollibut, who served the whole companie for a dayes meate, and is dangerous meate for surfetting. And sounding about five leagues off from the shore, our leade brought up in the tallow a kinde of Corrall almost white, and small stones as bright as Christall: and it is not to be doubted but that this land may be found very rich and beneficial if it were throughly discovered, although we sawe no creature there but little birdes. It is a marvellous thing to behold of what great bignesse and depth some Ilands of yce be here, some seventie, some eightie fadome under water, besides that which is above, seeming Ilands more then halfe a mile in circuit. All these yce are in tast fresh, and seeme to be bredde in the sounds thereabouts, or in some lande neere the pole, and with the winde and tides are driven alongst the coastes. We found none of these Ilands of yce salt in taste, whereby it appeareth that they were not congealed of the Ocean Sea water which is alwayes salt, but of some standing or little mooving lakes or great fresh waters neere the shore, caused eyther by melted snowe from tops of mountaines, or by continuall accesse of fresh rivers from the land, and intermingling with the Sea water, bearing yet the dominion (by the force of extreame frost) may cause some part of salt water to freese so with it, and so seeme a little brackish, but otherwise the maine Sea freeseth not, and therefore there is no Mare Glaciale or frosen Sea, as the opinion hitherto hath bene. Our Generall prooved landing here twice, but by the suddaine fall of mistes (whereunto this coast is much subject) he was like to loose sight of his ships, and being greatly endangered with the driving yce alongst the coast, was forced aboord and faine to surcease his pretence till a better opportunitie might serve: and having spent foure dayes and nightes sayling alongst this land, finding the coast subject to such bitter colde and continuall mistes, he determined to spend no more time therein, but to beare out his course towardes the streightes called Frobishers streights after the Generals name, who

White Corrall got by sounding.

Monstrous Isles of yce, in taste fresh, where-hence they are supposed to come.

The opinion of the frosen seas is destroyed by experience.

being the first that ever passed beyond 58 degrees to the Northwardes, for any thing that hath beene yet knowen of certaintie of New found land, otherwise called the continent or firme lande land of America, discovered the saide straights this last yere 1576.

Betweene Frisland and the straights we had one great storme, wherein the Michaell was somewhat in danger, *The Stirrage of the Michaell broken by tempest.* having her Stirrage broken, and her toppe Mastes blowen over boord, & being not past 50 leagues short of the straights by our account, we stroke sayle & lay a hull, fearing the continuance of the storme, the winde being at the Northeast, and having lost companie of the Barkes *The first entrance of the straights.* in that flaw of winde, we happily met againe the seventeenth day of July, having the evening before seene divers Ilands of fleeting yce, which gave an argument that we were not farre from land. Our Generall in the morning from the maine top (the weather being reason- [III. 63.] able cleare) descried land, but to be better assured he sent the two Barkes two contrarie courses, whereby they might discry either the South or North foreland, the Ayde lying off and on at Sea, with a small sayle by an Iland of yce, which was the marke for us to meete togither againe. And about noone, the weather being more cleare, we made the North forland perfite, which *Halles Iland.* otherwise is called Halles Iland, and also the small Iland bearing the name of the sayde Hall whence the Ore was taken up which was brought into England this last yeere 1576 the said Hall being present at the finding & taking up thereof, who was then Maister in the Gabriell with Captaine Frobisher. At our arrivall here all the Seas about this coast were so covered over with huge quantitie of great yce, that we thought these places might onely deserve the name of Mare Glaciale, and be called the Isie Sea.

The description of the straights. This North forland is thought to be devided from the continent of the Northerland, by a little sound called Halles sound, which maketh it an Iland, and is thought little lesse then the Ile of Wight, and is the first entrance of the straights upon the Norther side, and standeth in the latitude of sixtie two degrees and fiftie minutes, and is reckoned from Frisland   leagues. God having blessed us with so happie a land-fall, we bare into the straights which runne in next hand, and somewhat further up to the Northwarde, and came as neere the shore as wee might for the yce, and upon the eighteenth day of July our Generall taking the Goldfiners with him, attempted to goe on shore with a small rowing Pinnesse, upon the small Ilande where the Ore was taken up, to proove whether there were any store thereof to be found, but he could not get in all that Iland a peece so bigge as a Walnut, where the first was found. But our men which sought the other Ilands thereabouts found them all to have good store of the Ore, whereupon our Generall with these good tidings returned aboord about tenne of the clocke at night, and was joyfully welcommed of the company with a volie of shot. He brought egges, foules, and a young Seale aboord, which the companie had killed ashore, and having found upon those Ilands ginnes set to catch fowle, and stickes newe cut, with other things, he well perceived that not long before some of the countrey people had resorted thither.

No more gold Ore found in the first Iland.

Egs & foules of Meta incognita. Snares set to catch birds withall.

Having therefore found those tokens of the peoples accesse in those parts, and being in his first voyage well acquainted with their subtill and cruell disposition, hee provided well for his better safetie, and on Friday the ninteenth of July in the morning early, with his best companie of Gentlemen and souldiers, to the number of fortie persons, went on shore, aswell to discover the Inland and habitation of the people, as also to finde out some fit harborowe for our shippes. And passing towardes the shoare with no small difficultie by reason of the abundance of yce which lay alongst the coast so thicke togither that hardly any passage through them might be discovered, we arrived at length upon the maine of Halles greater Iland, and found there also aswell as in the other small Ilands good store of the Ore. And leaving his boates here with sufficient guarde we passed up into the countrey about two English miles, and recovered the toppe of a high hill, on the top whereof our men made a Columne or Crosse of stones heaped up of a good heigth togither in good sort, and solemnely sounded a Trumpet, and saide certaine prayers kneeling about the Ensigne, and honoured the place by the name of Mount Warwicke, in remembrance of the Right Honorable the Lord Ambrose Dudley Earle of Warwick, whose noble mind and good countenance in this, as in all other good actions, gave great encouragement and good furtherance. This done, we retyred our companies not seeing any thing here worth further discoverie, the countrey seeming barren and full of ragged mountaines and in most parts covered with snow.

The building of a Columne, called Mount Warwicke.

And thus marching towards our botes, we espied certaine of the countrey people on the top of Mount Warwick with a flag wafting us backe againe and making great noise, with cries like the mowing of Buls seeming greatly desirous of conference with us: whereupon the Generall being therewith better acquainted, answered them againe with the like cries, whereat and with the noise of our trumpets they seemed greatly to rejoyce, skipping, laughing and dancing for joy. And hereupon we made signes unto them, holding up two fingers, commanding two of our men to go apart from our companies, whereby they might do the like. So that forthwith two of our men & two of theirs met togither a good space from company, neither partie having their weapons about them. Our men gave them pins and points and such trifles as they had. And they likewise bestowed on our men two bow cases and such things as they had. They earnestly desired our men to goe up into their countrey, and our men offered them like kindnesse aboord our ships, but neither part (as it seemed) admitted or trusted the others curtesie. Their maner of traffique is thus, they doe use to lay downe of their marchandise upon the ground, so much as they meane to part withal, and

The first sight of the countrie people, wafting with a flagge.

The meeting a part of two Englishmen, with two of that countrey.

The order of their traffique

292

so-looking that the other partie with whom they make trade should doe the like, they themselves doe depart, [III. 64.] and then if they doe like of their Mart they come againe, and take in exchange the others marchandise, otherwise if they like not, they take their owne and depart. The day being thus well neere spent, in haste wee retired our companies into our boates againe, minding foorthwith to search alongst the coast for some harborow fit for our shippes, for the present necessitie thereof was much, considering that all this while they lay off and on betweene the two landes, being continually subject aswell to great danger of fleeting yce, which environed them, as to the sodaine flawes which the coast seemeth much subject unto. But when the people perceived our departure, with great tokens of affection they earnestly called us backe againe, following us almost to our boates: whereupon our Generall taking his Master with him, who was *Another meeting of two of our men with two of theirs.* best acquainted with their maners, went apart unto two of them, meaning, if they could lay sure hold upon them, forcibly to bring them aboord, with intent to bestow certaine toyes and apparell upon the one, and so to dismisse him with all arguments of curtesie, and retaine the other for an Interpreter. The Generall and his Maister being met with their two companions togither, after they had exchanged certaine things the one with the other, one of the Salvages for lacke of better marchandise, cut off the tayle of his coat (which is a chiefe ornament among them) and gave it unto our Generall for a present. But he presently upon a watchword given with his Maister sodainely laid hold upon the two Salvages. But the ground underfoot being slipperie with the snow on the side of the hill, their handfast fayled and their prey escaping ranne away and lightly recovered their bow and arrowes, which they had hid not farre from them behind the rockes. And being onely two Salvages in sight, they so fiercely, desperately, and with such fury assaulted and pursued our Generall and his Master, being altogether unarmed, and not mistrusting their subtiltie

THE ENGLISH VOYAGES

that they chased them to their boates, and hurt the Generall in the buttocke with an arrow, who the rather speedily fled backe, because they suspected a greater number behind the rockes. Our souldiers (which were commanded before to keepe their boates) perceiving the danger, and hearing our men calling for shot came speedily to rescue, thinking there had bene a greater number. But when the Salvages heard the shot of one of our calivers (and yet having first bestowed their arrowes) they ranne away, our men speedily following them. But a servant of my Lorde of Warwick, called Nicholas Conger a good footman, and uncombred with any furniture having only a dagger at his backe over-

tooke one of them, and being a Cornishman and a good wrastler, shewed his companion such a Cornish tricke, that he made his sides ake against the ground for a moneth after. And so being stayed, he was taken alive and brought away, but the other escaped. Thus with their strange and new prey our men repaired to their boates, and passed from the maine to a small Iland of a mile compasse, where they resolved to tarrie all night; for even now a sodaine storme was growen so great at sea, that by no meanes they could recover their ships. And here every man refreshed himselfe with a small portion of victuals which was laide into the boates for their dinners, having neither eate nor drunke all the day before. But because they knewe not how long the storme might last, nor how farre off the shippes might be put to sea, nor whether they should ever recover them againe or not, they made great spare of their victuals, as it greatly behoved them : For they knew full well that the best cheare the countrey could yeeld them, was rockes and stones, a hard food to live withall, and the people more readie to eate them then to give them wherewithall to eate. And thus keeping verie good watch and warde, they lay there all night upon hard cliffes of snow and yce both wet, cold, and comfortlesse.

These things thus hapning with the company on land,

the danger of the ships at Sea was no lesse perilous. For within one houre after the Generals departing in the morning by negligence of the Cooke in over-heating, and the workman in making the chimney, the Ayde was set on fire, and had bene the confusion of the whole if by chance a boy espying it, it had not bene speedily with great labour and Gods helpe well extinguished.

The Ayde set on fire.

This day also were diverse stormes and flawes, and by nine of the clocke at night the storme was growen so great, & continued such untill the morning, that it put our ships at sea in no small perill : for having mountaines of fleeting yce on every side, we went roomer for one, and loofed for another, some scraped us, and some happily escaped us, that the least of a M. were as dangerous to strike as any rocke, and able to have split asunder the strongest ship of the world. We had a scope of cleare without yce, (as God would) wherein we turned, being otherwise compassed on every side about : but so much was the winde and so litle was our sea roome, that being able to beare onely our forecourse we cast so oft about, that we made fourteene bordes in eight glasses running, being but foure houres : but God being our best Steresman, & by the industry of Charles Jackman and Andrew Dyer the masters mates, both very expert Mariners, & Richard Cox ye maister Gunner, with other very carefull sailers, then within bord, and also by the helpe of the cleare nights which are without darkenesse, we did happily avoide those present dangers, whereat since wee have more marvelled then in the present danger feared, for that every man within borde, both better and worse had ynough to doe with his hands to hale ropes, and with his eyes to looke out for danger. But the next morning being the 20 of July, as God would, the storme ceased, and the Generall espying the ships with his new Captive and whole company, came happily abord, and reported what had passed a shoare, whereupon altogither upon our knees we gave God humble and hartie thankes, for that it had pleased him,

The great danger of those rockes of yce.

They made 14 tacks in 4 hrs.

[III. 65.]

Night without darknes in that countrey.

from so speedy peril to send us such speedy deliverance, and so from this Northerne shore we stroke over towards the Southerland.

The one and twentieth of July, we discovered a bay which ranne into the land, that seemed a likely harborow for our ships, wherefore our Generall rowed thither with his boats, to make proofe thereof, and with his goldfiners to search for Ore, having never assayed any thing on the South shore as yet, and the first small Iland which we landed upon. Here all the sands and clifts did so glister and had so bright a marquesite, that it seemed all to be gold, but upon tryall made, it prooved no better then black-lead, and verified the proverbe. All is not gold that glistereth.

Our first com-
ming on the
Southerland of
the sayd
straights.

A Mine of
Blacke lead.

Upon the two and twentieth of July we bare into the sayde sound, and came to ancker a reasonable bredth off the shore, where thinking our selves in good securitie, we were greatly endangered with a peece of drift yce, which the Ebbe brought foorth of the sounds and came thwart us ere we were aware. But the gentlemen and souldiers within bord taking great paines at this pinch at the Capstone, overcame the most danger thereof, and yet for all that might be done, it stroke on our sterne such a blow, that we feared least it had striken away our rudder, and being forced to cut our Cable in the hawse, we were faine to set our fore saile to runne further up within, and if our stirrage had not bene stronger then in the present time we feared, we had runne the ship upon the rockes, having a very narrow Channell to turne in, but as God would, all came well to passe. And this was named Jackmans sound, after the name of the Masters mate, who had first liking unto the place.

Upon a small Iland, within this sound called Smithes Iland (because he first set up his forge there) was found a Mine of silver, but was not wonne out of the rockes without great labour. Here our goldfiners made say of such Ore as they found upon the Northerland, and found foure sortes thereof to holde gold in good quantitie.

Upon another small Iland here was also found a great dead fish, which as it should seeme, had bene embayed with yce, and was in proportion round like to a Porpose, being about twelve foote long, and in bignesse answerable, having a horne of two yardes long growing out of the snoute or nostrels. This horne is wreathed and straite, like in fashion to a Taper made of waxe, and may truely be thought to be the sea Unicorne. This horne is to be seene and reserved as a Jewell by the Queenes Majesties commandement, in her Wardrope of Robes.

The finding of an Unicornes horne.

Tuesday the three and twentieth of July, our Generall with his best company of gentlemen, souldiers and saylers, to the number of seventie persons in all, marched with ensigne displayde, upon the continent of the Southerland (the supposed continent of America) where, commanding a Trumpet to sound a call for every man to repaire to the ensigne, he declared to the whole company how much the cause imported for the service of her Majestie, our countrey, our credits, and the safetie of our owne lives, and therefore required every man to be conformable to order, and to be directed by those he should assigne. And he appointed for leaders, Captaine Fenton, Captaine Yorke, and his Lieutenant George Beste : which done, we cast our selves into a ring, and altogither upon our knees, gave God humble thanks for that it had pleased him of his great goodnesse to preserve us from such imminent dangers, beseeching likewise the assistance of his holy spirite, so to deliver us in safetie into our Countrey, whereby the light and truth of these secrets being knowen, it might redound to the more honour of his holy name, and consequently to the advancement of our common wealth. And so, in as good sort as the place suffered, we marched towards the tops of the mountaines, which were no lesse painfull in climbing then dangerous in descending, by reason of their steepnesse & yce. And having passed about five miles, by such unwieldie wayes, we returned unto our ships without sight of any people, or likelihood of habitation. Here diverse of the Gentlemen desired our Generall to suffer them to the number of twentie or thirtie persons to march up thirtie or fortie leagues in the countrey, to the end they might discover the Inland, and doe some acceptable service for their countrey. But he not contented with the matter he sought for, and well considering the short time he had in hand, and the greedie desire our countrey hath to a present savour and returne of gaine, bent his whole indevour only to find a Mine to fraight his ships, and to leave the rest (by Gods [III. 66.] helpe) hereafter to be well accomplished. And therefore the twentie sixe of July he departed over to the Northland, with the two barkes, leaving the Ayde ryding in Jackmans sound, and ment (after hee had found convenient harborow, and fraight there for his ships) to discover further for the passage. The Barkes came the same night to ancker in a sound upon the Northerland, where the tydes did runne so swift, and the place was so subject to indrafts of yce, that by reason thereof they were greatly endangered, & having found a very rich Myne, as they supposed, and got almost twentie tunne of Ore together, upon the 28 of July the yce came driving into the sound where the Barkes rode, in such sort, that they were therewith greatly distressed. And the Gabriell riding asterne the Michael, had her Cable gauld asunder in the hawse with a peece of driving yce, and lost another ancker, and having but one cable and ancker left, for she had lost two before, and the yce still driving upon her, she was (by Gods helpe) well fenced from the danger of the rest, by one great Iland of yce, which came a ground hard a head of her, which if it had not so chanced, I thinke surely shee had beene cast upon the rockes with the yce. The Michael mored ancker upon this great yce, and roade under the lee thereof: but about midnight, by the weight of it selfe, and the setting of the Tydes, the yce brake within halfe the Barkes length, and made unto the companie within boord a sodaine and fearefull noyse. The next flood toward the morning we weyed ancker, and went further up the straights, and leaving our Ore behind us which we had digged, for hast left the place by the name of Beares sound after the Masters name of the Michaell, and named the Iland Lecesters Iland. In one of the small Ilands here we found a Tombe, wherein the bones of a dead man lay together, and our savage Captive being with us, & being demanded by signes whether his countreymen had not slaine this man and eat his flesh so from the bones, he made signes to the contrary, and that he was slaine with Wolves and wild beasts. Here also was found hid under stones good store of fish, and sundry other things of the inhabitants; as sleddes, bridles, kettels of fishskinnes, knives of bone, and such other like. And our Savage declared unto us the use of all those things. And taking in his hand one of those countrey bridles, he caught one of our dogges and hampred him handsomely therein, as we doe our horses, and with a whip in his hand, he taught the dogge to drawe in a sled as we doe horses in a coach, setting himselfe thereupon like a guide: so that we might see they use dogges for that purpose that we do our horses. And we found since by experience, that the lesser sort of dogges they feede fatte, and keepe them as domesticall cattell in their tents for their eating, and the greater sort serve for the use of drawing their sleds.

The twentie ninth of July, about five leagues from Beares sound, we discovered a Bay which being fenced on ech side with smal Ilands lying off the maine, which breake the force of the tides, and make the place free from any indrafts of yce, did proove a very fit harborow for our ships, where we came to ancker under a small Ilande, which now together with the sound is called by the name of that right Honourable and vertuous Ladie, Anne Countesse of Warwicke. And this is the furthest place that this yeere we have entred up

Beares sound.

Lecesters Iland.

A tombe with a dead mans bones in it.

Bridles, knives, and other instruments found hid among the Rockes.

They use great dogs to draw sleds, and litle dogs for their meat.

THE ENGLISH VOYAGES

within the streites, and is reckoned from the Cape of the Queenes foreland, which is the entrance of the streites not above 30 leagues.   Upon this Iland was found good store of the Ore, which in the washing helde gold to our thinking plainly to be seene: whereupon it was thought best rather to load here, where there was store and indifferent good, then to seeke further for better, and spend time with jeoperdie.   And therefore our Generall setting the Myners to worke,

*A good presi-
dent of a good
Captain
shewed by
Captain Fro-
bisher.*

and shewing first a good president of a painefull labourer and a good Captaine in himselfe, gave good examples for others to follow him: whereupon every man both better and worse, with their best endevours willingly layde to their helping hands.   And the next day, being the thirtieth of July, the Michaell was sent over to Jackmans sound, for the Ayde and the whole companie to come thither.   Upon the maine land over against the Countesses Iland we discovered and behelde to our

*The maner of
their houses in
this countrey.*

great marvell the poore caves and houses of those countrey people, which serve them (as it should seeme) for their winter dwellings, and are made two fadome under grounde, in compasse round, like to an Oven, being joyned fast one by another, having holes like to a Foxe or Conny berry, to keepe and come togither. They undertrenched these places with gutters so, that the water falling from the hilles above them, may slide away without their annoyance: and are seated commonly in the foote of a hill, to shield them better from the cold windes, having their doore and entrance

ever open towards the South.   From the ground upward they builde with whales bones, for lacke of timber, which bending one over another, are handsomely compacted in the top together, and are covered over with Sealesskinnes, which in stead of tiles, fence them from the raine.   In which house they have only one roome, having the one halfe of the floure raised with broad stones a foot higher than ye other, whereon strawing Mosse, they make their nests to sleep in.

They defile these dennes most filthily with their beastly
feeding, & dwell so long in a place (as we thinke)
untill their sluttishnes lothing them, they are forced to
seeke a sweeter ayre, and a new seate, and are (no
doubt) a dispersed and wandring nation, as the Tartarians, and live in hords and troupes, without any
certaine abode, as may appeare by sundry circumstances
of our experience.

[III. 67.]
The sluttish-
nesse of these
people.

Here our captive being ashore with us, to declare
the use of such things as we saw, stayd himselfe alone
behind the company, and did set up five small stickes
round in a circle one by another, with one smal bone
placed just in the middest of all: which thing when
one of our men perceived, he called us backe to behold
the matter, thinking that hee had meant some charme
or witchcraft therein. But the best conjecture we could
make thereof was, that hee would thereby his countreymen should understand, that for our five men which
they betrayed the last yeere (whom he signified by the
five stickes) he was taken and kept prisoner, which he
signified by the bone in the midst. For afterwards
when we shewed him the picture of his countreman,
which the last yeere was brought into England (whose
counterfeit we had drawen, with boate and other furniture, both as he was in his own, & also in English
apparel) he was upon the sudden much amazed thereat,
and beholding advisedly the same with silence a good
while, as though he would streine courtesie whether
should begin the speech (for he thought him no doubt
a lively creature) at length began to question with him,
as with his companion, and finding him dumb and
mute, seemed to suspect him, as one disdeinfull, and
would with a little helpe have growen into choller at
the matter, untill at last by feeling and handling, hee
found him but a deceiving picture. And then with
great noise and cryes, ceased not wondring, thinking
that we could make men live or die at our pleasure.

A signe set up
by the savage
captive, & the
meaning
therof.

The savage
captive amaz-
ed at his
countreimans
picture.

And thereupon calling the matter to his remembrance,

he gave us plainely to understand by signes, that he had knowledge of the taking of our five men the last yeere, and confessing the maner of ech thing, numbred the five men upon his five fingers, and pointed unto a boat in our ship, which was like unto that wherein our men were betrayed: And when we made him signes, that they were slaine and eaten, he earnestly denied, and made signes to the contrary.

The last of July the Michael returned with the Aide to us from the Southerland, and came to anker by us in the Countesse of Warwicks sound, and reported that since we departed from Jackmans sound there happened nothing among them there greatly worth the remembrance, untill the thirtieth of July, when certaine of our company being a shoare upon a small Island within the sayd Jackmans sound, neere the place where the Aide rode, did espie a long boat with divers of the countrey people therein, to the number of eighteene or twenty persons, whom so soone as our men perceived, they returned speedily aboord, to give notice thereof unto our company. They might perceive these people climbing up to the top of a hill, where with a flagge, they wafted unto our ship, and made great outcries and noyses, like so many Buls. Hereupon our men did presently man foorth a small skiffe, having not above sixe or seven persons therein, which rowed neere the place where those people were, to proove if they could have any conference with them. But after this small boate was sent a greater, being wel appointed for their rescue, if need required.

Another shew of twenty persons of that countrey in one boate.

As soone as they espied our company comming neere them, they tooke their boates and hasted away, either for feare, or else for pollicie, to draw our men from rescue further within their danger: wherefore our men construing that their comming thither was but to seeke advantage, followed speedily after them, but they rowed so swiftly away, that our men could come nothing neere them. Howbeit they failed not of their best endevour in rowing, and having chased them above two miles into the sea, returned into their ships againe.

The morning following being the first of August, Captaine Yorke with the Michael came into Jackmans sound, and declared unto the company there, that the last night past he came to anker in a certaine baye (which sithens was named Yorkes sound) about foure leagues *Yorkes sound.* distant from Jackmans sound, being put to leeward of that place for lacke of winde, where he discovered certaine tents of the countrey people, where going with his company ashore, he entred into them, but found the people departed, as it should seeme, for feare of their comming. But amongst sundry strange things which in these tents they found, there was rawe and new killed flesh of unknowen sorts, with dead carcasses and bones of dogs, and I know not what. They also beheld (to *The apparel* their greatest marveile) a dublet of Canvas made after *found againe* the English fashion, a shirt, a girdle, three shoes for *of our English* *men which the* contrary feete, and of unequall bignesse, which they well *yere before* conjectured to be the apparell of our five poore countrey- *were taken* men, which were intercepted the last yeere by these *captive.* Countrey people, about fiftie leagues from this place, further within the Straights. Whereupon our men being in good hope, that some of them might be here, and [III. 68.] yet living: the Captaine devising for the best left his mind behind him in writing, with pen, yncke, and paper also, whereby our poore captive countrymen, if it might come to their hands, might know their friends minds, and of their arrivall, and likewise returne their answere. And so without taking any thing away in their tents, *A good devise* leaving there also looking glasses, points, and other of *of Captaine* *Yorke.* our toyes (the better to allure them by such friendly meanes) departed aboord his Barke, with intent to make haste to the Aide, to give notice unto the company of all such things as he had there discovered: and so meant to returne to these tents againe, hoping that he might by force or policie intrappe or intice the people to some friendly conference. Which things when he had delivered to the whole company there, they determined forthwith to go in hand with the matter. Hereupon Captaine Yorke with the master of the Aide and his mate (who the night before had bene at the tents, and came over from the other side in the Michael with him) being accompanied with the Gentlemen and souldiors to the number of thirty or forty persons in two small rowing Pinnasses made towards the place, where the night before they discovered the tents of those people, and setting Charles Jackman, being the masters Mate, ashore with a convenient number, for that he could best guide them to the place, they marched over land, meaning to compasse them on the one side, whilest the Captaine with his boates might entrap them on the other side. But landing at last at the place where the night before they left them, they found them with their tents removed. Notwithstanding, our men which marched up into the countrey, passing over two or three mountaines, by chance espied certaine tents in a valley underneath them neere unto a creeke by the Sea side, which because it was not the place where the guide had bene the night before, they judged them to be another company, and besetting them about, determined to take them if they could. But they having quickly discried our companie, lanched one great & another smal boat, being about 16 or 18 persons, and very narrowly escaping, put themselves to sea. Wherupon our souldiers discharged their Calivers, and followed them, thinking the noise therof being heard to our boats at sea, our men there would make what speede they might to that place. And thereupon indeede our men which were in the boates (crossing upon them in the mouth of the sound whereby their passage was let from getting sea roome, wherein it had bene impossible for us to overtake them by rowing) forced them to put themselves ashore upon a point of land within the sayd sound (which upon the occasion of the slaughter there, was since named The bloody point) whereunto our men so speedily followed, that they had little leisure left them to make any escape. But so soone as they landed, ech of them brake his Oare, thinking by that meanes to prevent us, in carying away their boates for want of Oares. And desperatly returning upon our men, resisted them manfully in their landing, so long as their arrowes and dartes lasted, and after gathering up those arrowes which our men shot at them, yea, and plucking our arrowes out of their bodies incountred afresh againe, and maintained their cause untill both weapons and life fayled them. And when they found they were mortally wounded, being ignorant what mercy meaneth, with deadly fury they cast themselves headlong from off the rockes into the sea, least perhaps their enemies should receive glory or prey of their dead carcaises, for they supposed us belike to be Canibals or eaters of mans flesh. In this conflict one of our men was dangerously hurt in the belly with one of their arrowes, and of them were slaine five or sixe, the rest by flight escaping among the rockes, saving two women, whereof the one being old and ugly, our men thought shee had bene a devill or some witch, and therefore let her goe: the other being yong, and cumbred with a sucking childe at her backe, hiding her selfe behind the rockes, was espied by one of our men, who supposing she had bene a man, shot through the haire of her head, and pierced through the childs arme, whereupon she cried out, and our Surgeon meaning to heale her childes arme, applyed salves thereunto. But she not acquainted with such kind of surgery, plucked those salves away, and by continuall licking with her owne tongue, not much unlike our dogs, healed up the childes arme. And because the day was welneere spent our men made haste unto the rest of our company which on the other side of the water remained at the tents, where they found by the apparell, letter, and other English furniture, that they were the same company which Captaine Yorke discovered the night before, having removed themselves from the place where he left them.

And now considering their sudden flying from our

Yorkes sound.
A hot skirmish betweene the English and them of that countrey.

The desperate nature of those people.

The taking of the woman & her child.

A prety kind of surgery which nature teacheth.

men, and their desperate maner of fighting, we began to suspect that we had heard the last newes of our men which the last yere were betrayed of these people. And considering also their ravenous and bloody disposition in eating any kind of raw flesh or carrion howsoever stinking, it is to bee thought that they had slaine and devoured our men: For the dublet which was found in their tents had many holes therein being made with their arrowes and darts.

[III. 69.] But now the night being at hand, our men with their captives and such poore stuffe as they found in their tents, returned towards their ships, when being at sea, there arose a sudden flaw of winde, which was not a little dangerous for their small boates: but as God would they came all safely aboord. And with these good newes they returned (as before mentioned) into the Countesse of Warwicks sound unto us. And betweene Jackmans sound, from whence they came, and the Countesse of Warwicks sound betweene land and land, being thought *The narrowest* the narrowest place of the Straights were judged nine *place of the* leagues over at the least: and Jackmans sound being *Straites is 9.* *leagues over.* upon the Southerland, lyeth directly almost over against the Countesses sound, as is reckoned scarce thirty leagues *The Queenes* within the Straights from the Queenes Cape, which is *Cape.* the entrance of the Streits of the Southerland. This Cape being named Queene Elizabeths Cape, standeth in the latitude of 62 degrees and a halfe to the Northwards of New found land, and upon the same continent, for any thing that is yet knowen to the contrary.

The maner of Having now got a woman captive for the comfort *the meeting of* of our man, we brought them both together, and every *the two cap-* man with silence desired to behold the maner of their *tives, and their* *entertainment.* meeting and entertainment, the which was more worth the beholding than can be well expressed by writing. At their first encountring they beheld each the other very wistly a good space, without speech or word uttered, with great change of colour and countenance, as though it seemed the griefe and disdeine of their captivity had taken away the use of their tongues and utterance: the woman at the first very suddenly, as though she disdeined or regarded not the man, turned away, and began to sing as though she minded another matter: but being againe brought together, the man brake up the silence first, and with sterne and stayed countenance, began to tell a long solemne tale to the woman, whereunto she gave good hearing, and interrupted him nothing, till he had finished, and afterwards, being growen into more familiar acquaintance by speech, they were turned together, so that (I thinke) the one would hardly have lived without the comfort of the other. And for so much as we could perceive, albeit they lived continually together, yet they did never use as man & wife, though the woman spared not to doe all necessary things that appertained to a good houswife indifferently for them both, as in making cleane their Cabin, and every other thing that appertained to his ease: for when he was seasicke, she would make him cleane, she would kill and flea the dogs for their eating, and dresse his meate. Only I thinke it worth the noting, the continencie of them both: for the man would never shift himselfe, except he had first caused the woman to depart out of his cabin, and they both were most shamefast, least any of their privie parts should be discovered, either of themselves, or any other body. *The shamefastnes and chastity of those Savage captives.*

On Munday the sixth of August, the Lieutenant with all the Souldiers, for the better garde of the Myners and the other things a shore, pitched their tents in the Countesses Island, and fortifyed the place for their better defence as well as they could, and were to the number of forty persons, when being all at labour, they might perceive upon the top of a hill over against them a number of the countrey people wafting with a flag, and making great outcries unto them, and were of the same companie, which had encountred lately our men upon the other shore, being come to complaine their late losses, and to entreate (as it seemed) for restitution of *Another appearance of the countrey people.*

the woman and child, which our men in the late conflict had taken and brought away; whereupon the Generall taking the savage captive with him, and setting the woman where they might best perceive her in the highest place of the Island, went over to talke with them. This captive at his first encounter of his friends fell so out into teares that he could not speake a word in a great space, but after a while, overcomming his kindnesse, he talked at full with his companions, and bestowed friendly upon them such toyes and trifles as we had given him, whereby we noted, that they are very kind one to another, and greatly sorrowfull for the losse of their friends. Our Generall by signes required his five men which they tooke captive the last yere, and promised them, not only to release those which he had taken, but also to reward them with great gifts and friendship. Our Savage made signes in answere from them that our men should be delivered us, and were yet living, and made signes likewise unto us that we should write our letters unto them, for they knew very

well the use we have of writing, and received knowledge thereof, either of our poore captive countreymen which they betrayed, or else by this our new captive who hath seene us dayly write, and repeate againe such words of his language as we desired to learne: but they for this night, because it was late, departed without any letter, although they called earnestly in hast for the same. And the next morning early being the seventh of August,

they called againe for the letter, which being delivered unto them, they speedily departed, making signes with three fingers, and pointing to the Sunne, that they meant to returne within 3 dayes, untill which time we heard no more of them, & about the time appointed they returned, in such sort as you shal afterwards heare.

This night because the people were very neere unto us, the Lieutenant caused the Trumpet to sound a call, and every man in the Island repayring to the Ensigne, he put them in minde of the place so farre from their countrey wherein they lived, and the danger of a great multitude which they were subject unto, if good watch and warde were not kept, for at every low water the enimie might come almost dryfoot from the mayne unto us, wherefore he willed every man to prepare him in good readinesse upon all sudden occasions, and so giving the watch their charge, the company departed to rest.

I thought the Captaines letter well worth the remembring, not for the circumstance of curious enditing, but for the substance and good meaning therein contained, and therefore have repeated here the same, as by himselfe it was hastily written.

The forme of M. Martin Frobishers letter to the English captives.

IN the name of God, in whom we all beleeve, who (I trust) hath preserved your bodies and soules amongst these infidels, I commend me unto you. I will be glad to seeke by al means you can devise for your deliverance, either with force, or with any commodities within my ships, which I will not spare for your sakes, or any thing else I can doe for you. I have aboord, of theirs, a man, a woman, and a child, which I am contented to deliver for you, but the man which I caried away from hence the last yeere is dead in England. Moreover you may declare unto them, that if they deliver you not, I will not leave a man alive in their countrey. And thus, if one of you can come to speake with mee, they shall have either the man, woman, or childe in pawne for you. And thus unto God whom I trust you doe serve, in hast I leave you, and to him wee will dayly pray for you. This Tuesday morning the seventh of August. Anno 1557.

Yours to the uttermost of my power,

MARTIN FROBISHER.

I have sent you by these bearers, penne, ynke, and *Postscript* paper, to write backe unto me againe, if personally you cannot come to certifie me of your estate.

The cause why M. Frobisher entred no further within the Streits this yere.

Now had the Generall altered his determination for going any further into the Streites at this time for any further discovery of the passage, having taken a man and a woman of that countrey, which he thought sufficient for the use of language: & having also met with these people here, which intercepted his men the last yere, (as the apparell and English furniture which was found in their tents, very well declared) he knew it was but a labour lost to seeke them further off, when he had found them there at hand. And considering also the short time he had in hand, he thought it best to bend his whole endevour for the getting of Myne, and to leave the passage further to be discovered hereafter. For his commission directed him in this voyage, onely for the searching of the Ore, and to deferre the further discovery of the passage untill another time.

On Thursday the ninth of August we began to make a smal Fort for our defence in the Countesses Island, and entrenched a corner of a cliffe, which on three parts like a wall of good heigth was compassed and well fenced with the sea, and we finished the rest with caskes of the earth, to good purpose, and this was called Bests bulwarke, after the Lieutenants name, who first devised the same. This was done for that wee suspected more lest the desperate men might oppresse us with multitude, then any feare we had of their force, weapons, or policie of battel: but as wisedome would us in such place (so farre from home) not to be of our selves altogether carelesse: so the signes which our captive made unto us, of the comming downe of his Governour or Prince, which he called Catchoe, gave us occasion to foresee what might ensue thereof, for he shewed by signes that this Catchoe was a man of higher stature farre then any of our nation is, and he is accustomed to be caried upon mens shoulders.

Bests bulwarke.

Their King called Catchoe.

How he is honoured.

About midnight the Lieutenant caused a false Alarme to be given in the Island, to prove as well the readines of the company there ashore, as also what help might be hoped for upon the sudden from the ships if need so required, & every part was found in good readines upon such a sudden.

Saturday the eleventh of August the people shewed themselves againe, & called unto us from the side of a hil over against us. The General (with good hope to heare of his men, and to have answere of his letter) went over unto them, where they presented themselves not above three in sight, but were hidden indeede in greater numbers behind the rockes, and making signes of delay with us to intrappe some of us to redeeme their owne, did onely seeke advantage to traine our boat about a point of land from sight of our companie: whereupon our men justly suspecting them, kept aloofe without their danger, and yet set one of our company ashore, which tooke up a great bladder which one of them offered us, and leaving a looking glasse in the place, came into the boate againe. In the meane while our men which stood in the Countesses Island to beholde, who might better discerne them, then those of the boate, by reason they were on higher ground, made a great outcrie unto our men in the boate, for that they saw divers of the Savages creeping behind the rockes towards our men, wherupon the Generall presently returned without tidings of his men.

Concerning this bladder which we received, our Captive made signes that it was given him to keepe water and drinke in, but we suspected rather it was given him to swimme and shift away withall, for he and the woman sought divers times to escape, having loosed our boates from asterne our ships, and we never a boate left to pursue them withall, and had prevailed very farre, had they not bene very timely espied and prevented therein.

After our Generals comming away from them they mustred themselves in our sight, upon the top of a hill, to the number of twenty in a rancke, all holding hands over their heads, and dancing with great noise and songs

[III. 71.]

A bladder changed for a looking glasse.

No newes of the English captives.

To what end the bladder was delivered.

Those people dancing upon the hil toppes.

311

together: we supposed they made this dance and shew for us to understand, that we might take view of their whole companies and force, meaning belike that we should doe the same. And thus they continued upon the hill tops untill night, when hearing a piece of our great Ordinance, which thundred in the hollownesse of the high hilles, it made unto them so fearefull a noise, that they had no great will to tarie long after. And this was done more to make them know our force then to doe them any hurt at all.

A skirmish shewed to those people.

On Sunday the 12 of August, Captaine Fenton trained the company, and made the souldiers maintaine skirmish among themselves, as well for their exercise, as for the countrey people to behold in what readines our men were alwaies to be found, for it was to be thought, that they lay hid in the hilles thereabout, and observed all the manner of our proceedings.

On Wednesday the fourteenth of August, our Generall with two small boates well appointed, for that hee suspected the countrey people to lie lurking thereabout, went up a certaine Bay within the Countesses sound, to search for Ore, and met againe with the countrey people, who so soone as they saw our men made great outcries,

Their flags made of bladders.

and with a white flag made of bladders sowed together with the guts and sinewes of beasts, wafted us amaine unto them, but shewed not above three of their company. But when wee came neere them, wee might perceive a great multitude creeping behinde the rockes, which gave us good cause to suspect their traiterous meaning: whereupon we made them signes, that if they would lay their weapons aside, and come foorth, we would deale friendly with them, although their intent was manifested unto us: but for all the signes of friendship we could make them they came still creeping towards us behind the rocks to get more advantage of us, as though we had no eyes to see them, thinking belike that our single wits could not discover so bare devises and simple drifts of theirs. Their spokesman earnestly perswaded us with many intising shewes, to come eate and sleepe ashore, with great arguments of courtesie, and clapping his bare hands over his head in token of peace and innocencie, willed us to doe the like. But the better to allure our hungry stomackes, he brought us a trimme baite of raw *Great offers.* flesh, which for fashion sake with a boat-hooke wee caught into our boate: but when the cunning Cater perceived his first cold morsell could nothing sharpen our stomacks, he cast about for a new traine of warme flesh to procure our appetites, wherefore he caused one of his fellowes in halting maner, to come foorth as a lame man from behind the rockes, and the better to declare his kindnes in carving, he hoised him upon his shoulders, and bringing him hard to the water side where we were, left him there limping as an easie prey to be·taken of us. His hope was that we would bite at this baite, and speedily leape ashore within their danger, wherby they might have apprehended some of us, to ransome their friends home againe, which before we had taken. The gentlemen and souldiers had great will to encounter them ashore, but the Generall more carefull by processe of time to winne them, then wilfully at the first to spoile them, would in no wise admit that any man should put himselfe in hazard ashore, considering the matter he now intended was for the Ore, and not for the Conquest: notwithstanding to proove this cripples footemanship, he gave liberty for one to shoote: whereupon the cripple having a parting blow, lightly recovered a rocke and went away a true and no fained cripple, and hath learned his lesson for ever halting afore such cripples againe. But his fellowes which lay hid before, full quickly then appeared in their likenesse, and maintained the skirmish with their slings, bowes and arrowes very fiercely, and came as neere as the water suffred them: and with as desperate minde as hath bene seene in any men, without feare of shotte or any thing, followed us all along the coast, but all their shot fell short of us, and are of little danger. They had belayed all the coast along for us, [III. 72.]

THE ENGLISH VOYAGES

and being dispersed so, were not well to be numbred, but wee might discerne of them above an hundreth persons, and had cause to suspect a greater number. And thus without losse or hurt we returned to our ships againe.

Now our worke growing to an end, and having, onely with five poore Miners, and the helpe of a few gentlemen and souldiers, brought aboord almost two hundreth tunne of Ore in the space of twenty dayes, every man therewithall well comforted, determined lustily to worke a fresh for a bone voyage, to bring our labour to a speedy and happy ende.

And upon Wednesday at night being the one and twentieth of August, we fully finished the whole worke. And it was now good time to leave, for as the men were well wearied, so their shooes and clothes were well worne, their baskets bottoms torne out, their tooles broken, and the ships reasonably well filled. Some with over-straining themselves received hurts not a little dangerous, some having their bellies broken, and others their legs made lame. And about this time the yce began to congeale and freeze about our ships sides a night, which gave us a good argument of the Sunnes declining Southward, & put us in mind to make more haste homeward.

It is not a little worth the memorie, to the commendation of the gentlemen and souldiers herein, who leaving all reputation apart, with so great willingnesse and with couragious stomackes, have themselves almost overcome in so short a time the difficultie of this so great a labour. And this to be true, the matter, if it bee well weyed without further proofe, now brought home doth well witnesse.

Thursday the 22 of August, we plucked downe our tents, and every man hasted homeward, and making bonefires upon the top of the highest Mount of the Island, and marching with Ensigne displayed round about the Island, wee gave a vollie of shotte for a farewell, in honour of the right honourable Lady Anne, Countesse of Warwicke, whose name it beareth : and so departed aboord.

The 23 of August having the wind large at West, we set saile from out of the Countesses sound homeward, *They returne.* but the wind calming we came to anker within the point of the same sound againe.

The 24 of August about three of the clocke in the morning, having the wind large at West, we set saile againe, and by nine of the clocke at night, wee left the Queenes Foreland asterne of us, and being cleere of the Streites, we bare further into the maine Ocean, keeping our course more Southerly, to bring our selves the sooner under the latitude of our owne climate.

The wind was very great at sea, so that we lay a hull all night, & had snow halfe a foote deepe on the *Snow halfe a* hatches. *foote deepe in August.*

From the 24 until the 28 we had very much wind, but large, keeping our course Southsoutheast, and had like to have lost the Barkes, but by good hap we met againe. The height being taken, we were in   degrees and a halfe.

The 29 of August the wind blew much at Northeast, so that we could beare but onely a bunt of our foresaile, and the Barkes were not able to cary any sayle at all.

The Michael lost company of us and shaped her course towards Orkney because that way was better knowne unto them, and arrived at Yermouth.

The 30 of August with the force of the wind, and a surge of the sea, the Master of the Gabriel and the *The Master* Boatswain were striken both overboord, & hardly was *of the Gabriel* the Boatswain recovered, having hold on a roape hang- *strooken over-* ing overboord in the sea, and yet the Barke was laced *boord.* fore and after with ropes a breast high within boorde.

This Master was called William Smith, being but a yong man and a very sufficient mariner, who being all the morning before exceeding pleasant, told his Captaine he dreamed that he was cast overboord, and that the

315

Boatswain had him by the hand, and could not save him, and so immediately upon the end of his tale, his dreame came right evilly to passe, and indeed the Boatswain in like sort held him by one hand, having hold on a rope with the other, untill his force fayled, and the Master drowned. The height being taken we found our selves to be in the latitude of   degrees and a halfe, and reckoned our selves from the Queenes Cape homeward about two hundreth leagues.

The last of August about midnight, we had two or three great and sudden flawes or stormes.

The first of September the storme was growen very great, and continued almost the whole day and night, and lying a hull to tarrie for the Barkes our ship was much beaten with the seas, every sea almost overtaking our poope, so that we were constrained with a bunt of our saile to trie it out, and ease the rolling of our ship. And so the Gabriel not able to beare any sayle to keepe company with us, and our ship being higher in the poope,

[III. 73.]

and a tall ship, whereon the winde had more force to drive, went so fast away that we lost sight of them, and left them to God and their good fortune of Sea. The second day of September in the morning, it pleased God of his goodnesse to send us a calme, whereby we per-

The Rudder of the Aide torne in twain.

ceived the Rudder of our ship torne in twaine, and almost ready to fall away. Wherefore taking the benefite of the time, we flung halfe a dozen couple of our best men over boord, who taking great paines under water, driving plankes, and binding with ropes, did well strengthen and mend the matter, who returned the most part more then halfe dead out of the water, and as Gods pleasure was, the sea was calme untill the worke was finished.

How the latitudes were alwayes taken in this voyage rather with the Staffe then Astrolabe.

The fift of September, the height of the Sunne being taken, we found our selves to be in the latitude of   degrees and a halfe. In this voyage commonly wee tooke the latitude of the place by the height of the sunne, because the long day taketh away the light not onely of the Polar, but also of all other fixed Starres. And here

316

the North Starre is so much elevated above the Horizon, that with the staffe it is hardly to bee well observed, and the degrees in the Astrolabe are too small to observe minutes. Therefore wee alwaies used the Staffe and the sunne as fittest instruments for this use.

Having spent foure or five dayes in traverse of the seas with contrary winde, making our Souther way good as neere as we could, to raise our degrees to bring our selves with the latitude of Sylley, wee tooke the height the tenth of September, and found our selves in the latitude of   degrees and ten minutes. The eleventh of September about sixe a clocke at night the winde came good Southwest, we vered sheat and set our course Southeast.

And upon Thursday, the twelfth of September, taking the height, we were in the latitude of   and a halfe, and reckoned our selves not past one hundred and fifty leagues short of Sylley, the weather faire, the winde large at Westsouthwest, we kept our course Southeast.

The thirteenth day the height being taken, wee found our selves to be in the latitude of   degrees, the wind Westsouthwest, then being in the height of Sylley, and we kept our course East, to run in with the sleeve or chanel so called, being our narrow seas, and reckoned us short of Sylley twelve leagues.

Sonday, the 15 of September about foure of the clocke, we began to sound with our lead, and had ground at 61 fadome depth, white small sandy ground, and reckoned us upon the backe of Sylley, and set our course East and by North, Eastnortheast, and Northeast among.

The sixteenth of September, about eight of the clocke in the morning sounding, we had 65. fadome osey sand, and thought our selves thwart of S. Georges channell a little within the banks. And bearing a small saile all night, we made many soundings, which were about fortie fadome, and so shallow, that we could not well tell where we were.

The seventeenth of September we sounded, and had forty fadome, and were not farre off the lands end, finding branded sand with small wormes and Cockle shells, and were shotte betweene Sylley and the lands ende, and being within the bay, we were not able to double the pointe with a South and by East way, but were faine to make another boord, the wind being at Southwest and by West, and yet could not double the point to come cleere of the lands end, to beare along the channel: and the weather cleered up when we were hard aboord the shore, and we made the lands end perfit, and so put up along Saint Georges chanel. And the weather being very foule at sea, we coveted some harborough, because

The arrival of the Aide at Padstow in Cornewall.

our steerage was broken, and so came to ancor in Padstow road in Cornewall. But riding there a very dangerous roade, we were advised by the countrey, to put to Sea againe, and of the two evils, to choose the lesse, for there was nothing but present perill where we roade: whereupon we plyed along the channell to get to Londy, from whence we were againe driven, being but an open roade, where our Anker came home, and with force of weather put to Seas againe, and about the three and twentieth

Our comming to Milford Haven.

of September, arrived at Milford Haven in Wales, which being a very good harborough, made us happy men, that we had received such long desired safetie.

About one moneth after our arrivall here, by order from the Lords of the Counsell, the ship came up to

The arrivall of the Gabriel at Bristow.

Bristow, where the Ore was committed to keeping in the Castel there. Here we found the Gabriel one of the Barkes, arrived in good safetie, who having never a man within boord very sufficient to bring home the ship, after the Master was lost, by good fortune, when she came upon the coast, met with a ship of Bristow at sea, who conducted her in safety thither.

The Michael arrived in the North parts.

Here we heard good tidings also of the arrivall of the other Barke called the Michael, in the North parts, which was not a little joyful unto us, that it pleased God so to bring us to a safe meeting againe, and wee lost in

all the voyage only one man, besides one that dyed
at sea, which was sicke before he came aboord, and was
so desirous to follow this enterprise, that he rather chose
to dye therein, then not to be one to attempt so notable
a voyage.

The third voyage of Captaine Frobisher, pretended for the discoverie of Cataia, by Meta Incognita, Anno Do. 1578.

He Generall being returned from the
second voyage, immediately after his arrivall in England, repaired with all hast
to the Court being then at Windsore, to
advertise her Majestie of his prosperous
proceeding, and good successe in this last
voyage, & of the plenty of gold Ore,
with other matters of importance which he had in these
Septentrionall parts discovered. He was courteously
enterteyned, and hartily welcommed of many noble men,
but especially for his great adventure, commended of her
Majestie, at whose hands he received great thankes, and
most gracious countenance, according to his deserts.
Her Highnesse also greatly commended the rest of the
Gentlemen in this service, for their great forwardnes in
this so dangerous an attempt: but especially she rejoyced
very much, that among them there was so good order
of governement, so good agreement, every man so ready
in his calling, to do whatsoever the General should command, which due commendation gratiously of her Majestie remembred, gave so great encouragement to all the
Captaines and Gentlemen, that they, to continue her
Highnesse so good and honourable opinion of them, have
since neither spared labour, limme, nor life, to bring this
matter (so well begun) to a happie and prosperous ende.
And finding that the matter of the golde Ore had appearance & made shew of great riches & profit, & the hope
of the passage to Cataya, by this last voyage greatly

THE ENGLISH VOYAGES

increased, her Majestie appointed speciall Commissioners chosen for this purpose, gentlemen of great judgement, art, and skill, to looke thorowly into the cause, for the true triall and due examination thereof, and for the full handling of all matters thereunto appertaining. And because that place and countrey hath never heretofore beene *A name given* discovered, and therefore had no speciall name, by which *to ye place new* it might be called and knowen, her Majestie named it *discovered.* very properly Meta Incognita, as a marke and bound utterly hitherto unknowen. The commissioners after sufficient triall and proofe made of the Ore, and having understood by sundrie reasons, and substantiall grounds, the possibilitie and likelyhood of the passage, advertised her highnesse, that the cause was of importance, and the voyage greatly worthy to be advanced againe. Whereupon preparation was made of ships and all other things necessary, with such expedition, as the time of the yeere then required. And because it was assuredly made accompt of, that the commoditie of Mines, there already discovered, would at the least countervaile in all respects *The hope of the* the adventurers charge, and give further hope & likely-*passage to* hood of greater matters to follow: it was thought *Cataya.* needfull, both for the better guard of those parts already found, and for further discovery of the Inland and secrets of those countreys, & also for further search of the passage to Cataya (whereof the hope continually more & more increaseth) that certaine numbers of chosen souldiers and discreet men for those purposes should *A forte to be* be assigned to inhabite there. Whereupon there was a *built in Meta* strong fort or house of timber, artificially framed, & *Incognita.* cunningly devised by a notable learned man here at home, in ships to be caried thither, wherby those men that were appointed to winter & stay there the whole yere, might aswell bee defended from the danger of the snow and colde ayre, as also fortified from the force or offence of those countrey people, which perhaps otherwise with too great multitudes might oppresse them. And to this great adventure and notable exploit many

well minded and forward yong Gentlemen of our
countrey willingly have offered themselves. And first
Captaine Fenton Lieutenant generall for Captaine Frobisher, and in charge of the company with him there,
Captaine Best, and Captaine Filpot, unto whose good
discretions the government of that service was chiefly
commended, who, as men not regarding peril in respect
of the profit and common wealth of their countrey, were
willing to abide the first brunt & adventure of those
dangers among a savage and brutish kinde of people, in
a place hitherto ever thought for extreme cold not
habitable. The whole number of men which had offered,
and were appointed to inhabite Meta Incognita all the *A hundreth*
yeere, were one hundreth persons, wherof 40 should be *men appointed*
mariners for the use of ships, 30 Miners for gathering *to inhabite*
the gold Ore together for the next yere, and 30 souldiers *there.*
for the better guard of the rest, within which last number
are included the Gentlemen, Goldfiners, Bakers, Carpenters, & all necessary persons. To each of the
Captaines was assigned one ship, aswel for the further
searching of the coast & countrey there, as for to returne
& bring backe their companies againe, if the necessity
of the place so urged, or by miscarying of the fleet the
next yere, they might be disappointed of their further
provision. Being therfore thus furnished with al necessaries, there were ready to depart upon the said voyage
15 saile of good ships, wherof the whole number was to *Fifteene sayle.*
returne again with their loding of gold Ore in the end
of the sommer, except those 3 ships, which should be
left for the use of those Captains which should inhabite
there the whole yere. And being in so good readinesse, [III. 75.]
the Generall with all the Captaines came to the Court,
then lying at Greenwich, to take their leave of her
Majestie, at whose hands they all received great
incouragement, and gracious countenance. Her highnesse besides other good gifts, and greater promises, *A chaine of*
bestowed on the Generall a faire chaine of golde, *gold given to*
and the rest of the Captaines kissed her hand, tooke *M. Frobisher.*

their leave, and departed every man towards their charge.

The names of the ships with their severall Captaines.

1	In the Aide being Amirall, was the Generall	Captaine Frobisher.
2	In the Thomas Allen Viceadmirall	Yorke.
3	In the Judith Lieutenant generall	Fenton.
4	In the Anne Francis	Best.
5	In the Hopewell	Carew.
6	In the Beare	Filpot.
7	In the Thomas of Ipswich	Tanfield.
8	In the Emmanuel of Exceter	Courtney.
9	In the Francis of Foy	Moyles.
10	In the Moone	Upcot.
11	In the Emmanuel of Bridgewater	Newton.
12	In the Salomon of Weymouth	Randal.
13	In the Barke Dennis	Kendal.
14	In the Gabriel	Harvey.
15	In the Michael	Kinnersley.

The sayd fifteene saile of ships arrived and met together at Harwich, the seven and twentieth day of May Anno 1578, where the Generall and the other Captaines made view, and mustred their companies. And every severall Captaine received from the Generall certaine Articles of direction, for the better keeping of order and company together in the way, which Articles are as followeth.

Articles and orders to be observed for the Fleete, set downe by Captaine Frobisher Generall, and delivered in writing to every Captaine, as well for keeping company, as for the course, the 31 of May.

1 INprimis, to banish swearing, dice, and card-playing, and filthy conmunication, and to serve God twice a day, with the ordinary service usuall in Churches of

England, and to cleare the glasse, according to the old order of England.

2 The Admiral shall carie the light, & after his light be once put out, no man to goe a head of him, but every man to fit his sailes to follow as neere as they may, without endangering one another.

3 That no man shall by day or by night depart further from the Admirall then the distance of one English mile, and as neere as they may, without danger one of another.

4 If it chance to grow thicke, and the wind contrary, either by day or by night, that the Admirall be forced to cast about, before her casting about shee shall give warning, by shooting off a peece, and to her shall answere the Viceadmirall and the Rereadmirall each of them with a piece, if it bee by night, or in a fogge; and that the Viceadmirall shall answere first, and the Rereadmirall last.

5 That no man in the Fleete descrying any sayle or sayles, give upon any occasion any chace before he have spoken with the Admirall.

6 That every evening all the Fleete come up and speake with the Admirall, at seven of the Clocke, or betweene that and eight, and if the weather will not serve them all to speake with the Admirall, then some shall come to the Viceadmirall, and receive the order of their course of Master Hall chiefe Pilot of the Fleete, as he shall direct them.

7 If to any man in the Fleete there happen any mischance, they shall presently shoote off two peeces by day, and if it be by night, two peeces, and shew two lights.

8 If any man in the Fleete come up in the night, & hale his fellow knowing him not, he shall give him this watch-word, Before the world was God. The other shal answere him (if he be one of our Fleete) After God came Christ his Sonne. So that if any be found amongst us, not of our owne company, he that first descrieth [III. 76.] any such sayle or sayles, shall give warning to the

Admirall by himselfe or any other that he can speake to, that sailes better then he, being neerest unto him.

9 That every ship in the fleete in the time of fogs, which continually happen with little winds, and most part calmes, shall keepe a reasonable noise with trumpet, drumme, or otherwise, to keepe themselves cleere one of another.

10 If it fall out so thicke ui mistie that we lay it to hull, the Admiral shall give warning with a piece, and putting out three lights one over another, to the end that every man may take in his sailes, and at his setting of sayles againe doe the like, if it be not cleere.

11 If any man discover land by night, that he give the like warning, that he doth for mischances, two lights, and two pieces, if it be by day one piece, and put out his flagge, and strike all his sailes he hath aboord.

12 If any ship shall happen to lose company by force of weather, then any such ship or ships shall get her into the latitude of   , and so keepe that latitude untill they get Frisland. And after they be past the West parts of Frisland, they shall get them into the latitude of   , and   , and not to the Northward of   ; and being once entred within the Streites, al such ships shal every watch shoote off a good piece, and looke out well for smoke and fire which those that get in first shall make every night, untill all the fleete be come together.

13 That upon the sight of an Ensigne in the mast of the Admirall (a piece being shot off) the whole fleete shall repaire to the Admirall, to understand such conference as the Generall is to have with them.

14 If we chance to meete with any enemies, that foure ships shall attend upon the Admirall, viz. the Francis of Foy, the Moone, the Barke Dennis, and the Gabriel: and foure upon my Lieutenant generall in the Judith, viz. the Hopewel, the Armenal, the Beare, and the Salomon: and the other foure upon the Vizadmirall, the

Anne Francis, the Thomas of Ipswich, the Emmanuel, and the Michael.

15 If there happen any disordred person in the Fleete, that he be taken and kept in safe custodie untill he may conveniently be brought aboord the Admirall, and there to receive such punishment as his or their offences shall deserve.

By me Martin Frobisher.

Our departure from England.

HAving received these articles of direction we departed from Harwich the one and thirtieth of May. And sayling along the South part of England Westward, we at length came by the coast of Ireland at Cape Cleare *Cape Cleare* the sixth of June, and gave chase there to a small barke *the sixt of* which was supposed to be a Pyrat, or Rover on the *June.* Seas, but it fell out indeede that they were poore men of Bristow, who had met with such company of Frenchmen as had spoiled and slaine many of them, and left the rest so sore wounded that they were like to perish in the sea, having neither hand nor foote hole to helpe themselves with, nor victuals to sustaine their hungry bodies. Our Generall, who well understood the office of a Souldier and an Englishman, and knew well what the necessitie of the sea meaneth, pitying much the miserie *A charitable* of the poore men, relieved them with Surgerie and salves *deede.* to heale their hurtes, and with meate and drinke to comfort their pining hearts; some of them having neither eaten nor drunke more then olives and stinking water in many dayes before, as they reported. And after this good deede done, having a large wind, we kept our course upon our sayd voyage without staying for the taking in of fresh water, or any other provision, whereof many of the fleete were not throughly furnished: and sayling towards the Northwest parts from Ireland, we mette with a great current from out of the Southwest, *Marke this* which caried us (by our reckoning) one point to the *current.* Northeastwards of our sayd course, which current seemed to us to continue it selfe towards Norway, and other the Northeast parts of the world, whereby we may be induced to beleeve, that this is the same which the Portugals meete at Capo de buona Speranza, where striking over from thence to the Streites of Magellan, and finding no passage there for the narrownesse of the sayde Streites, runneth along into the great Bay of Mexico, where also having a let of land, it is forced to strike backe againe towards the Northeast, as we not onely here, but in another place also, further to the Northwards, by good experience this yeere have found, as shalbe hereafter in his place more at large declared.

Now had we sayled about fourteene dayes, without sight of any land, or any other living thing, except certaine foules, as Wilmots, Nodies, Gulles, &c. which there seeme onely to live by sea.

[III. 77.] The twentieth of June, at two of the clocke in the morning, the General descried land, & found it to be *West Eng-* West Frisland, now named west England. Here the *land.* Generall, & other Gentlemen went ashore, being the first knowen Christians that we have true notice of, that ever set foot upon that ground: and therefore the Generall tooke possession thereof to the use of our Sovereigne Lady the Queenes Majestie, and discovered here a goodly harborough for the ships, where were also certaine little boates of that countrey. And being there landed, they espied certaine tents and people of that countrey, which were (as they judge) in all sorts, very like those of Meta Incognita, as by their apparell, and other things which we found in their tents, appeared.

The Savage and simple people so soone as they perceived our men comming towards them (supposing there had bene no other world but theirs) fled fearefully away, as men much amazed at so strange a sight, and creatures of humane shape, so farre in apparell, complexion, and other things different from themselves. They left in their tents all their furniture for haste behind them, where amongst other things were found a boxe of small nailes, and certaine red Herrings, boords of Firre tree well cut, with divers other things artificially wrought: whereby it appeareth, that they have trade with some civill people, or else are indeede themselves artificiall workemen.

Our men brought away with them onely two of their dogs, leaving in recompense belles, looking-glasses, and divers of our countrey toyes behinde them.

This countrey, no doubt, promiseth good hope of great commoditie and riches, if it may be well discovered. The description whereof you shall finde more at large in the second voyage.

Some are of opinion, that this West England is firme land with the Northeast partes of Meta Incognita, or else with Groenland. And their reason is, because the people, apparel, boates, and other things are so like to theirs: and another reason is, the multitude of Islands of yce, which lay betweene it and Meta Incognita, doth argue, that on the North side there is a bay, which cannot be but by conjoyning of the two lands together. *Frisland supposed to be continent with Groenland.*

And having a faire and large winde we departed from thence towards Frobishers Streites, the three and twentieth of June. But first wee gave name to a high cliffe in West England, the last that was in our sight, and for a certaine similitude we called it Charing crosse. Then wee bare Southerly towards the Sea, because to the Northwardes of this coast we met with much driving yce, which by reason of the thicke mistes and weather might have bene some trouble unto us. *The 23 of June.* *Charing crosse.*

On Munday the last of June, wee met with many great Whales, as they had bene Porposes.

This same day the Salamander being under both her corses and bonets, happened to strike a great Whale with her full stemme, with such a blow that the ship stoode still, and stirred neither forward nor backward. The Whale thereat made a great and ugly noyse, and cast up his body and taile, and so went under water, and within two daies after, there was found a great Whale dead *A Whale strooke a ship.*

swimming above water, which wee supposed was that which the Salamander strooke.

The second day of July early in the morning we had sight of the Queenes Foreland, and bare in with the land all the day, and passing thorow great quantity of yce, by night were entred somewhat within the Streites, perceiving no way to passe further in, the whole place being frozen over from the one side to the other, and as it *Frobishers* were with many walles, mountaines, and bulwarks of yce, *Streites choked* choked up the passage, and denied us entrance. And *up with yce.* yet doe I not thinke that this passage or Sea hereabouts is frozen over at any time of the yere: albeit it seemed so unto us by the abundance of yce gathered together, which occupied the whole place. But I doe rather suppose these yce to bee bred in the hollow soundes and freshets thereabouts: which by the heate of the sommers Sunne, being loosed, doe emptie themselves with the ebbes into the sea, and so gather in great abundance there together.

And to speake somewhat here of the ancient opinion of the frozen sea in these parts: I doe thinke it to be rather a bare conjecture of men, then that ever any man hath made experience of any such sea. And that which they speake of Mare glaciale, may be truely thought to be spoken of these parts: for this may well be called indeede the ycie sea, but not the frozen sea, for no sea consisting of salt water can be frozen, as I have more at large herein shewed my opinion in my second voyage, for *Salt water can-* it seemeth impossible for any sea to bee frozen, which *not freeze.* hath his course of ebbing and flowing, especially in those places where the tides doe ebbe and flowe above ten fadome. And also all these aforesayd yce, which we sometime met a hundreth mile from lande, being gathered out of the salt Sea, are in taste fresh, and being dissolved, become sweete and holesome water.

[III. 78.] And the cause why this yere we have bene more combred with yce then at other times before, may be by reason of the Easterly & Southerly winds, which brought us more timely thither now then we looked for. Which blowing from the sea directly upon the place of our Streites, hath kept in the yce, and not suffered them to be caried out by the ebbe to the maine sea, where they would in more short time have bene dissolved. And all these fleeting yce are not only so dangerous in that they wind and gather so neere together, that a man may passe sometimes tenne or twelve miles as it were upon one firme Island of yce: but also for that they open and shut together againe in such sort with the tides and sea-gate, that whilest one ship followeth the other with full sayles, the yce which was open unto the foremost will joyne and close together before the latter can come to follow the first, whereby many times our shippes were brought into great danger, as being not able so sodainely to take in our sayles, or stay the swift way of our ships.

We were forced many times to stemme and strike great rockes of yce, and so as it were make way through mighty mountaines. By which meanes some of the fleete, where they found the yce to open, entred in, and passed so farre within the danger thereof, with continuall desire to recover their port, that it was the greatest wonder of the world that they ever escaped safe, or were ever heard of againe. For even at this present we missed two of the fleete, that is, the Judith, wherein was the Lieutenant generall Captaine Fenton; and the Michael, whom both we supposed had bene utterly lost, having not heard any tidings of them in moe then 20 dayes before.

And one of our fleete named the Barke Dennis, being *Barke Dennis* of an hundreth tunne burden, seeking way in amongst *sunke.* these yce, received such a blow with a rocke of yce that she sunke downe therewith in the sight of the whole fleete. Howbeit having signified her danger by shooting off a peece of great Ordinance, new succour of other ships came so readily unto them, that the men were all saved with boats.

*Part of the
house lost.* Within this ship that was drowned there was parcell of our house which was to bee erected for them that should stay all the winter in Meta Incognita.

This was a more fearefull spectacle for the Fleete to beholde, for that the outragious storme which presently followed, threatned them the like fortune and danger. For the Fleete being thus compassed (as aforesayd) on every side with yce, having left much behinde them, thorow which they passed, and finding more before them, thorow which it was not possible to passe, there arose a sudden terrible tempest at the Southeast, which blowing from the maine sea, directly upon the place of the Streites, brought together all the yce a sea-boorde of us upon our backes, and thereby debard us of turning backe to recover sea-roome againe : so that being thus compassed with danger on every side, sundry men with sundry devises sought the best way to save themselves. Some of the ships, where they could find a place more cleare of yce, and get a little birth of sea roome, did take in their sayles, and there lay a drift. Other some fastened & mored Anker upon a great Island of yce, and roade under the Lee therof, supposing to be better guarded thereby from the outragious winds, and the danger of the lesser fleeting yce. And againe some where so fast shut up, and compassed in amongst an infinite number of great countreys and Islands of yce, that they were faine to submit themselves and their ships to the mercy of the unmercifull yce, and strengthened the sides of their ships with junckes of cables, beds, Mastes, plankes and such like, which being hanged over boord on the sides of their ships, might the better defend them from the outragious, sway and strokes of the said yce. But as in greatest distresse, men of best valour are best to bee discerned, so it is greatly worthy commendation and noting with what invincible minde every Captaine encouraged his company, and with what incredible labour the painefull Mariners and poore Miners (unacquainted with such extremities) to the everlasting renowne of our nation, did overcome the brunt of these so great and extreme dangers : for some, even without boord upon the yce, and some within boord upon the sides of their ships, having poles, pikes, pieces of timber, and Ores in their handes, stoode almost day and night without any rest, bearing off the force, and breaking the sway of the yce with such incredible paine and perill, that it was wonderfull to beholde, which otherwise no doubt had striken quite through and through the sides of their ships, notwithstanding our former provision : for plankes of timber of more then three inches thicke, and other things of greater force and bignesse, by the surging of the sea and billowe, with the yce were shivered and cut in sunder, at the sides of our ships, so that it will seeme more then credible to be reported of. And yet (that which is more) it is faithfully and plainely to bee prooved, and that by many substantiall witnesses, that our ships, even those of greatest burdens, with the meeting of contrary waves of the sea, were heaved up betweene Islands of yce, a foote welneere out of the sea above their watermarke, having their knees and timbers within boord [III. 79.] both bowed and broken therewith.

And amidst these extremes, whilest some laboured for defence of the ships, and sought to save their bodies, other some of more milder spirit sought to save the soule by devout prayer and meditation to the Almightie, thinking indeede by no other meanes possible then by a divine Miracle to have their deliverance : so that there was none that were either idle, or not well occupied, and he that helde himselfe in best securitie had (God knoweth) but onely bare hope remayning for his best safetie.

Thus all the gallant Fleete and miserable men without hope of ever getting foorth againe, distressed with these extremities remayned here all the whole night and part of the next day, excepting foure ships, that is, the Anne Francis, the Moone, the Francis of Foy, and the Gabriell, which being somewhat a Seaboord of the Fleete, and being fast ships by a winde, having a more scope of cleare, tryed it out all the time of the storme under sayle, being hardly able to beare a coast of each.

And albeit, by reason of the fleeting yce, which were dispersed here almost the whole sea over, they were brought many times to the extreamest point of perill, mountaines of yce tenne thousand times scaping them scarce one ynch, which to have striken had bene their present destruction, considering the swift course and way of the ships, and the unwieldinesse of them to stay and turne as a man would wish: yet they esteemed it their better safetie, with such perill to seeke Sea-roome, than without hope of ever getting libertie to lie striving against the streame, and beating amongst the Isie mountaines, whose hugenesse and monstrous greatnesse was such, that no man would credite, but such as to their paines sawe and felt it. And these foure shippes by the next day at noone got out to Sea, and were first cleare of the yce, who now enjoying their owne libertie, beganne a new to sorrow and feare for their fellowes safeties. And devoutly kneeling about their maine Mast, they gave unto God humble thankes, not only for themselves, but besought him likewise highly for their friendes deliverance. And even now whilest amiddest these extremities this gallant Fleete and valiant men were altogither overlaboured and forewatched, with the long and fearefull continuance of the foresayd dangers, it pleased God with his eyes of mercie to looke downe from heaven to sende them helpe in good time, giving them the next day a more favourable winde at the West Northwest, which did not onely disperse and drive foorth the yce before them, but also gave them libertie of more scope and Sea-roome, and they were by night of the same day following perceived of the other foure shippes, where (to their greatest comfort) they enjoyed againe the fellowship one of another. Some in mending the sides of their ships, some in setting up their top Mastes, and mending their sayles and tacklings; Againe, some complayning of their false Stemme borne away, some in stopping their leakes, some in recounting their dangers past, spent no small time & labour. So that I dare well avouch, there were never men more dangerously distressed, nor more mercifully by Gods providence delivered. And hereof both the torne ships, and the forwearied bodies of the men arrived doe beare most evident marke and witnesse. And now the whole Fleete plyed off to Seaward, resolving there to abide untill the Sunne might consume, or the force of winde disperse these yce from the place of their passage: and being a good birth off the shore, they tooke in their sailes, and lay adrift.

The seventh of July as men nothing yet dismayed, we cast about towards the inward, and had sight of land, which rose in forme like the Northerland of the straights, which some of the Fleete, and those not the worst Marriners, judged to be the North Foreland: howbeit other some were of contrary opinion. But the matter was not well to be discerned by reason of the thicke fogge which a long time hung upon the coast, & the new falling snow which yeerely altereth the shape of the land, and taketh away oftentimes the Mariners markes. And by reason of the darke mists which continued by the space of twentie dayes togither, this doubt grewe the greater and the longer perilous. For whereas indeede we thought our selves to be upon the Northeast side of Frobishers straights, we were now caried to the Southwestwards of the Queenes Foreland, and being deceived by a swift current comming from the Northeast, were brought to the Southwestwards of our said course many miles more then we did thinke possible could come to passe. The cause whereof we have since found, and it shall be at large hereafter declared.

Here we made a point of land which some mistooke for a place in the straightes called Mount Warwicke: but how we should be so farre shot up so suddainely within the said straights the expertest Mariners began to

Another assault.

Fogge, snow, and mistes hinder the Mariners markes.

A swift current from the Northeast.

marvell, thinking it a thing impossible that they could be so farre overtaken in their accounts, or that any current could deceive them here which they had not by former experience prooved and found out. Howbeit many confessed that they found a swifter course of flood then before time they had observed. And truely it was wonderfull to heare and see the rushing and noise that the tides do make in this place with so violent a force that our ships lying a hull were turned sometimes round about even in a moment after the maner of a whirlepoole, and the noyse of the streame no lesse to be heard afarre off, then the waterfall of London Bridge.

But whilest the Fleete lay thus doubtfull amongst great store of yce in a place they knew not without sight of Sunne, whereby to take the height, and so to know the true elevation of the pole, and without any cleere of light to make perfite the coast, the Generall with the Captaines & Masters of his ships, began doubtfully to question of the matter, and sent his Pinnesse aboord to *James Beare* heare each mans opinion, and specially of James Beare, *a good Mar-* Master of the Anne Francis, who was knowen to be a *iner.* sufficient and skilful Mariner, and having bene there the yere before, had wel observed the place, and drawen out Cardes of the coast. But the rather this matter grew the *Christopher* more doubtfull, for that Christopher Hall chiefe Pilot of *Hall chiefe* the voyage, delivered a plaine and publique opinion in *Pylot.* the hearing of the whole Fleete, that hee had never seene the foresayd coast before, and that he could not make it for any place of Frobishers Streits, as some of the Fleete supposed, and yet the landes doe lie and trend so like, that the best Mariners therein may bee deceived.

The tenth of July, the weather still continuing thicke and darke, some of the ships in the fogge lost sight of the Admirall and the rest of the fleete, and wandering to and fro, with doubtfull opinion whether it were best to seeke backe againe to seaward through great store of yce, or to follow on a doubtfull course in a Sea, Bay, or Streites they knew not, or along a coast, whereof by reason of the darke mistes they could not discerne the dangers, if by chance any rocke or broken ground should lie of the place, as commonly in these parts it doth.

The Viceadmirall Captaine Yorke considering the foresayd opinion of the Pylot Hall, who was with him in the Thomas Allen, having lost sight of the Fleete, turned backe to sea againe, having two other ships in company with him.

Also the Captaine of the Anne Francis having likewise lost company of the Fleete, and being all alone, held it for best to turne it out to sea againe, untill they might have cleere weather to take the Sunnes altitude, and with incredible paine and perill got out of the doubtfull place, into the open Sea againe, being so narrowly distressed by the way, by meanes of continuall fogge and yce, that they were many times ready to leape upon an Iland of yce to avoide the present danger, and so hoping to prolong life awhile meant rather to die a pining death.

Some hoped to save themselves on chestes, and some determined to tie the Hatches of the ships togither, and to binde themselves with their furniture fast thereunto, and so to be towed with the ship-bote ashore, which otherwise could not receive halfe of the companie, by which meanes if happily they had arrived, they should eyther have perished for lacke of foode to eate, or else should themselves have beene eaten of those ravenous, bloodie, and Men-eating people. *Hard shifts to save mens lives.*

The rest of the Fleete following the course of the Generall which led them the way, passed up above sixtie leagues within the saide doubtfull and supposed straights, having alwayes a faire continent upon their starreboorde side, and a continuance still of an open Sea before them. *The coast along ye Southside of Gronland 60 leagues.*

The Generall albeit with the first perchance he found out the error, and that this was not the olde straights, yet he perswaded the Fleete alwayes that they were in their right course, and knowen straights. Howbeit I suppose he rather dissembled his opinion therein then otherwise, *Mistaken straights which indeede are no straights.*

meaning by that policie (being himselfe led with an honourable desire of further discoverie) to induce the Fleete to follow him, to see a further proofe of that place. And as some of the companie reported, he hath since confessed that if it had not bene for the charge and care he had of the Fleete and fraughted ships, he both would and could have gone through to the South Sea, called Mar del Sur, and dissolved the long doubt of the passage which we seeke to find to the rich countrey of Cataya.

1 Of which mistaken straights, considering the circumstance, we have great cause to confirme our opinion, to like and hope well of the passage in this place. For the foresaid Bay or Sea, the further we sayled therein, the wider we found it, with great likelihood of endlesse continuance. And where in other places we were much troubled with yce, as in the entrance of the same, so after we had sayled fiftie or sixtie leagues therein we had no let of yce, or other thing at all, as in other places we found.

2 Also this place seemeth to have a marvellous great indraft, and draweth unto it most of the drift yce, and other things which doe fleete in the Sea, either to the North or Eastwards of the same, as by good experience we have found.

3 For here also we met with boordes, lathes, and divers other things driving in the Sea, which was of the wracke of the ship called the Barke Dennis, which perished amongst the yce as beforesaid, being lost at the first attempt of the entrance overthwart the Queenes forelande in the mouth of Frobishers straights, which could by no meanes have bene so brought thither, neither by winde nor tyde, being lost so many leagues off, if by force of the said current the same had not bene violently brought. For if the same had bene brought thither by tide of flood, looke how farre the said flood had carried it, the ebbe would have recarried it as farre backe againe, and by the winde it could not so come to

passe, because it was then sometime calme, and most times contrarie.

And some Mariners doe affirme that they have diligently observed, that there runneth in this place nine houres flood to three ebbe, which may thus come to passe by force of the sayd current: for whereas the Sea in most places of the world, doth more or lesse ordinarily ebbe and flow once every twelve houres with sixe houres ebbe, and sixe houres flood, so also would it doe there, were it not for the violence of this hastning current, which forceth the flood to make appearance to beginne before his ordinary time one houre and a halfe, and also to continue longer than his naturall course by an other houre and a halfe, untill the force of the ebbe be so great that it will no longer be resisted: according to the saying, Naturam expellas furca licet, usque recurrit. Although nature and naturall courses be forced and resisted never so much, yet at last they will have their owne sway againe.

Nine houres flood to three houres ebbe.

Moreover it is not possible that so great course of floods and current, so high swelling tides with continuance of so deepe waters, can be digested here without unburdening themselves into some open Sea beyond this place, which argueth the more likelihood of the passage to be hereabouts. Also we suppose these great indrafts doe growe and are made by the reverberation and reflection of that same current, which at our comming by Ireland, met and crossed us, of which in the first part of this discourse I spake, which comming from the bay of Mexico, passing by and washing the Southwest parts of Ireland, reboundeth over to the Northeast parts of the world, as Norway, Island, &c. where not finding any passage to an open Sea, but rather being there encreased by a new accesse, and another current meeting with it from the Scythian Sea, passing the bay of Saint Nicholas Westward, it doth once againe rebound backe, by the coastes of Groenland, and from thence upon Frobishers straights being to the Southwestwardes of the same.

The sea moveth from East to West continually.

5 And if that principle of Philosopie be true, that Inferiora corpora reguntur à superioribus, that is, if inferior bodies be governed, ruled, and caried after the maner and course of the superiors, then the water being an inferior Element, must needes be governed after the superior heaven, and so follow the course of Primum mobile from East to West.

Authoritie.

6 But every man that hath written or considered any thing of this passage, hath more doubted the returne by the same way by reason of a great downefall of water, which they imagine to be thereabouts (which we also by experience partly find) than any mistrust they have of the same passage at all. For we find (as it were) a great downefall in this place, but yet not such but that we may returne, although with much adoe. For we were easlier carried in one houre then we could get forth againe in three. Also by another experience at another time, we found this current to deceive us in this sort: That wheras we supposed it to be 15 leagues off, and lying a hull, we were brought within two leagues of the shore contrarie to all expectation.

Hard but yet possible turning backe againe.

Our men that sayled furthest in the same mistaken straights (having the maine land upon their starboord side) affirme that they met with the outlet or passage of water which commeth thorow Frobishers straights, and followeth as all one into this passage.

Some of our companie also affirme that they had sight of a continent upon their larboord-side being 60 leagues within the supposed straights: howbeit except certaine Ilands in the entrance hereof we could make no part perfect thereof. All the foresaid tract of land seemeth to be more fruitfull and better stored of Grasse, Deere, Wild foule, as Partridges, Larkes, Seamewes, Guls, Wilmots, Falcons and Tassel gentils, Ravens, Beares, Hares, Foxes, and other things, than any other part we have yet discovered, and is more populous. And here Luke Ward, a Gentleman of the companie, traded marchandise, and did exchange knives, bels, looking glasses, &c. with

Traffique.

338

those countrey people, who brought him foule, fish,
beares skinnes, and such like, as their countrey yeeldeth
for the same.   Here also they saw of those greater boats
of the countrey, with twentie persons in a peece.

Now after the Generall had bestowed these many [III. 82.]
dayes here, not without many dangers, he returned backe
againe.   And by the way sayling alongst this coast (being
the backeside of the supposed continent of America) and
the Queenes Foreland, he perceived a great sound to
goe thorow into Frobishers straights.   Whereupon he
sent the Gabriel the one and twentieth of July, to proove
whether they might goe thorow and meete againe with *Returne out of*
him in the straights, which they did : and as wee imagined *the mistaken*
before, so the Queenes foreland prooved an Iland, as *straights.*
I thinke most of these supposed continents will.· And
so he departed towardes the straights, thinking it were
high time now to recover his Port, and to provide the
Fleete of their lading, whereof he was not a little carefull,
as shall by the processe and his resolute attempts appeare.
And in his returne with the rest of the fleete he was so
intangled by reason of the darke fogge amongst a number
of Ilands and broken ground that lye off this coast, that
many of the shippes came over the top of rockes, which
presently after they might perceive to lie dry, having not
halfe a foote water more then some of their ships did
draw.   And by reason they could not with a smal gale
of wind stemme the force of the flood, whereby to goe
cleere off the rockes, they were faine to let an anker fall
with two bent of Cable togither, at an hundred and odde
fadome depth, where otherwise they had bene by the
force of the tydes caried upon the rockes againe, and
perished : so that if God in these fortunes (as a mercifull *Great dan-*
guide, beyond the expectation of man) had not carried us *gers.*
thorow, we had surely perished amidst these dangers.
For being many times driven hard aboord the shore
without any sight of land, untill we were ready to make
shipwracke thereon, being forced commonly with our
boats to sound before our ships, least we might light

thereon before we could discerne the same; it pleased God to give us a cleare of Sunne and light for a short time to see and avoyde thereby the danger, having bene continually darke before, and presently after. Manie times also by meanes of fogge and currents being driven neere upon the coast, God lent us even at the very pinch one prosperous breath of winde or other, whereby to double the land, and avoid the perill, and when that we were all without hope of helpe, every man recommending himselfe to death, and crying out, Lord now helpe or never, now Lord looke downe from heaven and save us sinners, or else our safetie commeth too late: even then the mightie maker of heaven, and our mercifull God did deliver us: so that they who have bene partakers of these dangers doe even in their soules confesse, that God even by miracle hath sought to save them, whose name be praysed evermore.

Long time now the Anne Francis had layne beating off and on all alone before the Queenes foreland, not being able to recover their Port for yce, albeit many times they dangerously attempted it, for yet the yce choaked up the passage, and would not suffer them to *Anne Francis* enter. And having never seene any of the fleete since *met with some* twenty dayes past, when by reason of the thicke mistes *of the fleete.* they were severed in the mistaken straights, they did now this present 23 of July overthwart a place in the straights called Hattons Hedland, where they met with seven ships of ye Fleete againe, which good hap did not onely rejoyce them for themselves, in respect of the comfort which they received by such good companie, but especially that by this meanes they were put out of doubt of their deare friends, whose safeties long time they did not a little suspect and feare.

At their meeting they haled the Admirall after the maner of the Sea, and with great joy welcommed one another with a thundring volly of shot. And now every man declared at large the fortunes and dangers which they had passed.

The foure and twentieth of July we met with the
Francis of Foy, who with much adoe sought way backe *Francis of Foy.*
againe, through the yce from out of the mistaken
straights, where (to their great perill) they prooved to
recover their Port. They brought the first newes of the
Vizadmirall Captaine Yorke, who many dayes with
themselves, and the Busse of Bridgewater was missing. *Bridgwater*
They reported that they left the Vizeadmirall reasonably *ship.*
cleare of the yce, but the other ship they greatly feared,
whom they could not come to helpe, being themselves so
hardly distressed as never men more. Also they told us
of the Gabriel, who having got thorow from the backside,
and Western point of the Queenes foreland, into Frobishers straights, fell into their company about the cape
of Good hope.

And upon the seven and twentieth of July, the ship of
Bridgewater got out of the yce and met with the Fleete
which lay off and on under Hattons Hedland. They
reported of their marvellous accidents and dangers, declaring their ship to be so leake that they must of
necessitie seeke harborow, having their stem so beaten
within their huddings, that they had much adoe to keepe
themselves above water. They had (as they say) five
hundreth strokes at the pump in lesse then halfe a watch,
being scarce two houres; their men being so over-
wearied therewith, and with the former dangers that they
desired helpe of men from the other ships. Moreover
they declared that there was nothing but yce and danger [III. 83.]
where they had bene, and that the straights within were
frozen up, and that it was the most impossible thing of *The Streits*
the world, to passe up unto the Countesse of Warwicks *frozen over.*
sound, which was the place of our Port.

The report of these dangers by these ships thus
published amongst the fleete, with the remembrance of
the perils past, and those present before their face,
brought no small feare and terror into the hearts of many
considerate men. So that some beganne privily to murmure against the Generall for this wilfull maner of

proceeding. Some desired to discover some harborow thereabouts to refresh themselves and reforme their broken vessels for a while, untill the North and Northwest windes might disperse the yce, and make the place more free to passe. Other some forgetting themselves, spake more undutifully in this behalfe, saying: that they had as leeve be hanged when they came home, as without hope of safetie to seeke to passe, and so to perish amongst the yce.

The Generall not opening his eares to the peevish passion of any private person, but chiefly respecting the accomplishment of the cause he had undertaken (wherein the chiefe reputation and fame of a Generall and Captaine *A valiant* consisteth) and calling to his remembrance the short time *mind of M.* he had in hand to provide so great number of ships their *Frobisher.* loading, determined with this resolution to passe and recover his Port, or else there to burie himselfe with his attempt.

Notwithstanding somewhat to appease the feeble passions of the fearefuller sort, and the better to entertaine time for a season, whilest the yce might the better be dissolved, he haled on the Fleete with beleefe that he would put them into harborow: thereupon whilest the shippes lay off and on under Hattons Hedland, he sought to goe in with his Pinnesses amongst the Ilandes there, as though hee meant to search for harborowe, where indeede he meant nothing lesse, but rather sought if any Ore might be found in that place, as by the sequele appeared.

In the meane time whilest the Fleete lay thus doubtfull without any certaine resolution what to do, being hard aboord the lee-shore, there arose a sodaine and terrible tempest at the Southsoutheast, whereby the yce began marvellously to gather about us.

Whereupon every man, as in such case of extremitie he thought best, sought the wisest way for his owne safety. The most part of the Fleete which were further shot up within the straights, and so farre to the leeward, as that they could not double the land, following the

course of the Generall, who led them the way, tooke
in their Sayles, and layde it a hull amongst the yce, and
so passed over the storme, and had no extremitie at all,
but for a short time in the same place.

Howbeit the other ships which plyed out to Seaward,
had an extreme storme for a longer season. And the
nature of the place is such, that it is subject diversly
to divers windes, according to the sundry situation of
the great Alps and mountaines there, every mountaine
causing a severall blast, and pirrie, after the maner of
a Levant.

In this storme being the sixe and twentieth of July,
there fell so much snow, with such bitter cold aire, that
we could not scarce see one another for the same, nor
open our eyes to handle our ropes and sayles, the snow *Snow in July.*
being above halfe a foote deepe upon the hatches of
our ship, which did so wet thorow our poore Mariners
clothes, that hee that had five or sixe shifts of apparell
had scarce one drie threed to his backe, which kind of
wet and coldnesse, togither with the overlabouring of
the poore men amiddest the yce, bred no small sicknesse amongst the fleete, which somewhat discouraged
some of the poore men, who had not experience of the
like before, every man perswading himselfe that the
winter there must needes be extreme, where they found *Extreme win-*
so unseasonable a Sommer.   *ter.*

And yet notwithstanding this cold aire, the Sunne *Great heat in*
many times hath a marvellous force of heate amongst *Meta Incog-*
those mountaines, insomuch that when there is no *nita.*
breth of winde to bring the colde aire from the dispersed yce upon us, we shall be wearie of the bloming
heate and then sodainely with a perry of winde which *Unconstant*
commeth downe from the hollownesse of the hilles, we *weather.*
shall have such a breth of heate brought upon our
faces as though we were entred within some bathstove
or hote-house, and when the first of the pirry and blast
is past, we shall have the winde sodainely a new blow
cold againe.

In this storme the Anne Francis, the Moone, and the Thomas of Ipswich, who found themselves able to hold it up with a saile, and could double about the Cape of the Queenes foreland, plyed out to the Seaward, holding it for better policie and safetie to seeke Sea roome, then to hazard the continuance of the storme, the danger of the yce, and the leeshoare.

[III. 84.]
And being uncertaine at this time of the Generals private determinations, the weather being so darke that they could not discerne one another, nor perceive which way he wrought, betooke themselves to this course for best and safest.

The General, notwithstanding the great storme, following his own former resolution, sought by all meanes possible, by a shorter way to recover his Port, and where he saw the yce never so little open, he gate in at one gappe and out at another, and so himselfe valiantly led the way thorow before to induce the Fleete to follow after, and with incredible paine and perill at length gat through the
The Generall recovereth his port.
yce, and upon the one and thirtieth of July recovered his long wished Port after many attempts and sundry times being put backe, and came to anker in the Countesse of Warwicks sound, in the entrance whereof, when he thought all perill past, he encountred a great Iland of yce which gave the Ayde such a blow, having a little before wayed her anker a cocke bill, that it stroke the anker flouke through the ships bowes under the water, which caused so great a leake, that with much adoe they preserved the ship from sinking.

At their arrivall here they perceived two ships at anker within the harborough, whereat they began much to marvell and greatly to rejoyce, for those they knew to be the Michael, wherein was the Lieutenant generall Captaine Fenton, and the small Barke called the Gabriel, who so long time were missing, and never heard of before, whom every man made the last reckoning, never to heare of againe.

Here every man greatly rejoyced of their happie meet-

ing, and welcommed one another after the Sea manner
with their great Ordinance, and when each partie had
ripped up their sundry fortunes and perils past, they
highly praysed God, and altogither upon their knees
gave him due, humble and hearty thankes, and Maister *Master Wolf-*
Wolfall a learned man, appointed by her Majesties *all Preacher.*
Councell to be their Minister and Preacher made unto
them a godly sermon, exhorting them especially to be
thankefull to God for their strange and miraculous
deliverance in those so dangerous places, and putting
them in mind of the uncertainetie of mans life, willed
them to make themselves alwayes readie as resolute men
to enjoy and accept thankefully whatsoever adventure his
divine Providence should appoint. This maister Wolfall
being well seated and setled at home in his owne
Countrey, with a good and large living, having a good
honest woman to wife and very towardly children,
being of good reputation among the best, refused not
to take in hand this painefull voyage, for the onely
care he had to save soules, and to reforme those Infidels
if it were possible to Christianitie : and also partly for the
great desire he had that this notable voyage so well
begunne, might be brought to perfection : and therefore
he was contented to stay there the whole yeare if occasion
had served, being in every necessary action as forward as
the resolutest men of all. Wherefore in this behalfe he
may rightly be called a true Pastor and minister of Gods
word, which for the profite of his flocke spared not to
venture his owne life.

But to returne againe to Captaine Fentons company, *The adven-*
and to speake somewhat of their dangers (albeit they be *tures of Cap-*
more then by writing can be expressed) they reported *taine Fenton*
that from the night of the first storme which was about *and his com-*
the first day of July untill seven dayes before the *panie.*
Generals arrivall, which was the sixe and twentith of the
same, they never saw any one day or houre, wherin they
were not troubled with continuall danger and feare of
death, and were twentie dayes almost togither fast

amongst the yce. They had their ship stricken through and through on both sides, their false stemme borne quite away, and could goe from their ships in some places upon the yce very many miles, and might easily have passed from one Iland of yce to another even to the shore, and if God had not wonderfully provided for
Extremitie causeth men to devise new arts and remedies. them and their necessitie, and time had not made them more cunning and wise to seeke strange remedies for strange kindes of dangers, it had bene impossible for them ever to have escaped: for among other devises, wheresoever they found any Iland of yce of greater bignesse then the rest (as there be some of more then halfe a mile compasse about, and almost forty fadome high) they commonly coveted to recover the same, and thereof to make a bulwarke for their defence, whereon having mored anker, they road under the lee therof for a time, being therby garded from the danger of the lesser
Hard shifts. driving yce. But when they must needes forgoe this new found fort by meanes of other yce, which at length would undermine and compasse them round about, and when that by heaving of the billow they were therwith like to be brused in peeces, they used to make fast the shippe unto the most firme and broad peece of yce they could find, and binding her nose fast thereunto, would fill all their sayles whereon the winde having great power, would force forward the ship, and so the shippe bearing before her the yce, & so one yce driving forward another, should at length get scope & searoome. And having by this meanes at length put their enemies to flight, they occupied the cleare place for a prettie season among sundry mountaines and Alpes of yce. One there was found by measure to be 65 fadome above water, which for a kind of similitude, was called Salomons porch.
[III. 85.] Some thinke those Ilands eight times so much under water as they are above, because of their monstrous
Strange wonders. weight. But now I remember I saw very strange wonders, men walking, running, leaping and shooting upon the mayne seas 40. myles from any land, without

any Shippe or other vessell under them. Also I saw fresh Rivers running amidst the salt Sea a hundred myle from land, which if any man will not beleeve, let him knowe that many of our company leapt out of their Shippe upon Ilandes of yce, and running there up and downe, did shoote at Buts upon the yce, and with their Calivers did kill great Seales, which use to lye and sleepe upon the yce, and this yce melting above at the toppe by reflection of the Sunne, came downe in sundry streames, which uniting together, made a pretie Brooke able to drive a Mill.

The sayde Captaine Fenton recovered his Port tenne dayes before any man, and spent good tyme in searching for Mine, and hee found good store thereof. He also discovered about tenne Miles up into the Countrey, where he perceived neither Towne, Village, nor likelihoode of habitation, but it seemeth (as he sayeth) barren, as the other parts which as yet we have entred upon: but their victuals and provision went so scant with them, that they had determined to returne homeward within seven dayes after, if the Fleete had not then arrived.

The Generall after his arrivall in the Countesses sound, spent no time in vaine, but immediatly at his first landing called the chiefe Captaines of his Councell together, and consulted with them for the speedier execution of such things as then they had in hand. As first, for searching and finding out good Minerall for the Miners to be occupyed on. Then to give good Orders to bee observed of the whole company on shore. And lastly, to consider for the erecting up of the Fort and House for the use of them which were to abide there the whole yeere. For the better handling of these, and all other like important causes in this service, it was ordeined from her Majestie and the Councell, that the Generall should call unto him certaine of the chiefe Captaines and Gentlemen in Councell, to conferre, consult and determine of all occurrents in this service, whose names are as here they follow.

Captaine Fenton.⎫　⎧Captaine Carew.
Captaine Yorke. ⎬　⎨
Captaine Best. ⎭　⎩Captaine Philpot.

And in Sea causes to have as assistants, Christopher
Hall and Charles Jackman, being both very good Pilots,
and sufficient Mariners, whereof the one was chiefe Pilot
of the Voyage, and the other for the discoverie. From
the place of our habitation Westward, Master Selman was
appointed Notarie, to register the whole maner of proceeding in these affaires, that true relation thereof might
be made, if it pleased her Majestie to require it.

The first of August every Captaine by order, from
the Generall and his councell, was commanded to bring
ashoare unto the Countesses Iland all such Gentlemen,
souldiers, and Myners, as were under their charge, with
such provision as they had of victuals, tents, and things
necessary for the speedy getting together of Mine, and
fraight for the shippes.

The Muster of the men being taken, and the victuals
with all other things viewed and considered, every man
was set to his charge, as his place and office required.
The Myners were appointed where to worke, and the
Mariners discharged their shippes.

Upon the second of August were published and
proclaymed upon the Countesse of Warwicks Iland with
sound of Trumpet, certaine Orders by the Generall and
his councell, appoynted to be observed of the company
during the time of their abiding there.

In the meane time, whilest the Mariners plyed their
worke, the Captaines sought out new Mynes, the Goldfiners made tryall of the Ore, the Mariners discharged
their shippes, the Gentlemen for example sake laboured
heartily, and honestly encouraged the inferiour sort to
worke. So that the small tyme of that little leisure
that was left to tarrie, was spent in vaine.

The second of August the Gabriel arrived, who came
from the Vizeadmirall, and beeing distressed sore with
Yce, put into Harborough neere unto Mount Oxford.

And now was the whole Fleete arrived safely at their Port, excepting foure, besides the Shippe that was lost: that is, the Thomas Allen, the Anne Francis, the Thomas of Ipswich, and the Moone, whose absence was some lette unto the workes and other proceedings, aswell for that these Shippes were furnished with the better sorte of Myners, as with other provision for the habitation.

The ninth of August the Generall with the Captaynes of his counsell assembled together, and began to consider and take order for the erecting up of the house or Fort for them that were to inhabite there the whole yeere, [III. 86.] and that presently the Masons and Carpenters might goe in hande therewith. First therefore they perused *Consultation* the Bils of lading, what every man received into his *for inhabiting* *Meta incog-* Shippe, and found that there was arrived onely the East- *nita.* side, and the Southside of the house, and yet not that perfect and entier: for many pieces thereof were used for fenders in many Shippes, and so broken in pieces whilest they were distressed in the yce. Also after due examination had, and true account taken, there was found want of drinke and fuel to serve one hundreth men, which was *An hundred* the number appoynted first to inhabite there, because *men appointed* *to inhabite.* their greatest store was in the Shippes which were not yet arrived. Then Captaine Fenton seeing the scarcitie of the necessary things aforesayd, was contented, and offred himselfe to inhabite there with sixtie men. Where- *No habitation* upon they caused the Carpenters and Masons to come *this yeere.* before them, and demanded in what time they would take upon them to erect up a lesse house for sixtie men. They required eight or nine weekes, if there were Tymber sufficient, whereas now they had but sixe and twentie dayes in all to remayne in that Countrey. Wherefore it was fully agreed upon, and resolved by the Generall and his counsell, that no habitation should be there this yeere. And therefore they willed Master Selman the Register to set downe this decree with all their consents, for the better satisfying of her Majestie, the Lords of the Counsell, and the Adventurers.

The Anne Francis, since shee was parted from the
Fleete, in the last storme before spoken of, could never
recover above five leagues within the streights, the winde
being sometime contrary, and most times the Yce compassing them round about. And from that time, being
about the seven and twentieth of July, they could neither
heare nor have sight of any of the Fleete, until the 3.
of August, when they descryed a sayle neere unto Mount
Oxford, with whom when they had spoken, they could
understand no newes of any of the Fleete at all. And
this was the Thomas of Ipswich, who had layne beating
off and on at Sea with very fowle weather, and contrary
windes, ever since that foresayd storme, without sight of
any man. They kept company not long together, but
were forced to loose one another againe, the Moone being
consort alwayes with the Anne Francis, and keeping very
good company plyed up together into the streights, with
great desire to recover their long wished Port : and they
attempted as often, and passed as farre as possible the
winde, weather, & yce gave them leave, which commonly
they found very contrary. For when the weather was
cleare and without fogge, then commonly the winde was
contrary. And when it was eyther Easterly or Southerly,
which would serve their turnes, then had they so great
a fogge and darke miste therewith, that eyther they could
not discerne way thorow the yce, or els the yce lay so
thicke together, that it was impossible for them to passe.
And on the other side, when it was calme, the Tydes
had force to bring the yce so suddenly about them, that
commonly then they were most therewith distressed,
having no Winde to cary them from the danger
thereof.

And by the sixt of August being with much adoe
got up as high as Leicester point, they had good hope
to finde the Souther shore cleare, and so to passe up
towards their Port. But being there becalmed and
lying a hull openly upon the great Bay which commeth
out of the mistaken streights before spoken of, they were

so suddenly compassed with yce round about by meanes
of the swift Tydes which run in that place, that they were
never afore so hardly beset as now.   And in seeking
to avoyde these dangers in the darke weather, the Anne
Francis lost sight of the other two Ships, who being
likewise hardly distressed, signified their danger, as they
since reported, by shooting off their ordinance, which the
other could not heare, nor if they had heard, could have
given them any remedie, being so busily occupied to
winde themselves out of their owne troubles.

The Fleeboate called the Moone, was here heaved *The Moone.*
above the water with the force of the yce, and received
a great leake thereby.   Likewise the Thomas of Ipswich,
and the Anne Francis were sore brused at that instant,
having their false stemmes borne away, and their ship
sides stroken quite through.

Now considering the continuall dangers and contraries,
and the little leasure that they had left to tarie in these
partes, besides that every night the ropes of their Shippes
were so frozen, that a man could not handle them without
cutting his handes, together with the great doubt they
had of the Fleetes safety, thinking it an impossibilitie for
them to passe unto their Port, as well for that they
saw themselves, as for that they heard by the former
report of the Shippes which had prooved before, who
affirmed that the streights were all frozen over within:
They thought it now very hie time to consider of their
estates and safeties that were yet left together.   And
hereupon the Captaines and masters of these Shippes,
desired the Captaine of the Anne Francis to enter into *The Anne*
consideration with them of these matters.   Wherefore *Francis, the*
Thomas of
Captaine Tanfield of the Thomas of Ipswich, with his *Ipswich and*
Pilot Richard Cox, and Captaine Upcote of the Moone, *the Moone con-*
with his master John Lakes came aboorde the Anne *sult.*
Francis the eight of August to consult of these causes. [III. 87.]
And being assembled together in the Captaines Cabin,
sundry doubts were there alledged.   For the fearefuller
sort of Mariners being overtyred with the continuall

labour of the former dangers, coveted to returne home-ward, saying that they would not againe tempt God so much, who had given them so many warnings, and delivered them from so wonderfull dangers: that they rather desired to lose wages, fraight, and all, then to continue and follow such desperate fortunes. Againe, their Ships were so leake, and the men so wearie, that to amend the one, and refresh the other, they must of necessitie seeke into harborough.

But on the other side it was argued againe to the contrary, that to seeke into harborough thereabouts, was but to subject themselves to double dangers: if happily they escaped the dangers of Rockes in their entring, yet being in, they were neverthelesse subject there to the danger of the Ice, which with the swift tydes and currents is caryed in and out in most harboroughs thereabouts, and may thereby gaule their Cables asunder, drive them upon the shoare, and bring them to much trouble. Also the coast is so much subject to broken ground and rockes, especially in the mouth and entrance of every Har-borough, that albeit the Channell be sounded over and over againe, yet are you never the neerer to discerne the dangers. For the bottome of the Sea holding like shape and forme as the Land, being full of hils, dales, and ragged Rockes, suffreth you not by your soundings to knowe and keepe a true gesse of the depth. For you shall sound upon the side or hollownesse of one Hill or Rocke under water, and have a hundreth, fiftie, or fourtie fadome depth: and before the next cast, yer you shall be able to heave your lead againe, you shall be upon the toppe thereof, and come aground to your utter confusion.

Another reason against going to harborough was, that the colde ayre did threaten a sudden freezing up of the sounds, seeing that every night there was new congealed yce, even of that water which remayned within their shippes. And therefore it should seeme to be more safe to lye off and on at Sea, then for lacke of winde to bring them foorth of harborough, to hazard by sudden frosts to be shut up the whole yeere.

After many such dangers and reasons alledged, and large debating of these causes on both sides, the Captaine of the Anne Francis delivered his opinion unto the company to this effect. First concerning the question *Captaine* of returning home, hee thought it so much dishonorable, *Bests resolu-* as not to grow in any farther question: and againe to *tion.* returne home at length (as at length they must needes) and not to be able to bring a certaine report of the Fleete, whether they were living or lost, or whether any of them had recovered their Port or not, in the Countesses sound, (as it was to bee thought the most part would if they were living) hee sayde that it would be so great an argument eyther of want of courage or discretion in them, as hee resolved rather to fall into any danger, then so shamefully to consent to returne home, protesting that it should never bee spoken of him, that hee would ever returne without doing his endevour to finde the Fleete, and knowe the certaintie of the Generals safetie. Hee *A Pinnisse for* put his company in remembrance of a Pinnisse of *the inhabiters.* five tunne burthen, which hee had within his Shippe, which was caryed in pieces, and unmade up for the use of those which should inhabite there the whole yeere, the which, if they could finde meanes to joyne together, hee offered himselfe to proove before therewith, whether it were possible for any Boate to passe for yce, whereby the Shippe might bee brought in after, and might also thereby give true notice, if any of the Fleete were arrived at their Port or not.

But notwithstanding, for that he well perceived that the most part of his company were addicted to put into harborough, hee was willing the rather for these causes somewhat to encline thereunto. At first, to search alongst the same coast, and the soundes thereabouts, hee thought it to be to good purpose, for that it was likely to finde some of the Fleete there, which being leake, and sore brused with the yce, were the rather thought likely to be

put into an yll harborough, being distressed with foule
weather in the last storme, then to hazard their uncertaine
safeties amongst the yce: for about this place they lost
them, and left the Fleete then doubtfully questioning
of harborough.

It was likely, also, that they might finde some fitte
harborough thereabouts, which might bee behoovefull
for them against another time. It was not likewise impossible to finde some Ore or Mine thereabouts wherewithall to fraight their Shippes, which would bee more
commodious in this place, for the neerenesse to Seaward,
and for a better outlet, then farther within the streights,
being likely heere alwayes to loade in a shorter time,
howsoever the streight should be pestered with yce
within, so that if it might come to passe that thereby
they might eyther finde the Fleete, Mine, or convenient
harborough, any of these three would serve their present
[III. 88.] turnes, and give some hope and comfort unto their
companies, which now were altogether comfortlesse. But
if that all fortune should fall out so contrary, that they
could neyther recover their Port, nor any of these
aforesayde helpes, that yet they would not depart the
Coast, as long as it was possible for them to tary there,
but would lye off and on at Sea athwart the place. Therefore his finall conclusion was set downe thus, First,
that the Thomas of Ipswich and the Moone should
consort and keepe company together carefully with the
Anne Francis, as neere as they could, and as true Englishmen and faithfull friends, should supply one anothers
want in all fortunes and dangers. In the morning
following, every Shippe to send off his Boate with a
sufficient Pylot, to search out and sound the harboroughs
for the safe bringing in of their Shippes. And beeing
arrived in harborough, where they might finde convenient
place for the purpose, they resolved foorthwith to joyne
and sette together the Pinnesse, wherewithall the Captaine
of the Anne Francis might, according to his former
determination, discover up into the streights.

After these determinations thus set downe, the Thomas of Ipswich the night following lost company of the other Shippes, and afterward shaped a contrary course homeward, which fell out as it manifestly appeared, very much against their Captaine Master Tanfields minde, as by due examination before the Lordes of her Majesties most honourable privie Counsell it hath since bene prooved, to the great discredite of the Pilot Cox, who specially persuaded his company against the opinion of his sayd Captaine, to returne home.

And as the Captaine of the Anne Francis doeth witnesse, even at their conference togither, Captaine Tanfield tolde him, that he did not a little suspect the sayd Pilot Cox, saying that he had opinion in the man neither of honest duetie, manhoode, nor constancie. Notwithstanding the sayde Shippes departure, the Captaine of the Anne Francis being desirous to put in execution his former resolutions, went with his Shippe boate (being accompanied also with the Moones Skiffe) to proove amongst the Ilands which lye under Hattons Hedland, if any convenient harborough, or any knowledge of the Fleete, or any good Ore were there to be found. The Shippes lying off and on at Sea the while under Sayle, searching through many sounds, they sawe them all full of many dangers and broken ground: yet one there was, which seemed an indifferent place to harborough in, and which they did very diligently sound over, and searched againe.

Here the sayde Captaine found a great blacke Iland, whereunto hee had good liking, and certifying the company thereof, they were somewhat comforted, and with the good hope of his wordes rowed cheerefully unto the place: where when they arrived, they found such plentie of blacke Ore of the same sort which was brought into England this last yeere, that if the goodnesse might answere the great plentie thereof, it was to be thought that it might reasonably suffice all the golde-gluttons of the world. This Iland the Captaine for cause of his good hap, called after his owne name, Bestes blessing, and with these good tydings returning aboord his Ship the ninth of August about tenne of the clocke at night, hee was joyfully welcommed of his company, who before were discomforted, and greatly expected some better fortune at his handes.

The next day being the tenth of August, the weather reasonably fayre, they put into the foresayde Harborough, having their Boate for their better securitie sounding before their Shippe. But for all the care and diligence that could bee taken in sounding the Channell *Anne Francis* over and over againe, the Anne Francis came aground *in danger.* upon a suncken Rocke within the Harborough, and lay thereon more then halfe drye untill the next flood, when by Gods Almighty providence, contrary almost to all expectation, they came afloat againe, being forced all that time to undersette their Shippe with their mayne Yarde, which otherwise was likely to overset and put thereby in danger the whole company. They had above two thousand strokes together at the Pumpe, before they could make their Shippe free of the water againe, so sore *The Moone in* shee was brused by lying upon the Rockes. The Moone *harborough.* came safely, and roade at anchor by the Anne Francis, whose helpe in their necessitie they could not well have missed.

Now whilest the Mariners were romaging their Shippes, and mending that which was amisse, the Miners followed their labour for getting together of sufficient quantitie of Ore, and the Carpenters indevoured to doe their best for the making up of the Boate or Pinnesse: which to bring to passe, they wanted two speciall and most necessarie things, that is, certaine principall tymbers that are called Knees, which are the chiefest strength of any Boate, and also nayles, wherewithall to joyne the plancks together. Whereupon having by chance a Smyth amongst them, (and yet unfurnished of his necessary tooles to worke and [III. 89.] make nayles withall) they were faine of a gunne chamber to make an Anvile to worke upon, and to use a pickaxe in stead of a sledge to beate withall, and also to occupy two small bellowes in steade of one payre of greater Smiths bellowes. And for lacke of small Yron for the easier making of the nayles, they were forced to breake their tongs, grydiron, and fireshovell in pieces.

The eleventh of August the Captaine of the Anne Francis taking the Master of his Shippe with him, went up to the toppe of Hattons Hedland, which is the highest land of all the streights, to the ende to descry the situation of the Countrey underneath, and to take a true plotte of the place, whereby also to see what store of Yce was yet left in the streights, as also to search what Mineral matter or fruite that soyle might yeeld : And the rather for the honour the said Captaine doeth owe to that Honourable name which himselfe gave thereunto the last yeere, in the highest part of this Hedland he caused his company to make a Columne or Crosse of stone, in token of Christian possession. In this place there is plentie of Blacke Ore, and divers pretie stones.

Hattons Hedland.

Pretie stones.

The seventeenth of August the Captaines with their companies chaced and killed a great white Beare, which adventured and gave a fierce assault upon twentie men being weaponed. And he served them for good meate many dayes.

A mightie white Beare.

The eighteenth of August the Pinnesse with much adoe being set together, the sayd Captaine Best determined to depart up the streights, to proove and make tryall, as before was pretended, some of his company greatly persuading him to the contrary, and specially the Carpenter that set the same together, who sayde that hee would not adventure himselfe therein for five hundreth pounds, for that the boate hung together but onely by the strength of the nayles, and lacked some of her principall knees and tymbers.

A Pinnesse there built.

These wordes somewhat discouraged some of the company which should have gone therein. Whereupon the Captaine, as one not altogether addicted to his owne selfe-will, but somewhat foreseeing how it might be afterwards spoken, if contrary fortune should happen him (Lo he hath followed his owne opinion and desperate resolutions, and so thereafter it is befallen him) calling the Master and Mariners of best judgement together, declared unto them how much the cause imported him in his credite to seeke out the Generall, as well to conferre with him of some causes of weight, as otherwise to make due examination and tryall of the goodnesse of the Ore, whereof they had no assurance but by gesse of the eye, and it was well like the other: which so to cary home, not knowing the goodnesse thereof, might be as much as if they should bring so many stones. And therefore hee desired them to deliver their plaine and honest opinion, whether the Pinnesse were sufficient for him so to adventure in or no. It was answered, that by carefull heede taking thereunto amongst the yce, and the foule weather, the Pinnesse might suffice. And hereupon the Masters mate of the Anne Francis called John Gray, manfully and honestly offering himselfe unto his Captaine in this adventure and service, gave cause to others of his Mariners to follow the attempt.

And upon the nineteenth of August the sayd Captaine being accompanied with Captaine Upcote of the Moone, and eighteene persons in the small Pinnesse, having convenient portion of victuals and things necessary, departed upon the sayd pretended Voyage, leaving their shippe at anchor in a good readinesse for the taking in of their fraight. And having little winde to sayle withall, they plyed alongst the Souther shore, and passed above 30. leagues, having the onely helpe of mans labour with Oares, and so intending to keepe that shore aboord until they were got up to the farthest and narrowest of the streights, minded there to crosse over, and to search likewise alongst the Northerland unto the Countesses sound, and from thence to passe all that coast along, whereby if any of the Fleete had bene distressed by wrecke of rocke or yce, by that meanes they might be perceived of them, and so they thereby to give them such

They adventure by the streight in a weake Pinnesse.

358

helpe and reliefe as they could. They did greatly feare, and ever suspect that some of the Fleete were surely cast away, and driven to seeke sowre sallets amongst the colde cliffes.

And being shotte up about fortie leagues within the Streights, they put over towardes the Norther shore, which was not a little dangerous for their small boates. And by meanes of a sudden flawe were dryven, and faine to seeke harborough in the night amongst all the rockes and broken ground of Gabriels Ilands, a place so named within the streights above the Countesse of Warwicks sound: And by the way where they landed, they did finde certaine great stones set up by the Countrey people as it seemed, for markes, where they also made many Crosses of stone, in token that Christians had bene there. The 22. of August they had sight of the Countesses sound, and made the place perfect from the toppe of a hill, and keeping along the Norther shore, perceived the smoke of a fire under a hils side: whereof they diversly deemed. When they came neere the place, they perceived people which wafted unto them, as it seemed, with a flagge or ensigne. And because the Countrey people had used to doe the like, when they perceived any of our boats to passe by, they suspected them to be the same. And comming somewhat neerer, they might perceive certaine tents, and discerne this ensigne to be of mingled colours, blacke and white, after the English fashion. But because they could see no Shippe, nor likelihood of harborough within five or sixe leagues about, and knewe that none of our men were woont to frequent those partes, they could not tell what to judge thereof, but imagined that some of the ships being carried so high with the storme and mistes, had made shipwracke amongst the yce or the broken Islands there, and were spoyled by the countrey people, who might use the sundry coloured flagge for a policie, to bring them likewise within their danger. Whereupon the sayd Captaine with his companies, resolved to recover the same ensigne, if it

40. leagues within the streights.

Gabriels Ilands.

[III. 90.]

359

were so, from those base people, or els to lose their lives, and all together. In the ende they discerned them to be their countreymen, and then they deemed them to have lost their Ships, and so to be gathered together for their better strength. On the other side, the company ashoare feared that the Captaine having lost his Shippe, came to seeke forth the Fleete for his reliefe in his poore Pinnisse, so that their extremities caused eche part to suspect the worst.

The Captaine now with his Pinnisse being come neere the shoare, commanded his Boate carefully to be kept aflote, lest in their necessitie they might winne the same from him, and seeke first to save themselves: for every *Proximus sum* man in that case is next himselfe. They haled one *egomet mihi.* another according to the manner of the Sea, and demaunded what cheere? and either partie answered the other, that all was well: whereupon there was a sudden and joyfull outshoote, with great flinging up of caps, and a brave voly of shotte to welcome one another. And truely it was a most strange case to see how joyfull and gladde every partie was to see themselves meete in safetie againe, after so strange and incredible dangers: Yet to be short, as their dangers were great, so their God was greater.

And here the company were working upon new Mines, *Captain Yorke* which Captaine Yorke being here arrived not long *arrived.* before, had found out in this place, and it is named the Countesse of Sussex Mine.

After some conference with our friends here, the Captaine of the Anne Francis departed towards the Countesse of Warwicks sound, to speake with the Generall, and to have tryall made of such mettall as he had brought thither, by the Goldfiners. And so he determined to dispatch againe towards his ship. And having spoken with the General, he received order for all causes, and direction as well for the bringing up of his Shippe to the Countesses sound, as also to fraight his Ship with the same Oare which he himselfe had found, which upon triall made, was supposed to be very good.

The 23. of August, the sayd Captaine mette together with the other Captaines (Commissioners in counsell with the Generall) aboorde the Ayde, where they considered and consulted of sundry causes, which being particularly registred by the Notarie, were appoynted where and how to be done against another yeere.

The 24. of August, the Generall with two Pinnisses and good numbers of men went to Beares sound, commanding the sayde Captaine with his Pinnesse to attend the service, to see if he could encounter or apprehend any of the people: for sundry times they shewed themselves busie thereabouts, sometimes with seven or eyght Boates in one company, as though they minded to encounter with our company which were working there at the Mines, in no great numbers. But when they perceived any of our Shippes to ryde in that roade (being belike more amazed at the countenance of a Shippe, and a more number of men) they did never shewe themselves againe there at all. Wherefore our men sought with their Pinnisses to compasse about the Iland where they did use, supposing there suddenly to intercept some of them. But before our men could come neere, having belike some watch in the toppe of the mountaines, they conveyed themselves privily away, and left (as it should seeme) one of their great dartes behinde them for haste, which we found neere to a place of their caves and housing. Therefore, though our Generall were very desirous to have taken some of them to have brought into England, they being now growen more wary by their former losses, would not at any time come within our dangers. About midnight of the same day, the captaine of the Anne Francis departed thence and set his course over the streights towards Hattons Hedland, being about 15. leagues over, and returned aboord his Shippe the 25. of August, to the great comfort of his company, who long expected his comming, where hee found his

None of the people will be taken.

THE ENGLISH VOYAGES

Shippes ready rigged and loden. Wherefore he departed from thence againe the next morning towards the Countesses sound, where he arrived the 28. of the same. By the way he set his Miners ashore at Beares sound, for the better dispatch and gathering the Ore togither: for that some of the ships were behind hand with their fraight, the time of the yeere passing suddenly away.

The thirtith of August the Anne Francis was brought aground, and had 8. great leakes mended which she had received by meanes of the rocks and yce. This day the Masons finished a house which Captaine Fenton caused to be made of lyme and stone upon the Countesse of Warwickes Island, to the ende we might prove against the next yeere, whither the snow could overwhelme it, the frost breake it up, or the people dismember the same. And the better to allure those brutish and uncivill people to courtesie against other times of our comming, we left therein divers of our Countrey toyes, as belles, and knives, wherein they specially delight, one for the necessary use, and the other for the great pleasure thereof. Also pictures of men and women in lead, men on horsebacke, looking glasses, whistles, and pipes. Also in the house was made an Oven, and bread left baked therein for them to see and taste.

We buried the timber of our pretended fort. Also here we sowed pease, corne, and other graine, to prove the fruitfulnesse of the soyle against the next yeere.

Master Wolfall on Winters Fornace preached a godly sermon, which being ended, he celebrated also a Communion upon the land, at the partaking whereof was the Captaine of the Anne Francis, and many other Gentlemen and Souldiers, Mariners, and Miners with him. The celebration of the divine mystery was the first signe, seale, and confirmation of Christs name, death, and passion ever knowen in these quarters. The said M. Wolfall made sermons, and celebrated the Communion at sundry other times, in severall and sundry ships, because the whole company could never meet together at any one place. The Fleet now being in some good readinesse for their lading, the Generall calling together the Gentlemen and Captaines to consult, told them that he was very desirous that some further discovery should be attempted, and that he would not onely by Gods helpe bring home his Ships laden with Ore, but also meant to bring some certificate of a further discovery of the Countrey, which thing to bring to passe (having sometime therein consulted) they found very hard, and almost invincible. And considering that already they had spent sometime in searching out the trending and fashion of the mistaken straites, therefore it could not be sayd, but that by this voyage they have notice of a further discovery, and that the hope of the passage thereby is much furthered and encreased, as appeared before in the discourse thereof. Yet notwithstanding if any meanes might be further devised, the Captaines were contented and willing, as the Generall shoulde appoynt and commaund, to take any enterprise in hand. Which after long debating was found a thing very impossible, and that rather consultation was to be had of returning homeward, especially for these causes following. First the darke foggy mists, the continuall falling snowe and stormy weather which they commonly were vexed with, and now daily ever more and more increased, have no small argument of the Winters drawing neere. And also the frost every night was so hard congealed within the sound, that if by evill hap they should bee long kept in with contrary winds, it was greatly to be feared, that they should be shut up there fast the whole yeere, which being utterly unprovided, would be their utter destruction. Againe, drinke was so scant throughout all the Fleet by meanes of the great leakage, that not onely the provision which was layd in for the habitation was wanting and wasted, but also each shippes severall provision spent and lost, which many of our company to their great griefe found in their returne since, for all the way homewards they dranke nothing but water. And the great cause of this leakage

Consultation for a further discovery.

and wasting was, for that the great timber and seacole, which lay so waighty upon the barrels, brake, bruised, and rotted the hoopes insunder. Yet notwithstanding these reasons alleaged the Generall himselfe (willing the rest of the Gentlemen and Captaines every man to looke to his severall charge and lading, that against a day appointed, they should be all in a readinesse to set homeward) went in a Pinnesse and discovered further Northward in the straights, and found that by Beares sound and Halles Island, the land was not firme, as it was *Broken Ilands* first supposed, but all broken Islands in maner of an *in maner of an* Archipelagus, and so with other secret intelligence to *Archipelagus.* himselfe, he returned to the Fleet. Where presently upon his arrivall at the Countesses sound, he began to take order for their returning homeward, and first caused certaine Articles to be proclaimed, for the better keeping of orders and courses in their returne, which Articles were delivered to every Captaine.

The Fleetes returning homeward.

HAving now received Articles and directions for our returne homewards, all other things being in forwardnesse and in good order, the last day of August
[III. 92.] the whole Fleete departed from the Countesses sound, excepting the Judith, and the Anne Francis, who stayed for the taking in of fresh water, and came the next day and mette the Fleete lying off and on, athwart Beares sound, who stayed for the Generall, which then was gone *Returne home-* ashore to dispatch the two Barkes and the Busse of *ward.* Bridgewater, for their loading, whereby to get the companies and other things aboord. The Captaine of the Anne Francis having most part of his company ashore, the first of September went also to Beares sound in his Pinnesse to fetch his men aboord, but the wind grewe so great immediatly upon their landing, that the shippes at Sea were in great danger, and some of them forcibly put from their ankers, and greatly feared to be utterly lost, as the Hopewell, wherein was Captaine Carew and

others, who could not tell on which side their danger
was most: for having mightie rockes threatning on the
one side, and driving Islands of cutting yce on the other
side, they greatly feared to make shipwracke, the yce
driving so neere them that it touched their bolt-sprit.
And by meanes of the Sea that was growne so hie, they
were not able to put to sea with their small Pinnesses
to recover their shippes. And againe, the shippes were
not able to tarrie or lie athwart for them, by meanes of
the outragious windes and swelling seas. The Generall
willed the Captaine of the Anne Francis with his company, for that night to lodge aboord the Busse of
Bridgewater, and went himselfe with the rest of his men
aboord the Barkes. But their numbers were so great,
and the provision of the Barkes so scant, that they
pestered one another exceedingly. They had great hope
that the next morning the weather would be faire,
whereby they might recover their shippes. But in the
morning following it was much worse, for the storme
continued greater, the Sea being more swollen, and the
Fleete gone quite out of sight. So that now their doubts
began to grow great: for the ship of Bridgewater which
was of greatest receit, and whereof they had best hope
and made most account, roade so farre to leeward of
the harborowes mouth, that they were not able for the
rockes (that lay betweene the wind and them) to lead
it out to Sea with a saile. And the Barks were already
so pestered with men, and so slenderly furnished with
provision, that they had scarce meat for sixe dayes for
such numbers.

The Generall in the morning departed to Sea in the
Gabriel to seeke the Fleete, leaving the Busse of Bridgewater, and the Michael behind in Beares sound. The
Busse set sayle, and thought by turning in the narrow
channell within the harborow to get to windward: but
being put to leeward more, by that meanes was faine
to come to anker for her better safetie, amongst a number
of rockes, and there left in great danger of ever getting

forth againe. The Michael set sayle to follow the Generall, and could give the Busse no reliefe, although they earnestly desired the same. And the Captaine of the Anne Francis was left in hard election of two evils: eyther to abide his fortune with the Busse of Bridgewater, which was doubtfull of ever getting forth, or else to bee towed in his small Pinnesse at the sterne of the Michael thorow the raging Seas, for that the Barke was not able to receive or relieve halfe his company, wherein his danger was not a little perillous.

So after hee resolved to commit himselfe with all his company unto that fortune of God and Sea, and was dangerously towed at the sterne of the Barke for many miles, untill at length they espyed the Anne Francis under sayle, hard under their Lee, which was no small comfort unto them. For no doubt, both those and a great number more had perished for lacke of victuals, and convenient roome in the Barks without the helpe of the sayd Ship. But the honest care that the Master of the Anne Francis had of his Captaine, and the good regarde of duetie towardes his Generall, suffered him not to depart, but honestly abode to hazard a dangerous roade all the night long, notwithstanding all the stormy weather, when all the Fleete besides departed. And the Pinnesse came no sooner aboord the shippe, and the men entred, but shee presently shivered and fell in pieces and sunke at the ships sterne, with all the poore mens furniture: so weake was the boat with towing, and so forcible was the sea to bruise her in pieces. But (as God would) the men were all saved.

At this present in this storme many of the Fleete were dangerously distressed, and were severed almost all asunder. Yet, thanks be to God, all the Fleete arrived safely in England about the first of October, some in one place and some in another. But amongst other, it was most marveilous how the Busse of Bridgewater got away, who being left behind the Fleete in great danger of never getting forth, was forced to seeke a way Northward thorow an unknowen channell full of rocks, upon the backe side of Beares sound, and there by good hap found out a way into the North sea, a very dangerous attempt: save that necessitie, which hath no law, forced them to trie masteries. This aforesayd North sea is the same which lyeth upon the backe side of Frobishers straits, where first the Generall himselfe in his Pinnesses, and after some other of our company have discovered (as they affirme) a great foreland, where they would have also a great likelihood of the greatest passage towards the South sea, or Mar del Sur.

An unknowen channell into the Northeast, discovered by the Busse of Bridgewater.

[III. 93.]

The Busse of Bridgewater, as she came homeward, to the Southeastward of Friseland, discovered a great Island in the latitude of 57 degrees and an halfe, which was never yet found before, and sailed three dayes alongst the coast, the land seeming to be fruitfull, full of woods, and a champion Countrey.

A fruitful new Island discovered.

There died in the whole Fleet in all this voyage not above forty persons, which number is not great, considering how many ships were in the Fleet, and how strange fortunes we passed.

A generall and briefe description of the Countrey, and condition of the people, which are found in Meta Incognita.

Aving now sufficiently and truly set forth the whole circumstance, and particuler handling of every occurrent in the 3. voyages of our worthy Generall, Captaine Frobisher, it shal not be from the purpose to speake somewhat in generall of the nature of this Countrey called Meta Incognita, and the condition of the savages there inhabiting.

First therefore touching the Topographical description of the place, It is now found in the last voyage, that Queene Elizabeths Cape being situate in latitude at 61.

A Topographicall description of Meta Incognita.

degrees and a halfe, which before was supposed to be part of the firme land of America, and also al the rest of the South side of Frobishers straites, are all severall Islands and broken land, and likewise so will all the North side of the said straites fall out to be as I thinke. And some of our company being entred above 60. leagues within the mistaken straites in the third voyage mentioned, thought certainely that they had discryed the firme land of America towards the South, which I thinke will fall out so to be.

These broken lands and Islands being very many in number, do seeme to make there an Archipelagus, which as they all differ in greatnesse, forme, and fashion one from another; so are they in goodnesse, colour, and soyle much unlike. They all are very high lands, mountaines, and in most parts covered with snow even all the Sommer long. The Norther lands have lesse store of snow, more grasse, and are more plaine Countreys: the cause whereof may be, for that the Souther Ilands receive all the snow, that the cold winds and percing ayre bring out of the North. And contrarily, the North parts receive more warme blasts of milder ayre from the South, whereupon may grow the cause why the people covet to inhabit more upon the North parts then the South, as farre as we can yet by our experience perceive

The people of Meta Incognita like unto Samoeds.

they doe. These people I judge to be a kind of Tartar, or rather a kind of Samoed, of the same sort and condition of life that the Samoeds bee to the Northeastwards beyond Moscovy, who are called Samoeds, which is as much to say in the Moscovy tongue as eaters of themselves, and so the Russians their borderers doe name them. And by late conference with a friend of mine (with whom I did sometime travell in the parts of Moscovy) who hath great experience of those Samoeds and people of the Northeast, I find that in all their maner of living, those people of the Northeast, and these of the

Their native colour.

Northwest are like. They are of the colour of a ripe Olive, which how it may come to passe, being borne in so cold a climate I referre to the judgement of others, for they are naturally borne children of the same colour and complexion that all the Americans are, which dwell under the Equinoctiall line.

They are men very active and nimble. They are a strong people and very warlike, for in our sight upon the toppes of the hilles they would often muster themselves, and after the maner of a skirmish trace their ground very nimbly, and mannage their bowes and dartes with great dexterity. They go clad in coates made of *Their apparel.* the skinnes of beasts, as of Seales, Deere, Beares, Foxes, and Hares. They have also some garments of feathers, being made of the cases of Foules, finely sowed and compact togither. Of all which sorts wee brought home some with us into England, which we found in their tents. In Sommer they use to weare the hairie side of their coates outward, and sometime goe naked for too much heate. And in Winter (as by signes they have declared) they weare foure or five folde upon their bodies with the haire (for warmth) turned inward. Hereby it appeareth, that the ayre there is not indifferent, but either it is fervent hote, or els extreme cold, & farre more excessive in both qualities, then the reason of the climate should yeeld. For there it is colder, being under 62. degrees in latitude, then it is at Wardhouse in the voyage to Saint Nicholas in Moscovie, being at above 72. degrees in latitude. The reason hereof perhaps *The acciden-* may be, that this Meta Incognita is much frequented *tall cause of the* and vexed with Easterne and Northeasterne winds, which *cold ayre at* from the sea and yce bringeth often an intollerable cold *Meta Incog-* ayre, which was also the cause that this yeere our straits *nita.* were so long shut up with so great store of yce. But there is great hope and likelihood, that further within [III. 94.] the Straights it will bee more constant and temperate weather.

These people are in nature very subtill and sharpe witted, ready to conceive our meaning by signes, and to make answere well to be understood againe. And if they have not seene the thing whereof you aske them, they will wincke, or cover their eyes with their hands, as who would say, it hath bene hid from their sight. If they understand you not whereof you aske them, they wil stop their eares. They will teach us the names of each thing in their language which wee desire to learne, and are apt to learne any thing of us. They

The Savages delight in Musicke.

delight in Musicke above measure, and will keepe time and stroke to any tune which you shall sing, both with their voyce, head, hand and feete, and will sing the same tune aptly after you. They will row with our Ores in our boates, and keepe a true stroke with our Mariners, and seeme to take great delight therein.

Hard kind of living.

They live in Caves of the earth, and hunt for their dinners or praye, even as the beare or other wild beastes do. They eat raw flesh and fish, and refuse no meat howsoever it be stinking. They are desperate in their fight, sullen of nature, and ravenous in their maner of feeding.

Their sullen & desperate nature doth herein manifestly appeare, that a company of them being environed by our men on the top of a hie cliffe, so that they could by no meanes escape our hands, finding themselves in this case distressed, chose rather to cast themselves headlong down the rocks into the sea, and so be bruised and drowned, rather then to yeeld themselves to our mens mercies.

Their weapons.

For their weapons to offend their enemies or kill their prey withall, they have darts, slings, bowes, and arrowes headed with sharpe stones, bones, and some with yron. They are exceeding friendly and kind hearted one to the other, and mourne greatly at the losse or harme of their fellowes, and expresse their griefe of mind, when they part one from another with a

Their chastity.

mourneful song, and Dirges. They are very shamefast in bewraying the secrets of nature, and very chaste in the maner of their living: for when the man, which wee brought from thence into England the last voyage, should put off his coat or discover his whole body for change, hee would not suffer the woman to bee present, but put her forth of his Cabin. And in all the space of two or three moneths, while the man lived in company of the woman, there was never any thing seene or perceived betweene them, more then might have passed betweene brother and sister : but the woman was in all things very serviceable for the man, attending him carefully when he was sicke, and he likewise in all the meates which they did eate together, woulde carve unto her of the sweetest, fattest, and best morsels they had. They wondred much at all our things, and were afraid of our horses and other beasts out of measure. They began to grow more civill, familiar, pleasant, and docible amongst us in very short time.

They have boates made of leather, and covered cleane *Their boates.* over saving one place in the middle to sit in, planked within with timber, and they use to row therein with one Ore, more swiftly a great deale, then we in our boates can doe with twentie. They have one sort of greater boates wherein they can carrie above twentie persons, and have a Mast with a saile thereon, which saile is made of thinne skinnes or bladders, sowed togither with the sinewes of fishes.

They are good Fishermen, and in their small Boates being disguised with their coates of Seales skinnes, they deceive the fish, who take them rather for their fellow Seales, then for deceiving men.

They are good marke-men. With their dart or arrow they will commonly kill a Ducke, or any other foule in the head, and commonly in the eye.

When they shoote at a great fish with any of their darts, they use to tye a bladder thereunto, whereby they may the better find them againe, and the fish not able to cary it so easily away (for that the bladder doth boy the dart) will at length be wearie, and dye therewith. *Traffique with*
some other
They use to traffike and exchange their commodities *nation un-*
with some other people, of whom they have such things *knowen.*

as their miserable Countrey, and ignorance of Art to make, denieth them to have, as barres of yron, heads of yron for their darts, needles made foure square, certaine buttons of copper, which they use to weare upon their forehads for ornament, as our Ladies in the Court of England doe use great pearle.

Gold.

Also they have made signes unto us, that they have seene gold, and such bright plates of mettals, which are used for ornaments amongst some people with whom they have conference.

We found also in their tents a Guiny Beane of redde colour, the which doth usually grow in they hote Countreys: whereby it appeareth they trade with other nations which dwell farre off, or else themselves are great travellers.

Their fewell.

They have nothing in use among them to make fire withall, saving a kinde of Heath and Mosse which groweth there.

[III. 95.]
How they make fire.

And they kindle their fire with continuall rubbing and fretting one sticke against another, as we doe with flints. They drawe with dogges in sleads upon the yce, and remoove their tents therewithall wherein they dwell in Sommer, when they goe a hunting for their praye and provision against Winter. They doe sometime parboyle

Their kettles and pannes.

their meat a little and seeth the same in kettles made of beasts skins: they have also pannes cut and made of stone very artificially; they use pretty ginnes wherewith they take foule. The women carry their sucking children at their backes, and doe feede them with raw flesh, which first they do a little chaw in their owne mouths. The women have their faces marked or painted over with small blewe spots: they have blacke and long haire on their heads, and trimme the same in a decent order. The men have but little haire on their faces, and very thinne beards. For their common drinke, they eate yce to quench their thirst withall. Their earth yeeldeth no

The people eate grasse and shrubs.

graine or fruit of sustenance for man, or almost for beast to live upon: and the people will eate grasse and shrubs of the ground, even as our kine doe. They have no wood growing in their Countrey thereabouts, and yet wee find they have some timber among them, which we thinke doth growe farre off to the Southwards of this place, about Canada, or some other part of New found land: for there belike, the trees standing on the cliffes of the sea side, by the waight of yce and snow in Winter overcharging them with waight, when the Sommers thaw commeth above, and also the Sea underfretting them beneath, which winneth dayly of the land, they are undermined and fall downe from those cliffes into the Sea, and with the tydes and currents are driven to and fro upon the coastes further off, and by conjecture are taken up here by these Countrey people, to serve them to planke and strengthen their boates withall, and to make dartes, bowes, and arrowes, and such other things necessarie for their use. And of this kind of drift wood we find all the Seas over great store, which being cut or sawed asunder, by reason of long driving in the Sea is eaten of wormes, and full of holes, of which sort theirs is found to be.

We have not yet found any venemous Serpent or other hurtful thing in these parts, but there is a kind of small flie or gnat that stingeth and offendeth sorely, leaving many red spots in the face, and other places where she stingeth. They have snow and haile in the best time of their Sommer, and the ground frosen three fadome deepe. *A strange kind of gnat.*

These people are great inchanters, and use many charmes of witchcraft: for when their heads doe ake, they tye a great stone with a string unto a sticke, and with certaine prayers and wordes done to the sticke, they lift up the stone from ground, which sometimes with all a mans force they cannot stirre, and sometime againe they lift as easily as a fether, and hope thereby with certaine ceremonious wordes to have ease and helpe. And they made us by signes to understand, lying groveling with their faces upon the ground, and making *Inchanters.*

THE ENGLISH VOYAGES

a noise downeward, that they worship the devill under them.

They have great store of Deere, Beares, Hares, Foxes, and innumerable numbers of sundry sorts of wild foule, as Seawmewes, Gulles, Wilmotes, Ducks, &c. wherof our men killed in one day fifteene hundred.

They have also store of haukes, as Falkons, Tassels, &c. whereof two alighted upon one of our ships at their returne, and were brought into England, which some thinke wil prove very good.

There are also great store of ravens, larkes, and partriges, wherof the Countrey people feed.

All these foules are farre thicker clothed with downe and fethers, and have thicker skinnes then any in England have: for as that countrey is colder, so nature hath provided a remedie thereunto.

Our men have eaten of the Beares, Hares, Partridges, Larkes, and of their wild foule, and find them reasonable good meat, but not so delectable as ours.

Their wild foule must be all fleine, their skins are so thicke: and they tast best fryed in pannes.

The Countrey seemeth to be much subject to Earthquakes.

The ayre is very subtile, piercing and searching, so that if any corrupted or infected body, especially with the disease called Morbus Gallicus come there, it will presently breake forth and shew it selfe, and cannot there by any kind of salve or medicine be cured.

Their longest Sommers day is of great length, without any darke night, so that in July al the night long, we might perfitly and easily write and reade whatsoever had pleased us, which lightsome nights were very beneficiall unto us, being so distressed with abundance of yce as we were.

The Sunne setteth to them in the Evening at a quarter of an houre after tenne of the clocke, and riseth againe in the morning at three quarters of an houre after one of the clocke, so that in Sommer their Sunne shineth to

them twenty houres and a halfe, and in the night is
absent three houres and a halfe. And although the
Sunne bee absent these 3. houres and a halfe, yet it is
not darke that time, for that the Sunne is never above   [III. 96.]
three or foure degrees under the edge of their Horizon:
the cause is, that the Tropicke of Cancer doth cut their
Horizon at very uneven and oblique Angles. But the
Moone at any time of the yeere being in Cancer, having   *A full revolu-*
North latitude, doth make a full revolution above their *tion of the*
Horizon, so that sometime they see the Moone above *Moone above*
their Horizon.
24. houres togither. Some of our company of the more
ignorant sort, thought we might continually have seene
the Sunne and the Moone, had it not bene for two or
three high mountaines.

The people are now become so warie, and so circum-
spect, by reason of their former losses, that by no meanes
we can apprehend any of them, although wee attempted
often in this last voyage. But to say trueth, wee could
not bestow any great time in pursuing them, because
of our great businesse in lading, and other things.

The Letters patents of the Queenes Majestie,
     granted to Master Adrian Gylbert and others,
     for the search and discovery of the North-
     west Passage to China.

Lizabeth by the grace of God of England,
France, and Ireland Queene, defender of
the faith, &c. To all, to whome these
presents shall come, greeting: Forasmuch
as our trustie and welbeloved subject
Adrian Gylbert of Sandridge in the
Countie of Devon, Gentleman, to his
great costes and charges, hath greatly and earnestly
travelled and sought, and yet doth travell and seeke,
and by divers meanes indevoureth and laboureth, that
the Passage unto China and the Iles of the Moluccas,
by the Northwestward, Northeastward, or Northward,

unto which part or partes of the world, none of our
loyall Subjects have hitherto had any traffique or trade,
may be discovered, knowen, and frequented by the
Subjects of this our Realme: Knowe yee therefore that
for the considerations aforesayd and for divers other
good considerations us thereunto specially mooving.
We of our grace especiall, certaine knowledge, and
meere motion, have given and granted, and by these
presents for us, our heires and successors, doe give
and grant free libertie, power, and full authoritie to the
sayd Adrian Gylbert, and to any other person by him
or his heires to be assigned, and to those his associates
and assistants, whose names are written in a Scedule
hereunto annexed, and to their heires, and to one
assignee of each of them, and each of their heires at all
times, and at any time or times after the date of these
presents, under our Banners and Ensignes freely, without let, interruption, or restraint, of us, our heires or
successors, any law, statute, proclamation, patent, charter,
or proviso to the contrary notwithstanding, to saile,
make voyage, and by any maner of meanes to passe
and to depart out of this our Realme of England, or
any our Realmes, Dominions, or Territories into all or
any Isles, Countreys, Regions, Provinces, Territories,
Seas, Rivers, Portes, Bayes, Creekes, armes of the Sea,
and all Havens, and all maner of other places whatsoever, that by the sayde Northwestward, Northeastward,
or Northward, is to be by him, his associates or assignes
discovered, and for and in the sayde sayling, voyage,
and passage, to have and use so many shippes, Barkes,
Pinnesses, or other vessels of any quantitie or burthen,
with all the furniture of men, victuals, and all maner
of necessary provision, armour, weapons, ordinance,
targets, and appurtinances whatsoever, as to such a
voyage shall or may be requisite, convenient or commodious, any lawe, statute, ordinance or proviso to the
contrary thereof notwithstanding. And also we doe
give and grant to the sayde Adrian Gylbert, and his

sayde associates, and to such assignee of him, and his heires, and to the heires and one assignee of every of his sayde associates for ever, full power and absolute authoritie to trade and make their resiance in any of the sayde Isles, Countreys, Regions, Provinces, Territories, Seas, Rivers, Portes, Bayes, and Havens, and all maner of other places whatsoever with all commodities, profites, and emoluments in the sayde places or any of them, growing and arising, with all maner of priviledges, prerogatives, jurisdictions and royalties both by sea and land whatsoever, yeelding and paying therefore unto us, our heires and successors, the tenth part of all such golde and silver oare, pearles, jewels, and precious stones, or the value thereof, as the sayd Adrian Gylbert and his sayd associates, their heires and assignes, servants, factors, or workemen, and every or any of them shall finde, the sayd tenth to bee delivered duely to our Customer, or other officers by us, our heires or successors thereunto assigned, in the Portes of London, Dartmouth, or Plimmouth, at which three places onely the sayde Adrian Gylbert, and his sayde associates, their sayde heires and assignes, shall lade, charge, arrive, and discharge all maner of wares, goods, and merchandizes whatsoever to the sayde voyage, and newe trade belonging or appertaining. And moreover, wee have given, granted, and authorized, and by these presents for us, [III. 97.] our heires and successors, of our grace especiall, certaine knowledge, and meere motion, doe give, graunt, and authorize the sayd Adrian Gilbert, and his sayd associats for ever, their heires and their said assignes & every of them, that if the aforesayd Iles, Countreys, Regions, Provinces, Territories, Seas, Rivers, Ports, Bayes, or Havens, or any other of the premisses by the sayd Adrian Gylbert or his associats, their heires and their said assignes or any of them, to be found by them, discovered and traffiqued unto by any trade as aforesayd, shall be by any other our subjects visited, frequented, haunted, traded unto or inhabited by the wayes afore-

sayd, without the special licence in writing of the said
Adrian Gylbert and his associats, and their heires and
assignes for ever, or by the most part of them, so
that the sayd Adrian Gilbert, his heires or assignes
be one of them, that then aswell their ship, or ships
in any such voyage or voyages be used, as all and
singuler their goods, wares, and marchandizes, or any
other things whatsoever, from or to any of the
places aforesayd transported, that so shall presume to
visit, frequent, haunt, trade unto, or inhabite, shall be
forfaited and confiscated, ipso facto, the one halfe of the
same goods and marchandizes, or other things whatsoever, or the value thereof to be to the use of us, our
heires or successours, and the other moytie thereof to
be to the use of the sayd Adrian Gylbert and his sayd
associats, their heires and assignes for ever: and unto
the sayd Adrian Gylbert and his sayd associats, their
heires and assignes wee impose, give, assigne, create
and confirme this name peculiar to be named by, to
sue and to be sued by, that is to wit, by the name
The collegues of the Colleagues of the fellowship for the discoverie
of the fellow- of the Northwest passage, and them for us, our heires
ship for the and successours by that name doe incorporate, and doe
discovery of the erect and create as one body corporate to have con-
Northwest tinuance for ever. Moreover unto the sayd Adrian
passage. Gylbert, and his said associats, and unto their heires
and their sayd assignes for ever, by name of the
Colleagues of the fellowship, for the discoverie of the
Northwest passage, we have given, granted, and confirmed, and doe by these presents give, grant, and
confirme full power and authoritie from time to time,
and at all times hereafter, to make order, decree and
enact, constitute and ordeine, and appoynt all such
ordinances, orders, decrees, lawes, and actes, as the
sayd new corporation or body politique, Colleagues
of the fellowship for the discoverie of the Northwest passage, shall thinke meete, necessary, and convenient, so that they or any of them be not contrary

to the lawes of this realme, and of this our present graunt.

And we by our Royall prerogative, and fulnesse of our authority, of our grace especiall, certaine knowledge and meere motion, do establish, confirme & ratifie all such ordinances, orders, decrees, lawes and acts to be in so full and great power and authority, as we, our heires or successours may or can in any such case graunt, confirme, or ratifie. And further for the better incouragement of our loving subjects in this discoverie, we by our Royall prerogative, and fulnesse of authority for us, our heires and successours, doe give, graunt, establish, confirme, ordeine, ratifie and allow by these presents, to the sayd Adrian Gylbert and to his associates, and to the heires and assignes of them and every of them for ever, and to all other person or persons of our loving subjects whatsoever that shall hereafter travaile, sayle, discover, or make voyage as aforesayd to any the Iles, Mainelands, Countreys or Territories whatsoever, by vertue of this our graunt to be discovered, that the heires and assignes of them and every of them being borne within any of the Iles, Mainelands and Countreys, or Territories whatsoever before mentioned, shall have and injoy all the privileges of free Denizens, as persons native borne within this *Free Deniza-* our Realme of England, or within our allegiance for *tion granted.* ever, in such like ample maner and forme, as if they were or had bene borne and personally resiant within our sayd Realme, any law, statute, proclamation, custome or usage to the contrary hereof in any wise notwithstanding.

Moreover, for the consideration aforesayd by vertue hereof, we give and graunt unto the sayd Adrian Gylbert, his heires and assignes for ever, free libertie, licence and privilege, that during the space of five *This Patent* yeeres next and immediatly ensuing the date hereof, it *remained in* shall not be lawfull for any person or persons what- *force five* soever, to visit, haunt, frequent, trade, or make voyage *yeeres.*

379

to any Iles, Mainlands, Countreys, Regions, Provinces, Territories, Seas, Rivers, Ports, Bayes, and Havens, nor to any other Havens or places whatsoever hitherto not yet discovered by any of our subjects by vertue of this graunt to be traded unto, without the special consent and good liking of the said Adrian Gylbert, his heires or assignes first had in writing. And if any person or persons of the associats of the sayd Adrian, his heires or assignes, or any other person or persons whatsoever, free of this discovery, shall do any act or acts contrary to the tenour and true meaning hereof, during the space of the sayd five yeeres, that then the partie and parties so offending, they and their heires for ever shall loose (ipso facto) the benefite and privilege of this our graunt, and shall stand and remaine to all intents and purposes as persons exempted out of this graunt.

[III. 98.]

And further by vertue hereof wee give and graunt, for us, our heires and successours at all times during the space of five yeers next ensuing the date hereof, *Authoritie to proceede at Sea against mutiners.* libertie and licence, and full authority to the sayd Adrian Gylbert, and his heires and assignes, that if it shall happen any one or moe in any ship or ships sayling on their sayd voyage, to become mutinous, seditious, disordered, or any way unruly to the prejudice or hinderance of the hope for the successe in the attempt or prosecuting of this discoverie or trade intended, to use or execute upon him or them so offending, such punishment, correction, or execution, as the cause shall be found in justice to require by the verdict of twelve of the companie sworne thereunto, as in such a case apperteineth: That expresse mention of the certaintie of the premisses, or of other gifts or graunts by us to the sayd Adrian Gylbert and his associats before this time made is not mentioned in these presents, or any other lawe, act, statute, proviso, graunt, or proclamation heretofore made or hereafter to be made to the contrary hereof in any wise notwith-

standing. In witnesse whereof we have made these
our Letters to bee made patents : Witnesse our selfe 1583.
at Westminster, the sixt day of Februarie, in the sixe
and twenty yeere of our reigne.

The first voyage of M. John Davis, undertaken in June 1585. for the discoverie of the Northwest passage, Written by M. John Janes Marchant, sometimes servant to the worshipfull Master William Sanderson.

Ertaine Honourable personages and worthy Gentlemen of the Court & Countrey, with divers worshipful Marchants of London and of the West Countrey, mooved with desire to advance Gods glory and to seeke the good of their native Countrey, consulting together of the likelyhood of the Discoverie of the Northwest passage, which heretofore had bene attempted, but unhappily given over by accidents unlooked for, which turned the enterprisers from their principall purpose, resolved after good deliberation, to put downe their adventures to provide for necessarie shipping, and a fit man to be chiefe Conductour of this so hard an enterprise. The setting forth of this Action was committed by the adventurers, especially to the care of M. William Sanderson Marchant of London, who was so forward therein, that besides his travaile which was not small, hee became the greatest adventurer with his purse, and commended unto the rest of the companie one M. John Davis, a man very well grounded in the principles of the Arte of Navigation, for Captaine and chiefe Pilot of this exployt.

Thus therefore all things being put in a readines, wee departed from Dartmouth the seventh of June, towards the discoverie of the aforesayd Northwest passage, with two Barkes, the one being of 50. tunnes,

named the Sunneshine of London, and the other being
35. tunnes, named the Mooneshine of Dartmouth. In
the Sunneshine we had 23. persons, whose names are
these following, M. John Davis Captaine, William Eston
Master, Richard Pope Masters mate, John Jane Mar-
chant, Henry Davie gunner, William Crosse boatswayne,
John Bagge, Walter Arthur, Luke Adams, Robert
Coxworthie, John Ellis, John Kelley, Edward Helman,
Musitians. William Dicke, Andrew Maddocke, Thomas Hill,
Robert Wats Carpenter, William Russell, Christopher
Gorney boy: James Cole, Francis Ridley, John Russell,
Robert Cornish Musicians.

The Mooneshine had 19. persons, William Bruton
Captaine, John Ellis Master, the rest Mariners.

The 7. of June the Captaine and the Master drewe
out a proportion for the continuance of our victuals.

The 8. day the wind being at Southwest and West
southwest, we put in for Falmouth, where we remained
untill the 13.

The 13. the wind blew at North, and being faire
weather we departed.

The 14. with contrary wind we were forced to put
into Silley.

The 15. wee departed thence, having the wind North
and by East moderate and faire weather.

The 16. wee were driven backe againe, and were
constrained to arrive at newe Grymsby in Silley: here
the winde remained contrary 12. dayes, and in that
space the Captaine, the Master and I went about all
the Ilands, and the Captaine did plat out and describe
the situation of all the Ilands, rocks and harboroughs
to the exact use of Navigation, with lines and scale
thereunto convenient.

They depart The 28. in Gods name we departed the wind being
from Silley. Easterly but calme.

July. The first of July wee sawe great store of Porposes;
The Master called for an harping yron, and shot twise
or thrise: sometimes he missed, and at last shot one

and strooke him in the side, and wound him into the [III. 99.]
ship: when we had him aboord, the Master sayd it
was a Darlie head.

The 2. we had some of the fish sodden, and it did
eat as sweete as any mutton.

The 3. wee had more in sight, and the Master went to
shoote at them, but they were so great, that they burst
our yrons, and we lost both fish, yrons, pastime and all:
yet neverthelesse the Master shot at them with a pike,
and had welnigh gotten one, but he was so strong that
he burst off the barres of the pike and went away:
then he tooke the boat-hooke, and hit one with that,
but all would not prevaile, so at length we let them
alone.

The 6. we saw a very great Whale, and every day
we saw whales continually.

The 16. 17. and 18. we saw great store of Whales. *Great store of*
The 19. of July we fell into a great whirling and *whales.*
brustling of a tyde, setting to the Northwards: and
sayling about halfe a league wee came into a very calme
Sea, which bent to the Southsouthwest. Here we heard
a mighty great roaring of the Sea, as if it had bene the
breach of some shoare, the ayre being so foggie and full of
thicke mist, that we could not see the one ship from the
other, being a very small distance asunder: so the
Captaine and the Master being in distrust how the tyde
might set them, caused the Mooneshine to hoyse out
her boate and to sound, but they could not finde ground
in 300. fathoms and better. Then the Captaine, Master,
and I went towards the breach, to see what it should be,
giving charge to our gunners that at every glasse they
should shoote off a musket-shot, to the intent we might
keepe our selves from loosing them. Then comming
nere to the breach, we met many Ilands of yce floting,
which had quickly compassed us about: then we went *The rouling of*
upon some of them, and did perceive that all the roaring *the yce together*
which we heard, was caused onely by the rowling of this *made a great*
yce together: Our companie seeing us not to returne *roaring.*

according to our appoyntment, left off shooting muskets, and began to shoote falkonets, for they feared some mishap had befallen us, but before night we came aboord *Yce turned into* againe with our boat laden with yce, which made very *water.* good fresh water. Then wee bent our course toward the North, hoping by that meanes to double the land.

The 20. as we sayled along the coast the fogge brake up, and we discovered the land, which was the most deformed rockie and mountainous land that ever we saw: The first sight whereof did shew as if it had bene in forme of a sugar-loafe, standing to our sight above the cloudes, for that it did shew over the fogge like a white liste in the skie, the tops altogether covered with snow, and the shoare beset with yce a league off into the Sea, making such yrkesome noyse as that it seemed to be the true patterne of desolation, and after the same our *The land of* Captaine named it, The land of Desolation.
Desolation.

The 21. the winde came Northerly and overblew, so that we were constrained to bend our course South againe, for we perceived that we were runne into a very deepe Bay, where wee were almost compassed with yce, for we saw very much toward the Northnortheast, West, and Southwest: and this day and this night wee cleared our selves of the yce, running Southsouthwest along the shoare.

Upon Thursday being the 22. of this moneth, about three of the clocke in the morning, wee hoysed out our boate, and the Captaine with six saylers went towards the shoare, thinking to find a landing place, for the night before we did perceive the coast to be voyde of yce to our judgement, and the same night wee were all perswaded that we had seene a Canoa rowing along the shoare, but afterwards we fell in some doubt of it, but we had no great reason so to doe. The Captaine rowing towards the shoare, willed the Master to beare in with the land after him, and before he came neere the shoare by the space of a league, or about two miles, hee found so much yce, that hee could not get to land by any

384

meanes. Here our mariners put to their lines to see if they could get any fish, because there were so many seales upon the coast, and the birds did beate upon the water, but all was in vaine: The water about this place *Very blacke* was very blacke and thicke like to a filthy standing poole, *water.* we sounded and had ground in 120. fathoms. While the Captaine was rowing to the shoare, our men sawe woods upon the rocks like to the rocks of Newfoundland, but I could not discerne them, yet it might be so very well: for we had wood floting upon the coast every day, *Floting wood.* and the Mooneshine tooke up a tree at Sea not farre from the coast being sixtie foote of length and foureteene handfuls about, having the roote upon it: After this the Captaine came aboord, the weather being very calme and faire we bent our course toward the South, with intent to double the land.

The 23. we coasted the land which did lie East-northeast and Westsouthwest.

The 24. the winde being very faire at East, we coasted the land which did lie East and West, not being able to come neere the shoare by reason of the great quantitie of yce. At this place, because the weather was somewhat *Colde by reason* colde by reason of the yce, and the better to encourage *of yce.* our men, their allowance was increased: the captaine and [III. 100.] the master tooke order that every messe, being five persons, should have halfe a pound of bread and a kan of beere every morning to breakfast. The weather was not very colde, but the aire was moderate like to our April-weather in England: when the winde came from the land, or the ice, it was some what colde, but when it came off the sea it was very hote.

The 25 of this moneth we departed from sight of this *They saile* land at sixe of the clocke in the morning, directing our *Northwest-* course to the Northwestward, hoping in Gods mercy to *ward above* finde our desired passage, and so continued above foure *foure dayes.* dayes.

The 29 of July we discovered land in 64 degrees *Land in 64* 15 minutes of latitude, bearing Northeast from us. The *degrees 15 min.*

winde being contrary to goe to the Northwestwards, we bare in with this land to take some view of it, being utterly void of the pester of yce and very temperate. Comming neere the coast, we found many faire sounds and good roads for shipping, and many great inlets into the land, whereby we judged this land to be a great number of Islands standing together. Heere having mored our barke in good order, we went on shoare upon a small Island to seeke for water and wood. Upon this Island we did perceive that there had bene people: for we found a small shoo and pieces of leather sowed with sinewes, and a piece of furre, and wooll like to Bever. Then we went upon another Island on the other side of our shippes: and the Captaine, the Master, and I, being got up to the top of an high rocke, the people of the countrey having espied us, made a lamentable noise, as we thought, with great outcries and skreechings: we hearing them, thought it had bene the howling of wolves. At last I hallowed againe, and they likewise cried. Then we perceiving where they stood, some on the shoare, and one rowing in a Canoa about a small Island fast by them, we made a great noise, partly to allure them to us, and partly to warne our company of them. Whereupon M. Bruton and the Master of his shippe, with others of their company, made great haste towards us, and brought our Musicians with them from our shippe, purposing either by force to rescue us, if need should so require, or with courtesie to allure the people. When they came unto us, we caused our Musicians to play, our selves dancing, and making many signes of friendship. At length there came tenne Canoas from the other Islands, and two of them came so neere the shoare where we were, that they talked with us, the other being in their boats a prety way off. Their pronunciation was very hollow thorow the throat, and their speech such as we could not understand: onely we allured them by friendly imbracings and signes of curtesie. At length one of them pointing up to the Sunne with his hand, would presently strike his breast so

The sound where our ships did ride was called Gilberts sound.

Musicians.

The people of the countrey came and conferred with men.

hard that we might heare the blow. This hee did many times before he would any way trust us. Then John Ellis the Master of the Mooneshine was appointed to use his best policie to gaine their friendship; who strooke his breast, and pointed to the Sunne after their order: which when he had divers times done, they beganne to trust him, and one of them came on shoare, to whom we threw our cappes, stockings and gloves, and such other things as then we had about us, playing with our musicke, and making signes of joy, and dauncing. So the night comming, we bade them farewell, and went aboord our barks.

The next morning being the 30 of July there came 37 *Thirty seven* Canoas rowing by our ships, calling to us to come on *Canoas.* shoare: we not making any great haste unto them, one of them went up to the toppe of the rocke, and leapt and daunced as they had done the day before, shewing us a seales skinne, and another thing made like a timbrell, which he did beat upon with a sticke, making a noise *Their musike.* like a small drumme. Whereupon we manned our boats and came to them, they all staying in their Canoas: we came to the water side were they were: and after we had sworne by the Sunne after their fashion, they did trust us. So I shooke hands with one of them, and he kissed my hand, and we were very familiar with them. We were in so great credit with them upon this single *Great famili-* acquaintance, that we could have any thing they had. *arity with the* We bought five Canoas of them: we bought their clothes *Savages.* from their backs, which were all made of seales skinnes & birds skinnes; their buskins, their hose, their gloves, all being commonly sowed and well dressed: so that we were fully perswaded that they have divers artificers among them. We had a paire of buskins of them full of fine wooll like bever. Their apparell for heat was made of birds skinnes with their feathers on them. We saw among them leather dressed like Glovers leather, and thicke thongs like white leather of a good length. We had of their darts and oares, and found in them that they would by no meanes displease us, but would give us whatsoever we asked of them, and would be satisfied with whatsoever we gave them. They tooke great care one of another: for when we had bought their boats, then two other would come and cary him away betweene them that had solde us his. They are very tractable people, void of craft or double dealing, and easie to be

brought to any civility or good order: but we judge them to be idolaters and to worship the Sunne.

During the time of our abode among these Islands we found reasonable quantity of wood, both firre, spruse and juniper; which whether it came floting any great distance to these places where we found it, or whether it grew in some great Islands neere the same place by us not yet discovered, we know not; but we judge that it groweth there further into the land then we were, because the people had great store of darts and oares which they made none account of, but gave them to us for small

trifles, as points and pieces of paper. We saw about this coast marveilous great abundance of seales skulling together like skuls of small fish. We found no fresh water among these Islands, but onely snow water, whereof we found great pooles. The cliffes were all of such oare as M. Frobisher brought from Meta incognita. We had

divers shewes of Study or Muscovy glasse shining not altogether unlike to Christall. We found an herbe grow-

ing upon the rocks, whose fruit was sweet, full of red juice, and the ripe ones were like corinths. We found also birch and willow growing like shrubbes low to the ground. These people have great store of furres as we judge. They made shewes unto us the 30 of this present, which was the second time of our being with them, after they perceived we would have skinnes and furres, that they would go into the countrey and come againe the next day with such things as they had: but this night the winde comming faire, the captaine and the master would by no meanes detract the purpose of our discovery. And so the last of this moneth about foure of the clocke in the morning in Gods name we set saile, and were all that day becalmed upon the coast.

The first of August we had a faire winde, and so pro- *August.* ceeded towards the Northwest for our discovery.

The sixt of August we discovered land in 66 degrees *Land in 66* 40 minuts of latitude, altogether void from the pester of *degrees 40* ice: we ankered in a very faire rode under a brave *min.* mount, the cliffes whereof were as orient as golde. This mount was named Mount Raleigh. The rode where our ships lay at anker was called Totnes rode. The sound which did compasse the mount was named Exeter sound. The foreland towards the North was called Diers cape. The foreland towards the South was named Cape Wal-singham. So soone as we were come to an anker in Totnes rode under Mount Raleigh, we espied foure white *Foure white* beares at the foot of the mount: we supposing them to *beares.* be goats or wolves, manned our boats and went towards them: but when we came neere the shore, we found them to be white beares of a monstrous bignesse: we being desirous of fresh victuall and the sport, began to assault them, and I being on land, one of them came downe the hill right against me: my piece was charged with hailshot & a bullet: I discharged my piece and shot him in the necke; he roared a litle, and tooke the water straight, making small account of his hurt. Then we followed him with our boat, and killed him with boare-speares, & two more that night. We found nothing in their mawes; but we judged by their dung that they fed upon grasse, because it appeared in all respects like the dung of an horse, wherein we might very plainly see the very strawes.

The 7 we went on shore to another beare which lay all night upon the top of an Island under Mount Raleigh, and when we came up to him he lay fast asleep. I levelled at his head, and the stone of my piece gave no fire: with that he looked up, and layed downe his head *A huge white* againe: then I shot being charged with two bullets, and *beare.* strooke him in the head: he being but amazed fell backwards: whereupon we ran all upon him with boare-speares, and thrust him in the body: yet for all that he gript away our boare-speares, and went towards the water; and as he was going downe, he came backe againe. Then our Master shot his boare-speare, and strooke him in the head, and made him to take the water, and swimme into a cove fast by, where we killed him, and brought him aboord. The breadth of his forefoot from one side to the other was foureteene inches over. They were very fat, so as we were constrained to cast the fat away. We saw a raven upon Mount Raleigh. We found withies also growing like low shrubs & flowers like Primroses in the sayd place. The coast is very mountainous, altogether without wood, grasse, or earth, and is onely huge mountaines of stone; but the bravest stone that ever we saw. The aire was very moderate in this countrey.

The 8 we departed from Mount Raleigh, coasting along the shoare, which lieth Southsouthwest, and East-northeast.

The 9 our men fell in dislike of their allowance, because it was too small as they thought: wherupon we made a new proportion; every messe being five to a messe should have foure pound of bread a day, twelve wine quarts of beere, six Newland fishes; and the flesh dayes a gill of pease more: so we restrained them from their butter and cheese.

[III. 102.]   The 11 we came to the most Southerly cape of this land, which we named The Cape of Gods mercy, as being the place of our first entrance for the discovery. The weather being very foggy we coasted this North land; at length when it brake up, we perceived that we were shot into a very faire entrance or passage, being in some places twenty leagues broad, and in some thirty, altogether void of any pester of ice, the weather very tolerable, and the water of the very colour, nature and quality of the maine ocean, which gave us the greater hope of our passage. Having sailed Northwest sixty leagues in this entrance we discovered certaine Islands standing in the midst thereof, having open passage on both sides. Wherupon our ships divided themselves, the one sailing on the North side, the other on the South side of the sayd Isles, where we stayed five dayes, having the winde at Southeast, very foggy and foule weather.

The 14 we went on shoare and found signes of people, for we found stones layed up together like a wall, and saw the skull of a man or a woman.

The 15 we heard dogs houle on the shoare, which we thought had bene wolves, and therefore we went on shoare to kill them. When we came on land the dogges came presently to our boat very gently, yet we thought they came to pray upon us, and therefore we shot at them, and killed two: and about the necke of one of them we found a leatherne coller, wherupon we thought them to be tame dogs. There were twenty dogs like mastives with prickt eares and long bush tailes: we found a bone in the pizels of their dogs. Then we went farther, and found two sleads made like ours in England: the one was made of firre, spruse and oken boords sawen *Timber* like inch boords: the other was made all of whale bone, *sawen.* & there hung on the tops of the sleads three heads of beasts which they had killed. We saw here larks, ravens, *Fowle.* and partridges.

The 17 we went on shoare, and in a little thing made like an oven with stones I found many small trifles, as a small canoa made of wood, a piece of wood made like an image, a bird made of bone, beads having small holes *An image.* in one end of them to hang about their necks, & other small things. The coast was very barren without wood or grasse: the rocks were very faire like marble, full of vaines of divers colours. We found a seale which was killed not long before, being fleane, and hid under stones.

Our Captaine and Master searched still for proba- *Probabilities* bilities of the passage, and first found, ‖ that this place *for the passage.* was all Islands, with great sounds passing betweene them.

THE ENGLISH VOYAGES

Secondly, the water remained of one colour with the maine ocean without altering.

Thirdly, we saw to the West of those Isles three or foure whales in a skull, which they judged to come from a Westerly sea, because to the Eastward we saw not any whale.

Also as we were rowing into a very great sound lying Southwest, from whence these whales came, upon the sudden there came a violent counter-checke of a tide from the Southwest against the flood which we came with, not knowing from whence it was mainteined.

Fiftly, in sailing twenty leagues within the mouth of this entrance we had sounding in 90 fadoms, faire grey osie sand, and the further we ran into the Westwards the deeper was the water; so that hard aboord the shoare among these Isles we could not have ground in 330 fadoms.

Lastly, it did ebbe and flow sixe or seven fadome up and downe, the flood comming from divers parts, so as we could not perceive the chiefe maintenance thereof.

The 18 and 19 our Captaine and Master determined what was best to doe, both for the safegard of their credits, and satisfying of the adventurers, and resolved, if the weather brake up, to make further search.

The 20 the winde came directly against us: so they altered their purpose, and reasoned both for proceeding and returning.

The 21 the winde being Northwest, we departed from these Islands; and as we coasted the South shoare we saw many faire sounds, whereby we were perswaded that it was no firme land but Islands.

The 23 of this moneth the wind came Southeast, with very stormy and foule weather: so we were constrained to seeke harborow upon the South coast of this entrance, where we fell into a very faire sound, & ankered in 25 fadoms greene osie sand. Here we went on shore, where we had manifest signes of people where they had made their fire, and layed stones like a wall. In this place we

LETTER FROM JOHN DAVIS TO WALSINGHAM, 3ʀᴅ OCTOBER, 1585

JOHN DAVIS

saw foure very faire faulcons; and M. Bruton tooke *Faulcons.*
from one of them his prey, which we judged by the
wings and legs to be a snite, for the head was eaten off.

The 24 in the afternoone, the winde comming somewhat faire, we departed from this road, purposing by
Gods grace to returne for England.

The 26 we departed from sight of the North land of *Their returne.*
this entrance, directing our course homewards untill the
tenth of the next moneth.

The 10. of September wee fell with The land of desola- *September.*
tion, thinking to goe on shoare, but we could get never [III. 103.]
a good harborough. That night wee put to sea againe
thinking to search it the next day: but this night arose
a very great storme, and separated our ships, so that we
lost the sight of the Mooneshine.

The 13. about noone (having tried all the night before *They saile*
with a goose wing) we set saile, & within two houres *from The land*
after we had sight of the Mooneshine againe: this day *of desolation to*
we departed from this land. *England in*
14. dayes.

The 27. of this moneth we fell with sight of England.
This night we had a marveilous storme and lost the
Mooneshine.

The 30. of September wee came into Dartmouth,
where wee found the Mooneshine being come in not
two houres before.

The second voyage attempted by M. John Davis
    with others, for the discovery of the North-
    west passage, in Anno 1586.

He 7. day of May, I departed from the
port of Dartmouth for the discovery of
the Northwest passage, with a ship of an
hundred and twentie tunnes named the
Mermayd, a barke of 60. tunnes named
the Sunneshine, a barke of 35. tunnes
named the Mooneshine, and a pinnesse
of tenne tunnes named the North starre.

And the 15. of June I discovered land in the latitude of 60. degrees, and in longitude from the Meridian of London Westward 47. degrees, mightily pestered with yce and snow, so that there was no hope of landing: the yce lay in some places tenne leagues, in some 20. and in some 50. leagues off the shore, so that wee were constrained to beare into 57. degrees to double the same, and to recover a free Sea, which through Gods favourable mercy we at length obtained.

The 29. of June after many tempestuous storms we againe discovered land, in longitude from the Meridian of London 58. degr. 30. min. and in latitude 64. being East from us: into which course sith it please God by contrary winds to force us, I thought it very necessary to beare in with it, & there to set up our pinnesse, provided in the Mermayd to be our scout for this discovery, and so much the rather because the yere before I had bene in the same place, and found it very convenient for such a purpose, wel stored with flote wood, & possessed by a people of tractable conversation: so that the 29. of this moneth we arrived within the Isles which lay before this land, lying North northwest, and South southeast, we know not how farre. This land is very high & mountainous, having before it on the West side a mighty company of Isles full of faire sounds, and harboroughs. This land was very litle troubled with snow, and the sea altogether voyd of yce.

The ships being within the sounds wee sent our boates to search for shole water, where wee might anker, which in this place is very hard to finde: and as the boat went sounding and searching, the people of the countrey having espied them, came in their Canoas towards them with many shoutes and cries: but after they had espied in the boat some of our company that were the yeere before here with us, they presently rowed to the boate, and tooke hold on the oare, and hung about the boate with such comfortable joy, as would require a long discourse to be uttered: they came with the boates to our ships, making signes that they knewe all those that the yeere before had bene with them. After I perceived their joy and small feare of us, my selfe with the Merchants & others of the company went a shoare, bearing with me twentie knives: I had no sooner landed, but they lept out of their Canoas and came running to mee and the rest, and embraced us with many signes of heartie welcome: at this present there were eighteene of them, and to eche of them I gave a knife: they offred skinnes to me for reward, but I made signes that they were not solde, but given them of courtesie: and so dismissed them for that time, with signes that they should returne againe after certaine houres.

Gentle and loving Savages.

The next day with all possible speede the pinnesse was landed upon an Isle there to be finished to serve our purpose for the discoverie, which Isle was so convenient for that purpose, as that we were very wel able to defend our selves against many enemies. During the time that the pinnesse, was there setting up, the people came continually unto us sometime an hundred Canoas at a time, sometime fourtie, fiftie, more and lesse, as occasion served. They brought with them seale skinnes, stagge skinnes, white hares, Seale fish, samon peale, smal cod, dry caplin, with other fish, and birds such as the countrey did yeeld.

An 100 Canoas with divers commodities.

My selfe still desirous to have a further search of this place, sent one of the shipboates to one part of the lande, and my selfe went to another part to search for the habitation of this people, with straight commandement that there should be no injurie offered to any of the people, neither any gunne shot.

[III. 104.]

The boates that went from me found the tents of the people made with seale skinnes set up upon timber, wherein they found great store of dried Caplin, being a litle fish no bigger then a pilchard: they found bags of Trane oyle, many litle images cut in wood, Seale skinnes in tan-tubs, with many other such trifles, whereof they diminished nothing.

Images, trane oyle, and Seale skins in tan tubs.

THE ENGLISH VOYAGES

They also found tenne miles within the snowy mounr-taines a plaine champion countrey, with earth and grasse, such as our moory and waste grounds of England are: they went up into a river (which in the narrowest place is two leagues broad) about ten leagues, finding it still to continue they knewe not howe farre: but I with my company tooke another river, which although at the first it offered a large inlet, yet it proved but a deepe bay, the ende whereof in foure houres I attained, and there leaving the boat well manned, went with the rest of my company three or foure miles into the countrey, but found nothing, nor saw any thing, save onely gripes, ravens, and small birds, as larkes and linnets.

The third of July I manned my boat, and went with fifty Canoas attending upon me up into another sound where the people by signes willed mee to goe, hoping to finde their habitation: at length they made signes that I should goe into a warme place to sleepe, at which place I went on shore, and ascended the toppe of an high hill to see into the countrey, but perceiving my labor vaine, I returned againe to my boat, the people still following me, and my company very diligent to attend us, and to helpe us up the rockes, and likewise downe: at length I was desirous to have our men leape with them, which was done, but our men did overleape them: from leaping they went to wrestling, we found them strong and nimble, and to have skil in wrestling, for they cast some of our men that were good wrestlers.

The fourth of July we lanched our pinnesse, and had fortie of the people to helpe us, which they did very willingly: at this time our men againe wrestled with them, and found them as before, strong and skilfull. This fourth of July the Master of the Mermayd went to certaine Ilands to store himselfe with wood, where *A grave with
a crosse layd
over.* he found a grave with divers buried in it, only covered with seale skinnes, having a crosse laid over them. The people are of good stature, wel in body proportioned, with small slender hands and feet, with broad visages,

and smal eyes, wide mouthes, the most part unbearded, *The Tartars*
great lips, and close toothed. Their custome is as often *and people of*
as they go from us, still at their returne to make a new *Japon are also*
truce, in this sort, holding his hand up to the Sun with *smal eyed.*
a lowd voice he crieth Ylyaoute, and striketh his brest
with like signes, being promised safety, he giveth credit.
These people are much given to bleed, and therefore
stop their noses with deeres haire, or the haire of an
elan. They are idolaters and have images great store,
which they weare about them, and in their boats, which
we suppose they worship. They are witches, and have
many kinds of inchantments, which they often used, but
to small purpose, thankes be to God.

Being among them at shore the fourth of July, one
of them making a long oration, beganne to kindle a fire
in this maner: he tooke a piece of a board wherein was
a hole halfe thorow: into that hole he puts the end of
a round stick like unto a bedstaffe, wetting the end
thereof in Trane, and in fashion of a turner with a piece *Their maner*
of lether, by his violent motion doeth very speedily *of kindling fire*
produce fire: which done, with turfes he made a fire, *like to theirs*
into which with many words and strange gestures, he *A fire made of*
put diverse things, which wee supposed to be a sacrifice: *turfes.*
my selfe and divers of my company standing by, they
were desirous to have me go into the smoke, I willed
them likewise to stand in the smoke, which they by no
meanes would do. I then tooke one of them, and thrust
him into the smoke, and willed one of my company to
tread out the fire, & to spurne it into the sea, which was
done to shew them that we did contemne their sorcery.
These people are very simple in all their conversation, *Great theeves.*
but marveilous theevish, especially for iron, which they
have in great account. They began through our lenitie
to shew their vile nature: they began to cut our cables:
they cut away the Moonelights boat from her sterne,
they cut our cloth where it lay to aire, though we did
carefully looke unto it, they stole our oares, a caliver, a
boare speare, a sword, with divers other things, wherat

the company and Masters being grieved, for our better securitie, desired me to dissolve this new friendship, and to leave the company of these theevish miscreants: whereupon there was a caliver shot among them, and immediatly upon the same a faulcon, which strange noice did sore amaze them, so that with speed they departed: notwithstanding their simplicitie is such, that within ten houres after they came againe to us to entreat peace; which being promised, we againe fell into a great league. They brought us Seale skinnes, and sammon peale, but seeing iron, they could in no wise forbeare stealing: which when I perceived, it did but minister unto mee an occasion of laughter, to see their simplicitie, and I willed that in no case they should bee any more

[III. 105.]

hardly used, but that our owne company should be the more vigilant to keepe their things, supposing it to be very hard in so short time to make them know their

Their rude diet.

evils. They eate all their meat raw, they live most upon fish, they drinke salt water, and eate grasse and ice with delight: they are never out of the water, but live in the nature of fishes, save only when dead sleepe taketh them, and then under a warme rocke laying his boat upon the

Their weapons.

land, hee lyeth downe to sleepe. Their weapons are all darts, but some of them have bow and arrowes and slings.

Strange nets.

They make nets to take their fish of the finne of a whale: they do all their things very artificially: and it should

These Islanders warre with the people of the maine.

seeme that these simple theevish Islanders have warre with those of the maine, for many of them are sore wounded, which wounds they received upon the maine land, as by signes they gave us to understand. We had

Copper oare.

among them copper oare, black copper, and red copper: they pronounce their language very hollow, and deepe in the throat: these words following we learned from them.

Their language.

Kesinyoh, Eate some.	Paaotyck, An oare.
Madlycoyte, Musicke.	Asanock, A dart.
Aginyoh, go fetch.	Sawygmeg, A knife.
Yliaoute, I meane no harme.	Uderah, A nose.
Ponameg, A boat.	Aoh, Iron.

JOHN DAVIS

Blete, An eye.
Unuicke, Give it.
Tuckloak, A stagge or ellan.
Panygmah, A needle.
Aob, The Sea.
Mysacoah, Wash it.
Lethicksaneg, A seale skinne.
Canyglow, Kisse me.
Ugnera, My sonne.
Acu, Shot.
Conah, Leape.
Maatuke, Fish.
Sambah, Below.
Maconmeg, Wil you have this.

Cocah, Go to him.
Aba, Fallen downe.
Icune, Come hither.
Awennye, Yonder.
Nugo, No.
Tucktodo, A fogge.
Lechiksah, A skinne.
Maccoah, A dart.
Sugnacoon, A coat.
Gounah, Come downe.
Sasobneg, A bracelet.
Ugnake, A tongue.
Ataneg, A seale.
Macuah, A beard.
Pignagogah, A threed.
Quoysah, Give it to me.

The 7. of July being very desirous to search the habitation of this countrey, I went myselfe with our new pinnesse into the body of the land, thinking it to be a firme continent, and passing up a very large river, a great flaw of winde tooke me, whereby wee were constrained to seeke succour for that night, which being had, I landed with the most part of my company, and went to the top of a high mountaine, hoping from thence to see into the countrey: but the mountaines were so many and so mighty as that my purpose prevailed not: whereupon I againe returned to my pinnesse, and willing divers of my company to gather muscles for my supper, whereof *Muscles.* in this place there was great store, my selfe having espied a very strange sight, especially to me that never before saw the like, which was a mighty whirlewinde taking up *A strange* the water in very great quantitie, furiously mounting it *whirlewinde.* into the aire, which whirlewinde, was not for a puffe or blast, but continual, for the space of three houres, with very little intermission, which sith it was in the course that I should passe, we were constrained that night to take up our lodging under the rockes.

The next morning the storme being broken up, we

went forward in our attempt, and sailed into a mighty great river directly into the body of the land, and in briefe, found it to be no firme land, but huge, waste, and Great Ilands. desert Isles with mighty sounds, and inlets passing betweene Sea and Sea. Whereupon we returned towards our shippes, and landing to stoppe a floud, wee found the burial of these miscreants; we found of their fish in bagges, plaices, and caplin dried, of which wee tooke onely one bagge and departed. The ninth of this moneth we came to our ships, where wee found the people desirous in their fashion, of friendship and barter: our Mariners complained heavily against the people, and said that my lenitie and friendly using of them gave them stomacke to mischiefe: for they have stollen an anker from us, they have cut our cable very dangerously, they have cut our boats from our sterne, and nowe since *Slings.* your departure, with slings they spare us not with stones of halfe a pound weight: and wil you stil indure these injuries? It is a shame to beare them. I desired them to be content, and said, I doubted not but al should be wel. The 10. of this moneth I went to the shore, the people following mee in their Canoas: I tolled them on shore, and used them with much courtesie, and then departed aboord, they following me, and my company. I gave some of them bracelets, & caused seven or eight [III. 106.] of them to come aboord, which they did willingly, and some of them went into the top of the ship: and thus curteously using them, I let them depart: the Sunne was no sooner downe, but they began to practise their devilish nature, and with slings threw stones very fiercely into the Moonelight, and strake one of her men then boatswaine, that he overthrew withall: where-at being moved, I changed my curtesie, and grew to hatred, my self in my owne boate well manned with shot, and the barks boat likewise pursued them, and gave them divers shot, but to small purpose, by reason of their swift rowing: so smally content we returned.

The 11. of this moneth there came five of them to make a new truce: the master of the Admiral came to me to shew me of their comming, and desired to have them taken and kept as prisoners untill we had his anker againe: but when he sawe that the chiefe ringleader and master of mischiefe was one of the five, he then was vehement to execute his purpose, so it was determined to take him: he came crying Iliaout, and striking his brest offered a paire of gloves to sell, the master offered him a knife for them: so two of them came to us, the one was not touched, but the other was soone captive among us: then we pointed to him and his fellowes for our anker, which being had, we made signes that he should be set at libertie: within one houre after he came aboord the winde came faire, whereupon we weyed and set saile, and so brought the fellow with us: one of his fellowes still following our ship close aboord, talked with him and made a kinde of lamentation, we still using him wel with Yliaout, which was the common course of curtesie. At length this fellow aboord us spake foure or five words unto the other and clapped his two hands upon his face, whereupon the other doing the like, departed as we suppose with heavie chere. We judged the covering of his face with his hands and bowing of his body downe, signified his death. At length he became a pleasant companion among us. I gave him a new sute of frize after the English fashion, because I saw he could not indure the colde, of which he was very joyfull, he trimmed up his darts, and all his fishing tooles, and would make okam, and set his hand to a ropes end upon occasion. He lived with the dry Caplin that I tooke when I was searching in the pinnis, and did eate dry Newland fish.

One of the people taken which after dyed.

All this while, God be thanked, our people were in very good health, onely one young man excepted, who dyed at sea the fourteenth of this moneth, and the fifteenth, according to the order of the sea, with praise given to God by service, was cast overboord.

*A huge quan-
titie of yce in
63. degrees of
latitude.*

The 17 of this moneth being in the latitude of 63. degres 8. minuts, we fell upon a most mighty and strange quantitie of yce in one intire masse, so bigge as that we knew not the limits thereof, and being withall so very high in forme of a land, with bayes and capes and like high cliffe land, as that we supposed it to be land, and therefore sent our pinnesse off to discover it: but at her returne we were certainely informed that it was onely yce, which bred great admiration to us all considering the huge quantitie thereof, incredible to be reported in trueth as it was, and therefore I omit to speake any further thereof. This onely I thinke, that the like before was never seene: and in this place we had very stickle and strong currents.

We coasted this mightie masse of yce untill the 30 of July, finding it a mighty barre to our purpose: the ayre in this time was so contagious and the sea so pestered with yce, as that all hope was banished of proceeding: for the 24 of July all our shrowds, ropes and sailes were so frosen, and compassed with yce,
onely by a grosse fogge, as seemed to me more then strange, sith the last yeere I found this sea free and navigable, without impediments.

Our men through this extremity began to grow sicke and feeble, and withall hopelesse of good suc-cesse: whereupon very orderly, with good discretion they intreated me to regard the state of this busines, and withall advised me, that in conscience I ought to regard the saftie of mine owne life with the preserva-tion of theirs, and that I should not through my over-boldnes leave their widowes and fatherlesse children to give me bitter curses. This matter in conscience did greatly move me to regard their estates: yet consider-ing the excellencie of the businesse if it might be attained, the great hope of certaintie by the last yeeres discovery, and that there was yet a third way not put in practise, I thought it would growe to my great disgrace, if this action by my negligence should grow into discredite: whereupon seeking helpe from God, the fountaine of all mercies, it pleased his divine majestie to move my heart to prosecute that which I hope shal be to his glory, and to the contentation of every Christian minde. Whereupon falling into consideration that the Mermaid, albeit a very strong & sufficient ship, yet by reason of her burthen was not so convenient and nimble as a smaller bark, especially in such desperate hazzards: further having in account her great charge to the adventurers being at 100.li. the moneth, and that in doubtfull service: all the premisses considered with divers other things, I determined to furnish the Moonelight with revictualling and sufficient men, and to proceede in this action as God should direct me. Whereupon I altered our course from the yce, and bare Eastsoutheast to recover the next shore where this thing might be performed: so with favourable winde it pleased God that the first of August we discovered the land in Latitude 66. degrees, 33. min. [III. 107.] and in longitude from the Meridian of London 70. degrees voyd of trouble without snow or ice.

The second of August wee harboured our selves in a very excellent good road, where with all speed we graved the Moonelight, and revictualled her: wee searched this countrey with our pinnesse while the barke was trimming, which William Eston did: he found all this land to be onely Ilands, with a Sea on the East, a Sea on the West, and a Sea on the North. In this place wee found it very hot, and wee were very much troubled *Great heat.* with a flie which is called Muskyto, for they did sting grievously. The people of this place at our first comming in caught a Seale, and with bladders fast tied to him sent him unto us with the floud, so as hee came right with our shippes, which we tooke as a friendly present from them.

The fift of August I went with the two Masters and others to the toppe of a hill, and by the way William

Eston espied three Canoas lying under a rocke, and went unto them : there were in them skinnes, darts, with divers superstitious toyes, whereof wee diminished nothing, but left upon every boat a silke point, a bullet of lead, and a pinne. The next day being the sixt of August, the people came unto us without feare, and did barter with us for skinnes, as the other people did : they differ not from the other, neither in their Canoas nor apparel, yet is their pronuntiation more plaine then the others, and nothing hollow in the throat. Our Savage aboord us kept himselfe close, and made shew that he would faine have another companion. Thus being provided, I departed from this lande the twelft of August at sixe of the clocke in the morning, where I left the Mermayd at an anker : the fourteenth sailing West about fiftie leagues, we discovered land, being in latitude

66. degrees
19. minutes.

66. degrees 19 minuts : this land is 70. leagues from the other from whence we came. This fourteenth day from nine a clocke at night till three a clocke in the morning, wee ankered by an Iland of yce, twelve leagues off the shore, being mored to the yce.

The fifteenth day at three a clocke in the morning we departed from this land to the South, and the eighteenth of August we discovered land Northwest from us in the morning, being a very faire promontory, in latitude 65. degrees, having no land on the South.

Great hope of
a passage.

Here wee had great hope of a through passage.

This day at three a clocke in the afternoone wee againe discovered lande Southwest and by South from us, where at night wee were becalmed. The nineteenth of this moneth at noone, by observation, we were in

64. degr. 20.
min.

64. degrees 20. minuts. From the eighteenth day at noone unto the nineteenth at noone, by precise ordinary care, wee had sailed 15. leagues South and by West, yet by art and more exact observation, we found our course to be Southwest, so that we plainely perceived

A great cur-
rent to the
West.

a great current striking to the West.

This land is nothing in sight but Isles, which increaseth our hope. This nineteenth of August at six a clocke in the afternoone, it began to snow, and so continued all night with foule weather, and much winde, so that we were constrained to lie at hull all night five leagues off the shore: In the morning being the twentieth of August, the fogge and storme breaking up, we bare in with the lande, and at nine a clocke in the morning wee ankered in a very faire and safe road and lockt for all weathers. At tenne of the clocke I went on shore to the toppe of a very high hill, where I perceived that this land was Islands: at foure *Ilands.* of the clocke in the afternoone wee weyed anker, having a faire North northeast winde, with very faire weather; at six of the clocke we were cleare without the land, and so shaped our course to the South, to discover the coast, whereby the passage may be through Gods mercy found.

We coasted this land till the eight and twentieth of *They runne 8.* August, finding it still to continue towards the South, *dayes South-* from the latitude of 67. to 57. degrees: we found *ward from 67* marveilous great store of birds, guls and mewes, incredible *upon the coast.* to be reported, whereupon being calme weather, we lay one glasse upon the lee, to prove for fish, in which space we caught 100. of cod, although we were but badly provided for fishing, not being our purpose. This eight and twentieth having great distrust of the weather, we arrived in a very faire harbour in the latitude of 56. *A harborough* degrees, and sailed 10. leagues into the same, being two *in 56. degrees.* leagues broad, with very faire woods on both sides: in this place wee continued until the first of September, in which time we had two very great stormes. I landed, & went sixe miles by ghesse into the countrey, and found that the woods were firre, pineapple, alder, yew, withy, *Faire woods.* and birch: here wee saw a blacke beare: this place yeeldeth great store of birds, as fezant, partridge, Barbary hennes or the like, wilde geese, ducks, black birdes, jeyes, thrushes, with other kinds of small birds. Of the partridge and fezant we killed great store with bow and arrowes: in this place at the harborough mouth we found great store of cod.

The first of September at tenne a clocke wee set saile, and coasted the shore with very faire weather. The thirde day being calme, at noone we strooke saile, and

let fall a cadge anker, to prove whether we could take any fish, being in latitude 54. degrees 30. minuts, in which place we found great abundance of cod, so that the hooke was no sooner overboord, but presently a fish was taken. It was the largest and the best fed fish that ever I sawe, and divers fisher men that were with me sayd that they never saw a more suavle or better skull of fish in their lives: yet had they seene great abundance.

The fourth of September at five a clocke in the afternoone we ankered in a very good road among great store of Isles, the countrey low land, pleasant and very full of fayre woods. To the North of this place eight leagues,

we had a perfect hope of the passage, finding a mightie great sea passing betweene two lands West. The South land to our judgement being nothing but Isles: we greatly desired to goe into this sea, but the winde was directly against us. We ankered in foure fathome fine sand. In this place is foule and fish mightie store.

The sixt of September having a faire Northnorthwest winde, having trimmed our Barke we purposed to depart, and sent five of our sailers yong men a shore to an Island, to fetch certaine fish which we purposed to weather, and therefore left it al night covered upon the Isle: the brutish people of this countrey lay secretly lurking in the wood, and upon the sudden assaulted our men: which when we perceived, we presently let slip our cables upon the halse, and under our foresaile bare into the shoare, and with all expedition discharged a double musket upon them twise, at the noyse whereof they fled: notwithstanding to our very great griefe, two of our men

were slaine with their arrowes, and two grievously wounded, of whom at this present we stand in very great doubt, onely one escaped by swimming, with an arrow shot thorow his arme. These wicked miscreants never offered parly or speech, but presently executed their cursed fury.

This present evening it pleased God further to increase our sorowes with a mighty tempestuous storme, the winde being Northnortheast, which lasted unto the tenth of this moneth very extreme. We unrigged our ship, and purposed to cut downe our masts, the cable of our shutanker brake, so that we onely expected to be driven on shoare among these Canibals for their pray. Yet in this deepe distresse the mightie mercie of God, when hope was past, gave us succour, and sent us a faire lee, so as we recovered our anker againe, and newe mored our ship: where we saw that God manifestly delivered us: for the straines of one of our cables were broken, and we only roade by an olde junke. Thus being freshly mored a new storme arose, the winde being Westnorthwest, very forcible, which lasted unto the tenth day at night.

The eleventh day with a faire Westnorthwest winde we departed with trust in Gods mercie, shaping our course for England, and arrived in the West countrey in the beginning of October.

Master Davis being arrived, wrote his letter to M. William Sanderson of London, concerning his voyage, as followeth.

Ir, the Sunneshine came into Dartmouth the fourth of this moneth : she hath bene at Island, and from thence to Groenland, and so to Estotiland, from thence to Desolation, and to our Marchants, where she made trade with the people, staying in the countrey twentie dayes. They have brought home five hundred seale skinnes, and an hundred and fortie halfe skinnes and pieces of skinnes. I stand in great doubt of the pinnesse, God be mercifull

unto the poore men, and preserve them, if it be his blessed will.

I have now experience of much of the Northwest part of the world, & have brought the passage to that likelihood, as that I am assured it must bee in one of foure places, or els not at all. And further I can assure you upon the perill of my life, that this voyage may be performed without further charge, nay with certaine profite to the adventurers, if I may have but your favour in the action. I hope I shall finde favour with you to see your Card. I pray God it be so true as the Card shal be which I will bring you: and I hope in God, that your skill in Navigation shall be gaineful unto you, although at the first it hath not proved so. And thus with my humble commendations I commit you to God, desiring no longer to live, then I shall be yours most faithfully to command. Exon this fourteenth of October. 1586.

Yours to command

JOHN DAVIS.

[III. 109.] The relation of the course which the Sunshine a barke of fiftie tunnes, and the Northstarre a small pinnesse, being two vessels of the fleete of M. John Davis, helde after hee had sent them from him to discover the passage betweene Groenland and Island, written by Henry Morgan servant to M. William Sanderson of London.

May.

He seventh day of May 1586. wee departed out of Dartmouth haven foure sailes, to wit, the Mermaid, the Sunshine, the Mooneshine, & the Northstarre. In the Sunshine were sixteene men, whose names were these: Richard Pope Master, Marke Carter Masters mate, Henry Morgan Purser, George Draward, John Mandie, Hugh Broken, Philip Jane, Hugh Hempson, Richard Borden,

John Philpe, Andrew Madock, William Wolcome, Robert Wag carpenter, John Bruskome, William Ashe, Simon Ellis.

Our course was Westnorthwest the seventh and eight dayes: and the ninth day in the morning we were on head of the Tarrose of Silley. Thus coasting along the South part of Ireland the 11. day, we were on head of the Dorses: and our course was Southsouthwest untill sixe of the clocke the 12. day. The 13. day our course was Northwest. We remained in the company of the Mermaid and the Mooneshine until we came to the latitude of 60. degrees: and there it seemed best to our Generall M. Davis to divide his fleete, himself sayling to the Northwest, and to direct the Sunshine, wherein I was, and the pinnesse called the Northstarre, to seeke a passage Northward betweene Groenland and Island to the latitude of 80. degrees, if land did not let us. So the seventh day of June wee departed from them: and the ninth of the same we came to a firme land of yce, which we coasted along the ninth, the tenth, and the eleventh dayes of June: and the eleventh day at sixe of the clocke at night we saw land which was very high, which afterward we knew to be Island: and the twelft day we harboured there, and found many people: the land lyeth East and by North in 66. degrees.

M. Davis in the latitude of 60. deg. divideth his fleete into 2. parts.

The 7. of June.

Island descryed.

66. degrees.

Their commodities were greene fish, and Island lings, and stockfish, and a fish which is called Scatefish: of all which they had great store. They had also kine, sheep and horses, and hay for their cattell, and for their horses. Wee saw also their dogs. Their dwelling houses were made on both sides with stones, and wood layd crosse over them, which was covered over with turfes of earth, and they are flat on the tops, and many of these stood hard by the shore. Their boates were made with wood and yron all along the keele like our English boates: and they had nayles for to naile them withall, and fish-hookes and other things for to catch fish as we have here in England. They had also brasen kettles, and girdles

Their commodities.

Their dwell-ings.

Their boats,

and purses made of leather, and knoppes on them of copper, and hatchets, and other small tooles as necessary as we have. They drie their fish in the Sun, and when they are dry, they packe them up in the top of their houses. If we would goe thither to fishing more then we doe, we should make it a very good voyage: for wee got an hundreth greene fish in one morning. Wee found heere two English men with a shippe, which came out of England about Easter day of this present yeere 1586, and one of them came aboord of us, and brought us two

M. John Roydon of Ipswich. lambs. The English mans name was M. John Roydon of Ipswich marchant: hee was bound for London with his ship. And this is the summe of that which I

They departed from Island Northwest. observed in Island. We departed from Island the sixteenth day of June in the morning, and our course was Northwest, and we saw on the coast two small barkes going to an harborough: we went not to them, but saw them a farre off. Thus we continued our course unto the end of this moneth.

July. The third day of July we were in betweene two firme lands of yce, and passed in betweene them all that day untill it was night: and then the Master turned backe againe, and so away we went towards Groenland. And

Groneland discovered. the seventh day of July we did see Groenland, and it was very high, and it looked very blew: we could not come to harborough into the land, because we were hindered by a firme land as it were of yce, which was along the shoares side: but we were within three leagues of the land, coasting the same divers dayes together. The seventeenth day of July wee saw the place which our Captaine M.

The land of Desolation. John Davis the yeere before had named The land of Desolation, where we could not goe on shore for yce. The eighteenth day we were likewise troubled with yce, and went in amongst it at three of the clocke in the

Groenland coasted from the 7. till the last of July. morning. After wee had cleared our selves thereof, wee ranged all along the coast of Desolation untill the ende of the aforesayd moneth.

August. The third day of August we came in sight of Gilberts sound in the latitude of 64. deg. 15. min. which was the place where wee were appoynted to meete our Generall and the rest of our Fleete. Here we came to an harborough at 6. of the clocke at night.

The 4. day in the morning the Master went on shore [III. 110.] with 10. of his men, and they brought us foure of the people rowing in their boats aboord of the ship. And in the afternoone I went on shore with 6. of our men, and there came to us seven of them when we were on land. We found on shore three dead people, and two of them had their staves lying by them, and their olde skinnes wrapped about them and the other had nothing lying by, wherefore we thought it was a woman. We also saw their houses neere the Sea side, which were made with *The houses of* pieces of wood on both sides, and crossed over with poles *Gronland.* and then covered over with earth: we found Foxes running upon the hilles: as for the place it is broken land all the way that we went, and full of broken Islands.

The 21. of August the Master sent the boate on shore for wood with sixe of his men, and there were one and thirtie of the people of the countrey which went on shore to them, & they went about to kill them as we thought, for they shot their dartes towards them, and we that were aboord the ship, did see them goe on shore to our men: whereupon the Master sent the pinnesse after them, and when they saw the pinnesse comming towards them, they turned backe, and the Master of the pinnesse did shoote off a caliver to them the same time, but hurt none of them, for his meaning was onely to put them in feare. Divers times they did wave us on shore to play with them *Our men play* at the football, and some of our company went on shore *at footeball* to play with them, and our men did cast them downe as *with the* soone as they did come to strike the ball. And thus *Savages.* much of that which we did see and do in that harborough where we arrived first.

The 23. day wee departed from the Merchants Isle, where wee had beene first, and our course from thence was South & by West, and the wind was Northeast, and we ran that day and night about 5. or 6. leagues, untill we came to another harborough.

The 24. about eleven of the clocke in the forenoone wee entred into the aforesayd new harborow, and as wee came in, we did see dogs running upon the Islands. When we were come in, there came to us foure of the people which were with us before in the other harborough, and where we rode, we had sandie ground. We saw no wood growing, but found small pieces of wood upon the Islands, & some small pieces of sweete wood among the same. We found great Harts hornes, but could see none of the Stagges where we went, but we found their footings. As for the bones which we received of the Savages I cannot tell of what beasts they be.

Sweete wood found.

The stones that we found in the countrey were black, and some white, as I thinke they be of no value, neverthelesse I have brought examples of them to you.

The 30. of August we departed from this harborough towards England, & the wind tooke us contrary, so that we were faine to go to another harborough the same day at 11. of the clocke. And there came to us 39. of the people, and brought us 13. Seale skins, and after we received these skins of them, the Master sent the carpenter to change one of our boates which wee had bought of them before, and they would have taken the boate from him perforce, and when they sawe they could not take it from us, they shot with their dartes at us, and stroke one of our men with one of their dartes, and John Filpe shot one of them into the brest with an arrow. And they came to us againe, and foure of our men went into the shipboate, and they shot with their dartes at our men: but our men tooke one of their people in his boate into the shipboate, and he hurt one of them with his knife, but we killed three of them in their boates: two of them were hurt with arrowes in the brests,

A skirmish between the Savages and our men.

and he that was aboord our boat, was shot in with an arrow, and hurt with a sword, and beaten with staves, whome our men cast overboord, but the people caught him and carried him on shore upon their boates, and the other two also, and so departed from us. And three of them went on shore hard by us, where they had their dogs, and those three came away from their dogs, and presently one of their dogs came swimming towards us hard aboord the ship, whereupon our Master caused the Gunner to shoote off one of the great pieces towards the people, and so the dog turned backe to land and within an houre after there came of the people hard aboord the ship, but they would not come to us as they did come before.

The 31. of August we departed from Gylberts sound for England, and when we came out of the harborough there came after us 17. of the people looking which way we went.

The 2. of September we lost sight of the land at 12. of the clocke at noone. *September.*

The third day at night we lost sight of the Northstarre our pinnesse in a very great storme, and lay a hull tarying for them the 4. day, but could heare no more of them. Thus we shaped our course the 5. day South-southeast, and sayling untill the 27. of the sayd moneth, we came in sight of Cape Clere in Ireland. *The pinnesse never returned home.*

The 30. day we entred into our owne chanell.

The 2. of October we had sight of the Isle of Wight.

The 3. we coasted all along the shore, and the 4. and 5.

The 6. of the said moneth of October wee came into the river of Thames as high as Ratliffe in safetie God be thanked. [III. 111.]

[The third

The third voyage Northwestward, made by M.
John Davis Gentleman, as chiefe captaine &
Pilot generall, for the discovery of a passage
to the Isles of the Moluccas, or the coast of
China, in the yeere 1587. Written by M.
John Janes.

May.

He 19. of this present moneth about
midnight wee weyed our ankers, set
sayle, and departed from Dartmouth with
two Barkes and a Clincher, the one
named the Elizabeth of Dartmouth, the
other the Sunneshine of London, and the
Clincher called the Helene of London:
thus in Gods name we set forwards with the wind at
Northeast a good fresh gale. About 3. houres after our
departure, the night being somewhat thicke with darknesse, we had lost the pinnesse: the Captaine imagining
that the men had runne away with her, willed the Master
of the Sunshine to stand to Seawards, and see if we could
descry them, we bearing in with the shore for Plimmouth.
At length we descried her, bare with her, and demanded
what the cause was: they answered that the tiller of their
helme was burst. So shaping our course Westsouthwest,
we went forward, hoping that a hard beginning would
make a good ending, yet some of us were doubtfull of it,
falling in reckoning that she was a Clincher; neverthelesse we put our trust in God.

The 21. we met with the Red Lion of London, which
came from the coast of Spaine, which was afrayd that we
had bene men of warre, but we hailed them, and after a
little conference, we desired the Master to carie our
letters for London directed to my uncle Sanderson, who
promised us a safe deliverie. And after wee had heaved
them a lead and a line, whereunto wee had made fast our

letters, before they could get them into the ship, they fell into the Sea, and so all our labour and theirs also was lost; notwithstanding they promised to certifie our departure at London, and so we departed, and the same day we had sight of Silley. The 22. the wind was at Northeast by East with faire weather, and so the 23. and 24. the like. The 25. we layd our ships on the Lee for the Sunneshine, who was a romaging for a leake, they had 500. strokes at the pumpe in a watch, the wind at Northwest.

The 26. and 27. wee had faire weather, but this 27. the pinnesses foremast was blowen overboord. The 28. the Elizabeth towed the pinnesse, which was so much bragged off by the owners report before we came out of England, but at Sea she was like a cart drawen with oxen. Sometimes we towed her because she could not saile for scant wind.

The 31. day our Captaine asked if the pinnesse were stanch, Peerson answered that she was as sound and stanch as a cup. This made us something glad, when we sawe she would brooke the Sea, and was not leake.

June.

THe first 6. dayes wee had faire weather: after that for 5. dayes wee had fogge and raine, the winde being South. The 12. wee had cleare weather. The Mariners in the Sunneshine and the Master could not agree: the Mariners would goe on their voyage a fishing, because the yeere began to waste: the Master would not depart till hee had the companie of the Elizabeth, whereupon the Master told our Captaine that hee was afrayd his men would shape some contrary course while he was asleepe, and so he should lose us. At length after much talke and many threatnings, they were content to bring us to the land which we looked for daily.

The 14. day we discovered land at five of the clocke *Land descried.* in the morning, being very great and high mountaines, the tops of the hils being covered with snow. Here the wind was variable, sometimes Northeast, Eastnortheast, and East by North: but we imagined ourselves to be 16. or 17. leagues off from the shore.

The 16. we came to an anker about 4. or 5. of the clocke after nonne, the people came presently to us after the old maner, with crying Ilyaoute, and shewing us Seales skinnes. The 17. we began to set up the pinnesse that Peerson framed at Dartmouth, with the boords which hee brought from London.

The 18. Peerson and the Carpenters of the ships began to set on the plankes. The 19. as we went about an Island, were found blacke Pumise stones, and salt kerned on the rockes, very white and glistering. This day also the Master of the Sunneshine tooke of the people a very strong lusty yoong fellow.

Salt kerned on the rockes.

[III. 112.]

The 20. about two of the clocke in the morning, the Savages came to the Island where our pinnace was built readie to bee launched, and tore the two upper strakes, and carried them away onely for the love of the yron in the boords. While they were about this practise, we manned the Elizabeths boate to goe a shore to them: our men being either afrayd or amazed, were so long before they came to shore, that our Captaine willed them to stay, and made the Gunner give fire to a Saker, and layd the piece levell with the boate which the Savages had turned on the one side because wee should not hurt them with our arrowes, and made the boate their bulwarke against the arrowes which we shot at them. Our Gunner having made all things readie, gave fire to the piece, and fearing to hurt any of the people, and regarding the owners profite, thought belike hee would save a Sakers shot, doubting wee should have occasion to fight with men of warre, and so shot off the Saker without a bullet: we looking stil when the Savages that were hurt should run away without legs, at length wee could perceive never a man hurt, but all having their legges could carrie away their bodies: wee had no sooner shot off the piece, but the Master of the Sunneshine manned his boate, and came rowing toward the Island, the very sight of whom made each of them take that hee had gotten, and flee away as fast as they could to another Island about two miles off, where they tooke the nayles out of the timber, and left the wood on the Isle. when we came on shore, and saw how they had spoiled the boat, after much debating of the matter, we agreed that the Elizabeth should have her to fish with-all: whereupon she was presently caryed aboord, and stowed.

Now after this trouble, being resolved to depart with the first wind, there fell out another matter worse then all the rest, and that was in this maner. John Church-yard one whom our Captaine had appoynted as Pilot in the pinnace, came to our Captaine, and master Bruton, and told them that the good ship which we must all hazard our lives in, had three hundred strokes at one time as she rode in the harbour: This disquieted us all greatly, and many doubted to goe in her. At length our Captaine by whom we were all to be governed, deter-mined rather to end his life with credite, then to returne with infamie and disgrace, and so being all agreed, wee purposed to live and die together, and committed our selves to the ship. Now the 21. having brought all our things aboord, about 11. or 12. of the clocke at night, we set saile and departed from those Isles, which lie in 64. degrees of latitude, our ships being all now at Sea, and wee shaping our course to goe, coasting the land to the Northwards upon the Easterne shore, which we called the shore of our Marchants, because there we met with people which traffiqued with us, but here wee were not without doubt of our ship.

The 24. being in 67. degrees, and 40. minutes, wee had great store of Whales, and a kinde of sea birds which the Mariners call Cortinous. This day about sixe of the clocke at night, we espied two of the countrey people at Sea, thinking at the first they had bene two great Seales, untill wee sawe their oares

Isles in 64. degrees.

Store of Whales in 67 degrees.

glistering with the Sunne: they came rowing towardes us, as fast as they could, and when they came within hearing, they held up their oares, and cryed Ilyaoute, making many signes: and at last they came to us, giving us birdes for bracelets, and of them I had a darte with a bone in it, or a piece of Unicorns horne, as I did judge. This dart he made store of, but when he saw a knife, he let it go, being more desirous of the knife then of his dart: these people continued rowing after our ship the space of 3. howres.

The 25. in the morning at 7. of the clocke we descried 30. Savages rowing after us, being by judgement 10. leagues off from the shore: they brought us Salmon Peales, Birdes, and Caplin, and we gave them pinnes, needles, bracelets, nailes, knives, bels, looking glasses, and other small trifles, and for a knife, a naile or a bracelet, which they call Ponigmah, they would sell their boate, coates, or any thing they had, although they were farre from the shore. Wee had but few skinnes of them, about 20. but they made signes to us that if wee would goe to the shore, wee should have more store of Chichsanege: they stayed with us till 11. of the clocke, at which time wee went to prayer, and they departed from us.

The 28. and 29. were foggie with cloudes, the 30. day wee tooke the heigth, and found our selves in 72. degrees and 12 minutes of latitude both at noone and at night, the Sunne being 5. degrees above the Horizon. At midnight the compasse set to the variation of 28. degrees to the Westward. Now having coasted the land, which wee called London coast, from the 21. of this present, till the 30. the Sea open all to the Westwards and Northwards, the land on starboord side East from us, the winde shifted to the North, whereupon we left that shore, naming the same Hope Sanderson, and shaped our course West, and ranne 40. leagues and better without the sight of any land.

72. deg. 12. min.

The great variation of the compasse.
London coast.
Betweene Gronland & the North of America above 40. leagues.

July.

THe second of July wee fell with a mightie banke of yce West from us, lying North and South, which banke wee would gladly have doubled out to the Northwards, but the winde would not suffer us, so that we were faine to coast it to the Southwards, hoping to double it out, that wee might have run so farre West till wee had found land, or els to have beene thorowly resolved of our pretended purpose. *A mightie banke of yce lying North and South.*

The 3. wee fell with the yce againe, and putting off from it, we sought to the Northwards, but the wind crossed us.

The 4. was foggie: so was the 5. also with much wind at the North.

The 6. being very cleare, we put our barke with oares through a gap in the yce, seeing the Sea free on the West side, as we thought, which falling out otherwise, caused us to returne after we had stayed there betweene the yce. The 7. and the 8. about midnight, by Gods helpe we recovered the open Sea, the weather being faire and calme, and so was the 9. The 10. we coasted the yce. The 11. was foggie, but calme.

The 12. we coasted againe the yce, having the wind at Northnorthwest. The 13. bearing off from the yce, we determined to goe with the shoare and come to an anker, and to stay 5. or 6. dayes for the dissolving of the yce, hoping that the Sea continually beating it, and the Sunne with the extreme force of heat which it had alwayes shining upon it, would make a quicke dispatch, that we might have a further search upon the Westerne shore. Now when we were come to the Easterne coast, the water something deepe, and some of our companie fearefull withall, we durst not come to an anker, but bare off into the Sea againe. The poore people seeing us goe away againe, came rowing after us into the Sea, the waves being somewhat loftie. We truckt with them for a few skinnes and dartes, and gave them beads, nailes, pinnes, *Extreme heate of the Sunne.*

needles and cardes, they poynting to the shore, as though they would shew us some great friendship: but we little regarding their curtesie, gave them the gentle farewell, and so departed.

The 14. wee had the wind at South. The 15. there was some fault either in the barke, or the set of some current, for wee were driven sixe points beyond our course West. The 16. wee fell with the banke of yce West from us. The 17. and 18. were foggie. The 19. at one a clocke after noone, wee had sight of the land which we called Mount Raleigh, and at 12. of the clocke at night, we were thwart the streights which we discovered the first yeere. The 20. wee traversed in the mouth of the streight, the wind being at West, with faire and cleare weather. The 21. and 22. wee coasted the Northerne coast of the streights. The 23. having sayled threescore leagues Northwest into the streights, at two a clocke after noone wee ankered among many Isles in the bottome of the gulfe, naming the same The Earle of Cumberlands Isles, where riding at anker, a Whale passed by our ship and went West in among the Isles. Heere the compasse set at thirtie degrees Westward variation. The 23. wee departed, shaping our course Southeast to recover the Sea. The 25. wee were becalmed in the bottome of the gulfe, the ayre being extreme hot. Master Bruton and some of the Mariners went on shoare to course dogs, where they found many Graves and Trane spilt on the ground, the dogs being so fat that they were scant able to run.

The 26. wee had a prety storme, the winde being at Southeast. The 27. and 28. were faire. The 29. we were cleare out of the streights, having coasted the South shore, and this day at noone we were in 62. degrees of latitude. The 30. in the afternoone wee coasted a banke of yce, which lay on the shore, and passed by a great banke or Inlet, which lay between 63. and 62. degrees of latitude, which we called Lumlies Inlet. We had oftentimes, as we sailed alongst the coast, great ruttes, the

They were driven West sixe points out of their course in 67. degrees, 45. minutes. Mount Raleigh.

The Earle of Cumberlands Isles.

The variation of the compasse 30. deg. Westward.

The land trendeth from this place Southwest and by South. My lord Lumleys Inlet.

water as it were whirling and overfalling, as if it were the fall of some great water through a bridge.

The 31. as we sayled by a Headland, which we named Warwicks Foreland, we fell into one of those overfals *Warwicks* with a fresh gale of wind, and bearing all our sailes, wee *Foreland.* looking upon an Island of yce betweene us and the shoare, had thought that our barke did make no way, which caused us to take markes on the shoare: at length wee perceived our selves to goe very fast, and the Island of yce which we saw before, was carried very forcibly with the set of the current faster then our ship went. *A very forcible* This day and night we passed by a very great gulfe, the *current West-* water whirling and roaring as it were the meetings of *ward.* tydes.

August.

[III. 114.]

THe first of August having coasted a banke of ice which was driven out at the mouth of this gulfe, we fell with the Southermost cape of the gulfe, which we named Chidleis cape, which lay in 61 degrees and 10 minutes of *Chidleys cape.* latitude. The 2 and 3 were calme and foggie, so were the 4, 5, and 6. The 7 was faire and calme: so was the 8, with a litle gale in the morning. The 9 was faire, and we had a litle gale at night. The 10 we had a frisking gale at Westnorthwest. The 11 faire. The 12 we saw five deere on the top of an Island, called by us Darcies *The lord Dar-* Island. And we hoised out our boat, and went ashore to *cies Island.* them, thinking to have killed some of them. But when we came on shore, and had coursed them twise about the Island, they tooke the sea and swamme towards Islands distant from that three leagues. When we perceived that they had taken the sea we gave them over because our boat was so small that it could not carrie us, and rowe after them, they swamme so fast: but one of them was as bigge as a good prety Cow, and very fat, their feet as bigge as Oxe feet. Here upon this Island I killed with my piece a gray hare.

The 13 in the morning we saw three or foure white

421

beares, but durst not go on shore to them for lacke of a good boat. This day we stroke a rocke seeking for an harborow, and received a leake: and this day we were in 54 degrees of latitude.

The 14 we stopt our leake in a storme not very outragious, at noone.

The 15 being almost in 52 degrees of latitude, and not finding our ships, nor (according to their promise) any kinde of marke, token, or beacon, which we willed them to set up, and they protested to do so upon every head land, Island or cape, within twenty leagues every way off *The fishing* from their fishing place, which our captaine appointed to *place betweene* be betweene 54 and 55 degrees: This 15 I say we shaped *54 and 55 de-* our course homewards for England, having in our ship *grees of lati-* but litle wood, and halfe a hogshead of fresh water. Our *tude.* men were very willing to depart, and no man more forward then Peerson, for he feared to be put out of his office of stewardship: but because every man was so willing to depart, we consented to returne for our owne countrey: and so we had the 16 faire weather, with the winde at Southwest.

The 17 we met a ship at sea, and as farre as we could judge it was a Biskaine: we thought she went a fishing *Abundance of* for whales; for in 52 degrees or thereabout we saw very *whales in 52* many. *degrees.*

The 18 was faire, with a good gale at West.

The 19 faire also, with much winde at West and by South.

And thus after much variable weather and change of *They arrive at* winds we arrived the 15 of September in Dartmouth *Dartmouth the* anno 1587, giving thanks to God for our safe arrivall. *15 of Sep-* *tember.*

A letter of the sayd M. John Davis written to M. Sanderson of London concerning his fore-written voyage.

Ood M. Sanderson, with Gods great mercy I have made my safe returne in health, with all my company, and have sailed threescore leagues further then my determination at my departure. I have bene in 73 degrees, finding the sea all open, and forty leagues betweene land and land. The passage is most probable, the execution easie, as at my comming you shall fully know.

Yesterday the 15 of September I landed all weary; therefore I pray you pardon my shortnesse.

Sandridge this 16 of September anno 1587.

Yours equall as mine owne, which

by triall you shall best know,

JOHN DAVIS.

[A Traverse-Booke

[III. 115.] A Traverse-Booke made by M. John Davis in west passage.

Moneth. May.	Dayes.	Houres.	Course.	Leagues.	Elevation of the pole. Deg.	Min.	The winde.
	19		W. S. W. Westerly.		50	30	N. E.
	20						
	21	35	W. S. W. Westerly.	50	50		N. E.
	22	15	W. N. W.	14			N. E. by E.
	22	6	W. N. W.	6			N. E. by E.
	22	3	W. N. W.	2			
	23	15	N. W. by W.	18			N. E.
	23	39	W. N. W.	36	50	40	
		3	W. N. W.	2			N. N. E.
		6	N. W. by W.	5			N. E. by N.
		3	W. N. W.	3			N. N. E.
		12	W. N. W.	12			N. E.
Noone the	24	24	W. N. W. Northerly.	25	51	16	
		3	W. N. W.	3			N. N. E.
		3	W. N. W.	$2\frac{1}{2}$			N. by E.
		6	W. by N.	5			N.
		6	W. by N.	5			N.
		2	S.	$\frac{1}{2}$			N.
Noone the	25	24	W. by N.	20	51	30	
		3	W.	3			N. N. W.
		3	W. S. W.	2			N. W.
		1	S. W.	1			W. N. W.
		2	W. N. W.	$1\frac{1}{2}$			N.
		3	W. N. W.	$1\frac{1}{2}$			N.
		3					Calme.
		4	W. N. W.	4			S. S. E.
		5	W.	6			S. S. E.

his third voyage for the discoverie of the North-
Anno 1587.

THE DISCOURSE.

This day we departed from Dartmouth at two of the clocke at night.

This day we descried Silly N. W. by W. from us.

This day at noone we departed from Silly.

The true course, distance and latitude.

The true course, distance, and latitude.

Now we lay upon the lee for the Sunshine, which had taken a leake of 500 strokes in a watch.

The true course, distance and latitude.

Moneth. May.	Dayes.	Houres.	Course.	Leagues.	Elevation of the pole.		The winde.
					Deg.	Min.	
Noone the	26	24	W. by N. Westerly.	23	51	40	
		11	W.	16			S. S. E.
		6	W. N. W.	2			S. S. E.
		7	W.	5			S. E.
Noone the	27	24	W. Northerly.	23			
Noone the	28	24	W.	20	52	13	E. S. E.
Noone the	28	28	W. by N. Northerly.	43	52	13	
Noone the	29	24	N. W.	30			S. by E.
		6	N. W.	10			S.
		3	N. by W.	2			W. by N.
		3	W. by N.	3			W. by S.
		12	N. W.	12			S. S. W.
Noone the	30	48	N. W. by N.	65	54	50	
		9	N. W.	12			S. W.
		9	N. W. by W.	12			S. S. W.
		3	W. N. W.	3			N. N. E.
		3	W. by N.	4			N.
	30	24	W. N. W. Northerly.	27	55	30	
June	1	12	W.	10			N. N. W.
		9	N. W.	8			E. N. E.
		3	N. W.	2½			E. N. E.
	1	24	W. N. W. Westerly.	17	55	45	
		12	N. W.	16			E. S. E.
		6	N. W.	7			S.
		6	N. W.	8			S. S. W.
Noone the	2	24	N. W. Northerly.	32	56	55	
Noone the	5	72	W. by S. southerly.	45	56	20	
Noone the	6	24	S. W.	16			W. N. W.
		7	S. W. by W.	6			W. by N.

THE DISCOURSE.

The true course, distance, &c.

We lay at hull with much winde, raine, and fog.

The common course supposed.

We towed the pinnesse 18 houres of this day.

The true course, distance, &c.

The true course, &c.

The true course, &c.

The true course, &c.

The true course, &c.

The true course, &c. drawen from divers traverses.

427

Moneth. June.	Dayes.	Houres.	Course.	Leagues.	Elevation of the pole.		The winde.
					Deg.	Min.	
		5					Calme.
		3	W. N. W.	1			S.
Noone the	7	9	W. N. W.	12			S.
		12	W. N. W.	20			S.
		3	W. N. W.	4			S.
Noone the	8	9	W. N. W.	7			S.
		12	W. N. W.	5			S.
Noone the	9	12	W. N. W.	13			S. E.
Noone the	9	96	W. by N. northerly.	86	57	30	
		3	W. N. W.	4			S. E.
		3	W. N. W.	2			S. E.
		6	W. N. W.	1			Calme.
Noone the	10	12	W. N. W.	$16\frac{1}{2}$			E.
		7	W. N. W.	12			E.
		2	N. W.	2			E.
Noone the	11	15	N. W.	18			E. N. E.
		12	N. W.	12			E. N. E.
		12	N. W.	13			E. by S.
Noone the	12	72	N. W. by W. northerly.	78	59	50	
Noone the	13	24	N. N. W. Westerly.	26	60	58	E. by N.
Noone the	14	24	N. N. W.	32	62	30	N. E.
		9	W. N. W.	7			N.
		3	N. W.	2			N. N. E.
		3	N. W. by N.	2			N. E. by N.
	15	9	N. N. W.	8			N. E.
Noone the	15	24	N. W. Northerly.	23	63	20	

THE DISCOURSE.

The true course, distance, & latitude for 96 houres.

The true course, &c. for 72 houres.

This day in the morning at five of the clocke we discovered land being distant from us at the neerest place sixteene leagues.   This land in generall lay Northwest and to the Westwards, being very mountainous. The winde was this day variable, and the aire sometime foggie, and sometime cleere.   The foresayd land bare from us (so neere as we could judge) North, Northwest, and Southeast.

The true course, &c.

Moneth. June.	Dayes.	Houres.	Course.	Leagues.	Elevation of the pole.		The winde.
					Deg.	Min.	
Noone the 16	24		N. N. E. Easterly.	14	64		
17							
20							
*At mid- night ye 21	8		W. N. W.	7			S. E.
Noone the 22	4		N. W.	6			S. E.
13			N. W.	18			S. E.
11			N.	13			S. E.
Noone the 23	36		N. W. by N.	42	65	40	
Noone the 24	24		N. by E. Northerly.	41	67	40	S. S. E.
25							
Noone the 26	48		N.				S.
3			N. W.	2			S. W.
7			N. N. E.	10			S.
6			·N.	8			S. W.
8			W. N. W.	5			S. E.
Noone the 27	72		N. Westerly.	52	70	4	
Noone the 30	72		N.	43	72	12	
30							
July 1	30		W. by S. Westerly.	44	71	36	N. W. by N.
2	24		S. E.	12	71	9	
Noone the 3	8		N. N. W.	11	71	40	N.
Noone the 5	48		S. S. E.	36	70		N.

[III. 117.]

THE DISCOURSE.

The true course, &c. This 16 of June at 5 of the clocke in the after-noone, being in the latitude of 64 degrees, through Gods helpe we came to an anker among many low islands which lay before the high land. This 17 of June we set up our pinnesse. The 20 she was spoiled by the Savages. At midnight the 21 of June wee departed from this coast, our two barks for their fishing voyage, and my selfe in the pinnesse for the discovery. From midnight the 21 we shaped our course as followeth.*

At this time we saw great store of whales.

The true course, &c.

The true course, &c. Here the weather was very hot. This 24 of June at 6 of the clocke at night we met two savages at sea in their small canoas, unto whom we gave bracelets, and nailes, for skins & birds. At 9 of the clocke they departed from us. The next day at 7 of the clocke in the morning, there came unto us 30 savages 20 leagues off the shore, intreating us to goe to the shore. We had of them fish, birds, skinnes, darts, and their coats from their backs, for bracelets, nailes, knives &c. They remained with us foure houres, and departed.

The true course, &c. for 72 houres.

The true course, &c. Since the 21 of this moneth I have continually coasted the shore of Gronland, having the sea all open towards the West, and the land on ye starboord side East from me. For these last 4 dayes the weather hath bene extreame hot and very calme, the Sun being 5 degrees above the horizon at midnight. The compasse in this place varieth 28 degrees towards ye West.

The true course, &c. This day at noone wee coasted a mighty banke of ice West from us.

This day we fell againe with the ice, seeking to double it out by the North.

The True course, &c.

Moneth. July.	Dayes.	Houres.	Course.	Leagues.	Elevation of the pole.		The winde.
					Deg.	Min.	
	6	24	S. S. W.	22	69		Variable.
	7						
	8						
Noone the	9	72	E. S. E.	7	68	50	Calme.
Noone the	10	24	S. E. by S.	8	68	30	E. by N.
Noone the	11	24	E. N. E.	11½	68	45	Variable.
Noone the	12	24	S. S. E.	16	68		N. N. W.
	13	24	E. by S.	20			S.
Noone the	14	24	W. by N.	11	67	50	S.
Noone the	15	24	W. S. W.	5	67	45	E.
Noone the	16	24	S. W. by W. westerly.	23	67	10	S.
Noone the	18	48	S. by W.	30	65	33	N. fog.
Noone the	19	24	W. southerly.	13	65	30	S. fog.
	20						
	23						
	24						
	25						

THE DISCOURSE.

The true course, &c. This 6 of July we put our barke thorow the ice, seeing the sea free on the West side : and having sailed 5 leagues West, we fell with another mighty barre, which we could not passe : and therefore returning againe, we freed our selves the 8 of this moneth at midnight, and so recovered the sea through Gods favour, by faire winds, the weather being very calme.

The true course, &c.

The true course, &c. This day we coasted the ice.

The true course, &c.

The true course, &c.

This day the people came to us off the shore, and bartered with us. Being within the Isles, & not finding good ankorage, we bare off againe into the sea.

The true course, &c.

The true course, &c. This day a great current set us West 6 points from our course.

The true course, &c. This day we fell w^t a mighty banke of ice West of us.

The true course, &c. Collected by divers experiments.

The true course, &c. This 19 of July at one a clocke in the afternoone we had sight of the land of Mount Ralegh, and by 12. of the clocke at night wee were thwart the Streights which (by Gods helpe) I discovered the first yere.

The 20 day wee traversed in the mouth of the sayd Streights with a contrary winde, being West and faire weather.

This 23 day at 2 of the clocke in the afternoone, having sailed 60 leagues Northwest, we ankered among an huge number of isles lying in the bottome of the sayd supposed passage, at which place the water riseth 4 fadome upright. Here as we rode at anker, a great whale passed by us, and swam West in among the isles. In this place a S. W. by W. moone maketh, a full sea. Here the compasse varied 30 degrees.

The 24 day at 5 of the clocke in the morning we set saile, departing from this place, and shaping our course S. E. to recover the maine Ocean againe.

This 25 we were becalmed almost in the bottome of the Streights, & had the weather marvellous extreame hot.

Moneth. July.	Dayes.	Houres.	Course.	Leagues.	Elevation of the pole.		The winde.
					Deg.	Min.	
26							S. E.
27							S.
Noone the 29					64		
Noone the 30	24	S. S. W.	22	63			
31	24	S. by W.	27	62			N. W.
August. Noone the 1	24	S.E. by S.	16	61	10	W. S. W.
Noone the 3	48	S. S. E.	16	60	26	Variable.
Noone the 6	72	S. E. Southerly.	22	59	35	Variable w^t calme.
7	24	S. S. E.	22	58	40	W. S. W.
8	24	S. E.	13	58	12	W. fog.
9	24	S. by W.	13	57	30	Variable & calme.
10	24	S. S. E.	17	56	40	S. W. by W.
11	24	S. E. easterly.	40	55	13	W. N. W.
12	24	S. E. easterly.	20	54	32	W. S. W.
13	24	S. S. E.	4	54		N. W.

[III. 118.]

THE DISCOURSE.

This day being in the Streights, we had a very quicke storme.

Being still in the Streight, we had this day faire weather.

At this present we got cleere of the Streights, having coasted the South shore, the land trending from hence S. W. by S.

This day we coasted the shore, a banke of ice lying thereupon. Also this 30 of July in the afternoone we crossed over the entrance or mouth of a great inlet or passage, being 20 leagues broad, and situate betweene 62 & 63 degrees. In which place we had 8 or 9 great rases, currents or overfals, lothsomly crying like the rage of the waters under London bridge, and bending their course into the sayd gulfe.

This 31 at noone, comming close by a foreland or great cape, we fell into a mighty rase, where an island of ice was carried by the force of the current as fast as our barke could saile with lum wind, all sailes bearing. This cape as it was the most Southerly limit of the gulfe which we passed over the 30 day of this moneth, so was it the North promontory or first beginning of another very great inlet, whose South limit at this present wee saw not. Which inlet or gulfe this afternoone, and in the night, we passed over: where to our great admiration we saw the sea falling down into the gulfe with a mighty overfal, and roring, and with divers circular motions like whirlepooles, in such sort as forcible streames passe thorow the arches of bridges.

The true course, &c. This first of August we fell with the promontory of the sayd gulfe or second passage, having coasted by divers courses for our savegard, a great banke of the ice driven out of that gulfe.

The true course, &c.

The true course, &c.

The true course, &c.

The true course, &c.

The true course, &c.

The true course, &c.

The true course, &c.

This day seeking for our ships that went to fish, we strooke on a rocke, being among many iles, and had a great leake.

Moneth. August.	Dayes.	Houres.	Course.	Leagues.	Elevation of the pole.		The winde.
					Deg.	Min.	
Noone the	14	24	S. S. E.	28	52	40	N. W.
*Noone ye	15				52	12	S. S. W.
	16	20	E. S. E. halfe point S.	50	51		S. W.
	17	24	E. by S.	30	50	40	S.
	18	24	E. by N. northerly.	49	51	18	W.
	19	24	E. halfe point north	51	51	35	Variable W. & S.
	20	24	E. S. E.	31	50	50	S. W.
Noone the	22	48	E. by N.	68	51	30	S. S. W.
	23	24	E. by N. Northerly.	33	51	52	S.
	24	24	E. by N.	31	52	10	Variable.
Noone the	27	72	E. Northerly.	40	52	23	Variable & calme.
Noone the	29	48	E. S. E.	47	51	28	Variable W. & N.
Noone the	31	48	S. E. by E. Easterly.	14	51	9	Variable.
September	2	48	E. Southerly.	65	51		N. W.
	3	24	E. by S. Easterly.	24	50	50	W. N. W.
	4	24	S. E. by E.	20	50	21	N. N. E.
	5	24	S. E. by E.	18	49	48	N. N. E.
	6	24	E. by S.	15	49	40	N.
	7	24	E. S. E.	20	49	15	N. N. W.
	8	24	N. E.	18	49	40	
	9	24	W. S. W.	7	49	42	
	10	24	S. E. by E.	$8\frac{1}{2}$	49	28	Variable.

THE DISCOURSE.

This day we stopped our leake in a storme. The 15 of August at noon, being in the latitude of 52 degrees 12. min. and 16 leagues from the shore, we shaped our course for England, in Gods name, as followeth.*

The true latitude.

The true course, &c.

The true course, &c. This day upon the Banke we met a Biscaine bound either for the Grand Bay or for the passage. He chased us.

The true course, &c.

The true course, &c.

The true course, &c.

The true course, &c.

The true course, &c.

The true course, &c. This 24 of August observing the variation, I found the compasse to vary towards the East, from the true Meridian, one degree.

The true course, &c. for 72 houres.

The true course, &c.

The true course, &c.

The true course, &c.

The true course, &c.

The true course, &c.

The true course, &c. Now we supposed our selves to be 55 leagues from Sillie.

The true course, &c.

The true course, &c.

Moneth. September.	Dayes.	Houres.	Course.	Leagues.	Elevation of the pole.		The winde.
					Deg.	Min.	
	11	24	N. E. by E.	10	49	45	Variable.
	12	24	N. W. by W.	6	50		N. E.
	13	24	E. by S. southerly.	15	49	47	N. E.
	15						

Under the title of the houres, where any number exceedeth 24, it is the
next before, as conteine

THE DISCOURSE.

This 15 of September 1587 we arrived at Dartmouth.

summe or casting up of so many other dayes and partes of dayes going
the foresayd summe.

[A report

[III. 119.] A report of Master John Davis of his three
Voyages made for the discovery of the Northwest passage, taken out of a Treatise of his,
Intituled the worlds Hydrographicall description.

Ow there onely resteth the North parts of
America, upon which coast my selfe have
had most experience of any in our age:
for thrise I was that waye imployed for
the discovery of this notable passage, by
the honourable care and some charge of
Syr Francis Walsingham knight, princi-
pall secretary to her Majestie, with whom divers noble
men and worshipfull marchants of London joyned in
purse and willingnesse for the furtherance of that
attempt, but when his honour dyed the voyage was
friendlesse, and mens mindes alienated from adventuring
therein.

The 1. voyage.   In my first voyage not experienced of the nature of
those climates, and having no direction either by Chart,
Globe, or other certaine relation in what altitude that
passage was to be searched, I shaped a Northerly course
and so sought the same toward the South, and in that
my Northerly course I fell upon the shore which in
ancient time was called Groenland, five hundred leagues
distant from the Durseys Westnorthwest Northerly, the
land being very high and full of mightie mountaines all
covered with snow, no viewe of wood, grasse or earth to be
seene, and the shore two leagues off into the sea so full of
yce as that no shipping could by any meanes come neere
the same. The lothsome view of the shore, and irksome
noyse of the yce was such, as that it bred strange con-
ceites among us, so that we supposed the place to be wast
and voyd of any sensible or vegitable creatures, whereupon I called the same Desolation: so coasting this shore
towards the South in the latitude of sixtie degrees, I

found it to trend towards the West, I still followed the leading therof in the same height, and after fifty or sixtie leagues it fayled and lay directly North, which I still followed, and in thirtie leagues sayling upon the West side of this coast by me named Desolation, we were past al the yce and found many greene & pleasant Isles bordering upon the shore, but the hils of the maine were still covered with great quantities of snow, I brought my ship among those Isles and there mored to refresh our selves in our weary travell, in the latitude of sixtie foure degrees or there about. The people of the countrey having espyed our shippes came downe unto us in their Canoas, & holding up their right hand to the Sunne and crying Yliaout, would strike their breasts: we doing the like the people came aboard our shippes, men of good stature, unbearded, small eyed and of tractable conditions, by whome as signes would permit, we understood that towards the North and West there was a great sea, and using the people with kindenes in giving them nayles and knives which of all things they most desired, we departed, and finding the sea free from yce supposing our selves to be past al daunger we shaped our course Westnorthwest thinking thereby to passe for China, but in the latitude of sixtie sixe degrees we fell with another shore, and there found another passage of twenty leagues broad directly West into the same, which we supposed to be our hoped straight, we entered into the same thirty or fortie leagues, finding it neither to wyden nor streighten, then considering that the yeere was spent (for this was the fine of August) not knowing the length of the straight and dangers thereof, we tooke it our best course to returne with notice of our good successe for this small time of search. And so returning in a sharpe fret of Westerly windes the 29. of September we arived at Dartmouth. And acquainting master Secretary Walsingham with the rest of the honourable and worshipfull adventurers of all our proceedings, I was appointed againe the second yere to search the bottome of this straight, because by all likelihood it was the place and passage by us laboured for. In this second attempt the marchants of Exeter, and other places of the West became adventurers in the action, so that being sufficiently furnished for sixe moneths, and having direction to search these straights, untill we found the same to fall into another sea upon the West side of this part of America, we should againe returne: for then it was not to be doubted, but shipping with trade might safely be conveied to China, and the parts of Asia. We departed from Dartmouth, and ariving upon the South part of the coast of Desolation coasted the same upon his West shore to the latitude of sixetie sixe degrees, and there ancored among the Isles bordering upon the same, where we refreshed our selves, the people of this place came likewise unto us, by whom I understood through their signes that towards the North the sea was large. At this place the chiefe ship whereupon I trusted, called the Mermayd of Dartmouth, found many occasions of discontentment, and being unwilling to proceed, shee there forsook me. Then considering how I had given my faith and most constant promise to my worshipfull good friend master William Sanderson, who of all men was the greatest adventurer in that action, and tooke such care for the performance

thereof, that he hath to my knowledge at one time disbursed as much money as any five others whatsoever, out of his owne purse, when some of the companie have bene slacke in giving in their adventure: And also knowing that I should loose the favor of M. Secretary Walsingham, if I should shrink from his direction; in one small barke of 30 Tunnes, whereof M. Sanderson was owner, alone without farther company I proceeded on my voyage, and arriving at these straights followed the same 80. leagues, untill I came among many Islands, where the water did ebbe and flow sixe fadome upright, and where there had bene great trade of people to make traine. But by such things as there we found, wee knew that they were not Christians of Europe that had used

that trade: in fine by searching with our boat, we found
small hope to passe any farther that way, and therefore
recovered the sea and coasted the shore towards the
South, and in so doing (for it was too late to search
towards the North) we found another great inlet neere
40 leagues broad, where the water entred in with violent
swiftnesse, this we also thought might be a passage: for
no doubt the North partes of America are all Islands by *The North*
ought that I could perceive therein: but because I was *parts of*
alone in a small barke of thirtie tunnes, and the yeere *America, all*
spent, I entred not into the same, for it was now the *Islands.*
seventh of September, but coasting the shore towardes
the South wee saw an incredible number of birds:
having divers fishermen aboord our barke they all concluded that there was a great skull of fish, we being
unprovided of fishing furniture with a long spike nayle
made a hooke, and fastened the same to one of our
sounding lines, before the baite was changed we tooke
more then fortie great Cods, the fish swimming so abundantly thicke about our barke as is incredible to bee
reported, of which with a small portion of salt that we
had, we preserved some thirtie couple, or thereaboutes,
and so returned for England. And having reported to
M. Secretarie Walsingham the whole successe of this
attempt, he commanded me to present unto the most
honourable Lord high Treasurour of England, some
part of that fish: which when his Lordship saw, & heard
at large the relation of this second attempt, I received
favourable countenance from his honour, advising me to
prosecute the action, of which his Lordship conceived a
very good opinion. The next yere, although divers of
the adventurers fell from the Action, as all the Westerne
marchants, and most of those in London: yet some of
the adventurers both honorable & worshipfull continued
their willing favor and charge, so that by this meanes
the next yere two shippes were appointed for the fishing
and one pinnesse for the discoverie.

Departing from Dartmouth, through Gods mercifull *The 3. voyage.*

favour, I arrived at the place of fishing, and there
according to my direction I left the two ships to follow
that busines, taking their faithful promise not to depart
untill my returne unto them, which should be in the fine
of August, and so in the barke I proceeded for the
discoverie: but after my departure, in sixeteene dayes the
two shippes had finished their voyage, and so presently
departed for England, without regard of their promise:
my selfe not distrusting any such hard measure proceeded
for the discoverie, and followed my course in the free
and open sea betweene North and Northwest to the
latitude of 67 degrees, and there I might see America
West from me, and Gronland, which I called Desolation,
East: then when I saw the land of both sides I began
to distrust it would proove but a gulfe: notwithstanding
desirous to know the full certainty I proceeded, and in
68 degrees the passage enlarged, so that I could not see
the Westerne shore: thus I continued to the latitude
of 73 degrees, in a great sea, free from yce, coasting the
Westerne shore of Desolation: the people came continually rowing out unto me in their Canoas, twenty,
forty, and one hundred at a time, and would give me
fishes dryed, Salmon, Salmon peale, Cod, Caplin, Lumpe,
Stone-base and such like, besides divers kinds of birds,
as Partrige, Fesant, Guls, Sea birds and other kindes of
flesh: I still laboured by signes to know from them what
they knew of any sea toward the North, they still made
signes of a great sea as we understood them, then I
departed from that coast, thinking to discover the North
parts of America: & after I had sailed towards the
West 40 leagues, I fel upon a great banke of yce:
the winde being North and blew much, I was constrained to 'coast the same toward the South, not seeing
any shore West from me, neither was there any yce
towards the North, but a great sea, free, large very
salt and blew, & of an unsearchable depth: So coasting
towards the South I came to the place where I left
the ships to fish, but found them not.   Then being

forsaken & left in this distresse referring my self to the mercifull providence of God, I shaped my course for England, & unhoped for of any, God alone releeving me, I arrived at Dartmouth. By this last discovery it seemed most manifest that the passage was free & without impediment toward the North: but by reason of the Spanish fleet & unfortunate time of M. Secretaries death, the voyage was omitted & never sithens attempted. The cause why I use this particular relation of all my proceedings for this discovery, is to stay this objection, why hath not Davis discovered this passage being thrise that wayes imploied? How far I proceeded & in what forme this discovery lieth, doth appeare upon the Globe which M. Sanderson to his very great charge hath published, for the which he deserveth great favor & commendations.

The discoverie of the Isles of Frisland, Iseland, [III. 121.] Engroneland, Estotiland, Drogeo and Icaria: made by two brethren, namely M. Nicholas Zeno, and M. Antonio his brother: Gathered out of their letters by M. Francisco Marcolino.

N the yere of our Lord 1200 there was in the Citie of Venice a famous Gentleman, named Messer Marino Zeno, who for his great vertue and singular wisedome, was called and elected governour in certaine common wealths of Italy: in the administration whereof he bore himselfe so discretly, that he was beloved of all men, and his name greatly reverenced of those that never knew or saw his person. And amongst sundry his worthy workes, this is recorded of him, that he pacified certaine grievous civile dissentions that arose among the citizens of Verona: whereas otherwise, if by his grave advise and great diligence they had not bene prevented, the matter was likely to breake out into hot broyles of warre. He was the first Podesta, or Ruler, that the Common wealth of Venice appointed in Constantinople in the yeere 1205 when our state had rule thereof with the French Barons. This Gentleman had a sonne named Messer Pietro, who was the father of the Duke Rinieri, which Duke dying without issue, made his heire M. Andrea, the sonne of M. Marco his brother. This M. Andrea was Captaine Generall and Procurator, a man of great reputation for many rare partes, that were in him. He had a sonne M. Rinieri, a worthy Senatour and prudent Counsellour: of whom descended M. Pietro Captaine Generall of the league of the Christians against the Turkes, who was called Dragon, for that in his shield, in stead of a Manfronè which was his armes at the first, he bare a Dragon. He was father to M. Carlo Il grande the famous Procurator and Captaine generall against the Genowayes in those cruell warres, when as almost all the cheife Princes of Europe did oppugne and seeke to overthrow our Empire and libertie, wherein by his great valiancie and prowesse, as Furius Camillus delivered Rome, so he delivered his country from the present perill it was in, being ready to become a pray and spoile unto the enemie: wherefore he was afterward surnamed the Lyon, and for an eternall remembrance of his fortitude and valiant exploits he gave the Lyon in his armes. M. Carlo had two brethren, M. Nicolo, the knight and M. Antonio, the father of M. Dragon, of whom issued M. Caterino, the father M. Pietro da i Grocecchieri. This M. Pietro had sonnes M. Caterino, that died the last yere, being brother unto M. Francisco, M. Carlo, M. Battista, and M. Vincenzo: Which M. Caterino was father to M. Nicolo, that is yet living.

Now M. Nicolo, the knight, being a man of great courage, after this aforesaid Genouan warre of Chioggia that troubled so our predecessours, entred into a great desire and fansie to see the fashions of the worlde and to travell and acquaint himselfe with the maners of sundry nations and learne their languages, whereby afterwards upon occasions he might be the better able to doe service to his countrey, and purchase to himselfe credite and honour. Wherefore he caused a ship to be made, and having furnished her at his proper charges (as he was very wealthy) he departed out of our seas, and passing the straites of Gibraltar, he sailed for certaine dayes upon the Ocean, keeping his course still to the Northwards, with intent to see England and Flanders. Where being assalted in those Seas by a terrible tempest, he was so tossed for the space of many dayes with the sea and winde, that he knew not where he was, till at length he discovered land, and not being able any longer to susteine the violence of the tempest the ship was cast away upon the Isle of Friseland. The men were saved, and most part of the goods that were in the ship. And this was in the yere 1380. The inhabitants of the Island came running in great multitudes with weapons to set upon M. Nicolo and his men, who being sore weather-beaten and over-laboured at sea, and not knowing in what part of the world they were, were not able to make any resistance at all, much lesse to defend themselves couragiously, as it behooved them in such a dangerous case. And they should have bene doubtlesse very discourteously intreated and cruelly handled, if by good hap there had not beene hard by the place a prince with armed people. Who understanding that there was even at that present a great ship cast away upon the Island, came runing at the noyse and outcryes that they made against our poore Mariners, and dryving away the inhabitants, spake in Latine and asked them what they were and from whence they came, and perceiving that they came from Italy and that they were men of the said Countrey, he was surprised with marvelous great joy. Wherefore promising them all, that they should receive no discourtesie, and that they were come into a place where they should be well used and very welcome, he tooke

The ship of M. N. Zeno cast away upon Frisland in Anno 1380.

A forraine prince hapning to be in Frisland with armed men, when M. Zeno suffered shipwracke there came unto him and spake Latine.

Zichmni prince of Porland or Duke of Zorani.

them into his protection upon his faith. This was a great Lord, and possessed certaine Islands called Porland, lying on the South side of Frisland, being the richest and most populous of all those parts, his name was Zichmni: and beside the said little Islands, he was Duke of Sorani, lying over against Scotland.

[III. 122.]

Of these North parts I thought good to draw the copie of a Sea carde, which amongst other antiquities I have in my house, which although it be rotten through many yeeres, yet it falleth out indifferent well: and to those that are delighted in these things, it may serve for some light to the understanding of that, which without it cannot so easily be conceived. Zichmni being Lord of those Sygnories (as is said) was a very warlike and valiant man and above all things famous in Sea causes. And having the yere before given the over-throw to the king of Norway, who was Lord of the Island, being desirous to winne fame by feates of armes, hee was come on land with his men to give the attempt for the winning of Frisland, which is an Island much bigger then Ireland. Wherefore seeing that M. Nicolo was a man of judgement & discretion, and very expert both in sea matters and martiall affaires, hee gave him commission to goe aboord his Navy with all his men, charging the captaine to honour him and in all things to use his counsaile.

Frisland the King of Nor-wayes.

This Navy of Zichmni was of thirteene vessels, whereof two onely were rowed with oares, the rest small barkes and one ship, with the which they sayled to the Westwards and with little paines wonne Ledovo and Ilofe and divers other small Islands: and turning into a bay called Sudero, in the haven of the towne named Sanestol, they tooke certaine small barks laden with fish. And here they found Zichmni, who came by land with his armie conquering all the countrey as he went: they stayed here but a while, and led on their course to the Westwards till they came to the other Cape of the gulfe or bay, then turning againe, they found certaine Islandes and broken lands which they reduced al unto the Signorie & possession of Zichmni. These seas, forasmuch as they sailed, were in maner nothing but sholds & rocks, in so much that if M. Nicolo and the Venetian mariners had not bene their Pilots, the whole fleete in judgement of all that were in it, had bene cast away, so small was the skill of Zichmnis men, in respect of ours, who had bene trained up in the arte and practise of Navigation all the dayes of their life. Now the fleete having done such things as are declared, the Captaine, by the counsaile of M. Nicolo, determined to goe a land, at a towne called Bondendon, to understand what successe Zichmni had in his warres : where they heard to their great content, that he had fought a great battell and put to flight the armie of his enemie : by reason of which victory, they sent Embassadours from all parts of the Island to yeeld the còuntrey up into his handes, taking downe their ensignes in every towne and castle : they thought good to stay in that place for his comming, it being reported for certaine that hee would be there very shortly. At his comming there was great congratulation and many signes of gladnesse shewed, as well for the victory by land, as for that by sea : for the which the Venetians were honoured and extolled of all men, in such sort that there was no talke but of them, and of the great valour of M. Nicolo. Wherefore the prince, who was a great favourer of valiant men and especially of those that could behave themselves well at sea, caused M. Nicolo to be brought before him, and after having commended him with many honourable speeches, and praysed his great industrie and dexteritie of wit, by the which two things he acknowledged himselfe to have received an inestimable benefite, as the saving of his fleet and the winning of many places without any great trouble, he made him knight, and rewarded his men with many rich & bountiful gifts. Then departing from thence they went in tryumphing maner toward Frisland,

*N. Zeno,
made knight
by Zichmni.*

*Ships laden
with fish at
Frisland, for
Flanders,
Britain, Eng-
land, Scotland,
Norway and
Denmarke.
But not to be
proved that
ever any came
thence.
A letter sent by
M. N. Zeno,
from Frisland
to his brother
M. Antonio
in Venice.
The end of
the first
letter.*

the chiefe citie of that Island, situate on the Southeast side of the Isle, within a gulfe, as there are many in that Island. In this gulf or bay there is such great abundance of fish taken, that many ships are laden therewith to serve Flanders, Britain, England, Scotland, Norway, and Denmarke, and by this trade they gather great wealth.

And thus much is taken out of a letter, that M. Nicolo sent to M. Antonio his brother, requesting that he would seeke some meanes to come to him. Wherefore he who had as great desire to travaile as his brother, bought a ship, and directed his course that way: & after he had sailed a great while and escaped many dangers, he arrived at length in safetie with M. Nicolo, who received him very joyfully, for that he was his brother not onely in flesh and blood, but also in valour and good qualities. M. Antonio remained in Frisland and dwelt there for the space of 14 yeres, 4 yeres with M. Nicolo, and 10 yeres alone. Where they came in such grace and favour with the Prince, that he made M. Nicolo Captaine of his Navy, and with great preparation of warre they were sent forth for the enterprise of Estland, which lyeth upon the coast betweene Frisland and Norway, where they did many dammages: but hearing that the king of Norway was coming towardes them with a great fleet, they departed with such a terrible flaw of winde, that they were driven upon certaine sholds: were a great part of their ships were cast away, the rest were saved upon Grisland, a great Island but dishabited. The king of Norway his fleete being taken with the same storme, did utterly perish in those seas: Whereof Zichmni having notice, by a ship of his enemies that was cast by chance upon Grisland, having repayred his fleet, and perceiving himself Northerly neere unto the Islands, determined to set upon Island, which together with the rest, was subject to the king of Norway: but he found the countrey so well fortified and defended, that his fleete being so small, and very ill appointed both of weapons and men, he was glad to retire. And so he left that enterprise without performing

[III. 123.]

450

any thing at all: and in the same chanels he assaulted the other Isles called Islande, which are seven, Talas, Broas, Iscant, Trans, Mimant, Dambere, and Bres: and having spoyled them all, hee built a fort in Bres, where he left M. Nicolo, with certaine small barkes and men and munition. And now thinking he had done wel for this voyage, with those few ships which were left he returned safe into Frisland. M. Nicolo remaining nowe in Bres, determined in the spring to go forth and discover land: wherefore arming out three small barkes in the moneth of July, he sayled to the Northwards, and arrived in Engroneland. Where he found a Monasterie of *Engroneland.* Friers, of the order of the Predicators, and a Church *Preaching* dedicated to Saint Thomas, hard by a hill that casteth *Fryers of Saint* forth fire, like Vesuvius and Etna. *Thomas.*

There is a fountaine of hot burning water with the which they heate the Church of the Monastery and the Fryers chambers, it commeth also into the kitchin so boyling hot, that they use no other fire to dresse their meate: and putting their breade into brasse pots without any water, it doth bake as it were in an hot oven. They have also smal gardens covered over in the winter time, which being watered with this water, are defended from the force of the snow and colde, which in those partes being situate farre under the pole, is very extreme, and by this meanes they produce flowers and fruites and herbes of sundry sorts, even as in other temperate countries in their seasons, in such sort that the rude and savage people of those partes seeing these super-naturall effects, doe take those Fryers for Gods, and bring them many presents, as chickens, flesh, and divers other things, and have them all in great reverence as Lords. When the frost and snowe is great, they heate their houses in maner beforesaid, and wil by letting in the water or opening the windowes, at an instant temper the heate and cold at their pleasure. In the buildings of the Monasterie they use no other matter but that which is ministred unto them by the fire: for they take the burning stones that are cast out as it were sparkles or cinders at the fierie mouth of the hill, and when they are most enflamed, cast water upon them, whereby they are dissolved and become excellent white lime and so tough that being contrived in building it lasteth for ever. And the very sparkles after the fire is out of them doe serve in stead of stones to make walles and vautes: for being once colde they wil never dissolve or breake, except they be cut with some iron toole, and the vautes that are made of them are so light that they need no sustentaccle or prop to holde them up, and they will endure continually very faire and whole. By reason of these great commodities, the Fryers have made there so many buildings and walles that it is a wonder to see. The coverts or roofes of their houses for the most part are made in maner following: first they rayse up the wall up to his full height, then they make it enclining or bowing in by little and litle in fourme of a vaut. But they are not greatly troubled with raine in those partes, because the climate (as I have saide) is extreme colde: for the first *Winter of 9.* snow being fallen, it thaweth no more for the space of *moneths.* nine moneths, for so long dureth their winter. They feede of the flesh of wilde foule and of fish: for wheras the warme water falleth into the sea, there is a large and wide haven, which by reason of the heate of the water, doeth never freeze all the winter, by meanes whereof there is such concourse and flocks of sea foule and such aboundance of fish, that they take thereof infinite multitudes, wherby they maintaine a great number of people round about, which they kepe in continuall worke, both in building and taking of foules and fish, and in a thousand other necessarie affaires and busines about the Monasterie.

Their houses are built about the hill on every side, in forme round, and 25 foote broad, and in mounting upwards they goe narower and narower, leaving at the top a litle hole, whereat the aire commeth in to give light to the house, and the flore of the house is so hot, that being within they feele no cold at all. Hither in the Summer time come many barkes from the Islands their about, and from the cape above Norway, and from Trondon, and bring to the Friers al maner of things that may be desired, taking in change thereof fish, which they dry in the sunne or in the cold, & skins of divers kindes of beasts. For the which they have wood to burne and timber very artificially carved, and corne, and cloth to make them apparell. For in change of the two aforesaid commodities all the nations bordering round about them covet to trafficke with them, and so they without any travell or expences have that which they desire. To this Monasterie resort Fryers of Norway, of Suetia and of other countreys, but the most part are of Islande. There are continually in that part many barks, which are kept in there by reason of the sea being frozen, waiting for the spring of the yere to dissolve the yce. The fishers boates are made like unto a weavers shuttle: taking the skins of fishes, they fashion them with the bones of the same fishes, and sowing them together in many doubles they make them so sure and substanciall, that it is miraculous to see, howe in tempests they will shut themselves close within and let the sea and winde cary them they care not whether, without any feare either of breaking or drowning. And if they chance to be driven upon any rocks, they remaine sound without the least bruse in the world: & they have as it were a sleeve in the bottome, which is tyed fast in the middle, and when there commeth any water into the boat, they put it into the one halfe of the sleeve, then fastening the ende thereof with two pieces of wood and loosing the band beneath, they convey the water forth of the boat: and this they doe as often as they have occasion, without any perill or impediment at all.

Moreover, the water of the Monastery, being of sulphurious or brimstonie nature, is conveyed into the lodgings of the principall Friers by certaine vesselles of brasse, tinne, or stone, so hot that it heateth the place

Trade in summer time from Trondon to S. Thomas Friers in Groneland. Resort of Fryers from Norway and Sueden, to the Monastery in Engroneland, called S. Tho.

M. Frobisher brought these kinde of boats from these parts into England.

[III. 124.]

as it were a stove, not carying with it any stinke or other noysome smell.

Besides this they have another conveyance to bring hot water with a wall under the ground, to the end it should not freeze, unto the middle of the court, where it falleth into a great vessel of brasse that standeth in the middle of a boyling fountaine, and this is to heat their water to drinke & to water their gardens, & thus they have from the hill the greatest commodities that may be wished: and so these Fryers employ al their travaile and studie for the most part in trimming their gardens and in making faire and beautifull buildings, but especially handsome and commodious: neyther are they destitute of ingenious and painefull artificers for the purpose; for they give very large payment, and to them that bring them fruits and seedes they are very bountifull, and give they care not what. So that there is great resort of workemen and masters in divers faculties, by reason of the good gaines and large allowance that is there.

In the Monastery of Saint Thomas most of them spake the Latine tongue. The end of the 2. letter.

The most of them speake the Latine tongue, and specially the superiours and principals of the Monastery. And this is as much as is knowen of Engroneland, which is all by the relation of M. Nicolo, who maketh also particular description of a river that he discovered, as is to be seene in the carde that I drew. And in the end M. Nicolo, not being used & acquainted with these cruell coldes, fel sicke, and a litle while after returned into Frisland, where he dyed. He left behind him in Venice, two sonnes, M. Giovanni and M. Toma, who had two sonnes, M. Nicolo the father of the famous Cardinal Zeno, and M. Pietro of whom descended the other Zenos, that are living at this day.

N. Zeno dyed in Frisland.

Now M. Nicolo being dead, M. Antonio succeeded him both in his goods, and in his dignities and honour: and albeit he attempted divers wayes, and made great supplication, he could never obtaine licence to returne into his countrey. For Zichmni, being a man of great courage and valour, had determined to make himself Lord of the sea. Wherfore using alwayes the counsaile and service of M. Antonio, he determined to send him with certaine barks to the Westwards, for that towards those parts, some of his fishermen had discovred certaine Islands very rich and populous: which discovery M. Antonio, in a letter to his brother M. Carlo, recounteth from point to point in this maner, saving that we have changed some old words, leaving the matter entire as it was.

Sixe and twentie yeeres agoe there departed foure fisher boats, the which, a mightie tempest arising, were tossed for the space of many dayes very desperately upon the Sea, when at length, the tempest ceasing, and the wether waxing faire, they discovered an Island called Estotiland, lying to the Westwards above 1000 Miles from Frisland, upon the which one of the boats was cast away, and sixe men that were in it were taken of the inhabitants and brought into a faire and populous citie, where the king of the place sent for many interpreters, but there was none could be found that understood the language of the fishermen, except one that spake Latine, who was also cast by chance upon the same Island, who in the behalfe of the king asked them what countreymen they were: and so understanding their case, rehearsed it unto the king, who willed that they should tary in the countrey: wherefore they obeying his commandement, for that they could not otherwise doe, dwelt five yeres in the Island, & learned the language, and one of them was in divers partes of the Island, and reporteths that it is a very rich countrey, abounding with all the commodities of the world, and that it is litle lesse then Island, but farre more fruitfull, having in the middle thereof a very high mountaine, from the which there spring foure rivers that passe through the whole countrey.

The inhabitants are very wittie people, and have all artes and faculties, as we have: and it is credible that in time past they have had trafficke with our men, for

The discoverie of Estotiland Westward. Sixe fishermen taken.

Fishermen of Frisland speake Latine.

Sixe were five yeeres in Estotiland. One of the fishers of Frisland reporteth of Estotiland. Estotiland rich, abounding with all the commodities of the world.

*Abundance
of golde.
Trade from
Estotiland, to
Engroneland:
Skins, brim-
stone, and
pitch : golde,
corne, and
beere, or ale.
Many cities
and castles.*

[III. 125.]
*A countrey
called Drogio.*

*The 6 fisher-
men of Fris-
land onely
saved, by
shewing the
maner to take
fish.
The chiefest
of the 6 fishers,
specified before
and his com-
panions.*

he said, that he saw Latin bookes in the kings Librarie, which they at this present do not understand : they have a peculiar language, and letters or caracters to themselves. They have mines of all maner of mettals, but especial they abound with gold. They have their trade in Engroneland, from whence they bring furres, brimstone & pitch : and he saith, that to the Southwards, there is a great populous countrey very rich of gold. They sow corne, and make beere and ale, which is a kinde of drinke that North people do use as we do wine. They have mighty great woods, they make their buildings with wals, & there are many cities and castles. They build small barks and have sayling, but they have not the load stone, nor know not the use of the compasse. Wherefore these fishers were had in great estimation, insomuch that the king sent them with twelve barks to the Southwards to a countrey which they call Drogio : but in their voyage they had such contrary weather, that they thought to have perished in the sea : but escaping that cruell death, they fell into another more cruell : for they were taken in the countrey and the most part of them eaten by the Savage people, which fed upon mans flesh, as the sweetest meat in their judgements that is.

But that fisher with his fellowes shewing them the maner of taking fish with nets, saved their lives : and would goe every day a fishing to the sea and in fresh rivers, and take great abundance of fish and give it to the chiefe men of the countrey, whereby he gate himselfe so great favour, that he was very well beloved and honoured of every one.

The fame of this man being spread abroad in the countrey, there was a Lord there by, that was very desirous to have him with him, and' to see how he used his miraculous arte of catching fish, in so much that he made warre with the other Lord with whom he was before, and in the end prevailing, for that he was more mightie and a better warriour, the fisherman was sent unto him with the rest of his company. And for the space of thirteene yeres that he dwelt in those parts, he *In the space* saith, that he was sent in this order to more then 25 *of 13 yeeres* Lords, for they had continuall war amongst themselves, *he served 25 lords of* this Lord with that Lord, and he with another, onely *Drogio.* to have him to dwell with them : so that wandring up and downe the countrey without any certaine abode in one place, he knew almost all those parts. He saith, that it is a very great countrey & as it were a new world : the people are very rude and voide of all goodnesse, they goe all naked so that they are miserably vexed with colde, neither have they the wit to cover their bodyes with beasts skins which they take in hunting, they have no kinde of mettal, they live by hunting, they cary certaine lances of wood made sharpe at the point, they have bowes, ye strings wherof are made of beasts skins : they are very fierce people, they make cruell warres one with another, and eate one another, they have governours & certaine lawes very divers among themselves. But the farther to the Southwestwards, the more civiltie there is, the ayre being somewhat temperate, so that there they have cities and temples to idols, wherein they sacrifice men and afterwards eate them, they have there some knowledge and use of gold and silver.

Now this fisherman having dwelt so many yeeres in those countreys purposed, if it were possible, to returne home into his countrey, but his companions despairing ever to see it againe, let him goe in Gods name, and they kept themselves where they were. Wherefore he bidding them farwell, fled through the woods towards Drogio, and was very well received of the Lord that dwelt next to that place ; who knew him and was a great enemie of the other Lord ; and so running from one Lord to another, being those by whom he had passed before, after long time & many travels he came at length to Drogio, where he dwelt three yeres. When as by good fortune he heard by the inhabitants, that there were certaine boates arrived upon the coast : wherefore entring into good hope to accomplish his intent, he went to the sea side, and asking them of what countrey they were; they answered of Estotiland, whereat he was exceeding glad, and requested that they would take him in to them, which they did very willingly, and for that he had the language of the countrey, and there was none that could speake it, they used him for their interpreter.

And afterward he frequented that trade with them in such sort, that he became very rich, and so furnishing out a barke of his owne, he returned into Frislande, where he made reporte unto this Lord of that wealthy countrey.

He returned from Estotiland to Frisland.

And he is throughly credited because of the mariners, who approve many strange things, that he reporteth to be true. Wherfore this Lord is resolved to send me forth with a fleet towards those parts, and there are so many that desire to go in the voyage, for the noveltie and strangenesse of the thing, that I thinke we shall be very strongly appointed, without any publike expence at all. And this is the tenor of the letter before mentioned, which I have here set downe to give intelligence of another voyage that M. Antonio made, being set out with many barkes, and men, notwithstanding he was not captaine, as he had thought at the first he should: for Zichmni went in his owne person: and concerning that matter I have a letter in forme following.

Zichmni minded to send M. Antonio Zeno with a fleete towards those parts of Estotiland.

One great preparation for the voyage of Estotiland was begun in an unlucky houre: for three dayes before our departure the fisherman died that should have bene our guide: notwithstanding this Lord would not give over the enterprize, but instead of the fisherman tooke certaine mariners that returned out of the Island with him: and so making our Navigation to the Westwards, we discovered certaine Islands subject to Frisland, and having passed certaine shelves we stayed at Ledovo for the space of 7 daies to refresh our selves, and to furnish the fleet with necessarie provision. Departing from thence we arrived the first of July at the Isle of Ilofe: and for that the wind made for us, we stayed not there, but passed

The 4 letter. The fisherman dyed that should have bene interpreter. Certaine mariners taken in his steede, which came with him from Estotiland.

Isle Ilofe.

forth, and being upon the maine sea, there arose immediately a cruel tempest, wherwith for eight dayes space we were miserably vexed, not knowing where we were : [III. 126.] & a great part of the barks were cast away, afterward the weather waxing faire, we gathered up the broken peices of the barks that were lost, and sayling with a prosperous winde we discovered land at West. Wherefore keeping *Zichmni his* our course directly upon it, we arrived in a good and *discoverie of* safe harborough, where we saw an infinit companie of *Icaria.* people ready in armes, come running very furiously to the water side, as it were for defence of the Island. Wherfore Zichmni causing his men to make signes of peace unto them, they sent 10 men unto us that could speake ten languages, but we could understand none of them, except one that was of Island. He being brought *An Island* before our prince and asked, what was the name of the *man in Icari.* Island, and what people inhabited it, & who governed it, answered, that the Island was called Icaria, and that all the kings that reigned there, were called Icari, after the *The kings of* name of the first king of that place, which as they say was *Icaria called* the sonne of Dedalus king of Scotland, who conquered *name of the* that Island, left his sonne there for king, and left them *first king of* those lawes that they retaine to this present, and after *that place,* this, he desiring to sayle further, in a great tempest that *who as they* arose, was drowned, wherefore for a memoriall of his *sonne to Deda-* death, they call those seas yet, the Icarian Sea, and the *lus king of* kings of the Island Icari, and for that they were contented *Scots.* with that state, which God had given them, neither *Icarian Sea.* would they alter one jote of their lawes and customes, they would not receive any stranger : wherefore they requested our prince, that hee would not seeke to violate their lawes, which they had received from that king of worthy memory and observed very duly to that present : which if he did attempt, it would redound to his manifest destruction, they being all resolutely bent rather to leave their life, then to loose in any respect the use of their lawes. Notwithstanding, that we should not thinke they did altogether refuse conversation and traffick with other

men, they tolde us for conclusion that they would
willingly receive one of our men, & preferre him to be one
of the chiefe amongst them, onely to learne my language
*The people of
Icaria desirous
of the Italian
tongue.
Ten men of
ten sundry
nations.*
the Italian tongue, and to be informed of our manners
and customes, as they had already received those other
ten of ten sundry nations, that came into their Island.
To these things our Prince answered nothing at all, but
causing his men to seke some good harbrough, he made
signes as though he would depart, and sayling round
about the Island, he espied at length a harbrough on the
East side of the Island, where hee put in with all his
Fleet: the mariners went on land to take in wood and
water, which they did with as great speede as they could,
doubting least they should be assaulted by the inhabitants,
as it fell out in deed, for those that dwelt therabouts,
making signes unto the other with fire and smoke, put
*Infinite multi-
tudes of armed
men in Icaria.*
themselves presently in armes and the other comming to
them, they came all running downe to the sea side upon
our men, with bowes and arrowes, and other weapons, so
that many were slaine and divers sore wounded. And
we made signes of peace unto them, but it was to no
purpose, for their rage increased more and more, as
though they had fought for land and living. Wherefore
*Zichmni
departed from
Icaria West-
wards.*
we were forced to depart, and to sayle along in a great
circuite about the Islande, being alwayes accompanyed
upon the hil tops & the sea coastes with an infinite
number of armed men: and so doubling the Cape of
the Island towards the North, we found many great
sholdes, amongst the which for the space of ten dayes we
were in continuall danger of loosing our whole fleet, but
that it pleased God all that while to send us faire weather.
Wherefore proceeding on till we came to the East cape,
we saw the inhabitants still on the hill tops and by the
sea coast keepe with us, and in making great outcryes
and shooting at us a farre off, they uttered their old
spitefull affection towards us. Wherefore wee determined to stay in some safe harborough, and see if wee
might speake once againe with the Islander, but our

determination was frustrate: for the people more like unto beasts then men, stood continually in armes with intent to beat us back, if we should come on land. Wherefore Zichmni seeing he could not prevaile, and thinking if he should have persevered and followed obstinately his purpose, their victuals would have failed them, he departed with a fayre wind and sailed sixe daies to the Westwards, but the winde changing to the Southwest, and the sea waxing rough, wee sayling 4 dayes with the wind the powp, and at length discovering land, were afraid to approch nere unto it, the sea being growen, and we not knowing what land it was: but God so provided for us, that the winde ceasing there came a great calme. Wherefore some of our company rowing to land with oares, returned & brought us newes to our great comfort, that they had found a very good countery and a better harborough: upon which newes we towed our ships and smal barks to land, and being entred into the harborough, we saw a farre off a great mountain, that cast forth smoke, which gave us good hope that we should finde some inhabitants in the Island, neither would Zichmni rest, although it were a great way off, but sent 100 souldiers to search the countrey and bring report what people they were that inhabited it, & in the meane time they tooke in wood and water for the provision of the fleet, and catcht great store of fish and sea foule and found such aboundance of birds egges, that our men that were halfe famished, were filled therewithall. Whiles we were riding here, began the moneth of June, at which time the aire in the Island was so temperate and pleasant as is impossible to expresse: but when we could see no people at al, we suspected greatly that this pleasant place was desolate and dishabited. We gave name to the heaven calling it Trin, and the point that stretched out into the sea, we called Capo de Trin. The 100 souldiers that were sent forth, 8 dayes after returned, and brought word that they had bene through the Island and at the mountaine, and that the smoke was a naturall thing pro-

100 men sent to discrie the countrey.

[III. 127.]

The 100 souldiers returned which had bene through the Island, report what they saw and found.

ceding from a great fire that was in the bottome of the hill, and that there was a spring from which issued a certaine water like pitch which ran into the sea, and that thereabouts dwelt great multitudes of people halfe wilde, hiding themselves in caves of the ground, of small stature, and very fearefull; for as soone as they saw them they fled into their holes, and that there was a great river and a very good and safe harborough. Zichmni being thus informed, and seeing that it had a holesome and pure aire, and a very fruitfull soyle and faire rivers, with sundry commodities, fell into such liking of the place, that he determined to inhabite it, and built there a citie. But his people being weary and faint with long and tedious travell began to murmure, saying that they would returne into their countrey, for that the winter was at hand, and if they entred into the harborough, they should not be able to come out againe before the next Summer. Wherefore he retaining onely the barks with Oares and such as were willing to stay with him, sent all *M. Antonio* the rest with the shippes backe againe, and willed that I, *Zeno, made* (though unwilling) should be their captaine. I therefore *chiefe captaine* departing, because I could not otherwise chuse, sayled for *of those ships* the space of twenty dayes to the Eastwards without sight *which went* of any land; then turning my course towards the South-*back to Fris-* east, in 5. dayes I discovered land, and found my selfe *land.* upon the Isle of Neome, and knowing the countrey, I perceived I was past Island: wherefore taking in some fresh victuals of the inhabitants being subject to Zichmni, I sayled with a faire winde in three dayes to Frisland, where the people, who thought they had lost their prince, because of his long absence, in this our voyage received us very joyfully.

What followed after this letter I know not but by conjecture, which I gather out of a piece of another letter, which I will set downe here underneath: That Zichmni built a towne in the port of the Island that he discovered, and that he searched the countrey very diligently and discovered it all, and also the rivers on

462

both sides of Engroneland, for that I see it particularly described in the sea card, but the discourse or narration is lost. The beginning of the letter is thus.

Concerning those things that you desire to know of *The 5 letter.* me, as of the men and their maners and customes, of the beasts, and of the countries adjoyning, I have made therof a particuler booke, which by Gods help I will bring with me: wherein I have described the countrey, the monstrous fishes, the customes and lawes of Frisland, Island, Estland, the kingdome of Norway, Estotiland, Drogio, and in the end the life of M. Nicolo, the knight our brother, with the discovery which he made, and the state of Groneland. I have also written the life and acts of Zichmni, a prince as worthy of immortall memory, as any that ever lived, for his great valiancie and singuler humanitie, wherein I have described the discovery of Engroneland on both sides, and the citie that he builded. Therefore I will speake no further hereof in this letter, hoping to be with you very shortly, and to satisfie you in sundry other things by word of mouth.

All these letters were written by M. Antonio to Messer Carlo his brother: and it grieveth me, that the booke and divers other writings concerning these purposes, are miserably lost: for being but a child when they came to my hands, and not knowing what they were, (as the maner of children is) I tore them, and rent them in pieces, which now I cannot cal to remembrance but to my exceeding great griefe. Notwithstanding, that the memory of so many good things should not bee lost: whatsoever I could get of this matter, I have disposed and put in order in the former discourse, to the ende that this age might be partly satisfied, to the which we are more beholding for the great discoveries made in those partes, then to any other of the time past, being most studious of the newe relations and discoveries of strange counteries, made by the great mindes, and industrie of our ancestours.

For the more credite and confirmation of the former

Historie of Messer Nicolas and Messer Antonio Zeni (which for some fewe respects may perhaps bee called in question) I have heere annexed the judgement of that famous Cosmographer Abraham Ortelius, or rather the yealding and submitting of his judgement thereunto: who in his Theatrum Orbis, fol. 6. next before the map of Mar del Zur, boroweth proofe and authoritie out of this relation, to shew that the Northeast parte of America called Estotiland, and in the original alwayes affirmed to bee an Islande, was about the yeere 1390 discovered by the aforesayd Venetian Gentleman Messer Antonio Zeno, above 100 yeeres before ever Christopher Columbus set saile for those Westerne Regions; and that the Northren Seas were even then sayled by our Europæan Pilots through the helpe of the loadstone: with divers

[III. 128.] other particulars concerning the customes, religion and wealth of the Southern Americans, which are most evidently confirmed by all the late and moderne Spanish Histories of Nueva Espanna and Peru.

ANd here I shall not (as I suppose) commit any great inconvenience, or absurditie, in adding unto this History of the new world, certaine particulars as touching the first discovery therof, not commonly known. Which discoverie al the writers of our time ascribe (& that not unworthily) unto Christopher Columbus. For by him

Estotiland first discovered. it was in a maner first discovered, made knowen, and profitably communicated unto the Christian world, in the yeere of our Lord 1492. Howbeit I finde that the North part thereof called Estotiland, (which most of all extendeth toward our Europe and the Islands of the same, namely, Groneland, Island, and Frisland,) was long ago found out by certaine fishers of the Isle of Frisland, driven by tempest upon the shore thereof: and

The second discoverie thereof. was afterward about the yeere 1390 discovered a new, by one Antonio Zeno a gentleman of Venice ; which sayled thither under the conduct of Zichmni king of the saide Isle of Frisland, a prince in those parts of great valour, and renowned for his martiall exploits and victories. Of which expedition of Zichmni there are extant in Italian certaine collections or abridgements gathered by Francisco Marcolino out of the letters of M. Nicolo and Antonio Zeni two gentlemen of Venice which lived in those partes. Out of which collections I doe adde concerning the description of Estotiland aforesaid these particulars following.

Estotiland (saith he) aboundeth with all things necessary for mankinde. In the mids thereof standeth an exceeding high mountaine, from which issue foure rivers that moisten all the countrie. The inhabitants are wittie and most expert in all Mechanicall arts. They have a kinde of peculiar language and letters. Howbeit in this Kings Librarie are preserved certaine Latine bookes, which they understand not, being perhaps left there not many yeeres before by some Europeans, which traffiqued thither. They have all kinde of mettals; but especially golde, wherewith they mightily abound. They trafficke with the people of Groneland: from whence they fetch skinnes, pitch and brimstone. The inhabitants report that towardes the South, there are regions abounding with gold, and very populous: they have many and huge woods, from whence they take timber for the building of ships and cities, whereof and of castles there are great store. The use of the loadstone for Navigation is unknowen unto them. They make relation also of a certaine region toward the South, called Drogio, which *Drogio.* is inhabited by Canibals, unto whom mans flesh is delicate meat: wherof being destitute they live by fishing, which they use very much. Beyond this are large regions, and as it were a newe world: but the people are barbarous and goe naked: howbeit against the colde they cloth themselves in beastes skinnes. These have no kinde of metall: and they live by hunting. Their weapons are certaine long staves with sharpe points, and bowes. They wage warres one against another. They have governours, and obey certaine lawes. But from hence more towardes the South the climate is much more temperate: and there are cities, and temples of idoles, unto whom they sacrifice living men, whose flesh they afterwards devoure. These nations have the use of silver and gold.

Thus much of this tract of landes out of the aforesaide collections or abridgements. Wherein this also is worthy the observation, that even then our Europæan Pilots sayled those seas by the helpe of the loadstone. For concerning the use thereof in Navigation, I suppose there is not to be found a more ancient testimonie. And these things I have annexed the rather unto this table of Mar del Zur; considering that none of those Authours which have written the Histories of the Newe world, have in any part of their writings, mentioned one word thereof. Hitherto Ortelius.